658

St

l

MORE PRAISE FOR BEST-PRACTICE EVA FROM FINANCE LEADERS

"I pride myself on being an early "EVA disciple." I have seen it applied with great success in management and incentive applications over many years. Even so, the new EVA-ratio framework covered in this book has challenged me to take my performance-management thinking and leadership to the next level. Best-Practice EVA is a stimulating, innovative and common sense playbook for any executive that genuinely cares about creating sustainable value for their stakeholders."

—Mark A. McCollum, Chief Financial Officer, Halliburton Company

"Ball's 20-year EVA journey has resulted in a disciplined capital allocation model, a shareholder-aligned incentive compensation program and significant long-term value creation for our shareholders. Bennett Stewart's new book explains the logic behind EVA and how it has helped us. It provides the most-up-to-date and practical roadmap that any CFO can use to adopt EVA and drive better business investment decisions and create more value. It's a winner."

—Scott Morrison, Senior Vice President and CFO, Ball Corporation

"We've used EVA to create a value-focused culture that pervades our company and that has been a real asset in communicating with our investors. I am excited about integrating the next generation of "best-practice" EVA metrics into our investor communications."

—Ann Scott, Director, Investor Relations, Ball Corporation

"We adopted EVA more than a decade ago and continue to employ it for investment decisions, measuring performance and providing incentives to a substantial percentage of our employees. It's been a great help to us, and yet I see that Best-Practice EVA takes EVA in important new directions. Once again, Bennett Stewart is several steps ahead of the rest of us in thinking through the best ways to align corporate performance, strategy and culture with creating wealth. My advice—read it, study it, and do it."

—Ken Trammell, Chief Financial Officer, Tenneco Inc.

MORE PRAISE FOR BEST-PRACTICE EVA FROM INVESTMENT EXPERTS

"The neglect of cost-of-capital is a truly remarkable shortcoming of traditional profitability measures. Bennett Stewart reveals a powerful solution, developed as a management tool over decades and now applied as well to investment management. Better still, he makes his case with highly readable case histories. Best-Practice EVA will give you a whole new perspective on how value is created."

—Martin Fridson, co-author of Financial
Statement Analysis: A Practitioner's Guide

"Best-Practice EVA provides a powerful lens to view and value corporate performance. It combines all the essentials of financial statement analysis into a framework with economic profit at its core. There is nothing wrong with this, and much to like about it."

—Frank J. Fabozzi, CFA, Editor, Journal of Portfolio Management,
Professor of Finance, EDHEC Business School, and Visiting Fellow,
Princeton University, Department of Operations Research and
Financial Engineering

Best-Practice EVA plainly shows how to convert accounting data into useful and reliable measures of true economic performance. The new EVA metric framework is a valuable innovation that will undoubtedly help business managers to make better operating and investment decisions

—Roger J. Grabowski, FASA, Managing Director,
Valuation Services, Duff & Phelps LLC, and co-author
of Cost of Capital: Applications and Examples.

MORE PRAISE FOR BEST-PRACTICE EVA FROM GOVERNANCE AUTHORITIES

"In this authoritative guide, Bennett Stewart demonstrates how CEOs can deploy EVA as a potent tool to measure and foster real economic value. It is clearly and convincingly written, and it filled with examples that will resonate with senior business leaders the world over."

—Wayne Cooper, Executive Chairman, Chief Executive Group

Bennett Stewart expands the repertoire of financial metrics available to executives and directors that want tie their strategies and incentives to creating shareholder value. The new EVA metrics may gain a footing in the compensation arena because they appear to capture all the key elements of the total performance story and can be applied in a fashion that can be relatively easy to understand and analyze. Bottom line – any practitioner, director, consultant, analyst or investor will derive a great deal of value from reading his new book. It's an excellent and important work

—James C. McGough, Partner, Meridian Compensation Partners, LLC

MORE PRAISE FOR BEST-PRACTICE EVA FROM BUSINESS EDUCATORS

There has long been a need to reconcile corporate finance and business strategy, and this book shows how to do it. It shows how EVA can be used to develop a culture that cares about allocating and managing capital as a core competency, how EVA Momentum can be used to focus attention on the right growth opportunities, and how EVA Margin can help ensure that strategy execution is truly a value-creating proposition. Bravo.

—John Percival, Adjunct Professor of Finance,
The Wharton School

"This book reflects two decades of refinements of EVA that make it a still more practical solution to value-based corporate management while still preserving the essential insight – if you focus on value creation using the right performance tools, good things follow."

—John D. Martin, Carr P. Collins Chair and Professor of Finance,
Baylor University, and co-author of Value Based Management
with Corporate Social Responsibility, Oxford University Press.

"Best-Practice EVA is an instant classic and the definitive must-read roadmap for anyone serious about acquiring a deep understanding of value-creation analysis. It is highly recommended for executives, security analysts, and business educators worldwide."

—Rob Weigan, Professor of Finance and Brenneman Professor of Business
Strategy, Washburn University School of Business

"Bennett Stewart's Best-Practice EVA goes right onto my required reading lists for my MBA and executive education courses. It's a real eye opener for anyone who wants to understand how value is created, and the best way to measure it and achieve it."

—Terry Campbell, Clinical Professor of Accounting,
Kelley School of Business, Indiana University

"Bennett Stewart has transformed EVA from a money measure of economic profit into a ratio-analysis framework for corporate investment analysis, planning and valuation that is powerful and practical. This book clearly spells out and illustrates the new and improved version of EVA that has a legitimate shot at bridging the corporate and investing worlds and becoming a new standard in corporate value-based governance."

—Donald Chew, Editor in Chief, *The Morgan Stanley Journal of Applied Corporate Finance*

Best-Practice
EVA

Founded in 1807, John Wiley & Sons is the oldest independent publishing company in the United States. With offices in North America, Europe, Australia, and Asia, Wiley is globally committed to developing and marketing print and electronic products and services for our customers' professional and personal knowledge and understanding.

The Wiley Finance series contains books written specifically for finance and investment professionals as well as sophisticated individual investors and their financial advisors. Book topics range from portfolio management to e-commerce, risk management, financial engineering, valuation, and financial instrument analysis, as well as much more.

For a list of available titles, visit our website at www.WileyFinance.com.

Best-Practice EVA

The Definitive Guide to Measuring and Maximizing Shareholder Value

G. BENNETT STEWART, III

EVA Dimensions LLC

WILEY

To Ling and Lauren, for love
To Jerome, for strength
To Al, for wisdom
To John, for faith
To Joel, for pointing the way

Contents

Preface   ix

CHAPTER 1
  EVA 101   1

CHAPTER 2
  EVA and Value   19

CHAPTER 3
  Accounting for Value   47

CHAPTER 4
  What's Wrong with RONA?   85

CHAPTER 5
  The New EVA Ratio Metrics   99

CHAPTER 6
  EVA Margin   123

CHAPTER 7
  Setting EVA Targets   157

CHAPTER 8
  Put Momentum into Planning   191

CHAPTER 9
  Dividing Multiples into Good and Bad   217

CHAPTER 10
  Put EVA into Capital Decisions and Acquisitions   223

CHAPTER 11
  EVA and the Buy Side   **245**

CHAPTER 12
  Become a Best-Practice EVA Company   **273**

APPENDIX A
  The Best-Practice EVA Software Toolkit   **287**

APPENDIX B
  Corrective Accounting Adjustments   **291**

APPENDIX C
  Accounting for Corporate Charges in Detail   **295**

Glossary   **299**

About the Author   **313**

Index   **315**

This book makes the case that there is a new and significantly better way to measure and maximize shareholder value that involves replacing traditional financial metrics and valuation tools with new ones. The framework I describe and illustrate can be used profitably by finance leaders, business operators, board members, and institutional investors alike. In fact, one of my prime objectives is to create a common ground—a new standard and shared vocabulary that will bridge value-based corporate management and stock market equity research and give all stakeholders in the corporate governance debate a better way to carry on the conversation. Right now, finance is a mishmash of measures that tell half the truth or hide the truth, with no agreement on any one of them. The market and management talk past each other, and directors and the media are caught in the cross fire. What is desperately needed is one measure and one framework that can accurately weigh all businesses and business decisions on a single scale, and gain common currency. That scale is EVA.

For the reader who may not be familiar with it, EVA,[1] pronounced E-V-A, for economic value added, is simply a different way to measure corporate profit that is better than all others. It measures profit according to economic principles and for the purpose of managing a business, and not by following accounting conventions; it is computed as net operating profit after taxes (NOPAT) less a charge for tying up balance sheet capital. Beyond that, EVA is a great way—I will argue it is the best way—not just to measure value, but to assist management in setting plans and making decisions that will maximize the net present value (NPV) of an enterprise.

EVA isn't new, of course. It has been a little over 20 years since I formally introduced EVA to the business community with my prior work, *The Quest for Value* (HarperBusiness, 1991). But most of the material in this book *is* new, and reflects a huge advance in the EVA framework that has

---

[1] EVA® is a registered service mark of EVA Dimensions LLC in the fields of corporate management software, financial data and rankings, valuation modelling, and investment management and research) and of Stern Stewart & Co. in financial and incentive consulting.

taken place over the past six years. For the first time, I lay out in comprehensive detail a set of important extensions to EVA that make it far easier to understand and use, and much more effective and wide ranging in its applications, than ever before. If you were exposed to EVA in the past but decided not to use it, this book will show you why you should reconsider your decision. And if you are new to EVA, don't worry—I cover all the basics as well as the enhancements. Indeed, this book is intended to function as a user's manual. It is a complete how-to guide to the very best and most practical techniques for measuring performance, valuing companies, choosing strategies, and running any business for maximum value. It is a book I hope you will want to refer back to again and again.

Let me roll back the clock and explain how we've arrived at this point. Although it is no longer the final word on the subject, *The Quest for Value* served the purpose of putting EVA firmly on the map when it was released in 1991. Up to then, almost no companies or investors were using EVA or anything like it. Measures like earnings per share (EPS), return on equity (ROE), profit margin, and cash flow dominated the financial landscape. But *The Quest* argued that EVA was a better financial management mousetrap, and it succeeded in convincing a number of early adopters to put it in place as the focal point of their management. The results were so impressive that the editors of *Fortune* magazine made EVA the cover article in the September 22, 1993, issue, with the tagline "EVA—it's the real key to creating wealth." That exposure, that imprimatur, was priceless. It brought about a tsunami of EVA adoptions the world over, which led the *Fortune* editorial board to develop a second tagline a few years later—"EVA is today's hottest financial idea, and getting hotter." Business schools incorporated EVA into their curricula, the Chartered Financial Analyst (CFA) exam that is the standard for stock research professionals required knowledge of it, and the level of interest in EVA was at a fever pitch. The Stern Stewart consulting organization of which I was a founding partner, and under whose banner I had published *The Quest*, expanded from 35 professionals to 235 five years later, with offices around the globe to help companies of all sizes, public and private, in virtually every industry, put EVA in place. Hundreds of companies adopted it and tied incentive pay to increasing it, and the results were usually quite stunning.

After all, what gets measured gets managed, and you do tend to get what you pay for. Confronted with the balance sheet charge that EVA imposes, managers understandably devoted considerable energy to animating the value of their assets. They also seeded more growth in profitable businesses that had been treading water to maintain existing high margins or high rates of return, which became irrelevant on the EVA scorecard. There are many other ways that EVA helps a business to operate more efficiently and effectively, and they will be chronicled in this book and substantiated with case studies. But the point is that managing for EVA was, and remains, a proven and universally applicable formula for running a business for better value.

Still, for all its phenomenal success through the 1990s and into the early 2000 decade, I began to notice a few chinks in the armor, deficiencies that were inhibiting EVA from being much more widely adopted. I knew that EVA had the potential to become the global standard of financial management and valuation excellence, but frankly, the uptick was much slower than it needed to be. I have the scars to prove it. After much soul-searching, I figured out why EVA was harder to adopt and harder to use than it should have been. Let me go over that list now, and then I will tell you how we licked every last one of those deficiencies to forge the new and improved version of EVA that is the subject of this book.

SHORTCOMINGS WITH FIRST-GENERATION EVA

The first and most glaring deficiency was that EVA was traditionally just a money measure of economic profit. Managers were simply being asked to increase the profit that they earned over the cost of capital as much as possible over a three- to five-year horizon. That was the essence of the message, and correct as far as it went. But EVA lacked a companion ratio indicator or, better, an entire ratio framework, to bring it to life. Let's face it. Ratios rule the business world, and the absence of EVA in a ratio format was a severe handicap.

For example, CFOs could not use EVA to compare performance over time and across lines of business or against public peers that differed in scale, so they tended to fall back on conventional ratio metrics instead. EVA also lost credibility with corporate directors who were unable to use it to calibrate bonus plans or reach informed judgments about the adequacy of business plan goals submitted by their management teams. How could they reach the right conclusions when they lacked the relevant statistics?

The ratio absence also meant that line managers found EVA a lot harder to understand and use than it should have been. They were unable to trace EVA to familiar levers and performance drivers, to connect it to measures like sales growth, gross margin, working capital days, plant turns, and the like. As a money measure, EVA was opaque when transparency was really needed. As a money measure, EVA tended to stand apart from the familiar performance ratio indicators when it needed to be joined to them at the hip.

The ratio deficiency was also a showstopper for investors. At the outset, many of them found EVA intellectually superior to the traditional financial metrics they were using, like earnings per share. Goldman Sachs and Credit Suisse First Boston started to run EVA calculations in their research departments, published primers about using EVA in stock valuation, and hosted conferences where I was invited to introduce EVA to their fund manager clients. Some fund managers, like Eugene Vessell of Oppenheimer Capital, began to recommend EVA to the companies in which they held major investments with the conviction that EVA would help the management teams improve the stock price and make everyone a winner.

But the investment community's interest in EVA was stillborn. To an even greater degree than business managers, investors require ratio indicators to compare, rank, sort, screen, and decide which stocks look relatively better to buy or sell across a broad universe of ever shifting opportunities. As a money measure, EVA failed that test. It was ill suited to fit into the decision processes employed at the major money houses. And one consequence of that failure was that even the most EVA-ardent CFOs and CEOs worried that if they spoke the EVA language, they would not be understood on Wall Street. Frankly, the evidence is overwhelming that EVA is the best measure to explain and drive share value, as I will show. But I can sympathize with the corporate managers who were reluctant go out on an EVA limb without assurance that investors would catch their drift.

EVA was also set back by a number of practical problems. Every company had to create its own software plumbing to calculate, track, analyze, and value EVA, which was time consuming, expensive to maintain, and error prone. An authoritative data file of EVA metrics covering public companies did not exist. EVA was a number, a data point, personal to each company. It was not a statistic computed according to a standard set of rules that boards, managers, investors, and consultants could trust and use with confidence.

Please do not misunderstand me. For all its shortcomings, the original EVA was leagues better than the alternatives, and many companies benefited immensely from putting it in place. As a measure of profit, EVA consolidates income efficiency and asset management into one net profit score. It is the only profit score that fully and correctly increases when balance sheet assets decrease. It is the only profit measure that builds in accountability for capital investments, because as more capital is invested, the charge for using it automatically ratchets up. The most important property is that the present value of a forecast for EVA is always *exactly the same* as the net present value of discounted cash flow. By its nature, EVA sets aside the profit that must be earned to recover the value of any capital that has been or will be invested, and thus it always discounts to net present value—to value net of invested capital. To increase EVA as a profit measure is to increase the net present value of the business and the wealth of the business owners, *by definition*.

The opportunity, then as now, is to focus on increasing EVA as the key corporate goal, applicable to all business units and all business decisions. The mission has been clear, but as I've said, the methods for using EVA and extracting the most value from it were not as effective as they needed to be. EVA could never become the global standard of financial excellence until the deficiencies I have outlined were addressed.

INTRODUCING THE NEW BEST-PRACTICE EVA MODEL

I left Stern Stewart in March 2006 to set up a new firm, EVA Dimensions. My objective was to start fresh and to figure out how all of the deficiencies I've outlined could be addressed head-on. I believe that we have succeeded. Innovations from EVA Dimensions have spawned a new and radically improved version of EVA, and a flourishing new ecosystem nourishing it, that now makes the adoption of EVA a far easier and more rewarding decision than it ever was before. It is not just a next-generation step worthy of a techy 2.0 designation, but a quantum leap forward. That's why I call it Best-Practice EVA. The goal of this book is to explain it in convincing detail.

The biggest advance is a set of headline EVA ratio statistics and a way to take them apart and elegantly trace them in steps to all the business performance factors that are moving the EVA needle. That has made EVA an open book that is brimming with managerial and valuation insights. It's fully transparent, and connected to business drivers in ways that are gaining a lot of converts in line operations where before there was resistance.

The new EVA metrics give CFOs an opportunity to streamline and amplify their management equations. The new ratios measure profitability performance so thoroughly and accurately, and they so closely align decisions to shareholder value, that all other financial ratio measures become obsolete. The old standbys, like gross margin, return on investment (ROI), or working capital turns, can be discarded or subordinated to the EVA cause. CFOs can also use the new EVA ratio framework as a superior method for analyzing and improving performance and stoking up the value of business plans—far more so than with the status quo financial technology. These may sound like exaggerated claims. But read the book and see if you don't end up agreeing with me.

A second major advance is the development of software tools that automate the Best-Practice EVA framework. It is now possible to test-drive, implement, and maintain EVA at world-class standards at a far lower cost and with more integrity than ever before. Related to that, EVA Dimensions now maintains a data file of EVA metrics covering 9,000 global companies over a 20-year history, with daily updates. It is a terrific research tool for corporate strategists and academic scholars. Frankly, this book could not have been written without the push-button access to EVA data that informs so many of the cases presented.

More important, the data file provides reliable reference points that turn EVA into a legitimate statistic for the first time. With it, directors can rate plans, judge results, and set goals through an EVA lens with trust and confidence. They can challenge management to perform up to a defined and documented market standard. A CFO can assess the company's EVA performance in light of the trends and accomplishments of public peers. The CFO can harvest irrefutable evidence about the company's relative standing and spotlight specific trends and improvement initiatives—ranked in terms of impact on value—to spur the company's line teams into action.

EVA Dimensions also is the source of a stock rating and analysis system that is gaining considerable traction in the professional investment community. Known as PRVit[2] (pronounced "prove it" and standing for the performance-risk-valuation investment technology), the model anticipates stock price movements on the premise that they are magnetically drawn to their fundamental EVA values. It's an important step in demonstrating that EVA applies to investors' buy and sell decisions just as well as it does to corporate decisions.

This is not just a theoretical exercise. The ratings have been featured on Bloomberg since 2006, and Fidelity Investments has made an abbreviated version available to online retail customers since 2008. More important, a rapidly growing number of institutional investors at the largest active U.S. equity managers are using EVA analysis in their buy and sell decisions. An institutional equity research service that EVA Dimensions launched at the beginning of 2012 has already established regular conversations with nearly 150 portfolio managers and research analysts, and the client roster is growing weekly. In the process of delivering valuation insights to clients, the research team is educating the buy-side community about the new ratio-based version of EVA and is helping to close the communication gap. Forward-looking CFOs and CEOs will start to talk the EVA language before their investors start asking them about it.

[2] PRVit® is a registered service mark of EVA Dimensions LLC

OUTLINE OF THE BOOK

This book is structured to tell the new EVA story from the ground up. It covers EVA essentials—the classic economic profit version of EVA—in the first three chapters. In Chapter 1, you learn how simple and intuitive EVA really is, how it is defined, and why it is better than all other measures of corporate profit and cash flow. You discover how it naturally guides managers into making all the right decisions—the ones that will maximize value. You even see how to use it in profit-sharing bonus plans that create the powerful incentives of an owner.

The next chapter shows how EVA can be used to determine—and improve— the intrinsic value of a business and the share price of a company. It also presents a precise formula that uses EVA to explain total shareholder returns, and proves that it works. This has been a missing link, and now it is firmly established: EVA, and changes in expectations for EVA, are the true drivers of shareholder returns. Cash flow and cash yield simply transmit the return that is in fact generated exclusively by the EVA performance ratios.

A major conclusion is that managers should stop making decisions according to cash flow analysis. I demonstrate why cash flow is not the answer—actually, why cash flow analysis is a big problem in corporate management—and why CFOs should start using forecasts for EVA to measure and improve the value of their plans, projects, acquisitions, and decisions.

The final foundational chapter provides a heavy indictment of conventional accounting profit measures along with what I hope is compelling evidence to convict them. The truth is that measures like earnings, earnings per share (EPS), earnings before interest and taxes (EBIT), and earnings before interest, taxes, depreciation, and amortization (EBITDA) so misrepresent economic value and so contradict commonsense business logic that they frequently lead managers way off the mark, and sometimes horribly so. The answer is not to start from scratch—that would be wildly impractical— but to repair the accounting flaws with a set of corrective adjustments that are built right into EVA and bring the real value of business decisions to the surface. Properly accounting for value may seem a dull topic best left to the finance crowd. It isn't. If you want to become a more informed director, a smarter manager, or a better investor, you will want to understand the decision traps cooked into accounting profit figures and how to avoid them.

Rate-of-return measures, in contrast, are beyond repair. They are so flawed, so misleading, and so dangerous that you should just put them aside. In Chapter 4 I show why ROI-minded managers have made some of the most tragic strategic and capital allocation blunders in business history and why you will surely make similar mistakes by using them.

If ROI or return on capital (ROC) isn't the right ratio to use, what is? The answer is EVA Momentum. It is introduced in Chapter 5, which is where the Best-Practice EVA framework first takes a bow. It is calculated by taking the *change* in EVA versus the prior period, and dividing by the revenues in the *prior period*. It measures the growth rate in EVA, scaled to the sales size of the business. It is the *only* corporate performance ratio where bigger always is better, because it gets bigger when EVA does, which means it should be every company's most important financial goal, the one ratio metric that everyone aims to maximize as the key measure of corporate success.

EVA Momentum is also the basis for an incredibly revealing diagnostic tool. It unfolds in stages to reveal all of the underlying performance factors that determine corporate value. It not only shows how much value has been created, but where and why. It is at once the measure that really matters and a portal to the many that can be managed. What's more, it is possible to determine the forward-looking EVA Momentum growth rate that is baked into share prices, and use that as a more reliable estimate of performance expectations than the old standbys, like consensus earnings per share. In this introductory chapter, I explain EVA Momentum in depth and why it is such a terrific answer to so many financial management questions, and illustrate it with an application to Amazon, which has been an amazing—and instructive—EVA Momentum performer.

Chapters 6 through 11 go through the nuts and bolts of Best-Practice EVA. They kick off with an in-depth look at EVA Margin, which is EVA expressed as a percentage of sales. It measures a business's true profit margin. It is a key productivity metric and my candidate to replace ROI. I call it the Momentum upshifter because analyzing it and improving it is a great way to put EVA Momentum into a higher gear. I look at it in depth for the Fifth Avenue jeweler Tiffany & Co., and take it apart like a fine watch to expose its inner workings.

Next up is the question of how to set corporate performance targets, a tedious but vital activity. Get the targets wrong, or set targets for the wrong measures, and bonus plans won't work, business plans won't be as good as they could be, and performance will not add to value. I show how to use the new EVA ratio metrics to get the targets right. I also show in detail how to put EVA Momentum into planning in truly effective ways. EVA Momentum is the single best measure of the quality and value of a business plan, and it is also a terrific tool—I would say the best one—for x-raying a business plan and seeing how to make it more valuable by making it more EVA capable. Best-Practice EVA also includes a new set of valuation multiples that can provide important reality checks on valuations and plan projections. They aren't perfect, but they are far, far better than the slippery and deceptive P/E ratio and EBITDA enterprise multiples that most finance departments use today.

A present-value version of EVA Margin, called NPV Margin, helps management to use EVA for more mundane tasks, like rating capital projects and evaluating any business decision where cost-benefit trade-offs spread out over time and across income statement and balance sheet effects. In the process, the old warhorse internal rate of return (IRR) is excused from service. It too has become obsolete and has no role to play in the Best-Practice EVA program. I also show why it is best to think of acquisitions as involving an *exchange of value* rather than the *exchange of earnings* that seems to be the fixation of the investment banking community, and how to use EVA to put a precise and accountable value on synergies.

The last link in the Best-Practice program is PRVit—the EVA market score report. In Chapter 11 I show how to read and interpret the report, how the score is determined, and why investors are turning to it to screen and rate stocks. I also show why it is finding a home with CFOs and investor relations (IR) directors who want insights into how the market is pricing their stock.

The book concludes with battle-tested tips from the firing line, practical suggestions for how you can test-drive and adopt Best-Practice EVA at your company, along with a checklist that investors can use to tell if a company is really on EVA or is only going through the motions.

THE BEST-PRACTICE EVA AGENDA

There is an underlying theme running through the book that I want to alert you to. I am calling on CFOs to put their financial management practices on a stringent diet, to slim them down and go really lean, and to resolutely focus on adding value by discarding an abundance of redundant and inferior measures and practices that have accumulated over the years. I am calling for CFOs to start fresh and end simple, with EVA at the core. There is a real logic and real value to adopting EVA as the key corporate mission, to using it as the prime decision tool, and to tossing out or at least subordinating all the conventional financial ratio metrics in favor of the EVA ratio metrics we've developed at EVA Dimensions. The consistent use of EVA for all those purposes will make it even simpler and even more effective as a corporate management framework. Even if you disagree, I think you will find much to like and take away from the Best-Practice EVA program outlined in this book.

In the past, EVA was something of a closed system, available to the select few. Now it is open architecture. All are welcome to join the Best-Practice EVA initiative. I call on investors and business consultants of all stripes, along with business school professors in finance, strategy, and general management, to join the cause. You can be incredibly influential change agents. And we, EVA Dimensions, have the software tools, reference data, training, and research services that can put you right on the cutting edge.

BENNETT STEWART
January 2013

CHAPTER 1

EVA 101

Many people think EVA (for economic value added) is just a performance measure. It is that, but it is a lot more. EVA has an application to every facet of corporate performance management. It is a technique for improving the planning process, and a framework for valuing decisions, gauging investments, and shaping strategies. It's the basis for bonus plans that turn managers and employees into charged-up, informed, enlightened owner/operators. It's a great way for a management team to credibly communicate its commitment to creating value to its investors. Using EVA pervasively—for all those applications and in substitution for other measures and methods—is what ultimately makes it so simple, so accountable, and so powerful. But true enough, EVA does begin as a performance measure, as simply a better way to gauge the true economic profit a business is earning. So let's begin there, with EVA 101—the money measure of EVA.

At its barest essence, EVA is a simple three-line computation of profit that anyone can understand:

> Sales
> – Operating costs
> – Capital costs

What remains is EVA. It is sales less operating costs less the full cost of financing business assets, as if the assets had been rented. It consolidates income efficiency and asset management into one net profit score. Increasing EVA is the name of the game. It's that simple. End of the story.

Well, not quite. To aerate a bit, observe that EVA starts with sales. Some critics have said EVA will motivate managers to shortcut customers. But how can that be? EVA cannot exist at the bottom line without generating sales at the top line, and there can be no sustained increase in EVA without sustained sales growth. Customer satisfaction, repeat business, innovation, and growth are essential to putting points on the EVA scorecard. But even that is not enough. EVA demands more. It is a higher calling. It is the most challenging measure of profit performance.

Operating costs must be covered, of course. Operating costs include all the materials and production costs, overhead and administration costs, and people and programming costs, but they also include depreciation and amortization and taxes. Physical assets wear out or become obsolete, and intangible assets are competed away and must be replaced, so true costs have to include an allowance for the consumption of both tangible and intangible assets. Corporate income taxes must also be paid before profits can really be counted. Note, however, that interest expense and any other financing charges are not included in this category; they are contained in the overall cost of capital, discussed next.

Most companies stop here or about here when they measure profit. They forget, or act as if they forget, that there is another critical cost to cover—the cost of using capital.

Capital is the total money that has been raised from lenders or shareholders or retained from the company's earnings and is used to finance the company's business assets. In other words, capital is the amount of money tied up in working capital such as inventories; in financing property, plant, and equipment; and in sundry business assets, including the goodwill premiums paid to acquire companies. And because balance sheets must balance, every time line teams go out and acquire more assets or increase inventories or purchase equipment or invest in writing software code, the treasury department must raise additional capital from lenders or shareholders, or retain more earnings instead of paying them out. The asset buys must be financed with capital sources. And to induce investors to put or leave their money in the business, a company must offer them a competitive return on their investment that stacks up favorably against other available opportunities on the market.

The cost of capital, in other words, is not a cash cost you can see and touch. It is not a cost that accountants actually deduct or ever will. It is an opportunity cost— the cost to the lenders and shareholders of giving up the returns they could otherwise *expect* to earn from investing their money in a stock and bond portfolio that has a risk profile the same as the company in question. Or put another way, capital has a cost because it is scarce; it is limited in the aggregate to the amount of money people and companies worldwide choose to save (less savings siphoned off to fund government deficits). For a company to create value, it must outperform the marginal project that is also competing for funding in the global capital markets.

Fortunately, the cost of capital can be determined without surveying investors or rank ordering investment projects. The market has already done the work for us, and the cost of capital is reflected in measurable market prices. Without going into the details, the cost of capital always starts with the prevailing yield on relatively safe long-range government bonds (to approximate the indefinite life of a business)—which today is about 2.5 percent in the United States, well below historic norms as it happens—plus a premium, an extra bump up in the rate of return to compensate investors for bearing the added risk of the business. The risk premiums generally range from 2 percent to 8 percent, depending on how exposed a company is to business cycles. Regulated electric and gas utilities, staples retailers like Wal-Mart and Costco, and established everyday food giants like Kellogg and General Mills that are comparatively isolated from business cycles (we all want to be warm and fed) come in at the low end, while home builders and semiconductor fabricators and theme park operators—companies that get whipsawed in a downturn—come in with very high costs of capital.

Though invisible to the naked eye, and out of the counting zone of the accountants, the cost of capital is a real cost that can be estimated with reasonable accuracy using modern financial techniques. Certainly we can do better than assuming that the cost of capital is zero, as profit measures like earnings before interest and taxes (EBIT) and earnings before interest, taxes, depreciation, and amortization (EBITDA) effectively do. Those measures assign no charge for using assets. Those measures provide no protection for the owners' interests. Those measures motivate managers to squander capital, when managers should be motivated to use scarce capital sparingly, imaginatively, and intelligently to achieve business goals. The truth is that until a company is covering the full cost of its debt and equity capital, it is really losing money no matter what the accountants may say. Investors, and that's all of us, expect a return on their investments, and that return requirement becomes an unavoidable cost faced by any company that uses capital in its business.

With this as background, let's now run a basic EVA calculation:

Sales	$1,250	Customer satisfaction, innovation, growth
– Operating costs	$1,100	Pricing power, purchasing power, efficiency
NOPAT	$ 150	Net Operating Profit After Taxes
– Capital costs (Cost of capital [%] × [$] Net business assets)	10% × $1,000	Working capital turns, plant productivity
= EVA	$ 50	

The simple sample company shown above—let's call it SSCo—generates $1,250 in sales with $1,100 of operating costs, leaving a $150 remainder called net operating profit after taxes (NOPAT). NOPAT is a resting point partway down the EVA schedule. It is the firm's operating profit, net of depreciation and amortization to make it sustainable, and after taxes on the operating profit are deducted. With NOPAT now defined, we can say that EVA is equal to NOPAT less a charge for capital.

The capital charge is computed by multiplying the cost of capital rate times the capital—that is, times the amount of money invested in the firm's *net* business assets, which is all the assets used in the business, net of, or less, the money advanced by trade suppliers. That being the case, the more a company is able to finance its working capital with interest-free credit from its suppliers, the less capital it will need to obtain from lenders and share-holders, and the higher its EVA will be.

Some may say it is not worthwhile to go into details like that and it would be better just to keep it simple. I disagree. I've seen real value in teaching team members about what goes into EVA and providing company-specific examples of how they can win. It's the simplest way to spread financial literacy company-wide and stimulate a lot of good thinking around how to improve performance in ways that may not have occurred to anyone before they were thinking in terms of EVA. Once they understand that trade credit reduces the capital charge, for instance, employees will naturally lean on suppliers for better terms without the need for constant prodding from the CFO. Granted, it takes some effort to instill EVA literacy, but it typically pays off in many ways, including saving the CFO for really strategic stuff. The bottom line is that EVA training is not an obstacle. It is a tremendous opportunity to improve performance.

To go back to the example, let's assume that SSCo's overall weighted average cost of capital is 10 percent, given its risk and capital structure. That is high by current standards but it is an easy figure to use. With $1,000 tied up in net business assets and a 10 percent cost, the firm must earn $100 in NOPAT to just break even. It's simple math. You just multiply the amount of capital times the cost of capital to determine the charge for the capital.

Now EVA can be computed. SSCo is earning $150 in NOPAT. The capital charge is $100. Therefore, its EVA is $50, the difference. That alone is telling us something very important. The company is earning a positive economic profit after covering all resource costs, something that is true of only about half of the public companies in the economy at any time. The other half generates negative or negligible EVA, yet many of those companies don't even know it. And even in profitable firms there are almost always EVA-sapping divisions that look great on other measures, like sales growth, operating margins, EBITDA, cash flow, and so on, but are actually destroying value. The bottom line is that EVA is a decidedly different and more accurate measure of performance that leads to profoundly different and more reliable impressions about where to invest and grow and where to restructure and retrench.

Before moving on, let's take a moment to appreciate how important and helpful the capital charge is. For one thing, there would be no point in working to reduce working capital or to improve plant turns if not for the charge. Why would management even bother and why would investors care, if capital had no cost? But with the charge, a whole new world of opportunities is opened for line teams to create value by better managing balance sheet assets. What at first appears daunting is very soon exhilarating and liberating. There are more levers to pull, more trade-offs to consider, and more ways to win.

A second point is that the capital charge is where accountability enters the EVA system. In many companies, getting a capital project approved is viewed as a win. With EVA, the approval of capital spending creates a visible ongoing obligation to cover the cost of the added capital.

A third insight is that the capital charge represents the amount of NOPAT profit that a company needs to earn in order to pay the interest due on its borrowed capital, after tax, while leaving a profit remainder that gives its shareholders a competitive return on the equity money they've invested in the firm. In other words, the firm's financing costs are not separate considerations outside the purview of EVA; they are baked right into the capital charge. As a result, operating people need not be concerned with interest payments, debt amortization, dividends, share buybacks, and the like. If they simply focus on covering the capital charge in the decisions they make, they are doing their job, and the financing costs will take care of themselves.

Moreover, if a firm raises capital and invests it in ways that increase its EVA, it is guaranteed to generate enough operating profit to pay interest on the money it borrowed and to provide share owners the minimum return they seek, and then some, on the additional capital they've funneled into the firm. EVA growth is always self-financing—it always attracts the capital needed to finance it.

A fourth point about the capital charge is that it establishes what is effectively a target for NOPAT that automatically rises or falls as more or less capital is invested in the business. The operating profit target contained in EVA, in other words, is not set by the board or the budget or by negotiation. Rather, it is an objective standard that is obtained by benchmarking the business against all other opportunities on the market, and asking: How much NOPAT profit must the firm earn, given the amount of capital it uses and the risk it takes, to just stand on a par with its capital market competitors? And the operating profit target represented by the capital charge is applicable even for private companies. They too should be asking: How do our operations stand up in the global marketplace for capital?

Board directors devote a lot of time to benchmarking with peer companies, assessing their firm's performance, and establishing financial goals to grade the management team. But in so doing, most neglect to investigate the most essential benchmarking of all, which is: Are we meeting the market-set standard of excellence? In other words: Are we earning an EVA profit and are we increasing it over time at an acceptable pace, relative to our competitors and relative to expectations factored into our stock price? No other indicator establishes so bright a line between acceptable and unacceptable performance, because EVA is the only one that is benchmarked against the global market standard for investing and using capital, and the market price for bearing risk. This notion will become even more practical after EVA has been turned into a set of performance ratios that abstract the performance from the size of the company.

A key feature of the NOPAT profit target is that it *automatically* changes as capital changes. The NOPAT performance bar is set higher as more capital is invested in a business, and the capital charge is automatically set lower as capital is withdrawn. With all other measures, an appropriate target has to be established or reestablished as circumstances or capital change, and that is not easy. How much should sales increase as additional capital is invested, or how much margin expansion should be sought to compensate for an increase in capital intensity, for example? Absent EVA, there really is no objective standard or simple way for revising targets on the fly for measures like sales growth and operating margins, because measures like those and all others are incomplete; they have blind spots and tell only part of the story.

EVA is different. Since EVA is operating profit net of a market-set target, a sustained increase is real progress, a persisting decrease is real deterioration, and sideways movement is truly just spinning wheels. In light of this, every management team in every business can have one simple mission: *to increase its EVA as much as possible*. No other measure enables management to espouse so simple and meaningful a goal. Making a negative EVA business less EVA negative is just as valid a way to improve performance and create value as making a positive EVA more positive. Like venerable Total Quality Management (TQM) programs that emphasize the continuous improvement in products and processes, the goal of an EVA program is the greatest sustainable *improvement* in EVA over time. Improving a tough turnaround business is given the same recognition in EVA as making a star performer shine brighter. The improvement goal is applicable across the board, regardless of the legacy assets or inherited baggage that is there at the start. It provides all the right incentives.

What are the incentives, though, and do they make sense? How are managers guided into making better decisions? The short answer is: in all the ways that matter and none that don't. While there are countless ways that performance can be improved and wealth created, depending on the business and the times, all the possible ways at all times conveniently fall into one of three key categories that are readily recognized by EVA, which are:

1. **Operate efficiently.** Intelligently cut wasteful costs. Increase NOPAT without increasing capital. Almost all measures get this one right, but EVA gets it right, too. It's important, and it's there. Go for it.
2. **Grow profitably.** Invest capital, and build the business, but be sure to cover the full cost of the invested capital. In truth, the *only* way a company can increase its EVA over the long term is by investing, by growing, and by innovating, but the return on the new capital must exceed the full cost of raising the capital. The incentive, in short, is to take on as many positive net present value (NPV) projects as possible, but *only* positive NPV projects. Investments and strategies that don't cover the cost of capital and that diminish the firm's NPV are absolutely discouraged and penalized, as they should be. There is a real deterrent to misallocating or misusing capital, but there is also a real reward for *all* growth over the cost of capital.
3. **Purge ruthlessly.** The last big improvement category is to stop pouring money into, or to liquidate assets from, the uneconomic activities that can't cover the cost of capital. Find ways to turn working capital faster; to increase production yields and uptimes; to sell assets worth more to others; to bring technology and products to market faster; to prune marginal or unprofitable lines of business, plants, product lines, and customers; and outsource or restructure where it is economic to do so. By putting a charge on assets, EVA puts a visible premium on superior asset management and lean business models.

No other metric so succinctly, accurately, and completely captures all of the ways that performance can be improved and wealth created in any business. And that is why EVA, and EVA alone, can be used in an incredibly simple but extraordinarily powerful profit sharing bonus plan. Let's take a short but scenic detour to explore the contours.

In the classic plan, the bonus consists of a base bonus award—a certain percentage of base pay that is needed to bring the participant's total pay package up to a competitive market standard—plus a bonus kicker that is some set percentage of the EVA earned in the year less a target for EVA that is set by a formula. The simplest formula sets the EVA target to the prior year's EVA, so that the bonus kicker just is a percentage of year-over-year change in EVA. Other variations include incorporating a growth goal into the EVA target or adjusting the target to reflect for the performance of peers—I will cover those variations in more detail in Chapter 7, where setting targets is formally discussed. For now, though, just think of the bonus as a competitive base bonus award plus a percentage of delta (change in) EVA. That actually works fine for most companies.

No matter what form it takes, though, the bonus plan message is the same—more EVA is good, and less EVA is bad, so make EVA go up. It's extremely simple, it provides all the right incentives, it clearly links pay to performance, and it reinforces the message that managers should really use EVA in reporting, planning, and decision making. It is the one bonus plan where a bigger bonus is better all around, because when EVA gets bigger, the stock price get bigger, as I will establish very clearly later on. The underlying theme is: Let's create wealth by sharing the wealth with the people who create the wealth.

The plan also has a number of unique and interesting properties that are worth playing out. For example, if a company just earns the cost of capital on incremental growth and its EVA goes sideways, its managers will earn the base bonus from the plan. Said another way, when the owners break even and just obtain the minimum return they expect on incremental investments in the business, then the firm's managers break even, too, and just earn the normal bonus they expect. That's fair and sensible, but missing from most bonus plans.

Suppose now that management does succeed at increasing EVA compared to the prior year. Then, great, the team is rewarded with a premium bonus, as it should be. The team added value by increasing EVA in some way. But there's a catch.

In the next year, the prior year's elevated EVA automatically becomes the new standard of excellence. The EVA performance target is reset higher by operation of the formula. Management is unable to rack up another large bonus unless it manages to increase EVA once again, piling even more EVA on top of the prior year's improvement. Even the simplest EVA bonus plan builds in a double protection for the shareholders. EVA requires more profit be earned as more capital is invested, and the bonus plan requires more EVA as management proves it can produce it. And if the management team was able to increase EVA year after year and earn supersized bonuses according to the bonus formula, nothing would please shareholders more, because that would undoubtedly send the share price higher (be patient—I will definitely show this). In exuberant moments I have said that I am prepared to make the managers rich—so long as they make the shareholders filthy rich. The important point here is that EVA bonuses are always self-financing. They are paid out of and are a fraction of the added value, which is true of any real pay-for-performance incentive plan, but most incentive plans fail that basic test.

What happens if EVA takes a tumble? The bonus kicker turns negative and is deducted from the base bonus. The bonus could fall all the way to zero, depending on how far EVA fell. There is a definite penalty for a down-turn in EVA, and that hurts, as it should. The incentive is: be prepared to react fast, increase fixed costs reluctantly, establish contingency plans to hold the EVA line in case bad things happen, and never think that good times last forever. Those are all terrific incentives for managers that shareholders would applaud and that boards should be prepared to provide. The downside is that managers are exposed to business risk, but should it be otherwise? Isolate managers from risk, and there will be no real risk management. Expose them to risk, and they will anticipate and manage risks. Take risk out of the pic-ture, and it is impossible to link pay to performance. It sounds draconian, but there are good reasons why even corporate managers should prefer it above and beyond the fact that it does provide them with all the right incentives.

The first argument is that the cost of capital can often be dramatically simplified by using a bonus plan like this one. Knowing that their bonuses are linked to producing EVA, managers in riskier divisions will naturally want to factor a more sizable return cushion into the capital projects they propose. As a result, CFOs aren't necessarily forced to gin up the cost of capital for riskier divisions. Many find they can get away with using just one company-wide cost of capital rate or use just a few as a simplification. The general rule is that a well-constructed EVA bonus plan is often a better way to encourage managers to think about and manage risk than to engage in what is often a politically charged and ineffectual debate over ratcheting the cost of capital up or down.

Here's an example. For many years Coca-Cola used just one cost of capi-tal worldwide in its EVA calculation. The rate was set at 12 percent and was used to review all results once they were converted into U.S. dollars, because that made it convenient to charge all operations 1 percent a month on their capital. And in its EVA program, Siemens, although it was made up of a diversified mix of 13 sectors (and 162 underlying business units) at the time, consolidated them all into just three distinct cost-of-capital categories ranging from low to average to elevated. Even that was highly effective. Once the firm's semiconductor business was measured against the higher cost of capital stand-ard it was assigned, management realized it was not competitive, and sold it.

A second reason is that the bonus plan immediately forgives manage-ment for the sin of letting EVA go down (after whacking the current-year bonus, that is). After all, the objective is to expose managers to risk as a motivator and not to drive them away. It is imperative to retain the good people through the bad times and to motivate them to try hard. This is where EVA bonus plans are so clever, in my opinion, because the EVA per-formance bar is reset to accommodate the new normal. In the next year, the prior year's marked-down EVA automatically becomes the new starting point for earning an upside EVA bonus. The management team knows that it will be able to earn back what it lost by reversing the downturn, perhaps more if it has been investing for growth when other companies held back.

In effect, the total bonus award is not only what it pays in a year but also how it automatically translates the performance in the year into a higher or lower EVA performance target in the next year. EVA companies take advantage of that. They not only track the bonuses that are being earned as a year unfolds; they also project the bonus outlook for the next year or two based on how the EVA target will be reset as compared to rolling EVA forecasts. That's a great way to mitigate demoralization during downturns, to keep up the pressure to perform in the good times, and to encourage everyone to stay focused at all times on driving EVA with a two- to three-year forward horizon.

Unfortunately, most companies do not use bonus plans anything like this. Most pay managers for beating budget goals. It sounds sensible—pay managers for doing what all agree they should aim to do. But it really isn't a good idea at all. It corrupts the planning process. When plan goals are used as bonus bogeys, managers are perversely motivated to understate and underperform the true performance potential that exists in their businesses rather than shooting for the stars. Their real incentive is to shoot low and keep their powder dry to make it easy to earn a steady if uninspiring bonus year after year. Well aware of this, senior and subordinate are pitted as adversaries rather than as planning partners. Trust and candor are forfeit, starting with the board compensation committee and the top management team. Planning becomes far less strategic and far more tactical as the field of vision narrows to arm wrestling over budget goals for just the year ahead. Managers hem and haw, hedge, hide, and hate it, but they cannot do anything about it because they are captives of a counterproductive system that ties their bonuses to their budgets and plan goals.

None of those really bad things can happen when companies use the classic EVA bonus plan that I have described. EVA bonus plans absolutely reward breakaway thinking, achieving stretch goals, and openly collaborating. They truly lead to better, more energetic, more realistic, more imaginative, more strategic, and inherently more value-based budgets and plans. How?

Aside from rewarding EVA—which gives the managers all the right incentives and the fullest range of levers to pull—it comes from setting and resetting EVA performance targets by automatically adjusting formulas that can be modeled out not just for one year as I illustrated, but for years ahead. Managers are literally able to plot out a long-range business plan and compute the bonus they will be entitled to receive each year over even a three- to five-year horizon. They know that if they just achieve their plan, they will be entitled to receive a very large stream of EVA bonus awards over time. They are paid for delivering results and as a share of the value they add, and not for beating budgeted intentions. They are paid to think and act like owners—to put in the really hard hours, to take intelligent risks, to challenge the status quo, and to be prepared to transform the business model and innovate as necessary—because they are married to the corporate well being over a long time frame and not just for a series of one-night budget stands. Managers who are confident in their abilities and who sincerely want to build valuable business franchises prefer to be recognized when they are really successful and set loose to make it happen—which is just what the EVA bonus plan does so well.

I am sometimes asked if I advocate breaking the bonus link to budgets and using formula-based targets in order to deemphasize budgeting and planning. Not at all. It's quite the opposite. Budgeting and planning are so important that they should not be corrupted by also making them the basis for earning bonus awards. My point is that companies that tie management incentives to business plans are forfeiting some of the best means available for driving better results.

In case you are wondering, EVA is the only measure that fits into a formula-based bonus plan with an automatically adjusting performance target. That is because it's the only measure where bigger is always better, where more is unequivocally better than less. One reason for that is the capital charge, which resets the profit performance bar. And as I will show in Chapter 3, EVA also irons out a whole bunch of accounting distortions. For instance, EVA is based on spreading out research and development (R&D) spending instead of expensing it, so there is no incentive to cut the spending to make a near-term budget and bonus goal. That's just one example, and you will have to read the chapter to fully appreciate that the care taken to measure EVA as a true gauge of economic profit pays a big dividend in being able to use it in a formula-based bonus plan. No other measure passes the test at all. All the others—and those include book earnings, profit margins, sales growth, and return on investment (ROI)—can seemingly improve in ways that the company's true performance and real value are actually diminished, as I will further explain and illustrate throughout the book. This is just a huge win for EVA and a major reason to use it.

A very good example of a highly effective EVA bonus plan comes from Ball Corporation, a metal packaging and aerospace company with $9 billion in annual revenues. I am pleased to say that I led the effort to help Ball's management adopt EVA in 1992, and that Ball has used essentially the same EVA bonus plan ever since. It is a model plan. The bonus is based exclusively on EVA. The message it conveys is simple—increase EVA. It clearly ties pay to performance. And it motivates all team players to use EVA in modeling decisions and looking for ways to improve performance. And they do use it, right down to the hourly staff in the beverage can manufacturing plant, who watch their parts stores like hawks and pounce on downtime to maximize the run time.

As described in the proxy excerpt description of the plan that follows, Ball's bonuses are based on beating a performance target that is strictly a weighted average of EVA results over prior years, and without any linkage to the budget or business plan goals. All team players are motivated to increase EVA as much as possible rather than to waste time negotiating annual budget goals. And because the bonus is based on an automatically adjusting formula for EVA, the same plan with the same structure has endured through the ages, through the dot-com bubble and burst and recovery, through the housing bubble and burst and slow recovery, through a whole raft of acquisitions, through thick and thin. The bonus plan is like a boat with a deep keel. Whichever way the wind blows, the incentive plan has a strong stabilizing tendency that keeps bonus pay coming back to a base bonus for maintaining EVA and a bonus premium for increasing it.

BALL CORPORATION: DESCRIPTION OF ANNUAL EVA BONUS PLAN, 2012 PROXY, PAGES 28–29

This short-term pay-for-performance incentive is used to encourage and reward the CEO and other NEOs for making decisions that improve performance as measured by EVA. It is designed to produce sustained shareholder value by establishing a direct link between EVA improvement and incentive compensation.

EVA was selected as the measure for Ball's Annual Incentive Compensation Plan because it has been demonstrated to correlate management's incentive with share price growth and shareholder returns. EVA is computed by subtracting a charge for the use of invested capital from net operating profit after-tax as illustrated below:

$$\text{EVA} = \begin{array}{c}\text{Net Operating Profits minus}\\ \text{After Taxes}\\ \text{(``NOPAT'')}\end{array} \quad \begin{array}{c}\text{Capital Charge}\\ \text{(the Amount of Capital Invested}\\ \text{by Ball multiplied by Ball's}\\ \text{After-Tax Hurdle Rate)}\end{array}$$

Generating profits in excess of both operating and capital costs (debt and equity) creates EVA. If EVA improves, value has been created.

Performance Measures—Targets are established annually for each operating unit and for the Corporation as a whole based on prior performance. The Plan design motivates continuous improvement in order to achieve payouts at or above target over time.

The Corporation's and/or operating unit's EVA financial performance determines the amount, if any, of awards earned under the Annual Incentive Compensation Plan. Such awards are based on actual EVA performance relative to the established EVA target. For any one year, the EVA target is equal to the sum of the prior year's target EVA and one-half the amount of the prior year's EVA gain or shortfall relative to the prior year's EVA target and may be calculated as follows:

$$\text{Current Year's EVA Target} = \text{Prior Year's Target EVA} + \tfrac{1}{2} \left(\text{Prior Year's Actual EVA} - \text{Prior Year's Target EVA} \right)$$

Improvement in EVA occurs when the amount of net operating profit after-tax less a charge for capital employed in the business increases over time. It establishes a direct link between annual incentive compensation and continuous improvement of return on invested capital relative to a 9% after-tax "hurdle rate." The Corporation has established 9% as the "hurdle rate" when evaluating capital expenditures and strategic initiatives in most regions in which we do business. This "hurdle rate" is above the Corporation's true cost of capital.

For a given year, a payout at 100% of target annual incentive compensation is achieved when actual EVA is equal to the EVA target. Actual annual incentive payments each year can range from 0–200% of the targeted incentive opportunity based on corporate performance and/or the performance of the operating unit over which the executive has responsibility. For the Corporation's consolidated plan, a payout of 0% is realized when actual EVA is $104 million less than targeted EVA. A payout of 200% or greater may be achieved if actual EVA is $52 million or higher than target EVA. However any amounts over 200% of target are banked and remain at risk until paid over time in one-third increments whenever actual performance under the Annual Incentive Plan results in a payout of less than 200% of target.

In 2011, Ball's actual EVA performance exceeded our EVA target by $46 million and resulted in a payout of 188% of target, as shown below:

EVA Objectives for Fiscal 2011

Target	200% Payout	Actual
$96.3 million	$148.3 million	$142.3 million

Not surprisingly, Ball has produced oodles of EVA. You do tend to get what you pay for. EVA progressed from a *loss* of $52 million for the four-quarter period ending mid-1997 to profits of $63 million by mid-2003, $137 million for mid-2008, and $223 million for the four-quarter period ending mid-2012. Ball has been the top performer in its sector, way outpacing its rivals on EVA and on stock performance. The improvement came not only from improving profitability, but also from growth, including a string of acquisitions and a bout of global expansion.

I don't design bonus plans any longer. I had my turn at that. But I certainly like to talk about them and share best practices from my experiences over the years. This is not the final word in the book on using EVA in bonus plans; as I said, the topic is treated in more depth in Chapter 7 when the question of setting targets for EVA comes up.

A good example of how EVA provides managers with a tangible incentive to improve performance and add value comes from Coca-Cola. Coke adopted EVA in the early 1980s, the first large company to really embrace it. CEO Roberto Goizueta was a huge fan, and after Coke produced the greatest shareholder wealth of any company in 1994, according to a ranking that *Fortune* magazine published using our statistics, we asked him to accept a trophy that Stern Stewart & Company and *Fortune* had cast to celebrate this accomplishment. He said he would, on one condition. He insisted on telling the attendees at the presentation ceremony why he was so keen about EVA. We accepted.

"EVA is not just for the corporate head office to use," he told the audience. "We think it is a way for everyone in the company to get on the value bandwagon." And he gave an example. Coca-Cola traditionally shipped its concentrated syrup to its bottlers in stainless steel containers. The containers sat patiently on Coke's balance sheet and were slowly depreciated against earnings, which made them quite accommodating to book profits. But according to Goizueta, "Someone deep in the midmanagement ranks looked at this and said, 'Wait, we don't really care about book profit. We care about EVA profit. What if we switched over to cardboard containers?'"

Here's the issue. Cardboard containers are not reusable. They are used once, discarded, and charged to earnings. Switching to them would reduce Coke's accounting profit and profit margin and raise unit production costs compared to staying with the stainless steel containers. Goizueta raised his hands in the air, reminiscent of Charlton Heston parting the Red Sea as Moses in *The Ten Commandments*, and asked the conference attendees, "And how many of *you* at *your* companies would even consider a decision like that that would reduce your profit and profit margin and raise production costs in one swoop? But that is why you need EVA, because maybe you should take those hits. You need EVA so everyone can see the right decision amid a sea of conflicting indicators."

In this case, selling the steel containers reduced Coke's capital and capital charge so much that it way more than offset the profit lost by expensing the cardboard containers. It was firmly EVA positive, even if it was NOPAT negative, to make the switch. But how would you really know that without running the numbers, including the impact on the capital charge? And that is precisely why EVA bonus plans are so effective, and so much more effective than stock ownership. With EVA, team members can run the numbers and use a little math to figure the correct decision where trade-offs are involved, as they always are in any real decision. The team members can use EVA to determine how much product prices or profit margins would have to increase to maintain or increase EVA in case a customer makes a request that ties up more inventory or plant capital, for example. They can compute the EVA impact themselves and get it right. They may not know or care that they are increasing the stock price. They only need to know that they are rewarded for EVA and that EVA gives them a concrete way to get to the right answer, and they can let the stock price just take care of itself.

I'll give you a few other examples of where EVA correctly motivated managers and guided them into making much better decisions. One of my clients in the late 1990s was Best Buy. The company's business model has been squeezed in a vice of late by Apple, Amazon, and Wal-Mart. But back then Best Buy was in even worse shape. The company had a lot of operational and inventory problems and was not near earning its cost of capital. It had no discipline around capital investment or a common way to keep score to get everyone pulling on the same oar. People were working at cross-purposes in many instances. So I was asked to make a presentation to the management committee, including Dick Schulze, the founder and CEO at the time (and the man who is currently contemplating taking Best Buy private), and afterward Dick commissioned me to help Best Buy to adopt EVA as its polestar. This was in 1997 and 1998, and it happened at the very time management was considering adding musical instruments to the merchandise lineup.

It seemed a good idea. Operating margins on musical instruments were clearly quite a bit higher than in Best Buy's traditional lines, and management was on the verge of a go decision. But once EVA came along, management zeroed in on the fact that musical instruments turn slowly and tie up a lot of capital. Teens come in and drum and strum for some time before saving enough dough to make the buy. Not only that, but the average ticket price was higher than typical Best Buy fare and would tie up even more money than usual in the inventory supply chain. The bottom line was that a move into musical instruments would boost the firm's operating profit and margins but reduce its EVA. Thankfully, it was rejected, which management might not have done had operating margins remained the focus of attention.

Another example was the decision by CSX Corporation, the railroad company, to enter intermodal—the business of putting trucks on railcars to ship them around. Management for years dragged its feet because intermodal would produce a much lower profit margin than the firm's main rail business was earning, and management did not want to dilute the margin. But once EVA came along, management realized that intermodal could add lots to EVA even with a lower margin because it required much less capital than the main rail business. It would piggyback off the existing network of assets, as it were, and would be incrementally quite EVA positive.

Another EVA-inspired move for CSX was to spend more on maintenance. Prior to EVA, management's goal had been EBITDA, which meant that maintenance spending had been viewed as a necessary evil and a charge to be minimized. But EVA motivated management to consider the benefits, and not just the costs, of maintaining the equipment. Line teams figured that more and better maintenance spending could save capital and boost EVA. They arranged to have railcars and locomotives roll into the repair yards more frequently and leave more swiftly, with a substantial payoff in fleet uptime, reliability, and longevity. EVA paved the way for CSX managers to spend more money on their income statement to save money on their balance sheet.

The last example I'll cite for now is Briggs & Stratton. This was a long time back, but is still relevant. Briggs was reeling from Japanese intrusions into its markets in the 1980s, when firms like Honda started to sell gas-powered engines and lawn mowers in the United States. In defense, Briggs added upscale versions of its engines that were outside its manufacturing comfort zone, which only made matters worse. Enter EVA. All of a sudden, Briggs slashed and redirected capital spending. Why? "The guys are now spending the capital money like it's their own," admitted CEO Fred Stratton.

EVA prompted Briggs, which had been a very highly integrated company, making almost everything in the engine but the spark plugs, to hive off, sell off, even to spin off many of its internal manufacturing lines that just were not competitive compared to outside vendors. And most incredibly, Briggs decided to outsource the manufacture of its troublesome high-end engines to Daihatsu and Mitsubishi. "We decided to let the Japanese fend off the Japanese," quipped the CEO. "Even so, we probably never would have done that without EVA, for cultural reasons; and also, it took our margins way down, as we were only able to charge a much lower markup on the engines we bought and resold than the ones we made, but in so doing we released capital and increased our focus. It was very EVA positive for us—it tuned our engine, probably saved the company."

Getting everyone to focus their efforts on improving a single measure that completely and correctly consolidates all the pluses and minuses of decisions into one score is incredibly powerful—more than most CFOs or CEOs who have not lived with it would believe. And ironically, and again counterintuitively, the hard part is not really so much in adding EVA. EVA can be explained simply, illustrated, and made relevant, and with our software tools it is a snap to automate and start using the best practices. In my experience, the hard part is convincing everyone to let go of the other financial metrics they have come to cherish over the years, and to trust EVA and let it be the one key focal measure that really matters.

Let's face it—most companies don't do anything of the sort. Most CFOs track a disorganized jumble of performance metrics without a way to express that one matters any more than any other. I recall once visiting a company that was placing a 10 percent weight on each of 10 metrics in its bonus plan, and when I stated the view that that was quite a few, the executives said, "But they are all on our balanced scorecard, and they are all important." I said, "But brushing your teeth in the morning is important, too. Why not add that? Why not put a 1 percent weight on 100 measures and bring everything into the picture?"

The serious point I was trying to convey was that in their attempt to make everything important, nothing was. They had a scorecard without a score. They acted as if each measure should be increased and would add to value on its own, as if no trade-offs ever needed to be made. But in the real world and in real decisions, choices and trade-offs always have to be made—the most basic of which is that you generally cannot increase sales unless you increase capital. And that is why it is so essential to have one score that properly consolidates the pluses and minuses into a net sum.

Another criticism is that they had so broken down the management equation into a set of mini-metrics that they were micromanaging the business and inhibiting their team from taking initiatives. They were straitjacketing their managers into a preordained way of running the business. At best they were re-creating EVA by an imperfect and very complicated proxy. At worst they were treating their management team disrespectfully, as if they had to spoon-feed them every detail and manage their every decision. I call that marionette management—management by pulling on strings. I say cut the strings and let Pinocchio come to life. *Educate and empower* is the hallmark of an EVA company.

CHAPTER 2

EVA and Value

How does EVA determine a company's share price? Not directly. It is not, after all, a per share measure. But EVA *is* the best measure of all to compute share prices and to explain actual stock price performance. If that were not true, there would be no case for EVA.

EVA ties to share prices indirectly through a sister measure that I call MVA, standing for market value added. As it turns out, MVA is far more significant than stock price itself. Here's why. MVA is the dollar difference between the total cash that investors have put or left in a business, and which now stands on its balance sheet as its invested capital, and the present value of the cash that they can expect to take out of the business, as indicated by the firm's share price. For example, if a company has a total market value or enterprise value of $1 billion, and has invested $600 million of capital in net business assets, then it has created MVA of $400 million, the difference.

As I said, this is a really important measure. It shows, first, how much wealth the firm has created for its owners by comparing what they have put in with what they can get out. Put another way, MVA is *franchise value*, the value of the business above just putting the assets in a pile. It is also, mathematically, the market's assessment of the net present value (NPV) of all investments the company has made, those already in place plus those expected to materialize down the road. Put it all together, and MVA is more important than share price.

In fact, increasing MVA should be every company's most important financial goal. An increase in MVA reveals, as no other measure can, how successful management had been at allocating, managing, and redeploying scarce resources of all kinds so as to maximize the wealth of the owners by maximizing the net present value of the enterprise. That being the case, every board and top team should track it.

As mentioned, EVA ties to share prices through its link to MVA. How important is that? It is *all-important.* That's because EVA is the *only* performance measure that directly ties to MVA. The link between MVA and

EVA exists because EVA also is the only measure that ties to NPV—to net present value. I call this the fundamental principle of wealth creation, and it states: *The present value of a forecast for EVA is always mathematically identical to the net present value of discounted cash flow, or to what is the same thing, MVA at the corporate level.* Why is that? By virtue of the capital charge, EVA sets aside the profit that must be earned to recover the value of the capital that has been or will be invested, and as a result, EVA *always* discounts to the net present value of a project or decision. It always discounts to the market value *above* the invested capital. And at the corporate level a forward plan projection of EVA always discounts to the consolidated company's MVA. You will see an example of that in just a minute.

I say this with great conviction and emphasis because we have developed a software tool that automatically calculates NPV and MVA both ways, by discounting cash flow and by discounting the EVA, and it always produces the same answer for a given forecast. The equality I am stressing is not a theory or something you might or might not believe. It is a mathematical truth, just as $2 + 2 = 4$. And as you will see later on, projecting and discounting EVA is at the heart of value-based planning and decision making.

Putting the math aside for a moment, consider the implications. If a company, a line of business, or a capital investment project is forecast to just break even on EVA—to just earn the cost of capital—then it breaks even on NPV. It will only be worth the book value of the capital invested in it. There is no NPV, no franchise value, no owners' wealth, and no MVA without EVA. You can grow everything else. You can expand sales, earnings, EBITDA, and margins all you want. But if you are not growing EVA you are not creating value—you are at best only preserving it.

On the bright side, once EVA turns positive and a firm generates more profit with its capital than its investors could earn by investing it on their own, then value is being added, wealth created, and a real franchise value established. And the greater the EVA and the faster, surer, and longer it grows, the greater the NPV and MVA will be. This is why *Fortune* magazine dubbed EVA "the real key to creating wealth" in the cover story that introduced EVA to its readers in September 1993.

Let's examine the EVA/MVA connection for Ball Corporation over the period from midyear 1997 to midyear 2012 as an example. The top chart in Exhibit 2.1 plots Ball's market value as the light bar versus its capital as the dark bar. The spread between the two is MVA, the market value added to the capital, and it is shown on the bottom chart.

By market value I mean the total value the market is assigning to all the capital invested in the firm's net business assets. It starts with the market capitalization of the common equity given the share price and also includes debt and other liabilities and the present value of rents on leased facilities and equipment, less excess cash. In other words, market value is what it

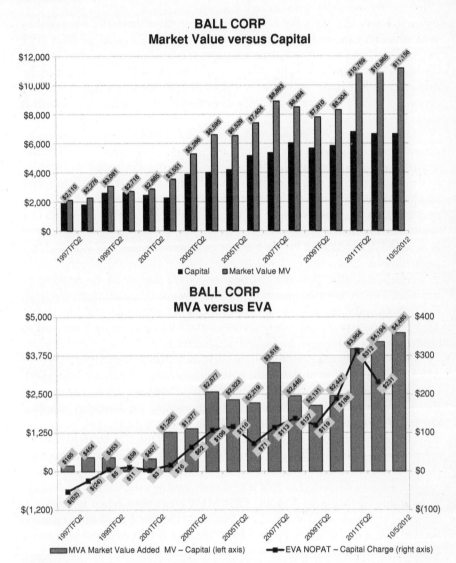

EXHIBIT 2.1   Ball Corporation's Market Value, MVA, and EVA (dollars in millions)

would cost to buy the business, debt and rent free and free of excess cash, at prevailing market prices. Capital is the corresponding investment in the firm's net business assets, including rented assets, and also net of excess cash, so that the two measures correspond, and MVA is simply the difference between the two.

Ball's MVA is plotted as the ascending bar on the left scale in the lower chart, and the firm's EVA profit is traced by the line on the right scale. MVA increased over the years because Ball's market value generally increased by *more* than its capital increased. Ball added to the stock of its positive NPV investments, and as a result, Ball added to the stock of its owners' wealth. As important, it added to its MVA by adding to its EVA. Ball's MVA increased hand in hand with the demonstrated ability to earn and increase economic profit. As expected, EVA was indeed the key to creating wealth at Ball Corporation.

Let's zoom in on details. In midyear 1997, Ball's market value and its capital both stood at about $2 billion (top chart), and thus its MVA was virtually nil at a time when EVA was negative but beginning to improve (bottom chart). EVA rose fairly steadily and certainly impressively after that, reaching a peak of over $300 million for the four-quarter period ending in mid-2011. In response, starting from a standstill, Ball's MVA ascended to a wealth premium that is now over $4 billion. Ball is thus a good example of how an EVA bonus plan forges a direct link between pay and value-adding performance.

Note, also, that Ball did not generate EVA and MVA by milking its business, but by nourishing growth. Management invested aggressively, as the firm's capital base increased from about $2 billion in 1997 to nearly $6.5 billion 15 years later in order to expand its business globally and to consummate a number of important acquisitions.

In the most recent period, Ball's EVA turned down somewhat and yet its MVA held up. Ball is in the process of an aggressive expansion campaign, and capital investment costs have temporarily depressed EVA. The market, though, has looked beyond that and is impounding the long-run expected stream of EVA into the current MVA. As an EVA company, Ball has earned a measure of credibility that enables it to make significant strategic investments while retaining investors' confidence that management is batting with their interests in mind.

In case you suspect that Ball was simply surfing an EVA wave common to its industry, take a look at the EVA/MVA chart for Crown Holdings, a principal competitor in the metal can business (Exhibit 2.2). Without getting bogged down in the year-to-year details, the fact is that over the long term, Crown's EVA has essentially moved sideways, and MVA as well. The picture is starkly different from Ball's.

The two cases illustrate a general rule. In the real world, changes in MVA are best explained by changes in EVA, far better than measures like growth in sales, earnings or EBITDA, margins, and returns. EVA measures wealth creation, in principle and in practice. And as a result, managers can analyze, project, and discount EVA to measure NPV and owner wealth with the confidence that they are focusing on the measure that really matters and accurately simulating how the market will respond.

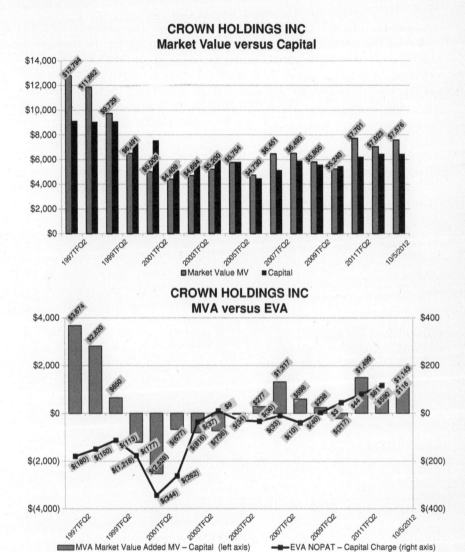

EXHIBIT 2.2   Crown Holdings' Market Value, MVA, and EVA (dollars in millions)

One company that does that is Volkswagen, which also makes Audi, Bentley, Bugatti, and Lamborghini branded vehicles, among others. The company's financial management is governed by EVA. The criteria for new investments and initiatives is to approve only those where the NPV—as measured by the present value of the projected EVA—is positive after considering project-specific risks and company-wide consequences.

Managers, moreover, are instructed to improve and optimize NPV by improving the stream of EVA profit that the investment can be configured to generate. The procedure to do that is described in the firm's EVA manual, an excerpt of which is shown in Exhibit 2.3. It shows that Volkswagen will forecast line-of-business net operating profit after taxes (NOPAT) and the charge for the incremental capital employed over the product life cycle, and then discount the resulting EVA at a 9 percent hurdle rate to measure net present value that is the basis for decision making. Incidentally, you can download a full PDF copy of the manual from the company's website at www.volkswagenag.com/content/vwcorp/info_center/en/publications/2010/ 08/Finanzielle_Steuerungsgroessen.bin.html/binarystorageitem/file/ Financial+Control+System+3e.pdf.

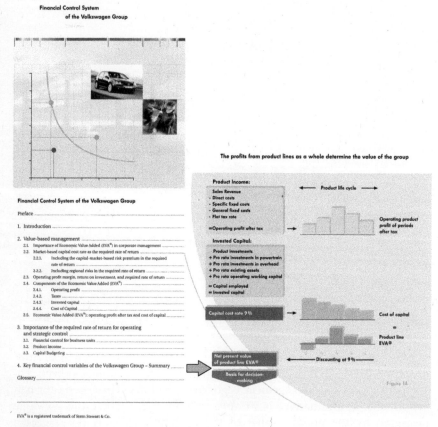

EXHIBIT 2.3 Volkswagen Financial Control System

As the Volkswagen example suggests, the present value of EVA is indeed identical to the net present value of discounted cash flow. I have said that is so because EVA sets aside the cost of capital needed to recover the value of the invested capital. But still, at a more fundamental level, why is the present value of a forecast for EVA always identical to discounted cash flow and NPV?

You can grasp it without a complicated proof. I like to put it in banking terms. Suppose I lend you $100 and then I say you have two choices. You can pay back the loan right away or you can take your time. Pay me back over 10 years, say, at a rate of $10 a year. As long as you pay me a market rate of interest on the unpaid loan balance, the present value of getting paid back right away and getting paid back over time with interest is exactly the same, by definition.

What is the analogy? The cash flow that is discounted to measure NPV is computed as if the loan was paid back right away. Investment spending is deducted from cash flow when it is forecast to be spent. EVA, on the other hand, is like paying the loan back over time, as assets are depreciated or charged through cost of goods sold and with a market rate of interest assessed on the outstanding loan balance. The present value is *always* the same, and regardless of the depreciation period chosen, from expensing right away to no depreciation at all to anything in between. This being the case, everything that validates cash flow or discounted cash flow as a management and valuation tool automatically validates EVA as well. Discard EVA, and you might as well discard discounted cash flow, for they come to the same thing.

I want to make the case, though, that *EVA is actually far better than cash flow* as a decision and analysis tool, because EVA better matches cost and benefit. It spreads the charge for using capital over the time periods when the investments are expected to contribute to profit and add to the value instead of concentrating the charge for capital in the one period that the investment is made, as cash flow does. As a result, an increase or a decrease in EVA from one period to the next is generally a far more reliable indication than cash flow ever is of whether NPV is increasing or decreasing. Moreover, with a ratio analysis framework we'll cover later, EVA is better able to show *why* the NPV is increasing or decreasing from period to period. EVA is able to pinpoint and statistically quantify the individual value drivers, and that makes it easier for managers to use it to improve the net present value of a plan, an investment project, or even an acquisition, and not just to measure it.

In contrast, cash flow can do none of those things, because cash flow is a highly misleading if not completely meaningless measure of performance from period to period. In any one period, cash flow could go lower because the firm's NOPAT is falling, which is bad, or because management is investing even more capital to fuel more growth in EVA, which would be terrific.

In fact, many of the most valuable companies on the market operate for years on end with a negative cash flow after investment spending. And what is true in one period is true over many periods. You simply cannot tell, over any time horizon, and certainly not over three- to five-year spans, whether more or less net cash generation from a business is an improvement or a setback. And that's not just a theory. The correlation between changes in MVA and net cash flow generation over three years is less than 10 percent.

To give one example, consider Amazon, which produced the 38th highest shareholder return among the S&P 500 nonfinancials over the three years ending mid-2012. AMZN invested very aggressively in those years. Its capital surged from $3.4 billion to $13.0 billion, way outstripping internally generated sources. The spending was so intense that the Internet retailer's cash flow net of the investment spending—the cash flow that you discount to measure value and that I refer to as its free cash flow—was *negative* $4.65 billion over a time frame when the firm's stock price increased from $83.66 to $228.35 a share.

What explains why the stock performed so well while management was shoveling bucket loads of cash back into the business? The investments were paying off, and they were generating year-over-year increases in EVA. As is shown in Exhibit 2.4, AMZN's EVA increased fairly steadily from $731 million for the four-quarter year ending mid-2009 to $1.3 billion for the mid-2012 year. As with Ball, AMZN's EVA propelled MVA, which blossomed from $32 billion to $92 billion, for $60 billion of wealth created *above* all the capital infusions. AMZN illustrates a general rule: When cash flow goes down and EVA goes up, it's EVA that wins the argument.

The implication is perhaps startling. *You should stop using discounted cash flow analysis.* That's right. Stop using discounted cash flow. Cash flow is not wrong in principle. It does discount to NPV, after all, and NPV is still the goal. Cash flow just doesn't work well in practice.

The only time management assembles all of the cash flow numbers in one view is when an investment is first proposed. But once accepted and funded, the capital is buried on the firm's balance sheet and no one really seems to care too much about it. As a result, operating teams have a burning desire to get their hands on as much capital as possible, to build their businesses, pad their budgets, and grease the skids for bonuses and advancement. Knowing this, the CFO office deploys storm troopers to the field to check forecast assumptions. The field retaliates by raising the projections. The head office fires back with increases in the hurdle rates. And in the end, the whole process of capital budgeting is characterized by mutual deception and Kabuki theater—everyone is wearing a mask. And all of these shenanigans happen for a simple reason: because cash flow is being used to

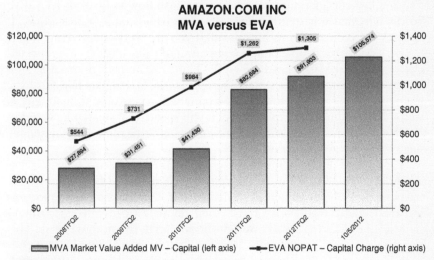

EXHIBIT 2.4 Amazon's MVA and EVA (dollars in millions)

calculate the value of the plans and projects when cash flow cannot be used to measure their performance after the fact.

What's better? EVA. Forecast, analyze, and discount EVA as the means to measure and improve the value of plans, projects, acquisitions, and decisions—as Volkswagen and Ball and many other EVA companies do—and then also measure EVA and reward improvements based on actual results. The NPV answer is always exactly the same. But unlike cash flow, EVA is able to forge a direct link between how decisions are made looking forward and how performance is measured and bonuses are awarded after the fact. It's all EVA-based. And that consistency in both directions is the key to keeping it simple and keeping it accountable.

The logic of this recommendation won't be fully apparent until I introduce the EVA performance ratios later on and show how they can be used to illuminate the moving parts that are driving EVA and driving the net present value. But the really important point for now is that, if you adopt the goal to increase EVA as the key profit performance measure, you are in fact motivating decisions that will maximize the discounted cash flow net present value of the business, and you can do that even better than using cash flow itself or any other financial measure.

VALUATION DETAILS

Establishing a connection from EVA to MVA and NPV, and to share price, is such a key consideration, and discarding cash flow in favor of EVA is so worthwhile, that it is worth going into more details on how this works. If you lack the patience for it, skip ahead. If you are on the quest, read on.

Let's revive the simple sample company and value it using cash flow and EVA. Recall that SSCo is earning NOPAT of $150 and has invested $1,000 in capital. Let's start with a simple example before layering on more realistic assumptions. We assume that the company will invest only to maintain its capital base and not for expanding it. It will spend only an amount equal to the depreciation of its physical assets and the amortization of its intangible ones, with two consequences.

First, its NOPAT profit will not grow. NOPAT will remain forever frozen at $150 because we are assuming there is no investment to grow the business; the only investment is to maintain it. Depreciation and amortization are deducted from NOPAT and equal amounts are invested to maintain the firm's productive capacity and profit potential, but nothing more. This leads to the second consequence, which is that the firm's capital is also constant. It runs at $1,000 forever. The maintenance capital-expenditure spending adds to capital each year, but that merely offsets the depreciation and amortization for the year, so that the net capital balance does not change.

The result is that the company's free cash flow (FCF) is also frozen at $150. FCF is the net cash generated from operations after investment spending. It is the net cash available for investor distribution. And last, it is the cash flow that is discounted at the cost of capital to measure value.

The formula to compute FCF is to take the NOPAT earned on the income statement and to deduct the period-to-period change in the capital employed on the balance sheet. Since the net change in capital is zero in this case, the distributable free cash flow is simply the firm's NOPAT profit. This reveals NOPAT's true significance. It measures the after-tax operating profit that can be sustained indefinitely and distributed as a return to investors each year while preserving the integrity of the underlying capital base.

What is the value of the company under these circumstances? The company is like a bond that promises to pay $150 annually forever. The formula to compute the value of a forever payment is to divide it by the cost of capital. In this case, take the NOPAT of $150 and divide it by the cost of capital of 10 percent, and the company is worth $1,500. It is worth $1,500 because at that value, the $150 in NOPAT the firm earns and pays out each year always provides investors with the 10 percent return they are seeking.

Incidentally, the NOPAT that is capitalized to measure the value should represent the firm's midcycle profit power, or the average NOPAT it will earn over a cycle. As a result, the return the investors earn on the market value they pay will actually fluctuate over business cycles, and won't be an even 10 percent a year even if it is an average of 10 percent a year, which is why the expected NOPAT is discounted at the cost of capital risk rate and not at the risk-free government bond rate.

What is the firm's MVA? The firm's market value is $1,500 and its invested capital is $1,000. MVA is $500, the difference. The company has added $500 to the value of its invested capital. It has created a positive franchise value and has added to its owners' wealth. This is depicted in Exhibit 2.5.

Now let's use EVA to value the company with the same assumptions. EVA, recall, is $50. It is the $150 NOPAT less the $100 capital charge required to earn a 10 percent return on the $1,000 of invested capital. Since we've assumed NOPAT and capital remain the same forever, EVA will, too. It will run at $50 as far as the eye can see. The present value of earning $50 per year, discounted at the 10 percent cost of capital, is $500. Voilà, as advertised, the present value of EVA does indeed equal the value added to

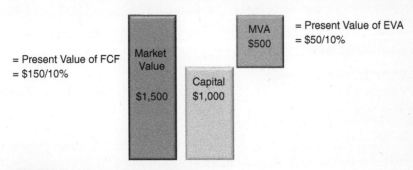

EXHIBIT 2.5   Market Value and MVA

the capital. It discounts to NPV and MVA because EVA sets aside the profit that must be earned to recover the value of the capital.

Incidentally, the $500 MVA we just computed goes by another name. I call it CVA, for current value added. CVA is the MVA that comes from assuming EVA will hold steady at its current level and never grow or shrink, which is what we assumed in this special case. MVA can be greater than that, however, if investors expect that EVA will grow, which is the case we will now take up.

Let's consider a more realistic example where the company invests capital and grows NOPAT and EVA. To keep it simple, assume that in addition to its normal replenishment spending to maintain the assets every year, the company makes a single growth investment of $100 in forecast year 1. Assume the payoff is that the NOPAT increases from $150 in year one to $165 in year 2 and then it holds steady thereafter (we're assuming for simplicity that it takes a year from the time of the investment until the return kicks in).

FCF Valuation	History	P1	P2	P3 and …
NOPAT	$150	$150	$165	$165
Capital	$1,000	$1,100	$1,100	$1,100
Δ Capital		$100	$0	$0
FCF (NOPAT − ΔCapital)	$150	$50	$165	$165
PV Factor @10%		0.90909	0.82645	8.2645
Present Value of FCF	$1,545.45	$45.45	$136.36	$1,363.64
Capital	$1,000.00			
MVA	$545.45			

EVA Valuation	History	P1	P2	P3 and …
NOPAT	$150	$150	$165	$165
Capital	$1,000	$1,100	$1,100	$1,100
Capital Charge @10%		$100	$110	$110
EVA (NOPAT − Capital Charge)	$50	$50	$55	$55
PV Factor @10%		0.90909	0.82645	8.2645
Present Value of EVA	$545.45	$45.45	$45.45	$454.55

The company's free cash flow (FCF) takes a major wallop in the first projection period. FCF drops from $150 to $50 as the $100 growth investment is deducted from NOPAT. Thereafter, assuming no more investment above maintenance spending, FCF continues forever at the new NOPAT of $165. Question: Is the company's value higher or lower, assuming the forecast assumptions given are accurate? Cash flow per se does not help to answer that question. It is lower up front, and more later, so who knows? Cash flow provides an insight only when the stream of cash flow is discounted to a present value. So let's do that, one last time.

As shown in the table, the FCF projected for years 1 and 2 is discounted to present value using conventional present value (PV) factors at the 10 percent cost of capital. The value of receiving $1 in year 1 is 90.90 cents today, and the value of a $1 in year 2 is 82.65 cents today. The trick is the PV factor for the third projected period, which is 8.2645. That says that each $1 of NOPAT that goes on forever starting in the third period is worth $8.2645 today. How so?

First, compute the value of receiving $1 of NOPAT per year forever at the 10 percent cost of capital. That is $1 divided by 10 percent, or $10. A 10:1 valuation multiple is put on each $1 of NOPAT. But that's the valuation multiple as of the end of the second period, and we want the valuation now. We need to bring the valuation back two more periods to the present value. That's easy. Just multiply the 10× multiple by the present value factor for the prior year, which recall is 0.82645, and sure enough, 10 times 0.82645 is the advertised 8.2645. That factor automatically computes the value of receiving $1 in NOPAT per year in perpetuity starting in period 3 and discounts it back two more years to present value. It is the present value of the enterprise multiple.

Multiply that factor times the projected perpetual NOPAT of $165, and the total present value is $1,363.64. Now add in the present values for FCF computed for the first two years, and the total present value of the cash to be cast off over the entire life of the business is $1,545.45, compared to a cash flow value of $1,500 before. The investment will bring an increase in net present value and MVA and increase the stock price. Just the prospect of the investment will increase the current wealth of the owners to a revised market-to-book spread of $545.45 versus $500 before.

That is all well and good, but *why* is that the answer? Why has the net present value increased? Cash flow tells us the value is higher but is silent on why. It swoons as the investment is made, surges as the return materializes, then flattens forever. What does the zigzag pattern tell us about the company's performance and its value? Absolutely nothing. As I have said, cash flow gives an NPV answer but without any insight and without any accountability or line of sight back to how performance can be measured and rewarded. It is arid and isolated, and it must go. Let's now take a look at how EVA values the same forecast, which appears in the bottom table.

As the $100 investment is added to the capital till, the capital charge increases by $10, from $100 to $110. That's where the accountability comes into play. The cost of the added capital becomes a new and ongoing charge to the EVA earnings, and managers know they must beat that. In this case the increase in the capital charge is more than covered by the projected $15 increase in NOPAT. EVA is projected to increase by $5, from $50 to $55. The investment is EVA positive, and hence it is by definition NPV positive. The increase in EVA from $50 to $55 is a clear proxy for the added value. That is the insight that EVA offers that cash flow does not.

Using the exact same PV factors to discount the projected EVA as we used to discount cash flow, the present value sum is identical. The PV of EVA is the same $545.45 MVA that was derived from discounting the cash flow. NPV and owner wealth have increased from $500 to $545.45 because the present value of the stream of EVA has been projected to increase. EVA can do everything cash flow does as far as measuring NPV and value is concerned, but it also provides a period-by-period measure to explain why the value has increased or decreased. Outside a firm's treasury department, which must be concerned with cash flow and how it will be financed and disposed of, there is no need for line teams to ever use it or be confused by it.

All other investments and returns are just variations on this simple example. It serves to show, I hope convincingly, that the present value of projected EVA always equals NPV at the investment project level and always equals MVA at the corporate level, no matter how complicated the pattern of investments and returns becomes.

Incidentally, there is a name for the added value we projected in this example. The extra $45.45 in MVA is called FVA, standing for future value added. It is present value of the *growth* in EVA over its current level. To put this in symbols, MVA = CVA + FVA. In this case, MVA = $545.45. That is the total NPV and wealth created. CVA = $500, and is the NPV value of the embedded EVA; FVA is the balance, $45.45, and is the NPV of the projected growth in EVA from $50 to $55.

In this example, FVA came entirely from the growth in EVA that was projected to occur in just a single period. In reality, FVA is the present value of the EVA growth that is expected *over the entire life of a business*. Does this require the clairvoyance of a Delphic oracle? Must EVA be forecast forever? Fortunately, no. EVA growth forecasts can be truncated as a practical matter. Here's why.

Investors have learned from painful experience that competition, saturation, substitution, fading fads, bureaucratic creep, overpriced acquisitions, and outright management blunders are among the factors that eventually undermine a firm's ability to continue growing its EVA. Like people, companies mature and lose their mojo. And when companies reach the point where their EVA can no longer grow, or are projected to reach that status, the EVA earned up to that point can be assumed to persist and be very simply valued in perpetuity. All business valuation methods do this, in effect. They reach a point where a *terminal value* is determined. But the justification for that lies in the EVA model and only in the EVA model. In all other models the rationalization for the terminal value is essentially a great mystery.

It is not just the saturation of the product and service markets that the company serves that sets limits on EVA growth. It is not that there is a given finite pool of economic profit to exploit, like a reservoir of oil to be tapped. The EVA reservoirs all have leaks. Emerging superior technologies and shifting tastes are always working to siphon EVA away underground and in an invisible way.

Think of it like this. When the world begins to value hot new things, the value it attaches to existing things cools, of necessity. Each consumer gets only so many votes to spend on the world market, and if consumers start to vote for the hot new things, like, for example, investments in social networking businesses, then they are implicitly withdrawing votes and subtracting economic profits from every other product and service and business out there. Think of EVA as the signal the market bestows on what it values and what deserves access to the available scarce resources for growth. Not everything can be a priority. As new businesses emerge and new technologies arise, the priorities change, the votes shift, and the EVA moves. Existing businesses wake up to find they have less pricing power and that they have become more like a commodity that can just cover its full costs, including the cost of capital, but no more. This can be frustrating. Management sees no reason for it. No bell goes off. But that is why it is so essential to monitor the movements of EVA at the margin.

Later on, in Chapter 7, Setting EVA Targets, we review statistics for the Russell 3000 companies over a 20-year history. You will see that EVA profits of individual companies definitely tend to cool and converge to long-run norms over time, and that the expectations factored into stock prices reflect that tendency. It is not just a theory.

Granted, some companies have managed to defy the gravitational pull on profits for a very long time. Coca-Cola is still increasing its EVA after well over a century in business, for example; but such companies are rare exceptions. Just think General Motors, Sears, Kodak, and RadioShack. Even once-revered tech giants like Hewlett-Packard, Dell, and Xerox have been just treading EVA water in recent years. Their EVAs are moving sideways as their products become more perfunctory. Their EVA glory runs appear to be at an end unless management can pull off a miraculous revival. Hope springs eternal, and some may succeed. But when real money is on the line, investors almost always assume that a company's EVA will eventually crest, and they will not take the risk of assuming it will grow forever.

This is the hard part of the valuation business. How long do you forecast it will take before Wal-Mart exhausts its profitable growth opportunities and its EVA no longer grows, for example? Are Best Buy and Dell already at the end of their EVA growth curves, or will they revive? And perhaps the biggest question of all: How long before Apple becomes like Whirlpool, a maker of everyday appliances in a crowded competitive market where increasing EVA is really hard to do?

Bear in mind that we are talking about growth in EVA and when that stops. Companies may continue to expand for quite a while, open new stores, add new customers, develop new products, increase sales and earnings, and so on, and yet see their EVA go sideways as they just earn the cost of capital on net on all new investments. This is far from a question of forecasting when a bankruptcy will occur. It is a question of when a sector becomes so competitive that the prices companies can charge will just cover the total cost of all resources they use. At that point there is no incentive for a new entrant to jump in and make matters worse, but neither is there an incentive for investors to pay a premium for growth even though the growth in sales and earnings per share (EPS) may continue for quite a while. All other measures are blissfully ignorant of the competitive change that has made growth irrelevant to the valuation of the company. But not EVA.

Please understand that EVA does not make valuations harder by asking these questions. Quite the opposite. EVA helps make valuations easier and more accurate by bringing the question of when growth will no longer add value and when EVA will crest into sharp relief. Other models simply ignore the issue or obscurely bury it in indeterminate valuation multiples.

Let's probe the question a little further. The EVA growth horizon that investors forecast typically involves some judgment about a particular company, but with heavy overtones from a probabilistic and pooled estimate. Stocks, in other words, are priced a lot like life insurance policies. No one can predict when any one person will expire, but the pool is predictable. You can look it up in actuarial tables. The same is true of stocks. Firms of a certain character, ones for example that have long-established profitable franchises and economic moats that protect them from encroachment, are as a group assumed to live longer EVA lives. They are the nonsmokers in the valuation crowd with healthy DNA. Some of the firms in the pool may sustain EVA growth for longer than the median estimate, others less, but the market will tend to get the pool right on average. And for well-endowed firms like these, the market generally prices seven to 12 years of EVA growth into the stock, but those estimates are revised all the time.

On the other side are firms in highly competitive businesses with many rivals and with little lasting opportunity for differentiation. Think of airlines or grocery chains, for instance. The firms are for the most part run by intelligent, dedicated, and creative people, but it is very easy for competitors to imitate what works. There are exceptions like Alaska Air and Whole Foods—that is where the company overlay comes in—but in the main, the market will not embed any significant expected EVA growth into the MVA of these stocks at any time.

The next category covers firms whose EVA profits are purely cyclical or commodity-price-driven phenomena, like fertilizer or forest products companies. From experience, the market assumes that any windfall or shortfall in the EVA profits is temporary and will be swiftly competed away or reversed as a normal supply/demand balance is restored. But putting the cycles aside, the EVA growth horizon for those firms is really nearly always zero.

In between the EVA-endowed franchises and the EVA-lean cyclical or commodity firms are two other categories. The first I call the flashes in a pan—companies that get hot and ride a wave and produce impressive EVA profits for a while, but are highly vulnerable—think Research In Motion (BlackBerry) or Nokia or Motorola in the cell phone business, or Green Mountain Coffee with its Keurig machines (now that Starbucks is on its tail). Their EVA can disappear in a blink of an eye and often does. The market always fears that will happen and factors the possibility into an actuarially limited EVA growth horizon, which is one reason why the managers in those firms are always dissatisfied with their market valuations.

The last category of note are the middle-of-the-roaders, the everyday firms operating in businesses that still have modest to above-average growth prospects, and where technological or brand or organizational capabilities confer the ability to sustain EVA growth over some reasonable horizon. How long? The general rule is five years. For most companies, the market is willing to pay for about five years of growth in EVA, and then assumes, either literally or effectively, that EVA flattens there forever (EVA may actually be forecast to continue growing for a while longer but then to fade, with the same valuation effect as if it was level forever). Even if you can sit down with your computer and forecast 50 years (Excel is a wonderful extrapolation tool), the market is apt to pay for only five, except in special cases. It is particularly important to recognize this limitation when you are pricing an acquisition candidate. It is easy to overpay by assuming EVA will grow for a longer stretch than the market will ever pay for.

Now let's return to the conversation about FVA—the portion of the value that is due to growth in EVA. It can be derived from discounting a projection of EVA, taking account of the appropriate growth horizons per the earlier discussion. That is what we did in the simple valuation example we just covered. But there is also a way to derive FVA from share prices to see what the market thinks it is. To do that, we compute MVA from the company's share price and then deduct its CVA—the MVA portion determined by capitalizing the firm's most recent four-quarter EVA at its cost of capital. The remainder is the firm's implied FVA, and it measures the total present value of the growth in EVA that *investors* are implicitly forecasting. This calculation is a way to free ride on the research that investors have done and have registered in stock price bets. It won't always be right, of course, but it is always worth consulting.

To illustrate, let's take a look at Apple. Its EVA and MVA are portrayed in Exhibit 2.6 with a breakout of MVA into the CVA and FVA components.

EXHIBIT 2.6 Apple's Market Value, MVA, and EVA (dollars in millions)

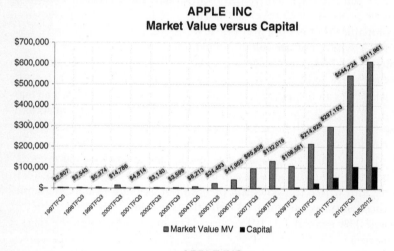

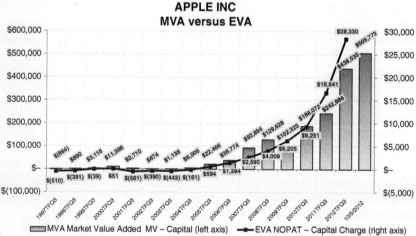

EXHIBIT 2.6 (Continued)

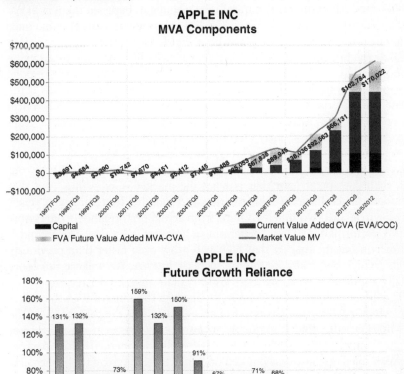

APPLE INC
MVA Components

APPLE INC
Future Growth Reliance

No surprises here—Apple has been a prodigious producer of EVA and MVA, the most prodigious ever. As shown in the lower left chart, Apple's EVA—the line—was running at a sizable *loss* as recently as 2003, just nine years ago. But since then it accelerated to, gulp, over $28 billion for the four-quarter period ending in June 2012. That's Apple's EVA profit, not its sales, ladies and gentlemen. And whereas 15 years ago, in 1997, Apple's MVA— the bar on the lower left chart— was negative, as of late summer 2012 it stood at, phew, $524 billion of created wealth and counting. As expected, Apple's MVA increased in lockstep with its EVA.

The upper left chart plots Apple's aggregate market value as the light bar. The dark bar is the firm's capital. The visual gap between them is MVA. Now look at the upper right chart. The line is aggregate market value once again, but now the bar below it has been divided into three segments, with capital at the bottom and a CVA component, which is the capitalized value of the EVA that Apple earned over the trailing four quarters, in the middle. The top portion of the bar is a plug residual component, FVA, which is the present value of the growth in EVA that investors are forecasting the firm will earn. That, too, increased from under $10 billion as little as eight years ago to $170 billion as of early October 2012.

Apple has not only performed magnificently. Steve Jobs and his successors brilliantly positioned the company to generate ever larger pools of EVA profit down the pike—or at least that is what the market is expecting. And that illustrates a general rule. Wealth creation and shareholder returns can generally come from just two sources. One is from actual performance, from raising the EVA performance bar and generating a greater CVA value. The second is from convincing the market that EVA will grow even faster than previously thought, which will translate into an increase in FVA. We will see this more formally a little later when we use EVA to explain shareholder returns.

The lower right chart in Exhibit 2.6 displays the ratio of FVA to market value, which I call Future Growth Reliance (FGR). It is the percentage of the firm's market value that is implicitly counting on—and is at the risk of not getting—continued growth in EVA. As of early October 2012, 25 percent of Apple's market value was banked on projected EVA growth. In the early years, when EVA was negative, as much as 160 percent of the company's market value was premised on EVA growth. That was an indication of just how risky the stock really was at that time and how much, even then, the market was willing to gamble on Jobs pulling off a miracle.

As time passed, Jobs and his team worked their magic, and the forecast EVA materialized (actually, a whole lot more materialized than the market had forecast); a larger *proportion* of Apple's market value shifted from potential value into actual value, from FVA into CVA, into the value of the embedded and established EVA profit stream and away from the expected growth. Don't misunderstand this. A massive expectation for growth in EVA profits remains in the share price, but the *percentage* of the firm's market value that is represented by that and is premised on achieving further EVA growth has shrunk.

To conclude, then, Future Growth Reliance (FGR) is a ratio statistic that EVA Dimensions tracks and that CFOs and board members should monitor. It provides a convenient and reliable indication of the market's confidence in a company's turnaround plan or strategic positioning to grow EVA. Later on, we will take this a step further and show how to convert FGR into an even more usable statistic, which is the expected growth rate for EVA.

GETTING FROM EVA TO THE SHARE PRICE

At this point I am quite hopeful that you understand that projections of EVA can be used to model the NPV of capital projects and specific decisions, and that a consolidated EVA projection discounts to the corporate aggregate MVA. That still leaves the question of how to get from MVA to share price.

It's easy. A little fiddling with the MVA formula is all that's required. Recall that MVA is market value less capital, where capital is the net assets used in the business:

$$MVA = \text{Market Value} - \text{Capital}$$

Rearrange, and substitute for MVA:

$$\text{Market Value} = \text{Capital} + MVA$$
$$\text{Market Value} = \text{Capital} + \text{Present value of EVA}$$

In other words, the market value of a company as a going concern business is equal to the book value of the capital that has been put into the business plus a premium, or less a discount, to reflect the quality of capital management. Said another way, corporate market value is commodity capital value plus proprietary franchise value, where franchise value is measured by the present value of the projected economic profit. For example, the market value of Microsoft is the money spent developing the software code as if it were just random zeros and ones plus the franchise value of the code in the sense that it works and it enhances the productivity of Microsoft's customers.

The franchise value could come from technology and innovation, distinctive and trusted brands, exceptional customer service and satisfaction, operational excellence, or any of myriad operating or strategic elements that enable the company to charge a price in excess of the total resource cost and to earn a positive EVA profit. If an asset does not ever appear in EVA, then it is not a real asset. A brand, for instance, has value only if it can be, and at some point is, used to create EVA.

So to determine a company's share price, follow these steps:

First, determine the MVA of the company's *business* by forecasting the midpath EVA, or the probability-weighted EVA it will earn over various scenarios, and discounting it to a present value. Forecast EVA for as long as it can be confidently expected to grow, and then capitalize the eventual steady-state midcycle EVA profit you foresee

as a level perpetuity, and discount it all back to a net present value.
Once again, you must consider competition, saturation, substitution, fading fads, bureaucratic creep, management blunders, and overpriced acquisitions, and put an actuarial time limit on management's ability to continue to grow EVA in an unpredictable disruptive world.

Second, determine the *total* market value of the *company*. Add the predicted MVA to the stock of net business assets contained in its current capital account to measure the value of the *business*, and then fold in the market value of other assets that were held out of the EVA projection, like excess cash or inventoried real estate, for example, to determine the total value of the *company*.

Third, deduct the estimated market value of all debts and other claims that come ahead of shareholders, including contingent liabilities, to arrive at the residual value of the common equity. It is important to deduct the market value of the claims, not face value. Company bonds that pay higher than market interest will have a market value greater than face value, for instance, and it is the market value that must be deducted, not the book value or par value.

Fourth, divide by the number of common shares outstanding to arrive at the basic share price. If there are considerable options or other convertible instruments outstanding, a final step will be to use Black-Scholes or some other method to factor in the dilution in the share price that stems from sharing part of the corporate upside value with contingent claimants, but that is icing on the cake, generally.

Don't get lost in the recipe. Follow it through and you realize that since most of the factors don't change, at any point in time the stock price is essentially just a function of adding the projected MVA per share to the common book value per share (as adjusted for accounting distortions we'll get to in the next chapter). If a company has 100 common shares outstanding, a corrected common book value of $1,000 (i.e., $10 a share), and a projected MVA from discounting EVA of $500 (i.e., $5 per share), then the stock has an intrinsic value of $15 per share, the sum. And since the book value is set at any instant, the only way a company's stock price increases is if management can earn more EVA and credibly increase expectations for earning even more EVA, as I demonstrated with Apple and will quantify further in the next section.

Once you have gone from EVA to share price in the four-step process I've laid out, you may want to compute various multiples to see how the valuation stacks up with other companies. You may compute a price-to-book or price-to-earnings multiple, or an enterprise valuation multiple that divides total value by the firm's EBITDA, for instance. Fine, do that, and see how it stacks up. But don't confuse cause with consequence.

To take the prior example, if the firm's earnings per share are $1, and the stock is worth $15 based on discounting EVA, then the stock trades for 15 times earnings. Follow the words closely. I said it correctly. The stock is *not* worth $15 because it is worth 15 times earnings. It is worth 15 times earnings because EVA says the stock is worth $15. Accountants compute EPS. Price is determined by discounting EVA. The P/E multiple is just a plug—it's the arithmetic relationship between the earnings that accountants calculate and the share price that EVA determines. It is the result of the valuation, not the source of it.

Many CFOs get this backward and confuse cause with consequence. They assume their stock price is a result of the multiple. They will say, "Our stock trades for $15 *because* we trade for 15 times earnings." That's completely ass backwards. The word *because* is fatal; if you believe stock prices result from the market applying a multiple, then you believe the best way to increase your stock price is to increase the denominator of whatever multiple you like the most. And if you do that, odds are you will end up killing your EVA and your stock price.

If you cotton to P/E, you aim to increase the E, the earnings per share, and you move mountains to avoid diluting EPS. If enterprise multiple is what you fancy, then you go on a warpath for more EBITDA. You are willing to spend any amount on capital so long as you improve cash profit. And if price-to-book is your cup of tea, you grow the book value. You retain earnings and add assets that increase your capital charge and reduce your EVA. In each case, you are literally aiming at measures that will almost guarantee you will kill your firm's EVA and end up trading for a much lower multiple of whatever denominator measure you used as your performance goal.

THE TIE BETWEEN EVA AND SHAREHOLDER RETURNS

I've always thought it was obvious and uncontestable that the corporate mission is to maximize owner wealth—to allocate, manage, and deploy resources to maximize NPV, which at the corporate level is manifest in MVA. After all, the title of Adam Smith's book is *The Wealth of Nations*, not the returns of nations. Creating wealth is the name of the game, and has been from the beginning. And I always felt that if a manager took care of maximizing wealth, then the returns that the shareholders earned would be maximized, too, as a natural by-product and not as something separate and distinct to worry about.

Many CFOs are not satisfied with that answer, though. They are stuck on explaining shareholder returns, even though maximizing wealth and increasing MVA are the better goal. But the CFO is my client, so I decided one day to derive the exact link between EVA and shareholder returns. I burned out my pencil sharpener but finally got it. For those who can't sleep at night without knowing the answer, read on. All others can take my word for it and safely slip into the next chapter.

Let's start with the axiomatic assertion that shareholder returns are defined as the dividends shareholders receive plus the appreciation in value of their shares, divided by the share price at the beginning of the measurement period. The total shareholder return (TSR), in other words, is a function of cash yield and a cash-equivalent gain or loss. It's a cash-on-cash return, in effect. That is by definition.

EVA does not tie directly to TSR, but we can get there eventually. EVA actually ties to a broader definition of return, what I call the total investor return (TIR). It is the return the company generates on behalf of *all* investors—its lenders and shareholders combined. In other words, it is the return on the total enterprise value of the business. It's the return you'd get if you bought the stock *and* the bonds and held all of the liabilities of the company (except trade credit) in market value proportions.

Like TSR, TIR can be estimated from a cash-on-cash yield. It is the free cash flow (FCF) the business generates, plus the change in the firm's overall market value (ΔV), divided by its market value at the start of the period (V_0), again, by definition.[1] I write it like this: $TIR = (FCF + \Delta V)/V_0$.

Now let's play the substitution game. We know FCF is NOPAT less the change in capital (i.e., $FCF = NOPAT - \Delta Capital$). Since $EVA = NOPAT - Capital charge$, then $NOPAT = Capital charge + EVA$, so plug in:

$$\begin{aligned} TIR &= (FCF + \Delta V)/V_0 \\ &= (NOPAT - \Delta Capital + \Delta V)/V_0 \\ &= (Capital\ Charge + EVA - \Delta Capital + \Delta V)/V_0 \end{aligned}$$

And because $MVA = V - Capital$, and thus $\Delta MVA = \Delta V - \Delta Capital$, TIR reduces to:

$$TIR = (Capital\ Charge + EVA + \Delta MVA)/V_0$$

---

[1] In practice it gets a little more complicated when we consider excess cash holdings that are excluded from the definition of FCF but that can also be paid out or accumulated in a period, or if a company spins off a major line of business, and so on. But those are details that do not alter the insights I will explain.

The revised formula shows that the total return a firm generates for all investors is a function of three factors that all come from the EVA model. The first factor is the capital charge/beginning value. It comes from simply reversing the discounting process. As time passes, investors earn a return from the time value of the money. The charge for using capital that is built into EVA is in fact the basic source of the return to investors, which is why acknowledging and earning the charge is so essential to good corporate governance.

The second factor comes from earning EVA. The more EVA, the higher the return. It's one for one.

The third factor is the return that comes from *increasing* MVA. As I have already established, MVA increases when the expected present value stream of EVA increases from improvements in either CVA or FVA, or both. In other words, *the true drivers of shareholder returns, beyond just passively reversing the discounting process, are earning and increasing EVA and increasing expectations for earning even more EVA*. True, the returns are paid in the currency of cash and cash-equivalent value change. But don't be deceived—the cash is just the medium of exchange. The actual driver of shareholder return is (no surprise here) EVA all the way!

Let's put the simple formula through its paces. Suppose a company is just breaking even on EVA and is not expected to improve it. In that case, it trades at the value of its book capital. Its MVA is zero and is not expected to increase, because its EVA is zero and not expected to increase. TIR is reduced to just the capital charge yield on the value:

$$
\begin{aligned}
\text{TIR} &= (\text{Capital Charge} + \text{EVA} + \Delta\text{MVA})/V_0 \\
&= (\text{Capital Charge} + \$0 + \$0)/V_0 \\
&= (\text{Cost of Capital} \times \text{Capital} + \$0 + \$0)/\text{Capital} \\
&= \text{Cost of Capital}
\end{aligned}
$$

Since market value equals the capital in this case, the charge for capital delivers a cost-of-capital return on the value. TIR equals the cost of capital, every year, as expected.

Now suppose the company belches out a one-time unexpected EVA uptick that has no impact on expected future EVA and so none on MVA or market value as well. Then the investor return that year will increase by the one-time EVA uptick, but no more, and thereafter it will settle right back to the cost of capital. Nonrecurring profits pay a one-time bonus dividend but just don't move the market. There's an important message there. Managers should avoid spending a lot of time on generating one-time gains since the market will assign them a multiple of one, then none.

Now suppose the firm's EVA rises and investors consider the improvement permanent. The firm's MVA increases to incorporate the increase in projected EVA, and the investor return soars whenever investors are first convinced this will happen. Depending on the cost of capital, the MVA increase could be 7 to 20 times the increase in annual EVA.

Finally, suppose that investors not only expect the increase in EVA to be permanent, but they also believe that management has positioned the company to continue increasing EVA for some time. In this case, MVA is turbocharged as both CVA and FVA rev up. The investor return skyrockets when the long-run EVA trajectory is revised and impounded into the share price. That, of course, is exactly what happened to Apple. EVA increased prodigiously, and the market now projects it to continue growing for quite a while. But that was not the case at all 10 years back.

After such a run-up, TIR will be based off a much higher market value. To just earn the expected cost of capital, a company like Apple will need to continue to increase its EVA and hike up its MVA year over year just to stay on track with expectations. But that is the way markets work. And it is another reason why I think it is helpful to have incentive plans that reward managers not only for increasing the stock price but also for actually delivering the EVA profit growth the market is expecting.

Recall that TIR measures the return earned on behalf of all capital providers, including lenders, whereas TSR is the return just for the common share owners. It is easy to go from one to the other. TSR is simply a leveraged version of TIR. The formula is:

$$TSR = TIR + (TIR - BR) \times (D/E)$$

It says that TIR is first applied to pay interest expense and other prior claim returns (as represented by BR, standing for the overall average borrowing rate paid to senior claimants), and what's left over is then spread over the common equity portion of the market value, so the higher the firm's debt-to-equity (D/E) ratio, the more any TIR excess return is magnified, up or down, for good or ill, into the shareholder return.

For instance, suppose TIR is 26 percent, the average effective borrowing rate is 6 percent, and the D/E ratio is 50 percent. Then the TSR that year would be 36 percent.

$$TSR = 26\% + (26\% - 6\%) \times 50\% = 36\%$$

Leverage cuts both ways. If TIR is −14 percent, then the firm's TSR would be −24 percent.

$$TSR = -14\% + (-14\% - 6\%) \times 50\% = -24\%$$

The bottom line is that total shareholder return is still very directly a function of EVA and any changes in expectations for EVA, only with leverage thrown in to spice it up.

Let's test that proposition with an application to Ecolab, currently with about $7 billion in revenues from cleaning and sanitizing chemicals following its acquisition of Nalco. Exhibit 2.7 displays the total investor return computed each year from the capital charge, EVA, and change in MVA over the year, divided by the initial market value, and the total shareholder return computed the conventional way from dividends and capital gains on prior share price. The light dashed line is the ratio of market value to equity value, so, the larger it is, the more leveraged the firm was.

What is striking is how similar the two returns are, even though they are computed from two entirely different formulas. TIR is computed strictly from the EVA metrics related to the firm's overall market value, TSR from cash dividends and cash-equivalent capital gains on the share price. Yet, the two were extremely highly correlated for Ecolab. In other words, the math derivation works! And not just for Ecolab. If you run the correlation across all stocks, it is about 82 percent. Maximize EVA, maximize MVA, and the shareholder returns take care of themselves. I've said that for many years, without any mathematical proof, but now there it is. It must work as long as $2 + 2 = 4$.

The only notable exceptions to this rule for Ecolab were in the early 1990s because Ecolab was highly leveraged at the time. Back then, market value was around 2 times equity value, or, put another way, debt was 50 percent of market value. A surge in TIR in 1991 and a downdraft the year before were strongly amplified in TSR. But that's just noise and should not distract from the essential conclusion. EVA is, in principle and in practice, the true driver of shareholder returns. No other measure can make that claim.

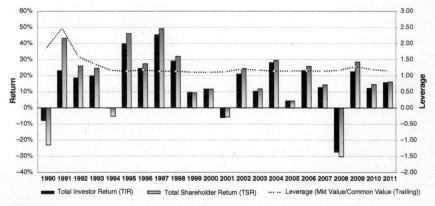

EXHIBIT 2.7 Ecolab's Total Shareholder Return and Total Investor Return

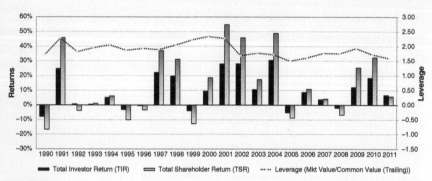

EXHIBIT 2.8 Ball Corporation's Total Shareholder Return and Total Investor Return

The same chart for Ball appears in Exhibit 2.8. The correlation between the up and down movements in the total EVA return on value and the total shareholder return is again very high, as expected. It is still EVA that is driving the returns. But the two return series are not as close in each period as they were for Ecolab because Ball has typically employed a lot more leverage. Keeping debt leverage high is one way that Ball's management has kept its overall cost of capital low to help keep its EVA high. And, in this case, the leverage has amplified mostly positive investor returns into even higher shareholder returns, which has been a blessing. If a management team is really confident about earning EVA, why share it? Use more debt and less equity to lavish the excess returns on the investors who get the EVA story.

CHAPTER 3

Accounting for Value

It is now time to have a little fun ribbing the accountants. One of my all-time favorite *New Yorker* cartoons—and this goes back to when Enron and WorldCom and a bunch of others were blowing up in a wave of accounting shenanigans—featured two comely misses at a bar, glancing over at two gentlemen, and one whispers to the other: "He has an air of danger about him. He's an accountant." Truer words were never spoken. Accounting *is* dangerous. But not for the reasons everyone assumes.

The real danger is not in the few fraudulent bad apples that make the headlines. It is in the great bulk of companies that hew honorably to generally accepted accounting rules. The danger stems from the fact that *mandated* accounting rules are flagrantly at odds with economic reality, distort performance measurement in a whole bunch of ways, and make valid comparisons across companies or business units virtually impossible. The real question for the thoughtful CFO—after complying with the law of the land, of course—is not whether to stick with the required accounting, but how to repair it. Aside from deducting the full cost of capital (COC), which is just essential, how else can reported accounting profits be modified (we are not about to throw out the whole system) so that EVA becomes an even more accurate barometer of value and a more effective guide to making better business decisions?

Before we get to the solutions, let me expose one incredible accounting defect that will show you that the emperor has no clothes. A fundamental reason accounting is so flawed as a management and shareholder valuation tool is that accounting statements cater to lenders rather than owners. Lenders want to get repaid even in the worst of circumstances, when the business has failed and it is a question of liquidating what's left of the carcass. Accounting rules create balance sheets that are intended for exactly those dire circumstances—to show the value that might be realized in a salvage sale.

But if we remove ourselves from the depressing company of Scrooge and Marley (the creditor class) and join the scintillating society of shareholders (the owner/proprietor class), the balance sheet changes before our eyes. As shareholders and as corporate managers, we are chiefly concerned with the company's performance and its value as a going-concern business enterprise. And from that perspective, we never expect to fully liquidate the assets. We need them to run our business—which means, strange as it may seem, that so-called assets aren't really assets at all. They are liabilities.

Assets tie up capital that must be financed at the cost of capital. A firm that ties up more assets on its balance sheet is perhaps more bankable— there's a greater reserve of blubber to cushion a fall—but as a business enterprise it is less valuable than a leaner outfit that earns the same profit with fewer assets. All else being equal, fewer assets mean more EVA, more real franchise value, and more wealth to the owners. Hence, accounting assets are actually liabilities. You want less of them, not more. The only true asset any company has is its ability to earn and increase EVA, which never appears on a balance sheet. If accountants have gotten even the most basic definition of an asset wrong, imagine how many other mistakes they've made. Take a deep breath. It's a long list. Let's talk through a few of them now.

MIXING OPERATING AND FINANCING DECISIONS

Another incredibly basic mistake accountants make is commingling the effects of financing decisions and business decisions, so that a business decision can appear good when it really isn't (or look bad when it really is good). For example, any investment financed with debt, such as a major acquisition, will contribute to accounting net income, increase earnings per share (EPS), and elevate the firm's reported return on equity (ROE) so long as it generates a rate of return that is anything over the after-tax cost of the borrowed funds—which these days could be 3 percent or even lower. A return on investment that low is hardly acceptable. The firm's stock price clearly will not be lifted until a much higher return standard has been met.

How is it, though, that the firm's stock price won't increase if its earnings per share do? If EPS goes up, then why doesn't the stock price go up, of necessity? Because debt-financed growth comes at a hidden cost. Adding leverage adds variability to the company's earnings. As more fixed interest payments are deducted from uncertain operating profits, the company's earnings and stock price become more volatile. They end up fluctuating more widely over the business cycle than if equity had been used to finance the growth or if equity was at least part of the financing mix. Confronted with the added financial risk, shareholders will understandably demand a higher return. Put simply, part of the hidden cost of adding debt is that it raises the cost of equity.

To earn a higher return to compensate for the added financial risk, shareholders will discount the firm's EPS at a higher rate and thus they will pay a lower multiple of the earnings. The P/E going down offsets the EPS going up. The bottom line is that an increase in EPS that arises from a *temporary* increase in leverage is not apt to increase the share price.

A *permanent* change in the debt-equity mix is another matter. A shift to a permanently higher leverage ratio, but one that is still within prudent limits, can reduce the overall cost of capital and increase the stock price, but not because EPS will go up. It's the tax subsidy that counts. Tax laws generally allow interest payments on debt, but not dividends, to be deducted from taxable income. Raise debt and retire equity, and keep it there, and the present value of the taxes saved by swapping debt for equity adds to the value of the company. Said differently, it is the equivalent of reducing the weighted average cost of capital. All the tax savings—and hence the value created by it—flow to shareholders as the claimants on all residual income.

One of my clients, Equifax, took advantage of this. Shortly after adopting EVA, the CFO at the time, Derek Smith, decided to *permanently* increase the firm's leverage ratio as a means of reducing the cost of capital. This was a firm that enjoyed a very strong cash flow, had paid continuing and increasing dividends since the 1920s, and had very little debt on its books because, first, it didn't need the money (growth was self-financing with internally generated cash) and, second, it was countercultural. Here was a company whose business was to rate credit now volunteering to reduce its own credit rating.

A confusion that trips up many a CFO is that when debt is raised to retire equity, the debt becomes riskier and more expensive (with a lower credit rating), and the equity does, too, as I have argued. How can it therefore ever be sensible to raise both the cost of borrowed money and the cost of the equity by raising the leverage target? The answer to the puzzle is that the weights are changing. There is more debt and less equity in the capital structure. While the cost of each rises as more debt comes into the picture, more weight is placed on the lower-cost debt than on the higher-cost equity, so that the *weighted average* cost comes down. This is entirely because corporate income taxes are saved.

It can be a trick to explain this to boards, but we did, and Equifax's directors approved the new higher leverage policy. But as Derek Smith rightly noted, nobody would believe the new policy was real unless it was put in place right away. So we fashioned an up-front and ongoing stock buyback program. The company announced the new higher leverage target, increased its debt to the target ratio, and used the proceeds to buy back a large block of stock. But more than that, management told investors that in subsequent years it would borrow even more money—that as it added to capital and continued to expand, it would continue to borrow money it did not really need and use it to buy back more stock in order to maintain the capital structure goal.

When and how did Equifax's stock price react? As soon as Equifax announced the new policy, the price increased 25 percent. The price jumped because the new policy was carefully explained, and the stock buyback made it credible. But note that the stock price increased not because of the buyback, but because of the new, lower-cost capital structure.

In fact, returning cash to investors in any form cannot really be of value, because the investors already own the company and own any cash it could distribute. It is like going to your bank, and taking cash out of your account, and asking, am I wealthier? You are more liquid, but you are not wealthier. The cash you have in your hand is cash you no longer have in the bank. You have changed the form but not the amount of your wealth. Likewise, Equifax shareholders obtained cash from the buyback, but the company had to borrow to pay it to them, and the debt would have to be repaid with priority out of cash flow that could otherwise have been paid to the shareholders down the road. It is always *how* a share repurchase is financed, and not the repurchasing of shares, that adds value. Consider another example. If management distributes surplus cash that the market fears would be used for high-priced acquisitions or other sub-EVA investments, the share price may rise, but again, the increase is all due to how the distribution is being financed, which in this case came from releasing capital that would otherwise be imprisoned in negative net present value (NPV) investments. Distributing cash is by itself always value neutral. You've got to go deeper, to the source of the distribution, to determine any impact on value.

MVA tells us that, too. A stock's market value goes down once the stock goes ex-dividend, and the book value of the equity goes down as the dividend is deducted from retained earnings. Market value and capital decline in equal and offsetting amounts, so there is no net effect on MVA, which is as it should be. If there is no effect on EVA, then there should be no effect on MVA. Paying out the fruits of our efforts, or even borrowing to prepay the fruits of our efforts, does not yield more fruit in and of itself. That is the truth that EVA and MVA see, but that other measures mangle horribly.

All this may sound like double-talk. If so, read it again. And remember, it is easy to be misled by EPS and return on equity (ROE) and accounting metrics that mix operating and financing decisions. Those measures do not discriminate between temporary and permanent changes in debt financing and debt policy. But the difference is crucial. And even with a permanent increase in leverage, a great portion of the increase in EPS and

ROE is needed just to compensate for the added risk and does not add to the share price.

How does EVA circumvent this? EVA is measured using a blended cost of debt and equity capital where the weights are not the actual proportions outstanding in any quarter or year, and where the full cost of the leverage ratio is reflected in the cost of the equity that is assumed. Ideally, the blend represents the target proportions management will employ on average over time. In our work we approximate that by using a running three-year average debt-to-equity ratio, but guidance from management would be most welcome by the market. The point here is that a transitory debt-financed stock buyback or debt-financed acquisition won't really move the EVA cost-of-capital needle, even though those maneuvers will temporarily and misleadingly spring load EPS and ROE.

DISCHARGE SURPLUS CASH

Another financing distortion comes from hoarding excess cash. Many successful companies, Apple and Microsoft among them, have accumulated vast cash reserves and invested them for pitifully low returns that mask how really profitable the underlying businesses are. Under EVA, excess cash is assumed to be invested in marketable securities bought at market prices that yield the return the market expects for the risk. The investments generate zero EVA, by definition. If the risk is low, the return will be low, but it is zero EVA nonetheless. In other words, this is a side game that really has nothing to do with the performance of the underlying business.

Accordingly, excess cash is removed from capital and the associated investment income taken out of net operating profit after taxes (NOPAT), so that the EVA measured is the EVA of the *business*. As a result, when a company with a cash hoard makes a massive cash payout as a dividend or share buyback, *nothing happens* to its EVA. It's a nonevent. In contrast, EPS and ROE go haywire, another example of how they confusingly mix operating and financing decisions and add a lot of noise to the business performance signal.

Incidentally, to be consistent, excess cash is also removed from market value as we measure it, so that when a firm pays out excess cash, nothing happens to the market value or to the capital we measure, so nothing happens to MVA, either. Wealth cannot be created or destroyed by transferring it from the left hand to the right hand. This is again as it should be. There is no change in EVA, and thus there should be no change in MVA, when excess cash is simply transferred from corporate coffers to investors' pockets.

TREAT LEASED ASSETS AS OWNED

Long before the International Financial Reporting Standards (IFRS) accounting rules came along or it became at all fashionable, EVA has treated
leased assets as if they were owned. This is another facet of separating operating performance from financing decisions.

To make the adjustment, the present value of rented assets is estimated
as a multiple of the rent expense. It is included in debt capital in the cost-of-
capital calculation, and it is added to net property, plant, and equipment to
become part of the net business-asset capital base that the operating team is
responsible for managing.

NOPAT is also adjusted as if the rented assets were owned. The interest
component of the rent expense is added back to NOPAT, but the depreciation part stays on as a deduction. Furthermore, the capital charge includes
the cost of capital applied to the present value of the rents.

When the dust settles, EVA is computed as if the rented assets were
owned. EVA is burdened with the depreciation and weighted average cost
of capital on the rented assets. The idea is that managers should allocate
and manage assets—and be judged on asset management performance—the
same way no matter how the assets have been financed. The objective also
is to make EVA into a purer, better, more comparable measure of profit performance that is insulated from differences in the mix of owning or leasing
assets that occur over time and from company to company.

REVERSE IMPAIRMENT CHARGES

Accountants are having a lot of fun these days valuing and revaluing the
book value of assets—which, as I have pointed out, is not the point at all, because assets are really liabilities. Why revalue a plant asset when other than
in liquidation, value is never in the plant, but in the EVA the plant earns?

Nevertheless, the bookkeepers are required to follow the rules and determine whether an asset is being carried at more than its fair value, and if
so, to write down the value. The value is never written up, of course, because
the accountants are in bed with bankers who only care about the dark, depressing side of life. The euphemism for the write-down is an *impairment
charge*. Just understand, it is a pure bookkeeping entry and has no effect
on cash flow, and thus it has no effect on value. But after the write-down,
a company can all of a sudden look a lot more profitable than it really is,
especially on measures like the rate of return on the now-depleted equity. It's
like playing golf and taking lots of mulligans. Anyone can beat par if you
ignore a lot of the wild swings that didn't pan out.

EVA puts the mulligans back on the scorecard. It reverses the impairment charge. The charge is removed from earnings and added back to balance sheet capital, as if the charge had never happened. It is a nonevent in the EVA world because accounting is not reality, and nothing actually happened.

What if a company really did overpay for an acquisition and the goodwill it has recorded on the books is not really worth it? Shouldn't the company take an impairment charge and write it down? My answer is still no. Leave it to EVA. In this case the company will be unable to earn the NOPAT needed to cover the cost of the acquisition capital it paid, and its EVA will be impaired. EVA will register the loss in value, not some accounting adjustment to balance sheet assets. We do not want the accountants to do the job of EVA and the security analyst.

A simple example may help. Suppose management buys a widget-making machine for $1,000 and expects to use it to generate a NOPAT of $150 (sound familiar?—it's SSCo, writ small). At a 10 percent cost of capital, the machine generates $50 in EVA and adds $500 to the net present value of the company. The company's book capital understates market value, but that never bothers the accountants. They don't write up the value of assets (and I am certainly not saying they should). What bothers the pencil pushers is what happens next.

Let's assume the very next day the price of widgets falls permanently, and the same machine is able to produce only $80 of NOPAT. Now EVA is –$20. The present value of EVA is a loss of $200, which means that the market value is only $800. It is the $1,000 book capital minus the $200 EVA valuation discount. EVA registers the profit loss, and the present value of EVA measures the impairment of value. There is no need for accountants to intervene here at all. But they do. International Accounting Standard No. 36 (IAS 36) mandates that they step in to write down the asset to its recoverable market value, and let's say that is $800. Now what would EVA show? Going forward, with NOPAT of $80, EVA would show up as $0 on an $800 book capital, and MVA would be $0, according to the accounting. But that is hardly useful or factual.

Impairment charges were not needed for the market or management to get the information that value had been lost. The decline and fall of EVA tells that plainly enough. Moreover, reducing the book value to market value is not helpful. It erases the memory of how we got to where we are. It misleadingly improves EVA from –$20 to $0. It reports MVA, the measure of wealth, as breaking even when the owners have actually lost $200. All these problems stem from accountants' mistaken belief that the balance sheet should record market value when balance sheet assets are always just a cost of doing business.

I have also found a few investors who seem confused about this. In one memorable meeting with a man who runs a China fund, he saw a problem with using EVA for evaluating Chinese companies because of widespread fraud (who knew?). He mentioned as an example one Chinese company that had recorded considerable asset acquisitions in recent years. When he visited the factory, he saw that the assets were no good at all. With further probing, he discovered that the company had bought the equipment at inflated prices from the CEO's son-in-law. My reaction was that all that meant was that the company had recorded a greater obligation on its balance sheet to earn a profit it cannot earn, which would make its EVA more negative and produce a greater MVA discount to be deducted from its book capital. In other words, it is exactly the same as the example I gave earlier. It would make no difference whether the widget-making asset lost value because the price of widgets went down or the widget machine was acquired for an inflated price to begin with. Either way, there is an impairment of value. And either way, it is manifest in EVA. Accountants, go away.

CAPITAL GAINS AND LOSSES GO TO THE CAPITAL ACCOUNT

Let's consider a variation on the accountants' impairment charge. What if an unrecognized loss in value is realized? What if an asset or business is sold and a book-value loss is recognized at the time of the sale? How is that treated in the EVA world?

Under EVA, an asset disposition loss is treated exactly the same as impairment accounting. The book loss is backed out of NOPAT and put back onto the balance sheet, but this takes a little more explanation.

Under standard accounting rules, a book-value loss on sale is charged against profit. That makes the decision to sell and exit always look bad, when it may be the best thing to do. The real news in the transaction may be that the asset is now worth more in the hands of another owner who is willing to pay a premium over what it is worth to the incumbent owner. It is also possible that the asset is being sold for too little. How can we tell the difference?

As with an impairment charge, a loss on a sale is reversed. The book loss is added back to reported earnings so that NOPAT measures the underlying ongoing earnings power of the business. But to be consistent, and to preserve the integrity of double-entry bookkeeping, the loss is also added back to balance sheet capital. In accounting terms, NOPAT is credited for the loss, and the capital account is debited in the same amount (I really am a frustrated accountant at heart). A special capital account is created for this purpose. We call it *cumulative unusual losses after tax*. It is a holding pen for all the one-time, nonrecurring write-downs and charges, and it, too, is subject to a capital charge.

Let's take a simple example. In fact, let's run through a make-believe analysis of Coca-Cola's decision to replace its stainless steel containers with disposable cardboard ones. I am going to set this up by ignoring a loss on the sale of the steel containers at first, and then bring the loss into the picture.

Suppose that the decision to switch to cardboard would reduce NOPAT by $10 a year, because expensing the cardboard containers is more costly than continuing to incur the depreciation expense on the steel containers. But suppose that the steel containers can be sold for $150, which is taken out of capital. If the cost of capital (COC) is 10 percent, Coke's owners would come out $5 a year better off making the switch, which is indicated by the increase in EVA:

$$EVA = NOPAT - COC \times Capital$$
$$\$5 = -\$10 \quad - 10\% \times -\$150$$

Note that since the cost of capital is deducted from NOPAT, the reduction in capital arising from the sale of an asset *adds* to EVA. And it adds to EVA regardless of what Coke does with the sale proceeds, because the EVA model always assumes that the company reinvests the cash to just earn the cost of capital and break even on EVA. As for judging the wisdom of the move, the calculation shown is the complete story.

Assuming that the proceeds are invested at the cost of capital is more sensible than you may imagine because, if nothing else, Coke could use the sale proceeds to retire its debt and buy back its equity in capital structure proportions, and let its investors earn the cost of capital by reinvesting the proceeds in a stock and bond portfolio of similar risk. In this example, Coke's investors could earn $15 a year on their own account by investing the $150 proceeds at the 10 percent cost of capital. Although accountants do not record that profit on Coke's books, that profit would be every bit as real to them as any profit that is actually earned inside the firm. EVA, in short, makes managers into partners with the owners. The goal is to maximize the joint profit of the firm and the profit opportunity available to the firm's owners with the capital outside of the firm. The bottom line in this example is, as long as Coke's NOPAT falls by less than the $15 in profit that the owners could earn investing the capital outside the firm, the owners will be better off, on net. If NOPAT falls by $10, as the example assumes, then on net, the owners are better off by $5, which is what EVA shows. This is one of the real attractions of EVA—by charging a company for using capital, EVA correctly credits the company for releasing capital and letting the firm's investors earn a return on it on their own. Measures like EPS and EBITDA are not even in the zip code of getting this right because they do not recognize the true opportunity cost of using or of releasing capital.

What if, to play the devil's advocate, Coke actually reinvested the proceeds in another project instead of paying them out? Then the two decisions should be split and not commingled. One decision is to sell the steel and shift to cardboard and pay the proceeds out to the owners, and the second decision is to raise capital from the owners at the cost of capital and invest it back into the business. Each decision should stand or fall on its own EVA merits. The value of each should not depend on the value of the other, because capital can be presumed to flow to and from the investors at the cost-of-capital rate.

Now let's bring a bookkeeping loss on sale into play. Suppose that all the facts are the same as before except for one thing. Suppose Coke's accountants are carrying the stainless steel containers on Coke's balance sheet at a $200 book value. This time, when the containers with a $200 book value are sold for $150 in after-tax proceeds, a $50 charge to earnings must be recorded. The question is: should recognizing the charge and reducing the book profit make any difference in the value of the decision?

Of course it makes no difference! It is just a bookkeeping entry. But let's follow this through. If we take the accounting at face value and run the $50 loss through the earnings, then instead of NOPAT falling by just $10, NOPAT would fall by $60, and instead of capital falling by the $150 in cash proceeds, it would fall by the full $200 book value that the accountants have written off the balance sheet. The result: while EVA actually goes up by $5, the accounting has EVA going down by $40:

$$\text{EVA} = \text{NOPAT} - \text{COC} \times \text{Capital}$$
$$-\$40 = -\$60 \quad - 10\% \times -\$200$$

This is clearly not what we want to see. EVA is intended to measure and motivate the right decisions, the ones that will maximize the company's net present value and stock price. And in this case, selling the steel and switching to cardboard is the right thing to do, but the raw accounting shows EVA taking it on the chin. What gives?

This is a perfect example of another accounting distortion known as "successful efforts," which means that only productive investments are admitted into the capital account, and unsuccessful ones are written off. In the accountants' world, assets are admitted to their exclusive balance sheet club only when they meet high standards. But that is not the real world, and it is not the purpose of the balance sheet as far as managers and owners are concerned. Remember, value is to be found in EVA, not on the balance sheet. The balance sheet is a cost, not an asset.

In the real world, finding winning investments and strategies requires investing in losers now and again. If you are running a retail business, not every store succeeds. Some of them just end up in the wrong location and must be closed. Or say you are drilling for oil in what a geologist would call a one-in-five success ratio prospect—that says you would have to drill five wells to have a very good shot at finding one that pays. What is the cost to find one good well? The cost of drilling five wells. You cannot as a matter of policy and practice locate one well without drilling five, or so the probability tells us. Investing in dry hole losers is an unavoidable part of the investment required to discover the winners. And though accountants write them off, investments in dry holes and losing stores and technology flops (even Apple has had a long string of misses over the years) are actually quite valuable in a way. We know not to drill there again. We do not put a store like that there again. We do not change map apps in the midst of new phone launch. We learn from our mistakes, or should.

In our knowledge-based economy, capital is knowledge, capital is discovery, capital is information, capital is learning, and capital is trial and error. It is not just bricks and mortar at all. In fact, today the really important capital investments are not in hard assets of the kind accountants recognize. We need to shift from a medieval definition of capital as the castle on the hill to the recognition that capital also includes investments in everything and anything that makes a company better and more capable of earning profits. And for that, EVA uses full-cost accounting. All investments, successful or not, are considered to be capital. And let me reiterate before you object to this that capital is not an asset and capital is not value. Capital is simply a raw material ingredient spent with the intention of creating value. Putting more ingredients into the capital accounts only sets up a higher capital charge hurdle for success. A greater profit must be earned to cover the full-cost capital that now appears on the balance sheet.

To convert from the successful efforts method that accountants prefer to the full-cost treatment that makes business sense and economic logic, losses on sales are added back to earnings and also added back to capital. It is double-entry bookkeeping, once again and always. The loss cannot be legitimately added back to pro forma the earnings without also making the corresponding add-back to the capital account. That wouldn't be cricket, and it would not be correct.

To continue with the Coke numbers, the $50 book loss is added back to NOPAT and also added back to capital. As a result, and as was originally the case, NOPAT is unaffected by the loss. It simply records the recurring profit stream from the business, which is a $10 reduction—the original effect of switching from steel to disposable paper containers. As for capital, the accountants reduced it by the $200 book value, but once the $50 loss is added back, capital decreases by only $150—by the after-tax cash proceeds. What shows through, thankfully, is the $5 increase in the EVA, which stands tall as a reliable measure of the merits of the decision.

$$\text{EVA} = \text{NOPAT} - \text{COC} \times \text{Capital}$$
$$-\$40 = -\$60 \quad - 10\% \times -\$200 \text{ (Accounting picture)}$$
$$+\$45 = +\$50 \quad - 10\% \times +\$50 \text{ (EVA adjustments)}$$
$$+\$5 = -\$10 \quad - 10\% \times -\$150 \text{ (Economic reality)}$$

It sounds complicated when you have to unwind the accounting, but that is because we have to undo the damage the accountants have done in the first place. Blame them, not me, for these complications. But also, to make it easier to understand what's really going on, think of it this way.

Under EVA, it is as if the only accounting entries were simply to debit the cash account by $150 to record the stainless steel sale proceeds coming in the door, and to credit (reduce) the capital account by $150 (leaving an unrecouped $50 of book value in capital). That's it. Nothing passes through the profit and loss (P&L) statement, because this is a capital gain or loss from a capital transaction, and capital gains and losses belong in the capital account—get it? Under EVA, the purpose of the balance sheet is not to show the assets; it is to record capital. It is simply to ask how much money has been put into the business with the hope and expectation it will create profit, generate EVA, and add to value, net of (less) any capital that has been retrieved from a sale or liquidation. When you start to think of your balance sheet as a capital account, and managers as stewards of capital, then you are getting closer to the EVA philosophy of management accounting.

Replacing generally accepted accounting principles (GAAP) balance sheets with the EVA accounting treatment for capital is an important way to unlock real value, in my experience. It tells managers to get rid of all assets that are really worth more to others and not to let bookkeeping losses stand in the way of their common sense. Instead, follow this rule: If the proceeds from disposal, reinvested at the cost of capital, produce more profit and a greater discounted EVA value than continuing to hold the asset, then sell it, and don't let accounting red ink stand in the way. That's the simple, clear thinking EVA brings to the fore.

I remember that up until we put EVA in place at Centura Bank of Rocky Mount, North Carolina (since acquired by RBC Bank), around 1997, management had been warehousing land in locations where it thought it might want to build branches down the road. Once EVA came in, management discovered that the bricks-and-mortar branches were not as EVA profitable as putting kiosks in Wal-Mart stores and other capital-conserving locations. The edifice complex was gone, just in time to take advantage of the swing to online banking. But rather than sitting on the land to avoid recognizing any loss, as many companies would have done, management stepped in aggressively to sell the properties and take a loss on the tax books that brought in more cash flow and reduced capital even more. It was a great EVA move that cleared a path into a whole new business model that might have been stymied had management let the appearance of an accounting loss stand in the way of realizing a real EVA gain.

Incidentally, gains are treated symmetrically. An unusual one-time gain on sale is removed from NOPAT, reducing it, and it is applied as a *reduction* of capital. It is an extra recovery of capital that permanently reduces the capital charge and increases EVA, presumably substituting for the earnings power lost by selling a productive asset for a gain, and making it possible to make a rational hold or sell decision.

Either way, with a gain or a loss, the EVA mandate is to dispose of assets where the after-tax sale proceeds, invested at the cost of capital, exceed the NOPAT earnings that are forfeited in the process. That is the correct, incremental, strategic NPV decision. It is easy for line teams to understand, and it motivates them to comb through their balance sheets and find tons of asset redeployment opportunities that might otherwise be off their radar screens.

RESTRUCTURING COSTS ARE INVESTMENTS, TOO

Management teams occasionally fashion an overall program to sell, cut, change, and transform in order to bring about a comprehensive redirection and restructuring of the company. Management will estimate the overall cost of the program, immediately charge it to earnings, and set up a restructuring reserve on its balance sheet to absorb the write-downs and cash costs as they occur.

The accounting for this kind of bold move is downright misleading and can even be a deterrent to restructuring a business line. Who wants to fess up to a large loss and pour red ink on the bottom line? Usually, no one other than a new CEO or division head who can blame the mess on his or her predecessor. But shareholders and directors don't want to wait for management changes in order to do the smart thing. And they don't have to when EVA is accounting for the consequences.

In the EVA world, the accounting for restructuring charges is much the same as for impairments or disposal losses The charges are added back to the earnings to reveal the underlying, ongoing earnings power of the business, and in exchange, the restructuring charges are folded into the same balance sheet capital account as is used for accumulating losses on sales. Think of it as a kind of goodwill account. It is abstract organizational capital, but it is capital nonetheless; it is money put into the business for an intended benefit, and it is subject to the cost-of-capital charge as a matter of maintaining accurate debit and credit bookkeeping.

Assuming that managers are judged—and rewarded—according to EVA measured this way, what are their incentives? Fail fast, and fail well. Step in and restructure and redeploy assets as soon as it is sensible to do so. Don't hesitate over fear of a mere bookkeeping charge. But, fail well. Just because accountants lump all the restructuring costs into a great one-time charge to earnings doesn't mean that managers have a license to spend wantonly.

I recall a recent conversation with the CFO of a major packaged goods company that was in the midst of planning the details of a comprehensive restructuring to consolidate product lines and streamline processes. He said, "Bennett, ever since I got board agreement for the restructuring program, my line guys have been looking for ways to take advantage of it. They are proposing to spend a lot more money on revising our processes and restructuring our businesses and paying out generous severance than they really should, just because they know it's all going to get lumped into a one-time charge to our earnings. They think it almost doesn't matter what we spend, that the market will digest it and move on. That cannot be true. Cash is cash. We've got to earn a return on it no matter how the accountants treat it. But the accounting is not helping me to get that message out."

He's right. Any cash outlay that does not directly or indirectly support current operations and that is spent with the intention that it will have a payoff stretching into future periods should be capitalized and written off over time, with interest. We can't do that comprehensively, of course. We'd suffocate under the details. But it certainly applies to one-time restructuring costs. You invest in a restructuring to streamline costs and increase profit performance. You have to earn a return on the capital invested in the restructuring and cover the cost of that capital the same as any other investment. If not, why are you doing it? If you cannot cover the cost of the capital invested in the transition, you might as well stick with the old ways, even if they are not as profitable as the new ones.

That is why under EVA we add restructuring costs to the balance sheet as an investment, subject to the capital charge, so that managers are pressured and obligated to earn a return on them. The EVA treatment removes the fear of failure, but it also sets a performance standard. The incentive is to spend only the restructuring dollars that will truly add an incremental return over the cost of capital. This is a sure cure for the "everything but the kitchen sink" syndrome.

Along these lines, I vividly recall a meeting with Victor Rice, at the time the chairman and CEO of Varity Corporation, the successor to Massey Ferguson, a Canadian farm implement manufacturer that had relocated to Buffalo, New York. I said, "Victor, I have bad news. According to my calculations, Varity's EVA is currently running at a loss of $150 million a year." He replied, "I am not surprised. This is a tough business. Farms are consolidating and the equipment is lasting longer. We've been in a consolidation phase so long that we kid ourselves by saying that a typical year in our business is worse than the year before but not as bad as year to come. Even so, we've continued to hope for the best," he said, "and we've put off plant consolidation and process rationalization for way too long. We desperately need a major revamping and restructuring, but we know that will lead to a lot of bookkeeping bloodletting, with major charges to our earnings. How can we demonstrate that we are winning when the accounting will say we are losing?"

I told Victor about using EVA and shielding the earnings from the restructuring charges and treating them as investments. He loved it. And his team did it. And over the next two years, Varity's EVA improved dramatically, from −$150 million to −$30 million, amid a sea of red accounting ink. Bonuses, based on the change in EVA, were very rich, and the managers were ecstatic, as I recall, but the shareholders were downright delirious because the stock increased 250 percent in value. True, EVA was still negative, but it had gotten a lot less negative a lot faster than investors had imagined it could, and the special EVA accounting for the restructuring was a real enabler for that to happen.

THE VARITY EXPERIENCE

The Varity experience with EVA offers other insights that, while off the mark of the accounting issues in this chapter, are worthwhile sharing. At one point in my engagement with Victor he asked me if I thought it made sense to put the sales and marketing team on the EVA bonus plan. At the time, I had too little experience to express an opinion, so I said, "Victor, I am not sure. I will ask them." And the sales and marketing bosses said, "No way. We drive sales. We want commissions on sales. Go away." I thought a second opinion might be helpful, so I asked the product line and plant managers. They said, "The sales team must absolutely be on the EVA plan, because all those bow tie types care about is driving more sales. They force us to make and stock every imaginable configuration of every possible product delivered any time

(continued)

and any way the customer wants at prices they prefer. But all that kills our manufacturing efficiency, loads up our inventory pipeline, and hurts our profits massively."

I said to Victor, "There are two points of view on this—the metal movers say 'nyet' and the metal producers say 'da'!" And when he heard the reasons he was fully in favor of putting the sales team on the company's EVA bonus plan. I said, "But, Victor, the sales guys will kick and scream. They like what they have." And he said, "You are right, so I will make it voluntary. They can volunteer to go on the EVA bonus plan or they can volunteer to leave the company. It's purely voluntary." Most stayed and prospered.

One contributor to prosperity was that, after everyone was on the EVA compensation plan, the sales chiefs asked for the first time to caucus with the production and product heads in a meaningful way, and together they quickly decided on how to slim down the product portfolio and take a lot of operating and capital costs out while preserving a huge portion of the revenue base and market appeal of the product lineup. Such communication and teamwork are a typical result of bringing EVA to the fore.

One last point on Varity: As I have said, I believe it is really quite helpful to simplify decision making and make it more accountable by discarding cash flow and instead to ask line teams to forecast, analyze, and discount EVA to measure and improve NPV. Victor understood that, but not everyone got it right away. One poor soul brought a capital project up for review with the standard cash flow analysis. Victor decided to make an example of him. He slammed his hand on the table, looked the subordinate in the eye, and emphatically said, "Don't you ever bring me the cash flow analysis again. I want to see all our decisions in terms of EVA. We are an EVA company. Got it?" Victor is tough. His father was a London chimney sweep, literally, and Victor worked his way up from the bottom. That would not be everyone's style. But the point is, word got around Varity very quickly that every decision had to be EVA framed. It does take leadership from the top to make it happen.

R&D AND BRAND SPEND ARE INVESTMENTS

What are the most important capital outlays at companies like Intel, Genentech, IBM, Coca-Cola, Nike, and Coach? Spending on research and innovation, on developing and launching products, and on building brands, of course. It's what differentiates the companies and enables them to charge premium prices and generate outstanding returns.

And yet, despite the obvious and even quantifiable value of the brands and technology, accountants immediately write off the money spent on developing them as a charge to earnings. They deduct the spending as if it has no enduring value and is just a period expense in support of current sales, which is patently false. We've already discussed successful efforts accounting, which is where accountants only allow oil and gas companies to record the money spent finding productive wells as assets and force them to expense the dry holes. The accountants are not even that generous with research and development (R&D) or brand building outlays. It is all expensed regardless of success. They assume failure is the norm. I call it "unsuccessful efforts accounting." Their justification, again, is that intangibles cannot be relied on to have a value in liquidation. That is growing increasingly untrue—witness all the talk about the value of the Twinkies brand when Hostess entered liquidation or Kodak's ability to auction off its brands and technology in bankruptcy—but accounting is a profession still stuck in the dark ages.

What is a better and more realistic answer? Under EVA, spending on R&D and brand building, on designing and launching new products, even on training programs, and, in some cases, on maintenance outlays that are deemed critical are added to balance sheet capital and are written off as a charge to earnings over time, subject to a capital charge on the unamortized balance. We generally write off R&D over five years and advertising and promotion spending over three years, but that varies for individual companies. In a typical example, if R&D spending increased $100 in a period, then it would turn into a $20 amortization charge per year over a five-year period, plus interest at the cost of capital charged on the unamortized balance. Spending on intangibles, in other words, is treated just like capital expenditure spending for plant and equipment, except that it is added to a special balance sheet account for intangible capital (which I discuss in more detail later on).

This follows an economist's view of the world, in which capital is defined as *any* cash outlay that is *expected* to generate benefits that extend over future periods. In principle, all spending that qualifies should be added to balance sheet capital and amortized against earnings over the expected payoff horizon. Those expectations may not be realized, but that is what EVA will tell us, not the balance sheet. I am not staking my claim to this EVA accounting treatment on theoretical grounds and by an emotional appeal to a higher economic calling. I want to be ruthlessly practical. I am advocating that you use the EVA accounting for intangibles because it will help your team to make better, and better informed, decisions with more accountability, clarity, and insight.

For instance, by spreading the cost over time, EVA discourages managers from opportunistically cutting the spending just to make a short-term earnings goal. Why cut $100 from R&D this year if it saves only $20 (plus interest) this year? That's just not an appealing or intelligent way to make budget, assuming that the R&D spending is worthwhile.

On the contrary, the EVA accounting treatment motivates managers to step up the spending if they think it will yield a high return on investment. Increase R&D by $100 this year, and the charge to EVA increases by only $20 in the current period, plus interest. The revised accounting treatment gives managers the time needed to make their proposed investments pay off rather than hitting them with the full expense right up front. It better matches cost and benefit.

In exchange for providing more freedom to invest in brands, people, processes, and technology, the EVA accounting also imposes more accountability for actually generating results. As President Reagan once put it in discussing nuclear disarmament, "Trust, but verify." With the EVA accounting, managers know that if they successfully lobby for the funding they will be obligated to cover the full cost, including interest, over time, and they know their success or failure will be transparently posted on the EVA scoreboard for all to see, and ideally, in the bonus awards they earn or fail to earn.

Managers in most companies define success as getting their proposed R&D, advertising, product launch, or training budgets approved. In the EVA company, success is defined as delivering value—actually getting a return on the investments and driving growth in EVA. Managers in most companies are loath to cut any spending for fear they could never get it back in their budgets. In the EVA-focused firm, managers are more likely to cut the spending that should be cut, knowing that they have the credibility to get it back should an appealing opportunity materialize down the road. Budgets are both more fixed and more flexible under EVA. There is a greater incentive to keep investing through thick and thin as long as the return is perceived to be there, and there is also more incentive and more credibility to alter the budget—up or down—as an honest reappraisal of the payoff dictates.

I will give you three examples of how the EVA accounting technique changed strategies for the better. Shortly after adopting EVA, Monsanto announced its intention to step up R&D spending by 40 percent at its G.D. Searle pharmaceutical unit. The unit had five drugs in stage-three clinical trials, and by stepping on the accelerator, Searle could prove the products faster and bring them to market sooner. The payoff could be big. Not only would the revenues and profits begin to accrue earlier, which counts as more discounted value, but they would likely last longer. The patent protection clock starts ticking from when the patent is first filed, so the sooner to market, the longer the effective patent life would be. In addition, doctors grow accustomed to prescribing the first therapy to market, which also sets up a barrier to deter new entrants or make it harder for them to gain share. In short, there are very good reasons to think that stepped-up R&D spending at that stage could drive significant EVA gains. But that rarely happens in practice because most pharmaceutical companies are afraid of the near-term negative impact on reported earnings per share. They let the accounting tail wag their business dog, as my former partner, Joel Stern, memorably put it.

Monsanto was well aware of the EPS impact, but did it anyway. CEO Robert Shapiro admitted in the press release that the increased R&D spending would significantly dilute the firm's reported earnings. Mark Wiltamuth, at the time a highly respected securities analyst at Natwest (now with Morgan Stanley), estimated that Monsanto's per-share earnings would drop from his prior estimate of $1.60 to $1.40 the next year, or by 12.5 percent. Yet Monsanto's stock price increased from about $38 to $40 a share that day, or about 2.5 percent. Put another way, Monsanto ended up trading for a 15 percent higher price-to-earnings (P/E) multiple, which more than countered the 12.5 percent EPS dilution. The market apparently responded favorably to the prospect of an increase in the present value of EVA rather than to the misleading near-term accounting appearance. And this is not an isolated example. Numerous empirical studies have shown that when accounting and economics diverge, the market responds to the expected long-run economic value in the short term—right away. The P/E gives way to the EVA.

The contrary view is what I call the accounting model of value, which I covered informally before. To be more precise, it says that a firm's share price, or P, equals its earnings per share (EPS) times its price-to-earnings (P/E) multiple, to wit, P = EPS × P/E. This is of course always true because the P/E multiple is solved for as a plug figure. A stock that trades for $10 a share, with $1 in per share earnings, trades for a P/E of 10. In fact, it is a tautology, not a valuation model. But some can't resist thinking it is a valuation model. Having written the formula down, it is tempting to conclude that an increase in EPS must translate into an increase in share price, and vice versa, because the P/E multiple is a given. Take EPS up to $1.10 a share, and the stock price rises to $11 a share, says the model. And don't dilute EPS to $0.90, because the stock price will nose-dive to $9. This screams at Monsanto to not step up the R&D and crush earnings. Of course, the EPS model was not right for Monsanto, and is not right in any case. But why is it wrong?

The accounting model makes a big assumption. It assumes that, regardless of what is driving the EPS up or down, the market is so simplistic and myopic and really so stupid that it just mechanically assigns the same P/E multiple no matter what. That is a highly theoretical proposition that turns out to be dead wrong in practice. P/E multiples change all the time to reflect a change in the *quality* of the earnings.

I have already discussed how an increase in a firm's leverage ratio, such as to borrow and buy back stock, reduces the multiple. It increases the volatility and decreases the quality of the bottom-line shareholder earnings, which renders EPS a poor guide to the stock price. An increase in spending on intangible assets has the opposite effect. A spending hike decreases EPS in the short term, but if an honest appraisal of the strategy shows that it is likely to increase EVA, then the company's share price will respond favorably, and right away, as it did with Monsanto, and the P/E multiple will more than take up the slack. In this case, there is an increase in the quality of reported earnings, because the current earnings are pregnant with the potential payoff from the current R&D spending. Once again, given this, a CFO or board member cannot really judge the value of a decision or how the market will respond by looking at near-term EPS. One must also ask what will happen to the P/E ratio. But how can one determine that?

Quite simply, abandon the idea that stock prices are set by putting a P/E multiple on EPS. Instead, forecast what will happen to EVA and discount that to determine the stock price, and then just derive the P/E ratio from that. If EVA shows a win, and the accountants inform us that EPS will be diluted for whatever reason, then you can safely conclude that the company will trade for a higher price-to-earnings multiple, that is all. You solve for it. You may not always be right, of course, but there is no question that you will more likely reach the right decision if you put it in terms of its impact on EVA than in terms of EPS.

To reiterate, the accounting model of valuation assumes that the P/E multiple is fixed, so EPS is all, while the EVA model assumes the present value of EVA is all, and the P/E multiple is just a plug. The evidence backs common sense. P/E ratios are plugs. EVA wins; EPS loses.

The second example I want to share comes from Kao USA, at the time known as Jergens Inc., the hand lotion company that had been acquired by the leading Japanese consumer products company, Kao Corporation, often referred to as the Procter & Gamble of Japan. I was invited in by the CFO to present EVA to the Japanese board that oversaw Jergens to help resolve a culture conflict.

The Japanese were uncomfortable with confrontation and did not like having to negotiate budget goals that became the basis for determining annual bonuses for the American management team. They felt, as I do, that that process is often highly counterproductive, that it tends to corrupt planning and make senior managers and subordinates into adversaries instead of partners. George Sperzel, the CFO at the time, saw EVA and the EVA bonus plan as the perfect way to reconcile the occidental demand for cash bonuses and the oriental aversion to confrontation and negotiation. I must have been good that day, because I was able to convince the board to commission the adoption of EVA and the bonus plan with automatic target resets. And it worked so well that a few years later, Kao became the first Japanese company to fully adopt EVA, but that is another story.

Shortly after adopting EVA, Jergens was launching a new skin cleansing patch developed in Japan named Biore. The marketing department followed standard procedure and prepared a typically aggressive plan to advertise and promote the product, which inevitably would lead to invitations to lavish dinners hosted by sundry fashion magazines and other media to pitch their advertising outlets. Sperzel stepped in and reminded the marketers that, under EVA, all the money they spent launching the new brand would be captured, capitalized, and written off over time, subject to cost of capital on the balance, so that if they overspent and did not deliver value, EVA would suffer and their bonuses would, too.

The gentle reminder led to a wholesale change in strategy, in effect from push to pull. In an about-face, the Jergens marketing team paid to entertain the magazine editors to sell them on the merits of articles describing the benefits of cleaning skin with an absorbent patch. Jergens stepped up trade show promotions and in-store displays and demonstrations. In short, Jergens looked for ways to make the product go viral before that was even a phrase. The result: Biore was EVA positive the third month from launch, which had never before happened in the company's marketing experience and was a key factor in the parent company's decision to adopt EVA in Japan.

A third way the EVA accounting produces better decisions is in neutralizing build versus buy choices. I recall going over the EVA treatment for capitalizing R&D spending with the vice-chair of a major tech company not long ago. After hearing me out, he confessed he wished we had spoken four years earlier. The company at that time had reached a critical juncture where it could either step up its tech spending to keep pace or punt. Management punted out of concern that a sharp increase in spending would be a drag on the firm's EPS record. The vice-chair said, "Bennett, now we have to go out and pay premium prices to buy the technology we could and should have developed on our own. The irony is that accounting says tech is an asset if you buy it but not if you develop it, but in the real world it is almost always the opposite. I really like your EVA approach. It puts buying and internal development on the same footing, so as a management team you are more inclined to make the right decision based on its economic value rather than its accounting appearance."

CFOs sometimes ask me to predict whether their company will spend more or less on intangibles with the EVA accounting treatment. As the examples show, it depends. Monsanto spent more, Jergens less. The answer is the company will spend differently and better.

A last point is that for any one company, the decision to capitalize and amortize the intangible investments depends on the facts and circumstances. For each type of intangible, ask: Is it material? Can we track it? Is it a variable that our managers can actually manage, and will they understand and respond to it? If not, keep it simple and just expense the outlay in accord with conventional accounting. But where the behavioral and managerial and analytical benefit is worth the extra tracking cost, then do it. At EVA Dimensions we've developed a set of software tools that automate the computations and correctly integrate them into the EVA metric set, which has reduced the cost of tracking the adjustments. For public companies, the software is coded to automatically amortize its reported R&D over five years (10 years for pharmaceutical and biotechnology companies) and advertising and promotion over three years (five years for pharma and biotech). That's the starting point, and it serves as a useful reference that any one company can alter and customize for internal use.

BAD DEBT RESERVES

Bankers have a curious practice. When they make a loan, they immediately write off one or two or three cents on the dollar as a loss. Why? Because they know loans are risky and some, inevitably, will not be repaid in full. But the banks don't just absorb the losses. They expect to offset the losses, plus cover their operating costs and interest expenses—heck, even to earn a decent return on capital—by jacking up the rates charged to all borrowers. Which raises the question: If the bankers prebook the losses they foresee on deadbeat loans, why aren't they prebooking the profits they expect to make off the loans that will be repaid? Because the accountant's motto is: when in doubt, debit. When in doubt, take a charge to earnings, set up a reserve, and be conservative.

But in running a business and in judging the shareholder value of a going concern, the better rule is not conservatism but realism. And in this case, the reality is that when times are good and profits are lush, managers inflate the provision for bad debts and squirrel away earnings in the reserve. Then when tough times hit, they underprovide for the actual losses they experience and draw down on the reserve, and that helps them smooth reported earnings. It is a classic example of the "cookie jar" reserve. While it may be a common practice, it is not a good idea at all. The practices don't just divorce reported profits from what is really happening at any given time. The manipulation is a transparent and fundamentally unethical attempt to paper over problems and fool the market, and to smooth bonuses. That is the slippery slope to the Enron zone.

EVA says, "Let there be light." The loan loss reserve is added back to the loans, so loans appear in the EVA capital base at the face value of what is owed. And instead of running the accounting estimate of losses—the so-called loan loss provision—through earnings, it is ignored and in its place the loans that actually go bad in a period are charged off against the EVA earnings. That way, if a loan is delinquent, the operating team is galvanized to collect it, because if they don't, it becomes a charge to that period's EVA earnings. And the next time they extend credit, they are motivated to think twice. In other words, this shifts attention from what the accountants can manage—the book provision—to what line managers manage—credit decisions and the ensuing actual losses and recovery efforts. The same applies in an operating company on its receivables and bad debt provision. It is the same EVA accounting, with the same beneficial consequences.

DEFERRING TAXES ADDS VALUE

There's nothing certain but death and taxes, so, given an alternative, let's talk tax. A problem is that companies never pay the tax that their accountants say they pay. Accountants compute tax as if it was due on the book income they measure, while companies actually pay tax on their taxable income, which is figured with a different set of rules using a different set of books. One example is that companies are able to write off their plant and equipment faster on their tax books, which postpones taxes compared to the reported tax. Other rules lead to tax prepayments. For example, accountants deduct an estimate for warranty costs when a sale is made and accrue employee compensation costs, but tax rules allow deductions to lower taxable income only when the costs are actually paid, which occurs at a later date.

Accountants true up the difference between book taxes and cash taxes on the balance sheet. When tax payments are delayed, a so-called deferred tax liability account builds up on the financing side of the balance sheet ledger. That represents a claim on future cash flow. It says that down the pike the company will have to pay more tax than its accountants compute in order to make up for paying less tax in the past. On the other side, when a company prepays tax, a so-called deferred tax asset accumulates on the balance sheet. It is an asset because the company will eventually obtain a refund of the prepaid tax. Either way, the book tax number is just a fiction, and changes in the deferred balance sheet accounts reconcile the accounting earnings fiction to the economic reality of when taxes are actually being paid.

Here's the rub. There is a real value to paying taxes later rather than sooner (i.e., for building up a deferred tax liability), because no interest is charged on the deferred tax liability. It is effectively interest-free capital. It reduces the amount of debt and equity capital the company would need to finance its net business assets and that would otherwise burden EVA with a capital charge.

The opposite applies for a deferred tax asset. There is a real added cost to finance the tax prepayment with capital. And yet, again, sadly, accounting books just completely ignore the timing value of when taxes are actually paid. This is a gross error, because industrial companies materially benefit from deferring lots of taxes, while others, like retailers, don't have nearly as many tax advantages. Systematic errors in judging performance are introduced if deferred taxes are buried on the balance sheet and essentially ignored, as most performance measures do. EVA gets it right.

There are three ways to recognize the timing value in EVA. The first approach, which I do not recommend, is to convert the book tax provision to cash taxes. For instance, if a company started with a net deferred tax liability balance of $70 and ended the year at $100, the $30 buildup would be added to NOPAT, and the $100 deferred tax liability balance-sheet account would be moved into equity capital, just as if the accounting provision for tax had been equal to the cash tax payments all along.

That is correct as far as it goes, but it introduces a lot of unwanted volatility into the EVA earnings because cash taxes fluctuate, sometimes by a lot. There are many reasons why that happens. Companies occasionally negotiate tax settlements that trigger a one-time tax payment or credit. Another is that U.S. tax rules have recently offered a temporary incentive to acquire equipment, called bonus depreciation. Another technical problem is that deferred tax accounts change when assets are acquired or sold to reconcile differences in the book tax carrying values. Whatever the reason, measuring EVA with cash taxes misrepresents sustainable profitability and distorts performance comparisons.

The second approach avoids that problem. The procedure is to include the deferred tax asset accounts in capital, subject to the capital charge, and to deduct deferred tax liability accounts from capital to offset the capital charge. The more money a firm has tied up in prepaid taxes (i.e., in a deferred tax asset account), the lower its EVA is, while the more it has built up a deferred tax liability account to fund its business and reduce the need for capital, the bigger its EVA is. As with the cash tax procedure, this one provides the right incentive—find legitimate ways to pay taxes later rather than sooner—while avoiding its deficiencies. One-time or temporary blips in cash taxes are absorbed into the deferred tax accounts and converted into an annual earnings equivalent.

Although that is a perfectly legitimate way to handle deferred taxes, a disadvantage is that it complicates capital. Deferred tax asset accounts are mixed in with the operational assets that line teams manage, and deferred tax liabilities confoundingly offset capital. That adds a layer of complexity in explaining what goes into capital, which is already a bit of a struggle for operating people. Why compound that?

This leads to the approach EVA Dimensions recommends. It is to recognize the value of deferring taxes via a direct adjustment to the tax deducted from EVA. To do this, deferred tax assets are *not* included in capital, and deferred tax liabilities are *not* deducted from capital—capital remains operationally focused. Instead, the tax on NOPAT—and thus on EVA—is reduced by the cost of capital saved from the net balance sheet deferral of taxes.

For example, suppose a company carries a deferred tax liability on its balance sheet of $160 and recognizes a deferred tax asset of $40, for a net deferred tax liability of $120, and its cost of capital is 10 percent. Then $12— the cost of capital saved—is *deducted* from the NOPAT tax. This produces the same EVA as the prior method but without the capital complications. It just takes the cost of capital effect and dumps it right into the tax account.

Besides keeping taxes out of the capital accounts, all tax items are consolidated into one effective tax and tax rate rather than being spread over the income statement and throughout the balance sheet. As important, it preserves the correct incentives. Business managers are motivated to collaborate with the company's tax department to implement strategies that will legitimately postpone tax payments and reduce the tax on EVA. As one of my clients put it, "Now that we are measuring EVA posttax with this system, the tax department has become an EVA profit center for us. We've come to realize that a dollar of tax saved is just as valuable as a dollar of profit earned." Then he corrected himself. "That is not quite right. The dollar of tax saved is *better* than the dollar of profit earned, because profit is taxed."

SMOOTH TAXES

In any one year and for many reasons, companies may report taxes that are dramatically more or less than a normal amount. Here is one example taken from PepsiCo's 2008 Annual Report:

> In 2007, we recognized $129 million ($0.08 per share) of noncash tax benefits related to the favorable resolution of certain foreign tax matters.

In 2006, we recognized noncash tax benefits of $602 million ($0.36 per share), substantially all of which related to the Internal Revenue Service's (IRS) examination of our consolidated tax returns for the years 1998 through 2002.

There is nothing at all wrong with what Pepsi reported. Management was just following the rules and living with the natural give-and-take of negotiations with tax authorities. But that is the point. Unusual and nonrecurring items flow through computed tax provisions and into book profits all the time, which introduces an unwanted source of noise into corporate profit measurement. EVA quiets the noise by establishing a normal or standard corporate income tax rate and then applying that rate each year to the firm's pretax operating income to estimate the tax that is deducted from NOPAT. Mind, we do not want to ignore one-time tax events, but we do want to smooth them out and convert them to the equivalent of an annual earnings impact.

How? By deferring them, and crediting them with the cost of capital. To be specific, EVA creates a separate deferred tax account (I call it the created deferred tax account) to hold the accumulated difference between the assumed smoothed tax and the accountant's tax provision on operating profit. If the smoothed tax computed at the standard rate is more than the provision, then a deferred tax liability is created, because the company's provision was for some reason less than the normal rate that year, and vice versa. The created deferred tax account is then treated the same as the ordinary balance-sheet deferred tax accounts. The cost of capital saved on a net created deferred tax liability is applied as a reduction in the tax on NOPAT (and EVA), and vice versa.

An example will make it easy. Suppose we've established that a firm's normal, ongoing, effective tax rate on its operating profit runs at 33 percent. If it records $100 in operating profit, then $33 is deducted from its NOPAT and, by extension, from its EVA, as the normal or standard tax provision. Suppose, though, that the company's book tax provision on operating profit that year was only $25—perhaps due to a shift to foreign source income taxed at a lower rate, an unusually large R&D credit, or a one-time tax settlement like at Pepsi. Then the $33 tax charged to EVA overstates the actual tax provision by $8, and that is added to the created deferred tax liability account and is carried forward forever. The opposite applies if the actual tax provision on operating profit was greater than the EVA standard tax.

Over time, if the standard tax rate accurately reflects the company's typical tax rate, the plus and minus adjustments should offset, and the created account should approximate zero in the long run. But over the short term, there will be deviations—that is the whole point, to smooth the fluctuations—and a net created deferred tax liability (or asset) account will accumulate. It is treated the same way as the company's actual deferred tax accounts. Interest at the cost of capital rate on the net created deferred tax liability is applied as a separate reduction in the tax on NOPAT (and thus on EVA).

When the dust settles, the tax deducted from EVA is a smoothed tax (at the assumed standard rate) less a cost of capital credit for the overall net deferral of taxes relative to the assumed smoothed tax. We get there in three steps, but that is the net effect of what happens. This treatment provides for a consistent and comparable assessment of after-tax performance while providing line teams with all the desirable incentives to factor taxes into their decisions and to legitimately defer or permanently reduce taxes. And it does not make the mistake of mixing tax items that happen once in a while with items that happen all the time. A transitory reduction in tax is converted to ongoing earnings equivalent by multiplying it times the cost of capital.

FIX RETIREMENT COST DISTORTIONS

Perhaps nowhere is accounting more befuddled than in defined-benefit retirement plans. To clear this up takes a bit of huffing and puffing, I am afraid, but it also brings together many of the issues we've discussed. This is your final exam on correctly accounting for value. Feel free to skip ahead if this is not your cup of tea or if it is not applicable to your company.

What is the real operating expense a company incurs in a period from its defined-benefit retirement plans? It is the increase in the present value of the liability for future benefit payments that arises from employee services in the period. Fortunately, there is a name for that. It is called the service cost. It represents the amount of money that a company would have to set aside and invest in safe bonds to meet the estimated future obligations incurred during the year. And if a company actually did set aside that money and did invest it in low-risk government bonds that were maturity-matched to the obligations, its accounting cost would equal the service cost in every period.

When we measure EVA, we assume a company did that, regardless of whether it actually did. We pretend the plan sponsor did fund its service cost each year with safe bonds, and we recognize the service cost as the charge to EVA. We consider that to be the best measure of the expected cost of the service in that period. It also appealingly separates the operating cost from assumptions about how the cost is financed. It does not mix legacy issues and pension funding strategies into the measurement of operating profit performance.

Here's the rub. Most companies do not do that. They do not fully fund their plans each year with bonds. They speculate. They mismatch contributions to the retirement fund compared to the service cost, which means they are effectively either borrowing money from or lending money to the retirement plan, and, worse, they don't invest the retirement assets in safe bonds with maturities matched to the retirement liabilities. They typically go for a mix of bonds and stocks and alternative investments. And they do that for two reasons.

The first is that CFOs are convinced that they can earn a higher return by investing retirement assets in a diversified market portfolio than by investing in safe bonds. Why not earn a higher return to reduce the cost of funding the pension promises, if that is possible? Answer: because a higher return is available only from, and in compensation for, taking more risk, so that after considering the added risk, there is no benefit at all to earning the higher return. A company's shareholders would be as well off if the pension plan were invested in bonds as in stocks (in fact, there are good arguments that they would be better off, but that is a topic for another book).

The argument for investing retirement assets in a risky portfolio is seductive. It is like saying that if you have $1,000 to invest, never invest it in safe government bonds. At least invest your money in a portfolio of BBB-rated corporate bonds and snatch the higher return. Why invest $1,000 and earn just 2 percent on government paper these days when the available yield on a triple-B bond portfolio is 4 percent, let's say? Why would you ever settle for $20 in interest income when you could earn $40? Why not earn more?

The answer, obviously, is that triple-B bonds are riskier, and the market has set the price—available to anyone—to compensate for that risk. They are not as safe or liquid or stable as government bonds, and the transaction costs in and out are generally higher. Lower-rated bonds are more volatile— their value tends to rise and fall with the market and the economic cycle. They have nondiversifiable beta risk. And, worst of all, lower-rated bonds can go AWOL just when you need their assistance the most. Their yields may shoot up and their prices may fall much more precipitously when there is a flight to quality and liquidity. As a result, investors understandably expect and demand to earn a higher return for bearing the higher risk and illiquidity of the lower-rated bonds. But note that the higher return does not make the lower-rated bonds more valuable. The higher return is what is *required* to make them worth just the same. An investor pays the same $1,000 today for a corporate bond portfolio that promises to pay $40 in interest a year as for a low-risk government bond portfolio that promises to pay only $20. The value is the same because the 4 percent corporate bonds are discounted at a 4 percent cost of capital rate, and the 2 percent government bonds are discounted at 2 percent, as is appropriate for the risk. And this is precisely why there is no benefit to investing retirement assets in a risky stock market portfolio instead of safe bonds. In both cases you start off using the same amount of money to buy marketable securities at market prices and earn a market return that is commensurate with the risk. But many CFOs forget this fundamental truth and are seduced by the superficial prospect of earning a higher return.

The second reason CFOs speculate in pension plans is that the accountants have rigged the bookkeeping rules in favor of taking pension risk in two ways. First, accountants allow companies to offset the service cost and the accrual of interest on the accumulated service cost with an *assumed* rate of return on the retirement assets. As I have argued, the risk-adjusted rate of return should be the same regardless of the retirement portfolio, and should be the same as the rate used to discount the service cost liability, but accountants do not do that. They take the world at face value, and they allow companies to use a higher assumed rate of return if they invest the retirement assets in a risky market portfolio than in a bond portfolio. This accounting convention enables companies that invest in a market portfolio to reduce their reported retirement costs and report them as lower than what they really are, considering the risk.

It gets worse. The difference between the present value of the projected retirement benefits and the current market value of the retirement assets is a plan's so-called funded status. Funded status can swiftly turn negative if the stock market takes a swoon. Under current accounting rules, a funding deficit is recognized on the accounting books as a minimum liability and a corresponding reduction in book equity, but the charge to recognize the funding deficit does not pass through ordinary profit channels. It is recognized through a back-channel, rear-door profit measure called other comprehensive income (OCI). Out of sight is out of mind. CFOs basically ignore it because it does not affect reported earnings or earnings per share (EPS). The added risk of investing in a market portfolio compared to investing in safe bonds is swept right under the carpet and ignored. Okay, if the funding deficit gets really large, then the accountants are stirred to run a charge through conventional profit channels. But guess what? They amortize the deficit charge over very long time frames of up to 20 years. In other words, the accountants take the investment risk, which is always a short-term fluctuation, and morph it into an innocuous long-term nonevent. This is simply unforgivable nonsense.

Nevertheless, the accounting rules are the rules, and the rules have misled most companies into speculation that really has no economic substance or added market value. Funding a fixed obligation with an uncertain market return can generate excess returns only at excess risk. It doesn't pay. We've seen this movie before. This is another prime example of how a CFO can goose up reported earnings and earnings per share, yet gain no traction in the stock market, because the market will penalize the stock with a lower price-to-earnings (P/E) multiple. As with borrowing to buy back stock, the EPS gain from following a risky pension investment strategy is countered by a loss in P/E multiple. Here too, the market sees through the accounting appearance. How? With EVA, of course. EVA lifts the veil and shows the warts and all. We'll need three steps to do it.

First, as mentioned, the true retirement cost in a period is the service cost and not the retirement expense that accountants report. The reported cost is added back to the earnings to get rid of it, and the service cost is deducted instead. With that, the incentive to invest in a risky market portfolio is eliminated, and the true expected ongoing cost is used in its place. That is the appropriate charge to use when judging operations managers and when making forward-looking business decisions. Irrelevant prior funding gains or losses or funding decisions should not be intermingled with future incremental business decisions.

Second, all the retirement accounts that the accountants have unhelpfully spread all over the balance sheet are consolidated into one net liability account. All retirement assets are brought over as an offset to the retirement liability. The minimum liability charges buried in the OCI retained earnings account are removed from equity and deducted from the retirement liability (which was increased to recognize the minimum liability in the first place, and now is back to where it was before recognition of the minimum liability). The cumulative service cost is added to the net retirement liability account, and the cumulative reported retirement costs are deducted from it. In other words, the retirement liability (and common equity) is adjusted to what it would be if the service cost was the reported cost all along and as if no minimum liability had ever been recognized.

When the dust settles, the retirement liability account is the cumulative difference between the service cost that increases the liability and the cash contributions to the retirement plan that reduce it. It is the net borrowing from or lending to the retirement plan. If a company always fully funded its service cost and invested in safe, matched-maturity bonds, then the net retirement liability computed per the previous formula would be zero. If there is a net retirement liability, then the company has not fully funded its service cost, and is effectively borrowing from the retirement plan. And if it is negative, then the company has put more funding into its retirement plans than its service cost, which is generally not a good sign. It could be prefunding the plans, but more likely that means the returns on its retirement assets have been so low that the company has had to ante up a surplus just to stay in the game.

One more step to go. The third adjustment is to recognize the cost of closing a funding gap—or the earnings equivalent of a funding gain, if the company should be so lucky. This begins by measuring the difference between the off-balance-sheet funded status of the plan and the on-balance sheet net liability computed earlier. If the off-balance-sheet liability is greater, then the company will eventually need to pony up the difference to make the plan whole. The company would have to raise capital to do that. So, the last step is to deduct from EVA the cost of capital charge for the capital needed to close the funding gap, and vice versa for a gain.

For instance, suppose the net funding gap between a company's off- and on-balance-sheet liabilities is $100, and the cost of capital is 10 percent. Then a $10 after-tax charge is directly deducted from its EVA. The charge appears in our reports under the caption "capital charge on post-employment-benefit (PRB) funding loss (gain)." And in a forecast valuation of the company, the present value of the charge discounted at the cost of capital—which would come to $100 in this case, which is the net unrecognized funding liability—would be deducted from the firm's NPV and MVA. With this procedure, a funding liability reduces the company's value directly and visibly, through the present value of the line-item hit to EVA, rather than being sidetracked into the virtually invisible OCI account where accountants stuff it.

It's a lot to grasp, so let's step back and run an overall example, building up from a simple situation and layering in more nuance. Let's start with a firm that has an annual service cost of $100, and assume that management does not fund any of it (ERISA rules require it to, but this is an example). Suppose the safe bond discount rate is 2 percent. Then after two years the liability on the books has grown to $202. It is $100 from the first-year service cost, plus $100 for the second year, plus $2 in accrued interest (it would also be reduced for any benefits paid, but let's keep it simple).

The plan's funded status off the books matches the liability that shows up on the books. Here's how. The plan's projected benefit obligation recorded in the company's financial footnotes is $202 (it is the same as the accumulated service cost liability), and with no assets in the plan, that is also the plan's funded status. As a result, there is no actuarial funding gap as we compute it, because the $202 on-balance-sheet liability matches the $202 off-balance-sheet liability. No adjustment to EVA is made. All that is happening is the company is borrowing from its employees. It is paying them in promises, in effect issuing bonds to them that come due postretirement. There is no cash outlay, but there is a liability recorded that reduces the firm's common equity book value as the service charge passes through EVA and out of retained earnings, so nothing is missing.

Now suppose the company borrows $202 to contribute to the retirement plan. The entry is to credit the borrowing and debit the retirement liability, which makes the balance-sheet retirement liability zero. Off the books, the retirement plan funded status is now zero, too. The projected obligation is fully funded by the $202 that is now available to invest in a matched-maturity safe bond fund. Forevermore, following the same policies, the company will show a retirement cost that is equal to its service cost. The interest that accrues on the retirement liability plus changes in the value of the retirement liability are always perfectly offset by the total return on the matched bond fund from interest income and from the change in its market value. Life would be simple and sensible if this were the case, and the accounting would accurately and coincidentally mirror economic reality.

But what if, instead, the retirement plan is invested in a common stock/corporate bond/alternate asset mix, as is typical, and as a result, the assumed return on the pension fund is jacked up to 7 percent? The reported retirement cost is now magically less than the service cost. The retirement liability accrues interest at the 2 percent safe bond rate, but that is way more than offset by an assumed 7 percent return from the pension fund. On net, the reported retirement cost understates the true service cost in an amount of 5 percent of the retirement fund assets each year. Book profit, EPS, EBITDA, and ROE all get a nice but quite meaningless free ride. There's the allure to play the game. Of course, the EVA accounting says nothing of the sort. The cost is still the service cost. Operating decisions and financing decisions are kept separate, once again, as they ought to be.

Suppose, contrary to the assumed 7 percent return, the pension fund falls 10 percent in value. Ouch. Now there is a sizable funded status gap—but in this case to keep it simple we assume it is not so sizable that it triggers additional cost recognition. It will trigger balance sheet recognition, though. The reported retirement liability will be increased and the book equity decreased to recognize the funded status liability. Ironically, the company's return on equity is inflated even more because the reported book equity is reduced. Oh boy. Bottom line: it was a terrible decision in hindsight—it really wasn't a good decision in foresight either, as I have argued, but it turned out *very* badly—yet the accounting impact on ROE makes it seem brilliant. What baloney.

EVA once again glides into the sorry scene to put things right. It reverses the entries that gave rise to the minimum retirement liability. It restores the book equity back to what it was, and reduces the on-balance-sheet liability to what it was. It adds back the reported retirement cost to earnings and subtracts the higher service cost in its place, and reverses the difference out of the retirement liability as if that distortion had not occurred. Then, it glances off book to observe a weakened retirement fund, one that formerly stood toe-to-toe with the pension liability, but which has now shriveled to chest high. EVA realizes it will take nutritional sustenance to restore the fund to its former status. It computes the cost of financing the replenishment at the cost of capital rate, and then deducts the charge from EVA. Now we have the truth. This was a dumb decision with a bad outcome. Now EVA has penetrated the fog of the accounting and made it plain for everyone to see what is really going on. The cost of a retirement plan is the service cost. Funding strategies that deviate from investing in safe, matched-risk bonds are speculation. The market does not pay for speculation, since anyone can do that and hardly anyone wins it. Funding gaps created by actuarial and investment losses are real liabilities, all right, but let's recognize the liability as a charge to EVA funded at the cost of capital rate. Accounting is a distorted view of an imaginary world. EVA is the truth of the matter. It is the economic reality.

STRATEGIC INVESTMENTS

I define a strategic investment as one that takes a while to ramp up and fully bear fruit, though I do remember a meeting quite a while back with a former CFO of Teledyne who said, "Bennett, I thought strategic investments were the ones that were *never* going to pay off." Now that was the voice of experience. But to be fair, strategic investments happen all the time and quite frequently do pay off.

This recalls an assignment I had working for Jollibee Foods in the Philippines. At the time (1998), there were only two markets in the world where McDonald's did not sell the most fast food. One was Israel because a kosher firm did, and the other was the Philippines for no good reason other than that Tony Tan, a Chinese immigrant entrepreneur and founder of Jollibee, so out-hustled the Golden Arches and so localized the product that his fast-food chain was among the most highly respected of all firms in Southeast Asia. When I met Tony, he said he wanted to put in EVA, and when I had the temerity to ask why he needed it, he responded, "We are excellent because we adopt best practices, and EVA is a best practice." I was not going to argue with him.

But shortly after the project began he called to cancel it. I asked why. "Because it takes about 18 months for new stores to fully ramp up to expected traffic, and on the start-up we are not earning the cost of capital. My team is telling me EVA will choke our growth." I told him that depends on how you measure EVA. We sat down and developed a schedule that said for the first 12 months a restaurant is open, it will be charged for only 60 percent of its capital; for the next 12 months, 90 percent; and after that, for 120 percent. In other words, we figured how much capital could be supported in each period to spread out the expected EVA evenly over time, which meant pushing some of the capital from the front end to the back. I call it the "AAMCO adjustment." You can pay less now, but then you've got to pay more later—to preserve the present value of EVA.

Public utilities do this all the time. It may take five years or longer to construct a new electric plant, and in the meantime, the investment is held out of the rate-base capital and the required return on the capital is not charged to the customer. Instead, it accumulates in the capital account until such time as the plant is operational. Then the entire amount, the bricks and mortar and the accumulated interest in the capital account, is folded into the rate base to generate a return. It is a well-established (dare I say it) accounting practice. But my point is that it should not apply just to regulated public utilities.

Georgia-Pacific, for example, used it to meter in the capital invested when major new paper lines were added. Apparently you cannot add a small paper-making line; you can only add them in quantum lumps, and you understand that you always invest a little ahead of the market to stake out your claim. So holding back a portion of the up-front investment and then metering it back into capital according to a preset schedule was a simple adjustment that encouraged the right decisions about timing the investments while maintaining accountability for generating the planned results on time and with interest.

Ball Corporation also provides strategic relief, but in its case it is not so formulaic. A special corporate committee reporting to the CFO reviews capital deferral proposals submitted by the line teams. And it is used sparingly, and only in the most material and truly strategic of applications.

Events that qualify are acquisitions. CFO Scott Morrison explains: "When we make an acquisition we recognize that the price we pay cannot be fully justified by the first year's earnings. We look to integrate and grow the target, and that typically ramps up over three years. So we figure out how much of the purchase price is due to the value of the expected first-year EVA earnings, and we hold back the rest and meter it into capital over three years. That way, we can get the deals done without a penalty to our EVA, but that way we are all on the hook to deliver the added value over time."

Here's an example. Suppose Ball paid 16 times earnings, or $1.6 billion, for a business that was projected to earn a first-year NOPAT of $100 million. To keep it simple, suppose Ball used a 10 percent cost of capital (Ball actually uses 9 percent). Then management would figure that the first-year NOPAT was worth an even $1 billion, and would hold back the $600 million difference and meter it into capital over three years. That way, the first year's EVA would be zero if NOPAT was on plan. Over the next three years NOPAT would have to increase to cover the cost of any new capital put into the business, as usual, but in addition, it would have to increase by at least another $20 million a year—that's the 10 percent return on the $200 capital leg in each of the three years—just to remain EVA neutral. Metering the capital back in simulates, and requires, the growth in economic profit that was the basis for justifying the acquisition price in the first place.

Most CFOs understand the issue, but they take a different approach. They don't adjust the performance measure. Instead, they adjust their performance targets. They swallow hard and acquiesce in setting an initially lower return goal to get a strategic deal done and bring the capital onto their books. The trouble is, once the first year has passed, everyone has conveniently forgotten the rosy forecasts submitted to justify the transaction or the investment in the first place. Going forward, performance targets are renegotiated like any other year in the budget process, with no memory of past promises or any accountability for actually delivering the strategic value. Knowing that there's a free pass after the first year is up, line teams at most companies are just not as seriously committed to rigorously planning out and delivering deal value as they should be, and that creates an unfortunate tension with CFOs, who care about protecting their company's financial strength. The interests of the decision makers inside the company are simply not as aligned as they should be when they most need to be—at the time the decision is going to be made.

SIMPLE MEASURES MAKE FOR COMPLEX CONVERSATIONS

There is a larger point here: Simple measures make for complex conversations. Traditional, out-of-the-box, ready-to-eat performance measures do not adapt well to transforming events or one-time items, like restructuring a business, stepping up spending on intangibles, outsourcing decisions, asset sales, consummating a major acquisition, deferring taxes, changing a company's capital structure, and the like. In consequence, managers and board members must devote a lot of time debating how to adjust the targets for those measures as circumstances change in a delicate and in fact impossible balancing act. But with EVA the target is always the same—more is better than less; bigger is better. EVA incorporates adjustments that smooth out and accommodate life's little surprises, that better match cost and benefit, that reflect the true strategic cost of capital, and so forth, which is why Ball Corporation could have such a simple and unchanging EVA bonus plan for 20 years.

When people tell me that they are concerned EVA is too complex to understand, I say three things. First, that's not really true. EVA is just common sense, and it is fundamentally a lot more intuitively appealing to operating people than profit measured by accounting rules. It is basically a three-line calculation—sales less operating costs less the capital costs to rent the balance sheet. True, some of the adjustments we just went through, especially the ones for taxes and defined-benefit pensions, are bewildering. But that is only because it takes a lot of steps to reverse the distortions inherent in reported accounting. Where EVA ends up is actually far easier to understand. As for taxes, it tells operating people to make decisions based on their fundamental underlying tax rate, and to use legitimate means to defer tax. For pensions, EVA says the operating cost is the service cost in the period, and speculative funding gains or losses are isolated as a corporate concern. Those messages are clear and clearly measured with EVA, but not so with reported figures. If anything, EVA brings enlightenment to the dark corners of accounting.

Second, explaining EVA and how to measure it is actually a very good way to get buy-in, to increase business acumen and introduce a common language, and to propel the out-of-the-box thinking that can actually increase EVA. Training is not a challenge; it is an enormous opportunity, as I have said.

Third, life is complex. In the real world a CFO must choose between using a more sophisticated metric like EVA that is defined to measure the value added from period to period and to iron out the bumps, and negotiating targets for a bunch of conventional metrics that don't accurately measure much of anything and that are subject to jarring distortions. You don't avoid complexity by using simple standard measures. You are just forced to shift the complexity into debates over how to adjust the targets. I say, keep it simple. Focus on increasing EVA as the measure that matters, and define EVA so that, to the greatest extent practical, a year-over-year increase is a real win, and a decrease is a real loss.

Before concluding this chapter, I want to point out that the corrective adjustments I've discussed are *value neutral*. We insist that any adjustment must alter only the pattern but not the present value of EVA. The present value is the same if a tax deferral flows right into cash taxes or if a capital charge credit for the deferral is added to EVA each year, and is the same if R&D is expensed or if it is amortized over time with cost-of-capital interest added to the unamortized balance. EVA cannot be defined arbitrarily. The present value of EVA and the net present value of free cash flow must be equal, which means that even in the EVA world, debits and credits must still balance. It's a quality check and an anchor to reality, and something that a lot of CFOs who claim to measure EVA forget to do.

SUMMING UP

Accountants cannot serve multiple masters in one set of financial records. They cannot at the same time address the needs of share owners and business managers who are or should be interested in maximizing going-concern value, and the requirements of lenders who want to write loan covenants against assets recoverable in liquidation, of regulators and politicians who are interested in witch hunts, and, worst of all, misguided CFOs who lobby for rules that enable them to inflate and manage reported profits. As a business manager, CEO, or corporate board member, you simply cannot afford to take reported accounting results at face value. There is way too much cosmetic surgery standing between you and the truth. You'll be misdirected at every turn. You should use EVA to get under the skin and measure the real economic profit with far more consistency and reliability than whatever comes out of an accounting report.

When I began my business career at the Chase Manhattan Bank in 1976 and went through the management training program, my colleagues and I were taught to rip apart company financials, question every reported line item and footnote, and do everything we could to get to the root of the firm's cash-flow-generating ability to service our loans. I understood that that was how markets worked, that lenders and shareholders were generally intelligent, trained, financially sophisticated professionals and skeptical people who did not trust surface appearance and who knew how to look well beyond the accounting façade and deeply into the workings of business performance. They—we—didn't always get that right, but it wasn't for lack of trying.

Imagine my dismay when I first became a consultant in the late 1970s and went out to meet CFOs and CEOs to discover how many of them assumed that the market would react unthinkingly to their financials at reported face value, and that, in those innocent days, it was actually ethical to manipulate accounting (within the malleable principles, of course) to put the best face on their reported results. I knew from personal experience (plus a lot of evidence on stock market behavior) and Sunday school that that view was totally wrong.

And now that we've added an EVA stock rating model to our tool kit (covered at the end of the book), I have had the privilege of meeting with many of the smartest and most influential investors in the world. I can tell you most certainly that none of the ones I've met put much, if any, credence in book accounting profits. They are acutely aware of pitfalls such as I have discussed, and they earnestly want to get to the truth, because the truth enables them to make better buy/sell decisions a little ahead of the crowd.

Many of them are understandably drawn to EVA for consistently repairing the distortions and making it easier for them to size up how a company is really doing.

To close out this chapter, let me confess that I've been rather hard on the accountants, but I do not really mean to be. They are just following the rules and are caught in the middle of a political process. They are doing an admirable job to keep up with all the complexity. And besides, I particularly need the corporate accountants on my side to administer the corporate EVA programs. They are, as often as not, the keepers of the EVA flame. So, sorry, I take it all back. Let's be friends.

CHAPTER 4

What's Wrong with RONA?

RONA, ROI, ROE, IRR—take your pick.[1] Each is a way to measure the productivity of capital, to relate profit to invested capital, or cash flow to spending, and to quantify the rate of return earned after getting the investors' money back. Returns matter. Earning a return over the cost of capital is a prerequisite for earning EVA and adding value and enriching the owners. A CFO may also logically assume that a business line earning a higher return may be a better candidate than another for further investment and growth—assuming past results can be replicated. A higher projected return also provides assurance that a decision or plan is more secure, that a greater cushion exists to soften the blow should key assumptions prove untenable. And as an analytical tool, RONA can be traced to operating margins and asset turns in accord with the classic DuPont formula. It can be used to give line teams a rounded view of operating performance and balance-sheet asset management. For many reasons, return-type measures have earned a prominent role in financial management over the years, and are still very popular with CFOs the world over. But I come not to praise RONA. I come to bury it.

RONA and the other conventional return metrics are highly misleading and incomplete performance indicators, for reasons I will explain. And the deficiencies are far from academic. As you will see, companies that have aimed to increase RONA or maintain a high RONA have committed major blunders in strategy and resource allocation. And when RONA is judged from the bird's-eye view of how well it performs as an element in a firm's

---

[1] RONA stands for return on net assets. In effect, it is the same thing as return on capital (ROC). Both are computed as net operating profit after tax (NOPAT) divided by net assets or net capital, which are equivalent. ROI is return on investment, and is just a generic term for RONA or ROC. ROE is return on equity. IRR is internal rate of return, and is based on determining the rate that will discount all cash flows to zero net present value (NPV). All the measures are in the same school of measuring the productivity of capital as a yield that can be compared against the cost of capital.

overall management system, it fails, or at least it is far inferior to EVA, as I have been saying and will continue to elaborate.

RONA fundamentally fails because it is inconsistent with what is—or should be—the main mission of every firm, which is to maximize the wealth of its owners. It is to maximize the *difference* between the capital that investors have put or left in the business and the present value of the cash flow that can be taken out of it. In short, the goal is to maximize MVA by maximizing the stream of EVA, as I have said.

Here's the problem in a nutshell. RONA tells us about the *ratio* of market value to invested capital, but that is not the same thing as maximizing the *spread* between market value and invested capital, which is the true goal. A company that aims to maximize RONA will always tend to hold back and underinvest, underinnovate, underscale, and undergrow. It will leave value and growth on the table, and become vulnerable to a hostile takeover or a toppling by upstart rivals.

The glaring deficiency of RONA first became apparent to me in the early 1980s, when I had the privilege of advising the Coca-Cola Company. The beverage company at the time was fabulously profitable, earning nearly a 25 percent return on its capital, but also was a victim of its own success. Management was reluctant to put the Coke name on growth products like Cherry Coke, Diet Coke, and Caffeine-Free Coke because those products were reckoned to earn only a 20 percent return and would dilute the 25 percent return on the Coke brand. To complicate matters, the company needed to reverse a longstanding commitment. Coke's founders had granted perpetual franchise licenses to promote growth of the bottling and distribution network, but by 1980 the independent bottling franchisees were parsed into economically undersized territories, in many cases run by lackadaisical third-generation owners. Coke needed to buy them up, consolidate contiguous regions, install hungry operators, and revise its pricing formula. But again, the capital to be invested in that strategy could not approach the phenomenal return from one of the world's most valuable brands. So Coke was stuck because management was stuck on maintaining its high RONA.

The solution for Coke, as it is for every company, was to define success as growth in economic profit or EVA—*even when that comes at the expense of RONA*. RONA and EVA are cousins, not identical twins. RONA is the percentage ratio of operating profit to capital. It measures the productivity of capital. EVA is the *dollar spread* of operating profit net of the cost of capital. It is the total amount of value added over the cost of all resources. The distinction may appear subtle and effete. After all, EVA uses the same data as RONA—EVA measures profit less the cost of capital instead of profit divided by the capital. I've even had CFOs tell me they are using EVA when they are actually using RONA or return on capital. But in fact, the two are not the same at all. The differences are quite profound and incredibly far-reaching.

Let's go back to the Coke conundrum. Coke's weighted average cost of capital was about 10 percent at that time, and its RONA was running about 25 percent as I said, or 15 percent above the hurdle rate. Coke was thus earning an EVA profit of $150 for every $1,000 of invested capital. Suppose that to roll out the new products and acquire bottlers, Coke would double its invested capital while earning only a 20 percent return on the new money put into the business. Then its RONA would sink halfway between the two, from 25 percent to 22.5 percent, and its RONA spread over the cost of capital would narrow from 15 percent to 12.5 percent. But the percentage spread would be multiplied by twice the amount of capital, by $2,000. The EVA dollar spread would widen to $250, an *increase* of $100, and that is what counts. This is a classic example of where a decision sends RONA down while EVA and share price would go up.

By shifting to EVA and abandoning RONA, Coke decided in the early 1980s to expand its product portfolio and acquire its bottlers—which it might not have done had RONA remained the measure that mattered. The decision led the company to such a phenomenal improvement in its EVA profit that by 1994 Coke was producing the most MVA wealth of any American firm, as *Fortune* chronicled in a story titled "America's Best and Worst Wealth Creators" featuring Coke CEO Roberto Goizueta on its cover as one of the best.

Other companies were not so lucky, Anheuser-Busch among them. For years the beer behemoth had opportunities to invest, acquire, and grow globally, but turned down all of them, leaving the firm ring-fenced and vulnerable to a hostile takeover. On November 18, 2008, the company reluctantly succumbed to the Brazilian-Belgian brewing company InBev. Anheuser-Busch became a target because its CEO, August Busch III, refused to dilute the RONA the firm was garnering in its U.S. beer business by entering more competitive overseas markets. As one adviser close to the company explained it:

> When you have a business that was as profitable as his [August Busch III, CEO] was, where the returns were as strong as his were, I'm not sure anyone would be so smart to say, 'We've got to take over the world,'" said one A-B adviser. "We understand now why he should have, but it would have diluted his margins and his returns.
> —*Dethroning the King,* by Julie MacIntosh
> (John Wiley & Sons, 2010)

As an aside, InBev, the buyer, grew out of Brahma Beer, the first Brazilian company to adopt EVA. I helped Brahma to adopt EVA in 1996 after I got a call from the CEO, Marcel Telles, who became intrigued by it after Credit Suisse First Boston (CSFB) used EVA in an analyst report on Brahma. Telles was so curious he asked the CSFB analyst, "Where can I learn more about EVA?" which led to me. We spent about six months developing a program to measure EVA throughout the company, and it became a key asset and capability of the firm that helped it to successfully gobble up many other brewers and eventually become the world's largest and most successful brewing company.

Coke and Anheuser-Busch are not isolated examples. You may know that the favorite business book of Apple's Steve Jobs and Intel's Andrew Grove is *The Innovator's Dilemma* by Harvard professor Clayton Christensen. The book chronicles how established industry leaders almost always cede their top spots to upstarts that start small, in the low-margin end of the business, and then over time take over the whole thing. It persuaded Andrew Grove to coin the expression "Only the paranoid survive," which is perhaps one solution. But Christensen thought a more fundamental reason better explained why top dogs are systematically reduced to also-rans and would lead him to prescribe a remedy other than paranoia to cure the Innovator's Dilemma. His solution: managers must stop worshipping at the RONA church:

> After puzzling over this mystery for a long time, he finally came up with the answer: it was owing to the way the managers had learned to measure success. Success was not measured in numbers of dollars but in ratios. Whether it was return on net assets, or gross margin percentage, or internal rate of return, all these measures had, in the past forty years, been enshrined in a near-religion (he liked to call it the Church of New Finance), by partners in hedge funds and venture-capital firms and finance professionals in business schools. People had come to think that the most important thing was not how much profit you made in absolute terms but what percentage profit you made on each dollar you put in. And that belief drove managers to shed high-volume but low-margin products from their balance sheets ... this is why he called it a church—it was an encompassing orthodoxy that made it impossible for believers to see that it might be wrong.
>
> **"When Giants Fail—What Business Has Learned from Clayton Christensen," by Larissa MacFarquhar, *New Yorker*, May 14, 2012**

My favorite example of the Innovator's Dilemma is IBM in the late 1970s and early 1980s. It's still relevant because of the magnitude of the dilemma and for what the company's CFO at the time said. Recall that IBM pioneered a major breakthrough with large mainframe computers in the 1960s after taking a big risk to develop the legendary IBM 360. An elite sales and marketing organization grew up to sell and service large corporate purchasers of the big boxes. When Apple and other West Coast upstarts first came out with diminutive desktop-sized computers in the mid-1970s, IBM dismissed them as mere toys, appealing to hobbyists, but certainly with no future as serious business machines. By the late 1970s, as the affordable personal computers were beginning to make serious inroads everywhere, the argument shifted. IBM's CFO at the time, Dean Pfeifer, was quoted in *Business Week* magazine as saying, "For us to invest in personal computers and dilute the 25 percent return we are now earning in the mainframe business would undermine the quality of our earnings, and we would not be acting in the best interests of our shareholders."

What a gaffe. EVA says that as long as you have a better way to invest money than the market does, do it, and don't worry about the impact on your company's rate of return, or any other measure for that matter. But unlike Coke, IBM stuck to its ROI guns and delayed making an effort to enter the low end of the computer business until it was too late. Desperate to catch up, IBM belatedly formed a PC unit in 1980, relegated the team to offices in Florida, far from the corporate campus in Armonk, New York, and told them to develop a personal computer as fast as possible. And in their haste, they outsourced the software operating system to a tiny start-up called Microsoft. Holy mackerel. IBM gave away Microsoft. It is not an exaggeration to say that one of biggest mistakes in business history was due to a fixation on ROI.

I call this the Jose Reyes syndrome. Reyes was the New York Mets shortstop who won the National League batting title in 2011. And to ensure he did, in the last game of the season, he produced a drag bunt single, for him almost a sure thing, and then he just took himself out of the game to keep his average up. The best batter in baseball withdrew from the game to maintain a ratio? Hard to fathom, but that is essentially what IBM did, too.

A desire to drive returns can also lead to capital misallocations across internal lines of business. I discovered that when I met with Fred Butler, CEO of the Manitowoc Company, of Manitowoc, Wisconsin, in 1992. Fred had invited me to visit because the fund manager and occasional activist investor Mario Gabelli had taken a stake in the firm and was lobbying to break it up. The company consisted of three business lines—a Great Lakes ship repair business that was in the dumps, a crane manufacturing business that was also not doing well, and a crown jewel, the Manitowoc ice machine business, which held a large share of its market for hospitality ice machines and was earning about a 30 percent return on capital.

"How do you set goals, measure performance, pay bonuses?" I asked Fred. He replied, "It was previously based on growth in sales and earnings. But our managers spent capital so wantonly, we said we need to bring capital stewardship into the picture, and we switched to return on capital as our goal and compensation metric. But that has not worked, either."

Fred continued, "The poor performers keep asking us for more capital to spend their way out of their hole and raise their returns, even with projects that are well under our overall cost of capital. And our best business, the ice machine business, is just treading water and is milking its return and forgoing growth. We are literally starving our stars and feeding our dogs. I did not think that was how it was supposed to work." But that is how it works when RONA rules the roost.

I said, perhaps flippantly, "Well, then, it seems Gabelli has a good point about breaking up the firm." Fred admitted, "Yes, he does, but I was hoping you had a better answer than just splitting up. How do we beat him and make him go away?" The answer, as you can guess, was EVA. The new success measure was to increase EVA. It saved the company. Faced with a charge for capital, the ship repair business was improved and sold, and the crane businesses shaped up and grew into a global powerhouse. Given the opportunity to win with any investment over the cost of capital, the ice machine business accelerated its growth and became the foundation for adding a whole range of food service products, including Garland and Frymaster, for example. The company's stock soared along with its EVA, and Gabelli happily went away with a nice return. Nowadays, under the capable leadership of CEO Glen Tellock and CFO Carl Laurino, Manitowoc is in its 16th year of financial stewardship under the EVA banner. Manitowoc's EVA is currently depressed, given the firm's exposure to the construction cycles, but the company saw a turnaround coming a year ago, as the excerpt of its 2011 annual report shows (see Exhibit 4.1). I would bet on Manitowoc cooking up a terrific resurgence in EVA in coming years.

The bottom line is this: EVA is additive, but RONA is not. Add something good to something great and EVA is greater still. Add a low-margin business to a strong one, and EVA increases so long as the cost of capital is covered. It's value-additive. It is a measure to maximize, because more EVA is more net present value (NPV) and more owner wealth. But that's just not true of RONA. There is literally no way to tell whether a company or division is better off reporting a higher or lower RONA, taken by itself. You can always try to jerry-rig RONA by combining it with other factors like growth, but all you are really doing is re-creating EVA by imperfect proxy. Why not make it simpler and more accurate and more effective, and just go for the real thing? Why not focus on a single measure that accurately scores the actual total value added by a business, by a plan, or by a decision—which is exactly what EVA does?

The Manitowoc Company, Inc. | 15

VALUE CREATION *Both Manitowoc businesses strive to maximize shareholder wealth by generating consistent improvements in Economic Value-Added. With our businesses in the early stages of multi-year growth cycles, we expect strong operating leverage to drive margins higher.*

Carl J. Laurino
Senior Vice President
& Chief Financial Officer

2011: A Strong Start and a Stronger Finish

We expected 2011 to be a transition year, one in which Manitowoc would begin to see measurable improvements in revenue and earnings. But we certainly did not expect the varying degrees of optimism and pessimism that ensued.

The year started off strong, with solid showings at industry trade shows and first-quarter performance by both businesses. However, as 2011 progressed, concerns about sovereign debt created economic turbulence. This led to increasing caution among our customers and fluctuating demand for both businesses. We focused on executing our strategy and leveraging our recent investments in manufacturing capacity, process equipment, and operational excellence. This culminated in a strong fourth quarter that helped our businesses deliver solid year-over-year growth in revenue and operating earnings.

Progress in Foodservice

In Foodservice, revenue improved by 7 percent to $1.5 billion. Operating margins of 14.5 percent were essentially equal to the level achieved in 2010. This reflected two actions. The first was a reduction in our operating footprint. In 2011 we received the full-year benefit of prior actions that resulted in the closure or sale of five facilities in Europe, plus the consolidation of three more in North America and one in Asia. And second, we introduced numerous Lean initiatives to enhance efficiency and create state-of-the-art manufacturing processes.

Significant Improvement in Cranes

In Cranes, revenue increased by 29 percent to $2.2 billion, while operating margins of 4.9 percent waned slightly due primarily to higher input costs.

Also of note, Cranes ended 2011 with a backlog of $761 million. The 33 percent increase from the prior year was driven by heightened order activity from various emerging economies, as well as an improving demand from North America. Equally impressive, new orders of $676 million during the fourth quarter were our highest since the third quarter of 2008.

Reducing Leverage and Boosting Profitability

Even while managing through a year of fluctuating financial results, we took important steps to strengthen our capital structure. Since the Enodis acquisition in 2008, we have realized the benefits of lower leverage by paying down more than $1 billion in debt. As a result, our debt-to-EBITDA ratio improved by more than one turn. Strong cash flow in the fourth quarter, combined with Foodservice asset sales, enabled us to pay back $140 million in debt by the end of 2011.

We are equally committed to reducing our leverage by boosting profitability. In 2011 our consolidated operating margin was 6.1 percent, versus 6.6 percent in 2010. The benefit from higher product volume was offset by market pricing issues, material cost increases, and some inefficiencies in the Crane supply chain. Our focus for 2012 will be to build upon the improved operating results both businesses posted at the end of 2011.

Creating a Stronger Balance Sheet

In 2011 we continued to strengthen our balance sheet. In May, we opportunistically refinanced our bank credit agreement. This reduced our interest expense by $10 million and pushed out our maturities—from 2013 and 2014 to 2016 and 2017. We now have improved flexibility to make necessary investments in both of our businesses as we drive sustainable long-term growth.

At the same time, we are vigilantly managing our working capital. The goal is to appropriately balance debt reduction with investments that create long-term shareholder value. In 2011 we continued to invest in Lean initiatives across both businesses. Since beginning this program in 2007, we have trained nearly 1,400 employees in Six Sigma/Lean manufacturing principles. This is one key reason why operating margins in Cranes are significantly higher than they were during the previous cyclical trough in 2003. That higher baseline positions Manitowoc for even greater profitability as we enter the next growth cycle.

Investing in Growth

We also expect several other investments to pay dividends in 2012 and beyond. Manitowoc's market-leading innovation continues to be a major competitive advantage, as both businesses introduced revolutionary new products in 2011 that will fuel our future growth.

Foodservice is expanding its global manufacturing and service footprint with new test kitchens in India and Singapore to help customers develop enhanced menu offerings. In similar fashion, Cranes recently opened a new aftermarket contact center in India, and is nearing completion of a new 265,000 square-foot manufacturing facility in Brazil. And to drive greater efficiency throughout its business, Cranes is accelerating a multi-year enterprise resource planning initiative. This project will unite our global administrative, financial, and manufacturing operations under a single technology platform. In 2012 we will integrate the ERP platforms in our Brazilian and French operations along with our global Crane Care business onto the new system—with full realization of this system's benefits occurring in 2014, when the implementation is complete.

We look forward to 2012 as a period of continued growth. Both businesses will work to leverage their competitive advantages and benefit from the significant investments we have made to upgrade our global manufacturing network, introduce Lean processes, and drive product innovation. This year, we will also strive to optimize our cash flow, enhance debt paydown, leverage our leading market shares, and expand our presence in emerging markets. For Manitowoc, the best is yet to come.

EXHIBIT 4.1   Manitowoc's 2011 Annual Report Excerpt

RONA is not only a misleading and incomplete measure at the corporate or line-of-business level, as I have discussed so far. It also fails to provide the correct answers concerning the configuration of individual investment projects or strategic choices, particularly when questions of how big, how fast, how many, and how much come into play. The reason is that the payoffs from investments and strategies typically increase and then decrease with scale. Rates of return initially grow larger and larger as more money is invested and unavoidable fixed costs are covered and market traction is gained. But at some point diseconomies set in. Costs inflate, distances widen, markets saturate, and the return begins to tail off as investment spending continues to ramp up. As a result, companies that focus on RONA will always tend to underscale their investments compared to what is optimal and leave profitable growth and added value on the table.

Consider the decision of how high to build a building as an example. Suppose a financial projection shows that a 10-story building won't even cover the 10 percent cost of capital. The building is so small that the rental income cannot even cover the full fixed cost of the land. It's a negative NPV project, and not worth considering except as a stepping-stone.

On the next step up the ladder, a 20-story building costs $20 million, let's say, and it generates an 18 percent RONA and an NPV of $16 million. The return climbs because the additional rental income for the higher floors is gravy to cover the fixed costs. This is an example of *increasing returns to scale*.

But now it gets complicated. A 30-story building costs $40 million, or twice as much to construct. It's more expensive per floor, and generates a RONA of only 15 percent. Extra elevator banks must be added, which cut into rentable space on all floors. The building requires sturdier reinforcement and takes significantly longer to construct, which delays the start of revenues. All these elements conspire to reduce the overall RONA of the proposed 30-story building to less than the rate of return projected on the 20-story building. This is an example of *diseconomies of scale* creeping in. Nevertheless, the 30-story building does show a higher NPV. Its NPV is estimated to be $20 million, or $4 million more than for the 20-story building.

The final candidate is a gleaming 40-story tower, costing a whopping $70 million to construct and generating a RONA just matching the 10 percent cost of capital, for an NPV of $0, as even more diseconomies of scale set in. It is, however, a magnificent structure and it will generate gushers of cash flow and EBITDA after the investment is made.

So what's the correct decision—the 20-story edifice that maximizes RONA, the 30-story one that maximizes NPV, or the 40-story tower that maximizes revenue, profit, and EBITDA? If you cannot even agree on the correct objective, how can you ever make the right decisions as a management team? Is RONA, NPV, or EBITDA the real goal, since you cannot have them all?

True, the 20- and 30-story projects are both acceptable, being that both of them earn returns more than the cost of capital and generate positive NPVs. But the 30-story project is the *best* project, because it's the one that maximizes NPV. It maximizes the spread between capital put in and the value gotten out. It maximizes corporate MVA, owner wealth, franchise value, and societal well-being by using scarce resources up to the point where incremental value added just exceeds the incremental resource cost.

There are two ways to see this. Compared to the 20-story project, the 30-story project costs another $20 million in investment, but generates an extra $4 million in net present value on top of that. The incremental project to build from 20 to 30 stories is attractive in its own right. Why reject that opportunity to add value just to maximize RONA? And the same reasoning applies to why management should *not* build a 40-story tower, for that is the same as taking on the 30-story building, a positive NPV endeavor, and then adding another project to build up to the 40th floor, which is incrementally a negative NPV proposition that should be rejected.

The 30-story project is also distinguished by its larger EVA. EVA can be measured by taking the percentage spread between RONA and the cost of capital, and multiplying it times the capital that is earning the spread. For instance, the annual EVA profit of the 20-story building is its 18 percent RONA, less the 10 percent cost of capital, times the $20 million investment. Its EVA is $1.6 million per year (and the present value of the EVA, at 10 percent, is $16 million, the project's NPV, so it all checks out).

The EVA of the 30-story building is considerably higher, actually 25 percent higher. EVA is (15% − 10%) × $40 million, or $2 million. Capitalize the EVA at 10 percent, and you have the $20 million NPV, as stated. This is better. More NPV is better than less. True, the project will generate a lower overall rate of return, *but the return is earned on more capital*. Size matters, too. The right answer is always to choose more EVA, since that always translates into more NPV, which is why it is so important to use EVA not just to judge the performance of whole lines of business but also to use it for judging—and actually helping to improve—the value of individual projects.

But do not just take my word for it. The pitfalls of IRR and by extension RONA are well recognized in the finance literature. Scholars with no axes to grind join me in recommending that corporate managers stop using IRR and RONA. Consider this excerpt from world's best-selling corporate finance textbook, *Principles of Corporate Finance*, by Stewart C. Myers

(MIT Sloan), Richard A. Brealey (London Business School), and Franklin Allen (Wharton):

> Many firms use internal rate of return (IRR) in preference to net present value. We think that is a pity. ... Financial managers never see all the possible projects. Most projects are proposed by operating managers. A company that instructs nonfinancial managers to look first at project IRRs prompts a search for those projects with the highest IRRs rather than the highest NPVs. It also encourages managers to modify projects so their IRRs are higher. Where do you typically find the highest IRRs? In short lived projects requiring little up-front investment. Such projects may not add much value to the firm.

The bottom line is this: For decisions about how many SKUs to carry; how much advertising to do or research to perform; how big to build a warehouse, plant, or building; how many stores to open; and how much working capital to stock—in other words, whenever the dimensions of scale and growth must be weighed against margins and returns, or even a decision about how a product should be configured and priced or a production function fulfilled—then RONA- and IRR-minded managers are always apt to underscale, underinvest, and underinnovate compared to managers who are aiming to maximize EVA and NPV.

I was going over all this with Mike Archbold in the late spring of 2012. At the time he was serving as president and chief operating officer of Vitamin Shoppe, where he was instrumental in establishing a financial focus on EVA (Mike left in the summer of 2012 to become CEO of Talbots, and he was previously the CFO of AutoZone). "Bennett," Mike said, "your building example resonates with me, but we call it the 'S' curve. We see it all the time: declining returns, followed by ramping returns, followed by cresting returns. When I was CFO at AutoZone, we got EVA so embedded as a financial discipline that even the marketing department got quite sophisticated at projecting the 'S' curve on marketing campaigns and we'd always look for the point to maximize the EVA profit.

"And here at Vitamin Shoppe, we've used an outside vendor to help us with automatic inventory restocking, which is actually a complicated problem, or at least we think so, because we look for the solution that maximizes our EVA, taking account of all the trade-offs. You've got to balance lead times, order size, inventory investment, warehouse and shipping costs, and the risk you are stocked-out and lose a sale and disappoint a customer, which means that cost is more than just the lost sales, but a bad customer experience. But we told our vendors, we want to put a price on everything and solve the program to maximize the expected net EVA profit, and it worked fabulously for us.

"The vendors, though, were quite surprised by our request, because their clients always ask them to figure out how to maximize the in-store stocking rate, to make sure they have the product on the shelves to never miss a sale. But that unidimensional focus is just as wrong as focusing on the return on capital or RONA. I mean, if RONA was the answer, it would really discourage us from ever making labor-saving capital investments. Why invest capital, even if it's cheaper than the labor it replaces, when the capital goes into the denominator of the RONA computation and labor doesn't? That's nuts. And that's how I can tell if a business operator is really business savvy. If they get EVA, they get value, and I can trust them to get the right decisions done. And if they don't get EVA, what does that say?"

RONA can also be severely criticized for a number of mundane but very practical deficiencies. For example, RONA critically depends on how management decides to define the net assets in the denominator. Should excess cash or retirement assets or deferred tax accounts be included? How about off-balance-sheet leased assets? Should assets be measured net of impairment charges or at original value? Should assets be revalued or kept at historical costs? Should capital include all debt and equity or just equity? The answers to these questions can profoundly swing a RONA or ROI computation, and while EVA is not totally immune to these choices, it is far more resilient because capital is a cost, a deduction from the EVA profit, and does not enter into the denominator of a ratio. For instance, EVA is essentially the same whether leases are capitalized or expensed or whether capital is defined as debt plus equity or just equity alone. You can pay for capital either explicitly, by deducting rent expense or interest expense from the profit, or implicitly, as part of the weighted average capital charge deducted from EVA, and the resulting EVA is the same either way, whereas the RONA would be very different. And besides, the emphasis should always be on the *change* in EVA, and not EVA per se, which also makes the EVA goal even more immune to how the capital base is defined.

RONA is also highly distorted and essentially meaningless for new economy companies that tend to employ trivial amounts of capital. Over the past seven years, as shown in Exhibit 4.2, Apple's return on capital, for instance, has been phenomenally high and extremely volatile, and basically useless as a performance indicator because its new economy capital base is so lean and variable. Apple's EVA, by contrast, steadily increased from less than 8 percent of sales to 19 percent of sales as a clear indication of the increasing productivity and profitability of the firm's business model.

EXHIBIT 4.2   Contrasting Apple's Return on Capital and Its EVA/Sales Profit Margin

	2006 TFQ3	2007 TFQ3	2008 TFQ3	2009 TFQ3	2010 TFQ3	2011 TFQ3	2012 TFQ3
Return on Capital (ROC = NOPAT/Capital)	64.8%	105.4%	199.1%	275.0%	62.2%	53.2%	45.3%
EVA/sales	7.7%	11.5%	13.0%	16.1%	16.2%	16.6%	19.0%

There are also some firms, and certainly lines of business, that operate with negative capital. Later on, we will see one—Blue Nile—a discount Internet retailer. The cash from its sales and trade funding is so prodigious it exceeds the firm's meager investment in inventories and fixed assets. And with negative capital, its RONA is truly meaningless. Under EVA, though, negative capital simply counts as a profit rebate. EVA is credited with the value of investing the capital float at the firm's cost of capital. As a result, Blue Nile's EVA has been positive and generally increasing, and as a percentage of sales typically runs in the range of 3 percent to 4.5 percent, which puts Blue Nile's business model around the 65th to 75th percentile in terms of how capable it is of driving EVA profit to the bottom line per dollar of sales. Again, this is just a foreshadowing of the EVA profit margin measure that will be introduced later on with more fanfare.

Another practical problem with RONA is that it is very tricky to apply to internal divisions that must be assigned assets. The knee-jerk reaction of line operators is to reject the allocation of assets to their business units in order to keep their RONAs up. But when the emphasis is instead placed on increasing EVA, managers shift gears and want to be assigned all the assets that they can legitimately manage. An initial assignment of assets reduces their division's initial EVA, but that does not matter. What matters is whether they are able to better manage the assets they are assigned and improve their EVA going forward. EVA depoliticizes the management of the assets, and focuses on performance at the margin, ignoring irrelevant sunk costs. I have been in meetings where the operating teams literally changed their stripes on the spot, from vociferously rejecting the assignment of assets to their divisions to clamoring for more once they grasped the rules of the EVA game. RONA, by contrast, is inherently based on an accumulation of irrelevant sunk costs, and it encourages endless and fruitless arguing over the internal allocation of assets.

I must toss one last grenade in the RONA direction (I did come to bury it, after all). RONA is so inherently biased against integration and generally so in favor of outsourcing that it pushes activities outside the firm that should stay in.

To see how, let's return to our simple sample company for another telling example. Recall that the company has $1,000 in capital and is earning $150 in NOPAT for a 15 percent return on capital, and with a 10 percent cost of capital, its EVA is running at $50. Suppose management considers moving $200 in computer assets from in-house management to the cloud for the exact same total of operating and capital costs, and without recording any gain or loss, so that the firm's EVA remains the same, by definition. In the real world, outsourcing might pay or might not. The point of this exercise is simply to show that even if the decision to outsource is truly EVA and value neutral, RONA just won't see it that way. It is an inherently biased measure that is unprepared for a world of business model diversity and complex choices. In this case RONA is going to go up because the firm has hived off a commodity investment that earns less than the corporate average return. Let's work the numbers.

With the transfer of $200 in assets to the cloud, the company's capital costs drop by $20 (by the 10 percent cost of capital), but since the transaction is a wash for EVA, by assumption, the incoming charges from the cloud vendor are going to raise the firm's operating costs and reduce its NOPAT by $20. It's a pure break-even exchange. There is no compelling reason to keep the computer systems or get rid of them by outsourcing. The outside cost and the inside cost, including the cost of capital, are identical.

Even so, the firm's RONA *increases* from 15 percent to 16.25 percent. Although NOPAT falls from $150 to $130, the return is now calculated as a percentage of only $800 in capital. The outsourcing maneuver leads to a higher reported return on capital. That does not matter, though, because the higher return is earned on less capital. From a purely financial point of view, it must be value neutral— there's no greater NPV, MVA, or stock price, since there is no more EVA. RONA was tricked into paying the decision a compliment it did not deserve.

It's a contrived example, sure, but the insight is real. RONA is so biased in favor of outsourcing that it motivates firms to go bulimic, to become so lean and hollowed out that they eventually cut beyond the fat and into muscle, giving up essential long-run sources of competitive advantage, and really paying more for services they could perform more cheaply in-house, all costs included. EVA, by contrast, favors outsourcing only where a third-party partner has clear advantages that enable it to perform a function at a sufficiently lower total cost that it overcomes the disadvantages of having to contract and deal with an outside vendor.

I'll give you an example of where EVA correctly motivated an outsourcing move. As I mentioned before, one of my EVA clients in the early 1990s was Equifax, the credit reporting bureau. It was then run by Jack Rogers, a former IBM senior officer. He was intimately familiar with IBM's computer capabilities and thought that outsourcing Equifax's extensive computer operations to IBM could make sense, if properly structured, even though the move would be quite countercultural. But to his credit, rather than mandating the decision or asking his team to simply trust his business judgment, which was, by the way, considerable, he said, "We have to run the EVA on it—it could be good, it could be bad, it's EVA that will tell us." As it happened, the facts and figures clearly showed an EVA advantage to turning over the company's computers and operations to IBM, while Equifax retained its real franchise value in its hold on personal credit statistics and market presence. That was the very first large outsourcing transaction of its kind (which is why IBM for years used Equifax's decision to showcase the merits of its outsourcing solution, based on the EVA analysis). As Equifax demonstrates, moving assets into the cloud or offshore for that matter *can* make sense—if it generates more EVA, but never because it increases RONA. An improved RONA is at best a by-product of making the right NPV/EVA decision, but should never be the prime motivator.

To say it one last time, only EVA always gives the right answer, to sourcing decisions or any other, because it's the only measure that literally discounts to the net present value of discounted cash flow. There is no *a priori* reason to expect that RONA should give the right answer, and it frequently doesn't; and there is every reason to think EVA will give the right, value-maximizing answer, and in my experience, it does, and it does so with more clarity, simplicity, and accountability than any other approach.

Why do so many CFOs persist in using rate-of-return metrics when they are so malevolent? I think there are two reasons. First, they're ratios. They permit performance comparisons and investment rankings regardless of size. Their very defect is an advantage in giving CFOs a way to rate performance across divisions that differ in scale and to compare projects that vary in investment commitment. Ratio returns common-size the comparisons. Another reason is that a ratio replacement has not existed. For all its shortcomings, RONA or ROI was the best ratio kid on the block for ranking performance and investments. What was better?

Until recently, nothing. But now, a set of new ratio metrics developed by EVA Dimensions offers CFOs all the advantages of size-adjusted performance indicators without sacrificing the critical link to maximizing the money value of NPV, owner wealth, and overall corporate profit performance. The new ratios are, unsurprisingly, all based on EVA. The very good news is that the new EVA ratios can completely replace RONA and IRR and even operating margins and growth rates with a management framework that is fundamentally more accurate, simpler to use and understand, more informative, and considerably more effective as a practical framework for value-based corporate planning and decision making. Accept my premise, and there is no longer a reason to look at RONA, or ROI, ROE, or IRR, ever again.

CHAPTER 5

The New EVA Ratio Metrics

Let's face it. Ratios rule the business world. Managers, directors, and CFOs all need financial ratios to set goals and meter bonus pay; to measure, benchmark, and diagnose performance; to rate, probe, and improve business plans; and to judge risk, compare valuations, spot best practices, and isolate key trends, among other things. Most companies just use a jumble of standard, textbook financial ratios—growth rates, margins, returns, turnover rates, and so forth. I think we can do better—a lot better.

I think that finance ratios need to work in two directions. I describe the directions as *E Pluribus Unum* and *E Unum Pluribus,* from the many to the one, and from the one to the many. The solution I suggest is symbolically depicted in the American dollar bill. Apparently even the Founding Fathers were EVA advocates. It's pictured as shown in Exhibit 5.1.

On the left hand, we need a measure of all measures, a summit score that correctly consolidates all the pluses and minuses of corporate performance into a single overarching financial indicator. That's *E Pluribus Unum,* and it is writ in capitals across the banner above the eagle's head. It stands for from the many to the one. From many peoples, from the many states,

EXHIBIT 5.1   E Pluribus Unum and E Unum Pluribus

comes one nation. And in this case, we are looking to go from the many performance measures to the one score that really counts.

But as the pyramid on the dollar bill suggests, we also need to go the other way, from the one to the many, from *Unum* to *Pluribus*. We require an elegant means to deconstruct the all-seeing pinnacle score that stands at the apex and trace it step by step to foundational measures without ever losing sight of the big picture and while putting the individual measures in the context of all others. We don't want to suboptimize; we want to maximize the whole. We need not just a score, but a management tool, an analytical framework, a way to dissect performance and help managers to discover ways to improve it.

We need the game score and we need the game statistics.

And this is where I confess that EVA totally failed in the past. EVA was traditionally just a money measure of economic profit, and managers were asked to increase it. The message was correct as far as it went, and a great help to many firms. But the method was incomplete. EVA needed a companion set of ratio statistics that fulfilled the many-to-one and one-to-many requirement, but it did not exist. If EVA was winning hearts and minds, and it was, it was winning with one hand tied behind its back.

No longer. By adding a set of three interrelated ratio metrics to EVA, I believe we have reached the culmination of corporate value-based management. Together, the three key EVA metrics replace and subsume traditional ratio metrics with a superior and simpler framework. The table in Exhibit 5.2 highlights the three ratios I propose and the traditional metrics they displace.

EXHIBIT 5.2 The EVA Ratio Metrics Summary Table

EVA Ratio Metrics	Definition	Traditional Ratio Metrics	Benefits
EVA Momentum (EVA growth rate)	ΔEVA/prior sales	Growth in sales, earnings, EBITDA, EPS	Growth in EVA is more important than growth in any other measure.
EVA Margin	EVA/sales	Gross margin, operating margin, EBITDA margin, RONA, ROI, ROE	EVA Margin consolidates operating efficiency and asset management into a productivity score.
Market-Implied Momentum (MIM)	EVA growth rate implied by share price	Consensus EPS; P/E, EBITDA multiples	MIM is a more reliable, useful indicator of investor expectations.

Though they are billed as innovations, the new ratios are valuable not in making EVA more sophisticated and erudite or academically appealing. Their value is in making EVA fundamentally easier to understand and more effective as a decision support tool. It's the Apple iPad version of EVA. The ratios are not the last steps you should get to in adopting EVA after you've done the EVA basics. The ratios should be part and parcel of how you roll out and use EVA from the get-go. You should use them, for example, in the early stages to introduce EVA to your management team and directors and showcase its applications and benefits.

When I recently reviewed the new EVA ratio framework with the former CFO of a major retail company, he said, "I always liked EVA but thought it was too hard to use and for our people to relate to their decisions. I didn't think our operators would really get it, so I never brought it in. But the new EVA ratio program you've shown me really brings it to life. You've opened the curtain; you've really cracked the code." Let's see if you think he is right.

EVA MOMENTUM

The first new ratio, EVA Momentum, is the most important of them all. It is the *change* in EVA divided by *prior-period* sales. It is a way to measure the growth rate in EVA and make that into a ratable summary statistic. For example, say that a company had sales of $1,000 in 2010, and that its EVA increased from $30 to $50 from 2010 to 2011 (or from –$50 to –$30—it wouldn't matter because only the change counts). Then its EVA Momentum for the 2011 year would be 2 percent. That's the $20 increase in EVA over the $1,000 in prior-period sales. As I said, it measures the growth rate in EVA, scaled to sales. It can be measured quarter to quarter, year over year, over the past three to five years as a trend, and, even better, over the forecast life of a business plan. However measured, it is a simply magical metric in many ways.

First of all, and this is a real big deal, it is the *only corporate ratio indicator where bigger is always better*, because it gets bigger when EVA gets bigger, which means that a firm's NPV and MVA and shareholder return are getting bigger, too. It is the one ratio measure that completely and correctly summarizes the total performance of a business in all ways that it can add value or subtract from it. Managers can legitimately aim to maximize EVA Momentum without fear of being misled into making dumb decisions. It can serve as every company's most important financial goal and the overarching measure that matters. It is the *Unum*, the One. It's the pinnacle score on the pyramid of measures.

To be specific, it can and it should be used *instead* of RONA, operating margin or sales, or EPS growth as *the* measure of performance and *the* arbiter of the quality and value of business plans. Put simply, a business plan is better and more valuable if it can credibly generate a greater EVA Momentum growth rate over the three- to five-year plan horizon. The greater the planned EVA Momentum, the greater is the projected growth in EVA, and the greater is the NPV of the plan and contribution it will make to the firm's share price. CFOs are now using EVA Momentum to rank and grade the quality and value of their business plans and as a means to stimulate their line teams to plan for and deliver more EVA-capable and valuable business plans during the planning process. An entire chapter will be devoted to explaining just this aspect of EVA Momentum.

A second key attribute is that EVA Momentum focuses on change, on improvement, on turning points, on the news in the data, on performance *at the margin*. It is completely independent of inherited assets or legacy liabilities, and as such it is a more apt indicator of whether a business unit is a candidate for growth or contraction than RONA, because RONA incorporates the returns from all projects still on the books, no matter how distant, including by now highly irrelevant and outdated sunk costs.

By highlighting change, EVA Momentum also helps management to zero in on and magnify worrisome trends and to be more alert to emerging risks. Sales, net income, EPS, and certainly EBITDA can all continue to expand long after a business has really started to lose its economic vitality, but EVA Momentum turns down or at least slows down at the earliest stages of when a business is maturing or facing competitive pressures, or when its managers are overinvesting in incrementally undesirable growth opportunities. EVA Momentum brings all the pressure points into one score. It is like the proverbial canary in the coal mine, sniffing out trouble and raising a red flag before other measures get in the game, which gives management and directors more lead time to respond.

EVA Momentum also credits turnaround business divisions with adding value when they are able to make a negative EVA less negative. It gives managers overseeing troubled units the means to express the value they expect they can create by successfully reengineering their business model. It improves their ability to legitimately compete for funding on a par with other better-endowed divisions.

And on the other side of the track, EVA Momentum puts a Bunsen burner under the behinds of division managers in the most profitable business lines to keep innovating, investing, growing, and scaling to continue to increase their EVA rather than just coasting and milking the high returns and margins they already have. In short, EVA Momentum is the financial cure for the Innovator's Dilemma. It most certainly supersedes RONA in correctly combining profitability and profitable growth at the margin into one overall score.

Bottom line: EVA Momentum is the ideal spanning measure, the one and only metric that CFOs can apply to diverse business units to fairly grade their performances and appropriately challenge them, regardless of the capital intensity of the business models or the current state of their profitability. Larger, multidivisional companies, populated with distinct lines of business and a spectrum of business models, will certainly benefit the most from having one EVA Momentum ratio metric to legitimately sit at the very top of all their performance scorecards and positioned as the key metric that matters.

Like all ratios, EVA Momentum is a statistic, but this one has real meaning. Any positive EVA Momentum is good, because that means EVA has increased; any negative EVA Momentum is bad, for then EVA has decreased, and zero EVA Momentum is a true breakeven. It is preservation of EVA without any expansion of it. It is zero EVA growth at the margin. And that, as it so happens, is pretty close to what the median firm in the market actually accomplishes.

Our analysis reveals that the long-run average EVA Momentum for the median Russell 3000 firm—the company swimming in the middle of the EVA performance pack—has been just 0.2 percent per year over the past 20 years. That's all—just two-tenths of 1 percent. The typical firm just ekes out a slight rise in its EVA profit over time, once the full cost of capital is considered and accounting distortions are eradicated. In a world teeming with choices, change, and risk, it is apparently not easy to sustain gains in economic profit year after year. As economic theory predicts, the corrosive forces of competition, saturation, substitution, fading fads, bureaucratic creep, overpriced acquisitions, and management blunders tend to force returns back to the cost of capital over time and at the margin. This finding also legitimizes the default assumption used in EVA valuations: namely, that at some point almost all firms will find their EVA growth potential snuffed out and exhausted at the margin.

Not all firms are just treading EVA water, of course. Over almost any five-year interval about 40 percent of all firms increase EVA at a meaningful pace, and the better-managed or more fortunate firms increase it by quite a lot. Our research shows that the 75th percentile performer tends to run with an EVA Momentum growth pace between 1 percent and 1.5 percent per annum on average. That would be equivalent to generating cumulative EVA Momentum of 5 percent to 7.5 percent over a five-year stretch, meaning that a 75th percentile quality forward plan would have to produce a $50 million to $75 million *increase* in EVA for every $1 billion in sales. (One attraction of EVA Momentum statistics is that they can always be converted to a money target or benchmark for any one company or business division.) The 90th percentile EVA Momentum performance has been quite impressive, running at a 3 percent to 3.5 percent per year average rate over the course of rolling five-year spans. Then there are the truly rare and exceptional firms where EVA Momentum is inflating like an early stage of the universe. Just think Apple. Its EVA Momentum has been simply off the charts, averaging 22.8 percent per year over the past five years. It is a 19 sigma event, like having the four best men's tennis players of all time playing at the same time. Enjoy it while it lasts.

Besides those general reference points, EVA Dimensions maintains a full range of EVA and EVA Momentum statistics for 9,000 global firms that breaks out into benchmarks by industry group, by company size, and by stage of the business cycle. Directors and managers now have the ability to quantitatively rank actual performance results and statistically grade the quality of plans through an EVA lens.[1] We examine the statistics in depth in Chapter 7, Setting EVA Targets.

MARKET-IMPLIED EVA MOMENTUM

Stock prices can be reverse engineered to estimate the EVA growth rates that investors are implicitly projecting. It is a mathematical exercise to solve for the EVA stair-step increase that will discount back to the prevailing share price (technically, to FVA or future value added, the market-derived value of EVA growth), and then to divide that projected, expected EVA increment by the prevailing sales to compute a statistic called Market-Implied Momentum (MIM).[2]

For example, suppose the math shows that EVA must increase $10 million a year over 10 years, and then hold steady, to discount back to the

---

[1] Another interesting observation in the EVA Momentum data is convergence—a group of companies that earn upper-quartile EVA Momentum over a five-year interval are as a group likely to slow down and generate an EVA Momentum pace closer to the median over the next five years, which is why the market as a rule never assumes that a growth company will trade for the same multiple of earnings in five years that it does today, even though investment bankers' acquisition pricing models almost always assume they will. The point is that it is even easier and more accurate to think of the terminal value in a discounted valuation in terms of how much EVA Momentum is likely to persist after the formal forecast period is concluded.

[2] To be technical and to standardize the statistic, we solve for the annual increase in EVA that needs to prevail over a 10-year growth horizon in order to discount back to FVA—to the portion of MVA that is specifically due to the expected growth in EVA.

current share price. If the firm's sales are currently running at $1 billion, then its MIM rate is 1 percent. That's the EVA Momentum growth forecast that is implicitly embedded in its stock price.

MIM turns out to be a far more reliable and useful statistic to quantify investor expectations than so-called consensus EPS, which (let's face it) is not really a consensus, but an opinion survey of sell-side analysts that ignores buy-side investors who actually buy and sell stocks and set the prices, and as a flawed measure of short-term earnings, EPS hardly tells the whole value story. MIM, by contrast, literally discounts to the consensus stock price, and it gives a direct read for the expected growth in the firm's EVA profit that is useful in three ways.

First, the higher MIM is, the more confidence investors are registering in the quality and value of management's forward plan. CFOs and board members should monitor MIM over time to understand how well the company's forward plan value and investor communications are being received in the market, and to be alert to any negative trends in investor expectations.

Second, MIM also provides a concrete bogey against which a firm's actual EVA Momentum performance can be judged. A firm that is persistently underperforming the market's expected EVA growth rate is asking for trouble. Tectonic pressure is building that will eventually convince investors to mark down the company's stock price to reflect a more realistic expectation in line with the firm's actual performance capabilities.

Third, CFOs can use MIM readings for their company and for publicly traded competitors to establish a minimum performance goal for their consolidated forward plan, a topic covered at length in Chapter 7 on setting targets.

EVA MARGIN

The third EVA ratio is a headline financial statistic in its own right, but it is also a cog in the EVA Momentum wheel. It can also fully replace the DuPont ROI formula with an analysis framework that is simpler to understand, more informative, and more inherently value-based.

It is called EVA Margin. It is the ratio of EVA to sales. It is the percentage of sales that falls to the EVA bottom line after deducting all operating and capital costs. Put simply, it is a firm's true economic profit margin. It is a key summary measure of profitability and productivity, consolidating operating efficiency and asset management into a reliable and comparable net margin score. EVA Margin quite simply takes the mission of maximizing value and turns it into a sales-based, margin-based framework.

An alternative would be to divide EVA by capital, and develop a return on capital times capital-type analysis system. Although some might prefer it, I argue against it. I have already pointed out the many pitfalls of return on capital as a governing measure, and all those arguments speak against expressing EVA as a return on capital, too. But there are three more reasons why I believe a sales denominator is highly preferable to a capital denominator.

First, line managers don't tend to think in terms of allocating capital and earning returns on it. To their way of thinking, those are the results of their plans and decisions rather than how they frame their decisions. Line teams tend to think much more naturally in terms of driving sales and improving the margin they earn on the sales. So my first objection is: let's stop imposing a financial model of management on operating people.

A second reason to go with the sales and margin approach is that, with EVA, capital has already been accounted for as a cost, as a deduction from the EVA profit, so there is no need to divide EVA by capital. That would be redundant. What EVA says is: consider capital to be a cost, a charge to profit like any other, not a divisor. Make managers manage capital as a cost of doing business, as a deduction from their EVA and their EVA profit margin, rather than obscurely sticking it in the numerator of a ratio. Divide EVA by whatever factor is most appealing as a driver of EVA. My contention is that in most cases that would be sales (though of course other divisors may better suit, depending on the business model).

The third reason, and this is really the clincher, is that the EVA/sales ratio is a more reliable, transparent, and usable measure of business productivity than return on capital (or operating margin, for that matter). It is more neutral in more dimensions. It does not favor one type of business or business mix over another. It is less susceptible to accounting chicanery and distortions. It unfolds to reveal all of the business drivers more elegantly and recognizably. It is the door that leads from the *Unum* to the *Pluribus*. It is the pathway to walk the steps from the summit to the foundation of the EVA Momentum Pyramid. This will take some discussion and illustration to prove out. I will say a few words here, but the entire next chapter is devoted to singing the praises of EVA Margin, too.

I already discussed how RONA misleadingly increases whenever a firm outsources an activity that earns a return lower than the firm's average return. Ironically, outsourcing also tends to misleadingly *decrease* operating margins. Move computers to the cloud, for example, and what was a balance sheet charge is now paid through cost of goods sold and selling, general, and administrative (SG&A) expense. Traditional margin measures almost always take it on the chin when assets are outsourced, even when outsourcing makes sense. EVA Margin, though, gets this right because it folds the income and balance sheet effects into one score. It is fundamentally a better measure for determining how to draw the boundaries separating the corporation from its suppliers.

In a similar vein, EVA Margin neutralizes the capital difference among business models or between product lines and lets real performance productivity differences shine through. The capital charge is the great equalizer in this. Compare Intel and Wal-Mart, the one incredibly capital intensive with risky fabrication plants, the other incredibly lean with a rapid-turn, low-markup business model. The two cannot by any means be compared on any of their operating margins. But they can be compared on their EVA Margins, because, again, the capital charge is the great neutralizer. The key is that, in the end, and no matter what the business, all companies are really competing for EVA, so EVA Margin is the margin that matters.

Another thing that makes EVA Margin a better performance indicator is that it incorporates all the corrective accounting adjustments that make EVA a better measure of profit. We've covered these, so I will not enumerate them one by one. But consider just the fact that R&D and advertising spending are amortized over time with interest as a charge to the EVA Margin rather than being expensed. Tangible and intangible assets are put on the same footing in the EVA Margin model, as they should be. EVA Margins can thus be meaningfully compared between specialty chemical and commodity chemical companies, for instance. The specialty firms invest in R&D to generate higher gross margins, whereas the commodity-oriented firms invest heavily in efficient large-scale plant assets to drive their value added. It makes no difference to the EVA Margin. It treats the two the same and puts their different business models on a common performance rating scale.

Business models do not have to be as far apart as that to benefit from the consistency that EVA imparts. Try comparing Coke and Pepsi. You'd think a comparison of close peers wouldn't find much difference. But in fact, Coke reports that a materially higher percentage of its sales is spent on advertising and promotion than Pepsi. In exchange, Coke reports a far higher gross margin. EVA Margin correctly levels the comparison. Or consider that close rivals Google and Apple differ in key ways that would trip up the conventional measures. Google is not only far more fixed-asset intense, with tons more money tied up in servers and systems than Apple has. Google also spends oodles more than Apple on R&D and on advertising and promotion—erroneously expensed with conventional operating margins and RONA, but correctly amortized with interest with EVA. A board member or business manager who consults the traditional financial ratios to compare the firms could easily be misled, but not so with the EVA Margin. The bottom line is this: A comparison even of close cousins is more incisive and reliable when the EVA accounting treatments substitute for conventional accounting rules.

I often meet CFOs who lament that they have no close public peers against which they can benchmark their firm. If they are thinking about benchmarking with conventional metrics, I agree with them. A better answer, though, is that they can always benchmark by comparing their firm's overall EVA Margin performance (and EVA Momentum performance) against the statistics for the whole market. The whole market is relevant (and rough sector peers even more so) because, again, all companies are really in the same business of competing for EVA, and EVA Margin neutralizes differences in the business models, sourcing strategies, and accounting conventions, and provides a universally applicable scale to weigh performance.

Let me again cite the statistics for the Russell 3000 universe to give you a feel for the mile markers. Before I do, though, ask yourself this question: What do you think the typical running average EVA/sales margin ratio would be or should be for the *median* firm among the Russell 3000 companies? I usually get answers of 3 percent to 10 percent in my management presentations, but what do you think?

The average EVA Margin for the median Russell 3000 public company over the past 20 years has been—dramatic pause—just 0.4 percent! This is the major leagues, so producing a winning percentage over just break-even baseball is actually not bad. Product markets are quite competitive at the margin, way more than most managers appreciate. Most managers are accustomed to thinking in terms of EBIT or EBITDA margins, which give them a highly inflated impression of corporate profitability and how well they are doing. Those measures are unburdened by the cost of capital, uncharged for tax, and unsaddled with restructuring costs that EVA carries forward and considers to be part of capital. When the full economic costs of doing business are considered, the EVA Margins that surface are right on the razor's edge and quite close to par, as again an economist would expect to be the case. But the implications are unsettling.

If EVA Margin is zero or close to it, as is true of the median firm, all the sales growth and book profit expansion in the world do no good for growing EVA. There is no Momentum without a Margin. By focusing attention on the EVA Margin, top management is better able to direct growth resources to where they truly can add value and not just spin wheels. Management is better able to impress line teams with how close the game score really is in most cases, and galvanize the teams to stretch for every advantage across the full income statement and balance sheet. Operating margins and EBITDA are corpulent and induce complacency where EVA Margins are lean and spark urgency.

As with EVA Momentum, the evidence shows the best firms are clearly able to run ahead of the pack. It is a right-tailed distribution. The 75th percentile firm has tended to earn an impressive EVA Margin of between 4 percent and 4.5 percent. Companies that are operating right at that upper quartile break point as of mid-2012 include firms as wide-ranging as Dell, Parker-Hannifin, Crocs, J.B. Hunt, Kellogg, Dollar Tree, and Starwood, to name a few. The 90th percentile performers operate at another great leap ahead, typically racking up EVA Margins of 9 percent to 10 percent. They include firms like Hershey, Becton Dickenson, Domino's Pizza, Boston Beer, Nordson Corporation, AutoZone, and Idexx Labs. They again hail from all over the map. There are EVA winners and losers in almost every industry. Management and strategy and innovation and operational excellence and hustle can make a big difference. Industry is not destiny.

EVA Margins over 10 percent are rare and noteworthy, and that is where you will find Coca-Cola, Apple, Google, Coach, Visa, T. Rowe Price, Paychex, Microsoft, Dolby Labs, FactSet, and about 300 other true standouts among the Russell 3000 companies. Stepping down from those commanding heights, let me offer you the judgment that maintaining a bottom-line EVA Margin over 4 percent is darn good. In fact, I would venture to say that any company that sustains an EVA Margin that averages over 2 percent over a cycle is really not bad, not bad at all.[3]

Ask yourself these questions: How do the EVA Margins of your lines of business stack up against the broad market standards? Moreover, how do they stack up against your more relevant business peers? As important, what are the underlying drivers that account for the differences, and what priority should be attached to improving each? Later on, you will see how to take the EVA Margin engine apart and examine the moving parts that advance or retard the EVA needle. For now, though, let's consider a simple example to get a feel for the full array of EVA ratio metrics I've introduced thus far.

A FIRST LOOK AT EVA MOMENTUM

We'll do that by looking at the simple sample company once again, as is shown in the table in Exhibit 5.3.

---

[3] A more sophisticated approach would be to measure the average EVA Margin net of the standard deviation in the margin—what you might call the risk-adjusted EVA Margin—and look for that to be positive to know that the business was on the bright side of EVA.

2	**Key EVA Metrics**				
3	**Simple Sample Co**		*Fiscal Year Ends: JAN*		
4			*Currency: U.S. Dollar*		
5	Benchmark: Russell 3000		*Scale: Values in Millions*		
8	*EVA Computation*		2011TFQ3		2012TFQ3
9	**NOPAT**				$ 150
11	Capital	$	900	$	1,100
12	× Cost of Capital (COC)		10.0%		10.0%
19	**Capital Charge**				$ 100
21	**EVA (NOPAT – Capital Charge)**	$	30	$	50
33	*EVA Return on Sales*				
34	**Sales Growth Rate**				25.0%
37	**Sales**	$	1,000	$	1,250
38	**EVA Margin (EVA/Sales)**		3.0%		4.0%
42	*EVA Growth*				
43	**Change in EVA (ΔEVA)**				$ 20
44	**EVA Momentum (ΔEVA/Prior Sales)**				2.0%

EXHIBIT 5.3   Summary EVA Metrics for the Sample Company

Let's start with the money measures, and then build into the new ratio metrics. Recall that SSCo generated an EVA of $50 in its most recent four-quarter year, the result of NOPAT of $150 and a 10 percent cost of capital applied to capital of $1,000—technically, that is the *average* capital outstanding over the year. As is shown on line 11, the opening capital balance was $900 and ending balance was $1,100 for an average of $1,000.[4] Without showing the details, let's assume SSCo's EVA was $30 in the prior year, as shown on line 21.

These basic facts tell us two important things about the company right off the bat: it is profitable and it improved, as EVA increased from $30 to $50. But how significant a performance is that? Let's size-adjust the money measures to find out.

Start with the EVA Margin. I have assumed that the company's sales were $1,000 in the first year and $1,250 the next (line 37). Do the math. The EVA/sales profit margin was $30/$1,000 or 3 percent the first year and $50/$1,250 or 4 percent the next year (line 38). That's an increase from about a 65th percentile EVA Margin to 75th based on typical Russell 3000 statistics. It is an impressive improvement in performance productivity, to be sure—and we'll see where it comes from later—but that statistic understates the true extent of the firm's overall performance in the year.

---

[4] In our software, average capital is measured even more precisely as the average of the average capital outstanding at the beginning and end of reporting quarters.

Total performance progress is measured by EVA Momentum, which is the $20 increase in EVA divided by the $1,000 sale base in the prior year. The firm's EVA Momentum was 2 percent in the most recent year, as shown on line 44. That is comfortably above the 1 percent to 1.5 percent pace that typically marks the 75th percentile break point, but not up to the 3 percent to 3.5 percent demarcation line for the 90th percentile. It was quantitatively a very solid if not outstanding performance. The next question is: how did that happen? What performance factors were responsible? Eventually we will want to see them all. But let's take this a step at a time.

Inching down from the top of the Momentum Pyramid in Exhibit 5.4, the first step is to divide EVA Momentum into two main components, from which all other performance factors can be derived. The first is about running smarter, and the second is about running faster. The first one is called "Productivity Gains," and it comes from generating an increase in the EVA Margin, and the second is called "Profitable Growth," a multiplicative factor that comes from delivering positive sales growth at a positive EVA Margin (or from cutting back on sales that carry a negative EVA Margin). The EVA Pyramid chart lays out the two elements. It is the first step in going from *Unum* to *Pluribus*, from the one score to the many measures, with more details to follow. It shows that 1 percent of SSCo's EVA Momentum came from getting better and the other 1 percent came from getting bigger. There was, coincidentally, an even split between the two. It was not only an impressive overall performance, but also a balanced performance. The car ran faster and it entered and won more races.

Let's take a closer look at the productivity gains strut on the lower left side of the chart. It is the value added from increasing the EVA-to-sales ratio and from driving more EVA to the bottom line out of top-line sales. It is the value added from tuning up the business engine, expanding the EVA Margin, and enhancing the business model productivity through some combination

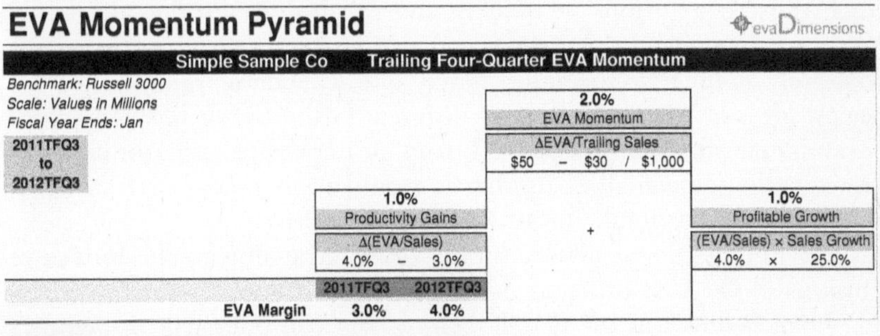

EXHIBIT 5.4 The EVA Momentum Pyramid

of what I like to call the "3-P's"—standing for price, product, and process. That says that EVA Margin expansion can come from earning and exerting *price power*, such as through leveraging brand, innovation, or service, or just getting prices right, or it can come from improving the *product mix* by putting an outstanding, all-star EVA-positive product lineup on the field (and benching products, and features, and customers that aren't EVA positive), or it can come from *process excellence*, from running a tight, lean, efficient ship from top to bottom, through operations excellence and asset management, and even covering taxes, restructuring investments, acquisition pricing discipline, and integration success as key processes to manage.

Note, though, it does take an *improvement* in the EVA Margin to propel EVA Momentum. Just sustaining excellent processes or holding on to a wide gross margin would only maintain the current Margin and would not add Momentum, at least not in this category. It takes real productivity progress to increase EVA and to drive EVA Momentum, because EVA Momentum measures performance at the margin and is the news in the data.

The other main EVA Momentum category measures the value added from profitable sales growth. As for the sample company, it added 25 percent to its sales and earned a 4 percent EVA Margin, a combination that contributed the missing 1 percent to its EVA Momentum. That precisely quantifies how much value was added from delivering quality growth, and conveniently expresses it on the exact same scale as productivity gains so that visualizing the trade-offs is a lot easier.

In sum, the windswept and austere summit of the EVA Momentum Pyramid that we've just surveyed reveals just how well a company is performing and *begins* to unravel the performance story. As for SSCo, we can see at a glance that the firm generated a significant increase in its economic profit, and that half of the added value came from making the business engine run better, with more torque and spark, and the other half from making it run faster, a one-two punch that generated significantly more EVA heft, EVA growth, and EVA Momentum at the margin. You would be hard-pressed to reach those conclusions so quickly and reliably using other measures. Clearly, an advantage of this format is that it enables a manager or analyst to accurately summarize the value added and dependably rank the performance progress of what may be very different businesses or business plans. For example, it puts the value added from an improving turnaround story on precisely the same analysis footing as would apply to a growth star. It is an analysis method suitable for all business missions.

The Pyramid summit also naturally draws attention to the bird's-eye conclusions as the first order of business and discourages managers from getting bogged down in the details before they can put them in perspective. It is always tempting to jump right into the weeds when reviewing performance, but the managers who do that not only are unable to see the forest, they can't even see the trees. They literally get lost in the weeds. The approach I advocate is: Let's take it a step at a time. Let's first grasp the big-picture essence of how successful the business was in driving economic profit growth and then fill in the why and how pixels second. Let's peel the onion in stages, but let's start off knowing we are holding an onion and not a tomato.

Let's consider a few alternative scenarios and see how easy it is to simulate EVA Momentum and how to drive it. Suppose that the sample firm's EVA Margin had remained stuck at 3 percent. How much would pulling the carpet out from under EVA Margin expansion have hurt its EVA Momentum? Quite a bit. EVA Momentum would have been only 0.75 percent instead of 2 percent. In the absence of the productivity gains, EVA Momentum would come only from the sales growth, but now at only the 3 percent EVA Margin rate. This illustrates how really important EVA Margin is to EVA Momentum. Increasing the EVA Margin not only directly increases the EVA derived from existing sales; it also makes sales growth all the more profitable. It pays a double dividend, or its absence exacts a double penalty. Profitability trumps growth to a large degree in the EVA Momentum math.

Another insight is that all sales growth is not created equal. If a firm's EVA Margin is zero or close to it, which is true of nearly half of all firms on the market, all the growth in the world adds nothing to EVA. Growth will propel sales, EBIT, EBITDA, and EPS, but will produce no EVA Momentum and therefore no added shareholder return at all (the shareholders will of course still earn the expected cost of capital return, but no more). Growth without a positive EVA Margin is the epitome of spinning wheels. Managers who start to see a low EVA Momentum score on their tally sheets will soon get the message—we've got to take better shots before we take more shots.

On the other side, even modest sales growth at a sizable EVA Margin can do more good than lots more growth at a lower EVA Margin. Consider Coca-Cola, a firm that is currently earning almost a 13 percent EVA Margin. Suppose its sales grow at a 7 percent a year clip (i.e., doubling in about 10 years, consistent with management's espoused strategic goals). Without any change in its EVA Margin, Coke's EVA Momentum would be 0.9 percent, close to the 75th percentile break point, and quite impressive for a firm that has been in business for over 100 years. Coke may not be a growth company judged by sales or EPS growth, but it is most definitely a growth stock judged by EVA Momentum.

What about a business with a far more modest but still quite respectable 2 percent EVA Margin that is delivering 30 percent sales growth? Its EVA Momentum rate is 0.6 percent. It is only two-thirds of the 0.9 percent

Momentum pace that Coca-Cola generates with only 7 percent sales growth. This company's sales and its EPS are expanding over four times faster than Coke's. But growth in sales and EPS does not matter. Growth in EVA does, and on that score, Coke wins by a landslide. EVA Momentum trumps EPS momentum every time.

This illustrates how hard it is to correctly judge how various business units are really performing with conventional performance metrics. I could give you all of the data on metrics like operating margins, RONA, sales and profit growth rates, and such, and you'd be scratching your head for quite a while to figure out, if you could see the right answer at all, what you'd be able to see very quickly and far more accurately on the EVA Momentum scorecard.

What about a firm that is operating with a negative EVA Margin? Bear in mind that the firm could show positive net income and EPS along with EPS growth as long as it is covering the after-tax cost of the money it borrows. But if it is failing to cover the overall cost of capital and its EVA Margin is in the red, then the growth in all the other measures is only detracting from its EVA and subtracting from its value. The EVA Margin message to the managers is to wake up and stop throwing more good money after bad. Sales growth at a negative EVA Margin will only dig a deeper hole. The first commandment must be to improve the EVA Margin. Go on a diet before you enter the race. Get better before you get bigger. Repair the business model, restructure, and streamline; do what it takes to move to an incrementally positive EVA Margin business model.

Most CFOs would like to convey messages like these to their line teams, but the guidance is hard to explain with conventional measures. Combining EVA as a money measure with EVA Margin and EVA Momentum as ratio indicators is a much easier and more effective way to get everyone to see the light.

MARKET METRICS

I beg your continued indulgence—we will very soon go into more depth on EVA Momentum drivers and apply them to Amazon. For now, though, I need to take you on a short detour to review the valuation metrics for our sample company and how they tie to EVA. After all, we do need to see how EVA ties to creating wealth.

Start with MVA. It's the spread between the market's valuation of the business, given its share price, and the capital invested in it (these appear on lines 50 and 51, respectively, in Exhibit 5.5). In Chapter 2 we valued the sample company under various scenarios for projecting and discounting its EVA. Now we are taking the opposite tack. We will use valuation statistics derived from hypothetical but realistic share prices to reach inferences about how investors perceive the sample company and view its prospects.

Two key findings are conveyed by the table in Exhibit 5.5. The sample firm's MVA is positive and it increased over the year, from $850 to $1,000. The company has transformed valuable inputs into more valuable outputs, and it has enriched its owners. But more than that, the MVA expansion indicates that the firm is now adding even more value, is creating even more wealth, has enlarged its franchise value, and has beefed up the corporate NPV larder, compared to the prior year. To repeat, MVA, and the change in

2	**Key EVA Metrics**				
3	**Simple Sample Co**		*Fiscal Year Ends: SEP*		
4			*Currency: U.S. Dollar*		
5	*Benchmark: Russell 3000*		*Scale: Values in Millions*		
8	**EVA Computation**		**2011TFQ3**		**2012TFQ3**
9	**NOPAT**				$ 150
	Capital		$ 900		$ 1,100
	× Cost of Capital (COC)		10.0%		10.0%
19	**Capital Charge**				$ 100
	EVA (NOPAT – Capital Charge)		$ 30		$ 50
33	**EVA Return on Sales**				
34	**Sales Growth Rate**				25.0%
37	**Sales**		$ 1,000		$ 1,250
38	**EVA Margin (EVA/Sales)**		3.0%		4.0%
42	**EVA Growth**				
43	**Change in EVA (ΔEVA)**				$ 20
44	**EVA Momentum (ΔEVA/Prior Sales)**				2.0%
48	**Wealth Creation**				
	Share Price		$ 17.50		$ 21.00
50	**Market Value (MV)**		$ 1,750		$ 2,100
51	**Capital**		$ 900		$ 1,100
	Market Value Added (MVA = MV – Capital)		$ 850		$ 1,000
	Current Value Added (CVA = EVA/COC)		$ 300		$ 500
	Future Value Added (FVA = MVA – CVA)		$ 550		$ 500
57	**MVA Spread (MVA/Capital)**		94%		91%
60	**MVA Margin (MVA/Sales)**		85%		80%
64	**Market Expectations**				
65	**Future Growth Reliance (FVA/MV)**		31%		24%
68	**Market-Implied EVA Momentum (MIM)**		0.7%		0.5%
71	Market-Implied EVA Improvement		$ 7.1		$ 6.3
73	**Cash Flow**				
74	**Free Cash Flow (FCF = NOPAT – ΔCapital)**				$ (50)
75	**FCF Generation (FCF/Capital)**				–5%

EXHIBIT 5.5 The Key EVA Metrics for the Sample Company

MVA, should be on the scorecard of every public company director. They are very telling measures.

Now let's bring EVA and MVA together. As I've said, at any point in time, MVA should equal the present value of the EVA profit that a firm can be expected to earn in the future, which means that over time, changes in MVA should be best explained by changes in EVA. It's no surprise, then, that the sample firm's MVA was positive and increased when its EVA was positive and increased. Again, it is a made-up example, but the two are joined in principle and in practice.

Recall that MVA can be divided into two components—CVA and FVA. CVA, for current value added, comes from assuming that the firm's EVA remains constant forever. In Chapter 2 we established that SSCo's CVA is $500 (as shown on line 55). It is the $50 in EVA profit recorded in the most recent year divided by the 10 percent cost of capital. FVA, or future value added, is the portion of MVA attributable to the expected growth in EVA. Here it is determined by simple subtraction, as MVA minus CVA, to see what the market thinks it is. In this case it is $1,000 – $500, or $500, too, by sheer coincidence. It is shown on line 56. FVA is the prepayment the market is making in anticipation of strategic growth in EVA that hasn't happened yet. It can be turned into two companion ratio statistics that quite usefully quantify investor expectations.

The first of those, as I discussed earlier, is Future Growth Reliance (FGR), or the ratio of FVA to market value. It is the proportion of the firm's market value that depends on continued EVA Momentum. For the sample company, as shown on line 65, the reliance ratio ended the year at 24 percent. That says the firm's market value would tumble 24 percent if investors became convinced that it would never be able to increase EVA above its current $50 level.

Reliance is a double-edged sword. On the one side, the higher the reliance percentage, the more confidence investors are registering in management's ability to grow EVA. It's the best defense against takeover and the most enticing invitation to raise capital for growth. An increase in reliance is also a key to increasing MVA and driving shareholder returns. The troubling bit is that when reliance is high, management actually needs to deliver significant EVA growth just to stay on target with investor expectations, and a slip, even a minor one, can precipitate a dramatic downturn in the firm's valuation and owner wealth. It is obviously a very telling statistic that any CFO or board member should want to monitor and benchmark against other like companies and the market.

The second ratio that can be derived from FVA is even more important. It is the performance expectations ratio I introduced earlier in this chapter. It is Market-Implied Momentum (MIM). It is the average annual

EVA Momentum growth rate that is implicitly baked into the stock price. Trust me on the math. The MIM rate impounded into the sample company's latest market value is 0.5 percent, which is equivalent to an expected annual increase in EVA over 10 years of $6.25 (0.5% × $1,250 in sales in the last period), as are shown on lines 68 and 71 in the table. Put another way, the MIM rate projects that EVA will progress from $50 to $56.25, $62.50, to $68.75, and so on, going up $6.25 a year, for 10 years, and then it is assumed to go flat. The firm's 0.5 percent MIM rate is above the 0.2 percent long-run average EVA Momentum delivered by the median firm in the Russell 3000 universe over the past 20 years. The market is apparently still expecting great things going forward for some time.

Future Growth Reliance and Market-Implied Momentum shrank over the most recent year. The reliance ratio ended up at 24 percent versus 31 percent the year before, and MIM dropped to 0.5 percent from 0.7 percent. Do those signal the market was losing confidence in SSCo's future growth potential? Strictly speaking, yes, but that is chiefly because so much of the EVA growth that was expected as of the end of the prior year was actually achieved in the recent year, which left relatively less growth on the come.

MIM was 0.71 percent at the end of the prior year (shown on line 68), which translated into an expected annual EVA increase of $7.1 million (line 71) on the $1,000 sales base. The sample company ended up producing a lot more than that. Its EVA increased $20 million and EVA Momentum hit 2 percent. With almost three years' worth of expected EVA growth coming in the one year, the EVA growth expected to come on top of that diminished somewhat, but still remained quite strong. Net net, what the company lost in expectations it more than made up with its actual performance. Put another way, the firm's EVA increased 66 percent in the period (from $30 to $50) and its MIM decreased 30 percent (from 0.71 percent to 0.50 percent), but the combination still left shareholders with a much higher share price and far larger MVA in its wake.

Incidentally, the sample company is not at all unusual in this regard. It is common to see a bout of EVA Margin expansion and EVA Momentum growth countered by a cooling in MIM expectations. Investors generally expect competition and maturation to pull high EVA Margins and abnormally high growth rates back toward the universal market norm (and vice versa). We will investigate this phenomenon in greater detail in Chapter 7 on target setting.

There are two other valuation ratios I'd like to cover before moving on. These quantify the relative size of the firm's MVA. The first one, shown on line 57 and labeled MVA Spread, is the ratio of MVA to capital. It is a wealth creation efficiency ratio. It is an improved version of the price-to-book ratio that avoids accounting distortions and leverage vagaries. In the most recent period it was 91 percent for SSCo, indicating every invested dollar had been transformed into 91 cents of added wealth, which is not bad by current standards. As of midsummer 2012, the MVA-to-capital ratio was 33 percent for the median Russell 3000 firm.

The second MVA indicator is MVA Margin, which (you guessed it) is the ratio of MVA to sales. It is the ratio of franchise value per dollar of revenue. It measures the efficiency with which the company is translating customer satisfaction into owner wealth. MVA Margin is 80 percent for the sample company in the latest period, also not bad; the mid-2012 market median ratio was half that, at 41 percent.

Although these are interesting statistics to quantify and benchmark wealth creation efficiency, be aware of their limitations. The table shows that the wealth indexes for the sample company decreased, but MVA increased and that is what really matters. As I have shown, it is the change in MVA that actually drives shareholder returns, and not changes in MVA ratios.

To complete the review, take a glance at the bottom section on the summary schedule. It shows a calculation of the company's free cash flow (FCF) on line 74. The company earned $150 in NOPAT but invested $200 in capital as capital increased from $900 to $1,100 over the year, leaving free cash flow at minus $50. Divide that by the $1,000 in average capital, and the firm's free cash flow generation rate, or net cash flow yield, shown on line 75, was −5 percent.

However expressed, the company invested beyond its internal cash sources, and was forced to tap external financing to fund growth. The cash flow indicators are bleeding red, and no doubt it was a hectic year for the firm's treasurer. Yet it was truly a terrific year for the operating team and for the owners. EVA increased, EVA Margin increased, and EVA Momentum was upper quartile and way above prior expectations. MVA and owner wealth increased handsomely, too. The sample company joins Amazon as another classic example of why free cash flow after investment spending is such a poor and actually irrelevant measure of corporate performance.

Free cash flow can, though, be used in the formula to measure the total investor return (TIR), although again in a way I think is misleading. Recall that TIR can be computed as $(FCF + \Delta V)/V_0$. Plug in for SSCo:

$$
\begin{aligned}
\text{TIR} &= (FCF + \Delta V)/V_0 \\
&= [-\$50 + (\$2,100 - \$1,750)]/\$1,750 \\
&= (-\$50 + \$350)/\$1,750 = 17.1\%
\end{aligned}
$$

It was a great year in terms of total investor return—over 17 percent. But the negative sign on FCF does not begin to explain why that is so. And now from the more helpful EVA point of view:

$$TIR = (Capital\ charge + EVA + \Delta MVA)/V_0$$

Plug in:

$$TIR = [\$100 + \$50 + (\$1,000 - \$850)]/\$1,750 = 17.1\%$$

The return is the same computed both ways, of course, but to reiterate the insight, cash flow and the cash-equivalent value change are merely the agents that transmit returns to investors. They are just the market's messenger boys. Reversing the capital charge, earning EVA, and driving MVA and EVA expectations higher—all positive in this case—are the real backroom bosses driving and determining the returns that are parceled out to investors. Cash flow does not matter. Earning and increasing EVA does. EVA Margin and EVA Momentum tell us how well a business is doing in those return-driving departments.[5]

LET'S GET REAL—A FIRST LOOK AT AMAZON

The table in Exhibit 5.6 presents the same key metrics table, but now for Amazon (AMZN), with one addition. There is now a section—starting on line 24—that reports the firm's return on capital. It is the ratio of NOPAT to average capital, or the return on capital (ROC), which is my preferred version of RONA (not that I prefer RONA at all). It's shown here to sound the drum I've already beaten, which is that RONA, ROI, or ROC (pick your poison) are lousy measures and you should stop using them. I'll get to that.

The table shows a five-year record, for years constructed from rolling four-quarter periods that conclude at the midpoint of 2012. The latest period shown, for example, is a composite of the last two quarters of 2011 plus the first two quarters of 2012, based on an analysis of 10-Q filings. Did I prepare this by hand? Heck no. I pushed a button and, presto, it appeared in a preconfigured Excel spreadsheet we call EVA *Express*. My team and I spent six years developing software that ingests reported financial data for

---

[5] In fact, it is possible to explain TIR as a function of the EVA Margin, the EVA Momentum, the MIM rate and change in the MIM rate, and the sales growth rate. Again, it all comes down to the key EVA ratio statistics.

2	**Key EVA Metrics**					
3	**AMAZON.COM INC**				*Fiscal Year Ends: DEC*	
4					*Currency: U.S. Dollar*	
5	*Benchmark: Russell 3000*				*Scale: Values in Millions*	
8	**EVA Computation**	2008TFQ2	2009TFQ2	2010TFQ2	2011TFQ2	2012TFQ2
9	NOPAT	$ 767	$ 1,007	$ 1,316	$ 1,788	$ 2,118
11	Capital	$ 3,142	$ 3,382	$ 5,018	$ 9,098	$ 12,983
12	x Cost of Capital (COC)	9.2%	8.9%	9.0%	8.9%	8.2%
19	Capital Charge	$ 223	$ 276	$ 332	$ 526	$ 813
21	EVA (NOPAT – Capital Charge)	$ 544	$ 731	$ 984	$ 1,262	$ 1,305
23	**EVA Return on Capital**					
24	Return on Capital (ROC = NOPAT/Capital)	31.6%	32.6%	35.7%	30.2%	21.5%
27	Cost of Capital (COC)	9.2%	8.9%	9.0%	8.9%	8.2%
29	EVA Spread (EVA/Capital = ROC – COC)	22.5%	23.6%	26.7%	21.3%	13.2%
33	**EVA Return on Sales**					
34	Sales Growth Rate	40.5%	19.7%	39.8%	40.5%	34.9%
37	Sales	$ 17,132	$ 20,509	$ 28,665	$ 40,277	$ 54,326
38	EVA Margin (EVA/Sales)	3.2%	3.6%	3.4%	3.1%	2.4%
42	**EVA Growth**					
43	Change in EVA (ΔEVA)	$ 216	$ 187	$ 253	$ 278	$ 43
44	EVA Momentum (ΔEVA/Prior Sales)	1.8%	1.1%	1.2%	1.0%	0.1%
48	**Wealth Creation**					
49	Share Price	$ 73.33	$ 83.66	$ 109.26	$ 204.49	$ 228.35
50	Market Value (MV)	$ 31,036	$ 34,833	$ 46,448	$ 91,783	$ 104,886
51	Capital	$ 3,142	$ 3,382	$ 5,018	$ 9,098	$ 12,983
53	Market Value Added (MVA = MV – Capital)	$ 27,894	$ 31,451	$ 41,430	$ 82,684	$ 91,903
55	Current Value Added (CVA = EVA/COC)	$ 6,369	$ 8,776	$ 11,473	$ 15,252	$ 17,996
56	Future Value Added (FVA = MVA – CVA)	$ 21,525	$ 22,675	$ 29,957	$ 67,432	$ 73,907
57	MVA Spread (MVA/Capital)	888%	930%	826%	909%	708%
60	MVA Margin (MVA/Sales)	163%	153%	145%	205%	169%
64	**Market Expectations**					
65	Future Growth Reliance (FVA/MV)	69%	65%	65%	73%	70%
68	Market-Implied EVA Momentum (MIM)	1.6%	1.3%	1.3%	2.0%	1.4%
71	Market-Implied EVA Improvement	$ 268.5	$ 271.7	$ 374.0	$ 809.7	$ 749.4
73	**Cash Flow**					
74	Free Cash Flow (FCF = NOPAT – ΔCapital)	$ (266)	$ 698	$ (547)	$ (2,038)	$ (2,067)
75	FCF Generation (FCF/Capital)	–11%	23%	–15%	–34%	–21%

EXHIBIT 5.6 EVA Metrics for Amazon

9,000 global public companies every night into a battery of servers, where a set of algorithms crunch the numbers according to our standard formulas for measuring the sacred EVA ratios. The next morning, while sipping my first cup of java, I can call up virtually any public company from all over the globe and see how it is faring on the EVA/MVA scorecard. The EVA data file also feeds a league-leading stock rating and ranking model we've developed, but more on that later.

Now, I'd like to ask a favor. It is your turn. Take a look at the vital statistics for AMZN. What do you observe, now that you've been schooled in the EVA ratio metric set? This is your big chance.

Okay, I never did my homework either, so here goes. AMZN has been amazing, in a nutshell. EVA is running at last polling at $1.3 billion, up from only $0.5 billion four years before, and it increased every year. EVA Momentum (line 44) has been strictly positive, a statistical rarity. Granted, the EVA Momentum pace has been slowing in recent years, and lately slipped well under the 1.4 percent or so MIM rate investors have baked into the firm's share price (line 68). If you want to get concerned, Amazon is running a performance deficit. It is banking promises to step up the pace of its EVA Momentum and make its investments pay off in future years.

But that is looking ahead. As for the actuals, not surprisingly, MVA has been consistently positive and more than tripled over the four-year interval, from just under $30 billion at the start to over $90 billion at the end. That is more than $60 billion in added owner wealth, thank you. And, as expected, MVA has risen pretty much hand in hand with the EVA. To sum it up, AMZN looks remarkably like the simple sample company. Its performance has been truly impressive in all the ways that count, and at the same time, and like the hypothetical firm, there are contrary and misleading indicators to consider and discard.

As has already been noted, and as is shown in the table, Amazon's FCF was negative—very negative in fact—and not just in the past two years. It was negative in four out of the five years, and cumulatively way negative. Investors have shoveled boatloads more cash into the firm than it has ever paid out. But none of that matters. Only growth in EVA and MVA matters.

But that is not all. After rising in the first two periods, AMZN's return on capital (line 24) has melted down in the past two years. The most recent ROC is a good 10 percentage points lower than it tended to be over the prior four years. It is running at only about 20 percent instead of over 30 percent. And yet, although ROC is now at a low point, Amazon's EVA, MVA, and share price are now at high points. Again, when ROC goes down and EVA goes up, it is EVA that wins the argument.

And what a case EVA makes. Amazon's cumulative EVA Momentum over the past five years—computed from the cumulative change in EVA divided by sales five years back—was an even 8 percent, or a 1.6 percent per year average, as is shown on the Momentum Pyramid in Exhibit 5.7. How good was that? It's 78th percentile versus the EVA Momentum accomplishments of all other Russell 3000 firms over that five-year span. The pace of EVA growth was really quite good, and yet productivity gains were a no-show in the performance, actually a slight hindrance, as EVA margin deteriorated by 30 basis points. The entire EVA Momentum—and more—was due to hyper sales growth—a compound annual growth rate (CAGR) of 34.7 percent and cumulative growth of 345 percent—at a slight but meaningfully positive EVA Margin.

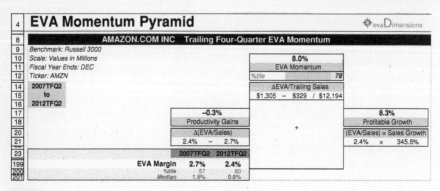

EXHIBIT 5.7   The EVA Momentum Pyramid for Amazon

The most significant aspect of Amazon's performance, which is the profitable growth element behind the $90 billion in wealth creation Amazon achieved, was totally off the RONA radar screen. And frankly, even the erosion in the EVA Margin, lamentable though it is, does not alter the basic conclusion, which is that AMZN produced a simply stunning performance and added value over the past five years. To put it in a tongue twister you can remember, the quantity of quality earnings matters more than the quality of the earnings. EVA Margin, too, is ultimately just a cog in the EVA Momentum wheel.

But what a cog it is. In the next chapter, I put EVA Margin under the microscope and show how it unfolds to reveal all the drivers of business model productivity in a step-by-step framework that is simple, informative, and practical as a management tool. It does the job so well it is my candidate to relieve from duty RONA and the DuPont ROI model.

CHAPTER 6

EVA Margin

EVA Margin is not the measure to maximize—EVA Momentum is. It is, though, an extremely important driver of EVA Momentum, as I have shown. But it is more than that. It is the critical pathway leading from the one to the many. It is the staircase that descends from the overall score into the engine-room drivers that managers can actually manage in order to construct a better-performing business model and shift EVA Momentum into a higher gear.

Let's begin with a quick look at the EVA Margin breakout we have designed for this purpose for the Simple Sample Co., shown in Exhibit 6.1. It is a format that expresses all business model productivity elements on a profit margin schedule. By design it starts on familiar ground—with the firm's cash operating margin, a variation of the classic EBITDA/sales ratio. In the example shown, that is 33.5 percent. It is a function of the firm's gross margin and overhead efficiency—which are breakout elements we'll get to later on.

While the cash profit margin is an interesting statistic for management to monitor, it is incomplete and misleading by itself because the capital charges

	33.5%	Cash Operating Profit Margin	Cost of Goods Sold SG&A
—	**27.4%**	Productive Capital Charges	Working Capital PP&E Capital Intangible Capital
=	**6.1%**	EVA Margin Before Tax	The Key Pre-Tax Productivity Measure
—	**2.1%**	Corporate Charges	Taxes Other EVA Goodwill and Restructuring Charges
=	**4.0%**	EVA Margin	The Key Bottom Line Profitability Measure

EXHIBIT 6.1 The EVA Margin Schedule in Brief

must be covered. One huge advantage of this approach lies in common-sizing the capital charges—dividing them by sales—so that the balance sheet assets used in running the business are made into the equivalent of a directly deductible charge against the cash operating margin. In the example, the charges for all of the productive capital elements sum to 27.4 percent of sales.

What's left over is called the EVA Margin Before Tax. It is 6.1 percent in the example. That is a key measure of business model productivity that consolidates operating efficiency and asset management into a net margin score. It is also a suitable statistic for grading line teams and benchmarking trends against peers, because it is measured before the rather abstract grab bag of corporate charges that comes next—for things like taxes, sundry income and expense items, and charges for goodwill and restructuring investments—again expressed as a percentage of sales, which sum to 2.1 percent in the example, leaving a 4 percent EVA Margin at the bottom line.

Although the method to compute it is very different, the EVA Margin measured on the ratio-formatted schedule is always the same as the simple ratio of EVA to sales. Management can use this ratio breakout schedule, and more detailed versions of it, with full confidence that if it maximizes its EVA Margin with the intelligence the schedule provides, it will maximize the EVA profit it earns per dollar of sales generated in the period.

Even at this high-level summary view, the EVA Margin starts to yield actionable intelligence as the result of breaking it into a number of measurable performance indicators and line-item summary statistics. Line teams are able to use it to understand the overall profitability of their business and the main drivers. But this view is only the beginning. In this chapter, you will learn how to take the EVA Margin apart and trace it step-by-step to all of the underlying performance factors that determine business profitability.

Incidentally, in the process of fleshing out the EVA Margin schedule, I intend to make the case that it is a far better performance analysis framework than the so-called DuPont return on investment (ROI) formula. For readers who may not be familiar with it, the DuPont ROI formula was developed by the iconic chemical conglomerate and put into use as far back as the 1920s as a means of summarizing and analyzing the performance of the firm's numerous business divisions. The formula, shown graphically in Exhibit 6.2, expresses return on investment (or return on net assets [RONA], which is the same thing) as the multiplicative product of operating margin and asset turnover.

DuPont's management team used it to quickly grasp the performance essentials of its divisions and manage far-flung business operations. It has been rightly hailed over the years as a key innovation in business management. I contend, though, it is time to retire the formula and replace it with

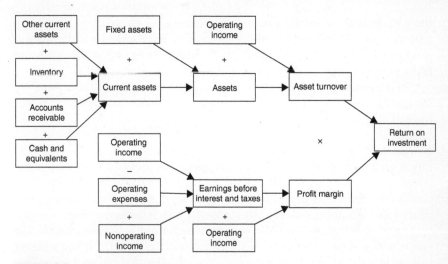

EXHIBIT 6.2 The DuPont Formula

the EVA Margin schedule. The argument flows through the remainder of the book, but grant me a few words now to set the stage.

I have already written at length about the shortcomings of RONA as a measure—that it is not a measure to maximize—and I have already made the case that it is more intuitive for operating managers to think in terms of sales growth and profit margins as the levers of value as opposed to return on capital and capital growth. But besides those deficiencies, the ROI formula fails on purely practical grounds. It is simply a far less effective performance analysis tool than the EVA Margin schedule is.

One obvious problem is that it expresses ROI as the *product* of profit margin and asset turns. It is multiplicative right at the start. The benefit of increasing asset turns depends on the size of the profit margin, and the benefit of increasing the profit margin is scaled by the turns. Each confusingly depends on the other. It is not clear what each contributes or how to make operational trade-offs, particularly when the factors vary from business to business.

With the EVA Margin schedule, by contrast, balance sheet assets are just a cost, a charge to profit and profit margin, the same as any other cost. And it's all simple plus-and-minus math, from the cash operating margin at the top to the EVA Margin at the bottom, with each performance factor along the way conveniently expressed on the same footing, as a common percentage of sales. Operating managers no longer have to perform mental FX transactions to compare the significance of improving working capital days, plant turns, gross margin, tax rates, and the like. As you will see, the EVA Margin schedule converts all performance elements to a common currency—to an understandable percentage-of-sales scale—which means it is way easier to answer questions like: "Which is more important—improve gross margin 0.3 percent or take 10 days out of working capital?"

ROI is, moreover, derived from an overall asset turnover ratio. Attributing the ratio to specific assets like inventories or property, plant, and equipment (PPE) is not easy or obvious (you'd have to weight the turns by the proportion of the total assets that the asset represented), but with the EVA Margin schedule, each category of capital and asset management opportunity is separately displayed and correctly priced as a charge that is naturally weighted according to its significance. All in all, the EVA Margin schedule is simply a better way to demystify the balance sheet and give managers a practical tool to manage it and consider trade-offs with other performance factors.

Another advantage to EVA Margin, which frankly I consider to be decisive, is that it ties right into EVA Momentum. Unlike ROI, it has a higher calling. It *is* the Momentum upshifter, after all. Analyzing it, and improving it, is a directly recognizable key to driving EVA and generating more EVA Momentum. It is part and parcel of the EVA Momentum model. It correctly positions the analysis of performance productivity as an element in a more encompassing measure of wealth creation that includes the value of profitable growth, again on the exact same percentage-of-sales scale. The point is that EVA Margin, like EVA Momentum, applies to all aspects of financial management, whereas ROI clearly doesn't.

All told, there are three principal applications of the EVA Margin schedule that I will discuss. The first one, explored in this chapter, is for reviewing actual performance results period by period or over a range of years for a strategic perceptive. The schedule, for example, provides an ideal format for organizing quarterly and annual performance reviews and keeping them focused on EVA and the drivers of EVA. It is also an ideal way to x-ray and benchmark business model performance across divisions or in comparison with public peers, as I also show in this chapter.

The second application is to use the EVA Margin schedule to deconstruct business plan projections. It is the most efficient and reliable template for isolating the value drivers and testing sensitivities, and for isolating and grading critical assumptions in the plan and judging how realistic it is. I will investigate these techniques in the upcoming planning chapter.

The third application is to use it for analyzing capital investment proposals using a special present value version. Instead of just measuring and analyzing EVA Margin by period, an overall EVA Margin is computed based on the projected present value of EVA and the present value of projected sales. This provides a single EVA Margin statistic that is characteristic of the overall profitability and net present value (NPV) of the project, like an internal rate of return (IRR), only better. The present value version also facilitates understanding the drivers and assumptions, as I will show in the chapter on EVA and decisions and acquisitions.

In sum, I contend that the EVA Margin schedule is the best way for CFOs and line teams to dissect business performance, to spot key trends and developments, and to benchmark with peers and size up relative strengths and weaknesses. It is the best tool for helping company teams to make decisions that involve trade-offs and formulate initiatives that target the best opportunities to increase EVA Momentum. Those are the claims. Now let's take a look and see if you agree.

Let's once again start with the Simple Sample Co. We'll use the same first-pass breakout of the EVA Margin that I introduced at the beginning of the chapter, but this time explaining the elements in more detail.

The schedule in Exhibit 6.3 starts with a top-line measure of the firm's cash operating profit margin that is called the EBITDAR margin (on line 32). EBITDAR is an improved version of EBITDA. It is EBITDA plus rent expense, plus a handful of other add-backs for things like research and development (R&D) and retirement distortions that make it a purer, better, more consistent, complete, and correct measure of the firm's underlying cash profit generation (I cover the details in the next section). Suffice it for now to say that it is not affected by shifts in owned versus leased assets, it is not affected by shifts in spending on intangibles, and it is not affected by retirement funding distortions. For the sample company, the EBITDAR margin increased from 33.0 percent to 33.5 percent of sales, and was one of the factors contributing to the expansion in the EVA Margin and the EVA Momentum performance chronicled in the prior chapter. Details will follow.

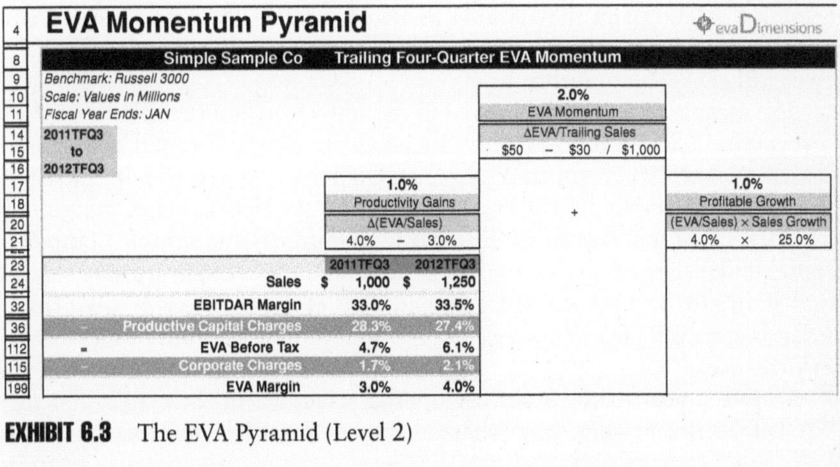

EXHIBIT 6.3 The EVA Pyramid (Level 2)

Next is the profit margin deduction to cover the total cost of all the capital employed in the firm's operating activities (line 36). This requires some explanation. First, the charge consists of the depreciation and amortization of the assets, plus the cost of capital on the assets—expressed as a percentage of sales. It combines capital maintenance and the necessary return on capital in one charge, and as such, it is the total cost incurred by using the assets in the period, and it is similar to the cost that would be incurred by renting the assets from third parties. The second point is that the charges arise just from the firm's "productive capital," as I call it, which isn't all the capital. It is the capital used to run the business and generate revenues. It consists of working capital; property, plant, and equipment (PPE) assets (including rented assets); and intangible capital (including R&D, ad spending, and other self-created intangible assets). It excludes goodwill and non-revenue-linked assets, such as excess cash balances, investments, deferred-tax assets, long-term receivables, retirement assets, and the like, that are handled farther down the schedule or simply put aside from the EVA calculation.

The productive capital charge, in other words, isolates the total cost associated with the assets that are in some way contributing to the EBITDAR margin, which effectively makes it a minimum performance barrier that must be surpassed before EVA can be created in the operations. In that spirit, the charges are computed, as I will explain in more detail, using a pretax cost of capital. That way, the charges are on the same footing as and directly deductible from the EBITDAR margin, which is also measured pretax.

As the chart shows, the sample firm needed to generate an EBITDAR margin in the 27 percent to 28 percent range just to cover the full charge to rent its productive capital. A company that operates in a more capital intense business would have to surpass an even greater EBITDAR margin threshold. A company that is able to manage its assets better, turn them faster, and generate a higher yield from them would face a comparatively lower EBITDAR margin threshold.

The sample firm actually moved in that direction and recorded a sizable performance gain in this category. Its productive capital rental charge decreased from 28.3 percent to 27.4 percent. That amounted to a 0.9 percent savings, and it added almost twice as much to the firm's pretax margin as the 0.5 percent increase in its EBITDAR margin. As the sample company typifies, balance sheet performance can and often does count for more than what shows up on the income statement. That is one reason why EBITDAR and its cousin EBITDA are woefully incomplete and misleading measures of performance.

At this point a line is drawn on the schedule, on line 112, for the EVA Before Tax margin. It is what remains of the EBITDAR margin after deducting the productive capital charges. It indicates, first, whether the company's operations are EVA positive or negative and by how much, and second, whether business model productivity is improving or waning. The sample company's pretax margin was a win on both counts. It was positive and strongly improved—from 4.7 percent of sales to 6.1 percent—because management was firing on both pistons and recording gains in income efficiency and asset management.

As I said, the pretax EVA Margin is a very significant performance indicator. It consolidates pricing power, product mix, and process excellence efficiency—the "3-P's"—into a net margin score that neutralizes business model differences and accurately reveals the overall value added or lost in the period with all operational factors considered. As such, it is a measure that CFOs can confidently use for judging operations managers during quarterly reviews, and for reaching conclusions about best practices and where to invest and grow. The corporate team, of course, remains responsible all the way down to the bottom-line EVA Margin, including the corporate charges, which we'll get into later on.

Let's now descend another level deeper on the path to the many. For this, we will use the level 3 breakout schedule shown in Exhibit 6.4. It's the same EVA Margin for the same sample company, just colored in with more detail and more insights.

4	**EVA Momentum Pyramid**							eva Dimensions
8			Simple Sample Co	Trailing Four-Quarter EVA Momentum				
9	Benchmark: Russell 3000							
10	Scale: Values in Millions				**2.0%**			
11	Fiscal Year Ends: JAN				EVA Momentum			
14	2011TFQ3				ΔEVA/Trailing Sales			
15	to				$50 − $30 / $1,000			
16	2012TFQ3							
17				**1.0%**			**1.0%**	
18				Productivity Gains			Profitable Growth	
20				Δ(EVA/Sales)	+		(EVA/Sales) × Sales Growth	
21				4.0% − 3.0%			4.0% × 25.0%	
23				2011TFQ3 2012TFQ3				
24			Sales	$ 1,000 $ 1,250				
26	−		COGS (Adjusted)	53.0% 53.0%				
29	−		SG&A (Adjusted)	14.0% 13.5%				
32			EBITDAR Margin	33.0% 33.5%				
36	−		Productive Capital Charges	28.3% 27.4%				
46	−		Working Capital Charge	3.8% 3.3%				
70	−		PP&E Charge	16.0% 15.0%				
91	−		Intangible Capital Charge	8.5% 9.0%				
112	=		EVA Before Tax	4.7% 6.1%				
115	−		Corporate Charges	1.7% 2.1%				
116	× (1−)		EVA Tax Rate	30.0% 30.0%				
133	+		Other EVA	0.5% 0.5%				
188	−		Goodwill & Unusual Items Charge	0.8% 0.8%				
199			EVA Margin	3.0% 4.0%				

EXHIBIT 6.4 The Pyramid (Level 3)

EBITDAR—CASH OPERATING PROFIT

The schedule starts as always with the EBITDAR margin, which merits further explanation at this point. As I said, EBITDAR is the classic EBITDA figure, the conventional earnings before interest, taxes, depreciation, and amortization measure, plus adjustments that make it an even better measure of cash operating profit. Here's how we convert raw EBITDA sugar cane into refined EBITDAR rum in four steps:

1. EBITDA is measured before interest and depreciation expense, but *after* deducting rent expense. It decreases when a company rents an asset but not when it buys one and incurs the depreciation and interest cost on its own books. EBITDA rewards investing in and owning assets instead of renting them, even when leasing would be advantageous. It distorts performance comparisons over time and between firms as the mix of owning and leasing assets varies.

   EBITDAR eliminates that distortion by adding rent expense to EBITDA. It is the same whether assets are owned or rented. It reflects the quality of asset management regardless of how the assets have been financed. The cost of the rented assets is not forgotten, of course. It is combined with the overall charge for fixed assets further down the schedule.

2. R&D and advertising and promotional spending are deductions from EBITDA, but shouldn't be. As I have discussed, the deductions are a source of noise that make it harder to tell how well underlying operations are doing when management decides to step up or pull back on the spending. In the worst cases it motivates managers to cut the spending in order to make a short-term earnings goal.

   EBITDAR is isolated from those distortions because the period spending for R&D and advertising and promotion (and, depending on the company, for other intangibles, such as training, launching new products, or ramping up new stores) is added back. Again, the spending is not forgotten. Like rented assets, it is charged off with interest further down the schedule.

3. Retirement distortions are backed out of EBITDAR. The company's reported retirement expense is added back to EBITDA, and the service cost is deducted in its place to better represent the true ongoing cost of operations in the period.

4. Accruals are converted to cash. Examples are that EBITDAR is measured after deducting the net charge-offs of bad debts instead of the bad debt provision and after converting last in, first out (LIFO) cost of goods sold (COGS) to first in, first out (FIFO) (and the FIFO value of inventories is used to measure capital).

For any one company, there may be more or fewer or different adjustments (our software handles them all automatically), but this list gives you a good feel for why EBITDAR, and hence the EBITDAR-to-sales margin, is a purer measure of operations excellence that is more comparable from period to period, from division to division, and from company to company.

EBITDAR can also be computed as sales less cost of goods sold (COGS) and less selling, general, and administrative (SG&A) charges that incorporate the same adjustments. The adjusted COGS figure shown in the table is measured predepreciation and prerent expense, for example, and SG&A is measured predepreciation, preamortization, prerent, pre-R&D, pre–ad spending, pre–retirement cost distortions, and so forth. The result is that even these two EBITDAR components are more telling than the standard figures.

PRODUCTIVE CAPITAL

Let's review the charge for productive capital in more detail. As I said, it includes the depreciation and amortization charges that must be set aside to replenish the base of assets that support the business operations and generate revenues, and it also includes the charge for the cost of capital on the productive capital elements, but computed at a pretax rate.

A pretax cost of capital rate is used so that the capital charges are equivalent to any other operating expense, like cost of goods sold, that is also measured pretax. Managers are thus better able to size up the significance of capital as a cost element and make decisions that involve trade-offs. Another benefit is that an improvement in asset management appears very simply as a reduction in the charge and an improvement in the pretax EVA margin, just as if product prices had increased or operating costs had been reduced. A 1 percent saving in productive capital charges is just as valuable as a 1 percent reduction in SG&A costs, for instance. The two are now perfectly equivalent.

Computing EVA pretax as a step along the road to bottom-line EVA is certainly a big improvement over the traditional way. In years gone by the standard method to compute EVA pitted an after-tax capital charge against an after-tax NOPAT. That approach made managing capital seem to be less important than it really is—like 40 percent less important—because the capital charge was computed and presented posttax rather than pretax. Another problem with that formulation is that after-tax EVA takes line teams out of the pretax revenue and cost world in which they tend to operate. It was another factor that kept EVA out of the operating manager's comfort zone.

Here's how we do it now. Suppose a firm has a 9 percent cost of capital after-tax, and we've established a 40 percent standard tax rate will apply to smooth the tax calculation. The 9 percent posttax rate is divided by 1 less the standard tax rate; that is, it is grossed up to 15 percent, and that higher pretax rate is used to compute the capital charges on all the productive capital elements. Even with today's lower cost of capital rates (due to low interest rates), once managers are charged for capital at eye-popping pretax rates, they start to pay a lot more attention to managing capital, or I should say that they start to give the balance sheet the *appropriate* amount of attention it deserved all along. You may be wondering: If EVA is charged for capital at the higher pretax cost of capital rate, how do we end up with the correct EVA after tax? Simple—the tax applied to pretax EVA is adjusted to rebate the difference between the pretax and posttax costs of capital. Trust me, it works. We always get the same bottom-line EVA while isolating pretax EVA performance as a more apt measure to judge operations.

So far we've been discussing productive capital as a single overall charge to the EVA Margin. Although that is a useful summary statistic, line teams need more details if they are to understand it and manage it. They need a way to trace the charge to specific assets and connect it with relevant balance sheet indicators. To do that, we follow four steps:

1. **Compartmentalize.** Balance sheet asset elements are assigned to distinct capital buckets that line teams can relate to and manage.
2. **Monetize.** The capital buckets are converted into pretax charges.
3. **Common-size.** The line item charges are expressed on a common percentage-of-sales margin scale.
4. **Personalize.** The capital cost drivers are supplemented with company-specific metrics and milestones that help the line teams to understand and manage the outcomes.

The EVA Margin schedule shows the results of following this procedure—at least through the first three steps. The schedule now shows separate pretax line-item charges for working capital, for PPE (including the rented assets), and for intangibles (including the home-grown ones), which sum to the overall productive capital charges. Let's discuss the components one by one.

WORKING CAPITAL

The pretax capital charge for working capital is computed by applying the pretax cost of capital times the average balance of working capital in the business, and expressing the charge as a percentage of sales. A 16.7 percent pretax cost of capital is used (that is the 10 percent posttax cost of capital, grossed up at the assumed 40 percent standard tax rate). Working capital includes transactional cash balances (leaving out excess cash), plus receivables at face value and inventories at current FIFO value, less the funding from trade payables. It's the net amount of capital that would have to be financed by lenders and shareholders to support the company's cash conversion cycle.

The EVA Margin schedule shows that the sample company's working capital charge decreased from 3.8 percent of sales to 3.3 percent, adding 50 basis points to the pretax EVA Margin. The breakout (call this level 4, presented in Exhibit 6.5) shows why. Improving working capital from an average of 83 days of sales on hand to 72 was the reason.

		2011TFQ3	2012TFQ3
46	Working Capital Charge	3.8%	3.3%
49	Cost of Capital Before Tax	16.7%	16.7%
50	Working Capital Days on Hand	83	72

EXHIBIT 6.5 The Working Capital Charge (Level 4)

Click again, dig deeper still, and look at level 5 now (shown in Exhibit 6.6). Cash conversion sped up because receivables were collected three days faster (line 53) and inventories turned five days quicker (line 56), but also because the proportion of receivables and inventories financed by the trade climbed from 21 percent to 26 percent (line 67), which gave the firm three more sales' days of interest-free funding (line 63). The big picture

23			2011TFQ3	2012TFQ3
46		Working Capital Charge	3.8%	3.3%
49		Cost of Capital Before Tax	16.7%	16.7%
50		Working Capital Days on Hand	83	72
53	=	Receivables Days	45	42
56	+	Inventory Days	60	55
59	=	Inventory Days (COGS)	113	104
62	×	COGS (Adjusted)/Sales	53.0%	53.0%
63	−	A/P Days	22	25
66	=	Receivables + Inventory Days DOH	105	97
67	×	Funding Ratio (AP/Inv+Rec)	21%	26%

EXHIBIT 6.6 The Working Capital Charge (Level 5)

is filling in with the details that resonate with line teams. Cash conversion counts, and now it counts quite visibly as an increase in the profit margin.

PROPERTY, PLANT, AND EQUIPMENT (PPE)

The next capital charge on the docket is for the physical asset base—labeled PPE, for property, plant, and equipment in the EVA Margin schedule. To be clear and to review, it covers, first, depreciation and amortization expense (the estimated annual cost to replace or refurbish wasting assets); second, the pretax cost of capital on the net plant base; and third, the same thing on the rented assets.

Whereas EBITDAR is computed as if all assets are owned, even the ones rented, the PPE charge is computed as if all the assets used in the business operations are rented, even the ones that are owned. As a result, the capital charge and the cash profit margin are unaffected by how assets are financed.

The EVA Margin schedule shows that the overall PPE charge fell from 16 percent of sales to 15 percent, a full 1 percent improvement. The questions are: how and why? The financials won't reveal all, but they can provide some insights, as is seen with the next mouse click, shown in Exhibit 6.7.

A prime improvement source was tying up less gross plant capital per dollar of sales, as shown on line 73. The sample firm's *gross* PPE—which is the original undepreciated cost it paid to acquire the fixed assets, plus the present value of its rented assets—dropped from 80 cents per sales dollar to 75 cents. Intensity dropped by 5 cents on 80 cents, or by 1/16, which accounts for the 1 percent savings on the capital charge, from 16 percent to 15 percent. Generating a greater revenue yield on the investment in PPE was thus a prime mover of the company's EVA Margin and EVA Momentum over the period.

A decrease in plant intensity such as this could come from improving yield and productivity and uptime and quality, or from a shift in product mix to faster-selling lines at higher prices, or to ones requiring less setups and changeovers, or from improving warehousing and transportation asset

23			**2011TFQ3**	**2012TFQ3**
70		PPE Charge	16.0%	15.0%
73		Gross PPE (Adjusted) per $1 Sales	0.80	0.75
76	×	Rental Rate	20.0%	20.0%
79		Depreciation Rate	7.5%	7.0%
82		Remaining Life (Net/Gross PPE)	75%	78%
85		Cost of Capital Before Tax	16.7%	16.7%

EXHIBIT 6.7 PPE Capital Charges (Level 5)

logistics, or from using information technology (IT) assets more efficiently, or moving IT assets to the cloud. There are any number of ways to do it. The financial numbers cannot provide deeper insights than just documenting the improvement but not pinpointing the underlying cause.

That is why our clients typically devise sister metrics to help them better explain and manage their PPE charge (and the other breakout lines on the schedule, too). To continue the analogy I have employed, they lay even deeper foundational stones under the base of the EVA Momentum Pyramid. A retailer, for example, might break out the gross PPE intensity ratio into construction cost per square foot divided by its average sales per square foot. The retailer, in other words, looks to manage PPE intensity by keeping construction costs under control or on target, and by maximizing the sales turns per square foot of space. Manufacturers bring in production yield, defect rates, capacity utilization, run time, setups, forecasting accuracy, product mix, and so on. Transportation companies embellish the schedule with metrics that reflect the total cost of maintenance versus replacement of rolling stock, fleet utilization, repair downtime, and the like. The ideal is to adorn and accessorize the EVA Margin schedule with a range of company-specific metrics that make it more useful as a reporting and management tool—and not just in the PPE section, but throughout.

Though increasing turns while decreasing PPE intensity is generally the dominant opportunity, other PPE variables can enter for good or ill. Without going through the math,[1] another means to reduce the PPE charge is to reduce the rate at which the PPE assets are being depreciated, as is reported on line 79 (for example, by using longer-lived assets or by finding ways to extend asset lives while keeping quality and productivity up). Another route would be to slow down asset replacement and stretch out the average age of the plant base, as would be indicated by a reduction in the net-to-gross PPE ratio shown on line 82 (the reason this enters is that the cost of capital

---

[1] To be specific, the PPE charge is shown on the breakout schedule as the product of the gross plant intensity ratio and the average effective rent rate, which combines depreciation and cost of capital into one overall rate. The cost of capital, though, is attenuated by (multiplied by) the ratio of net to gross plant, because the cost of capital applies to the net plant. To take an example, the sample company's first-year PPE charge of 16 percent was due to tying up 80 cents of gross plant per $1 of sales and having to pay an effective rental rate of 20 percent—you multiply those two together. The rental rate in turn was from the sum of the 7.5 percent depreciation rate and the 16.7 percent pretax cost of capital, age adjusted—that is, multiplied times 75 percent net to gross PPE ratio. In other words, in that year, 25 percent of the PPE assets had already been depreciated, and only 75 percent of the original cost was still on the books, so that reduced the effective cost of capital applied to the gross PPE assets.

charge is applied to the net depreciated asset base, so that older and more fully depreciated assets bear a smaller cost of capital charge at any given degree of gross asset intensity). That strategy, though, will work only for a while and up to a point, and must be balanced against other costs—the cost of poor quality, low yield, dwindling reliability, higher maintenance costs, increased raw material costs, and so forth. Again, any one metric must be viewed in the context of the trade-offs and ramifications across the whole business model.

INTANGIBLE CAPITAL

The third breakout bucket on the schedule is for intangible capital. The charge covers the amortization cost and the pretax cost of capital on the firm's book intangibles, except for goodwill (which is handled further down the schedule), and on its self-created ones, covering items like R&D and advertising and promotional spending that are treated as capital investments in the EVA model.

As an acquisitive, brand-rich and technology-rich firm, the sample company incurs substantial charges in this category. In the most recent year, the firm incurred a 1 percent charge from its reported book intangibles, a 5.7 percent charge to cover its investments in innovation (R&D), and 2.3 percent for its marketing outlays (advertising and promotional spending), for a total of 9 percent, up from 8.5 percent in the prior year (the breakout is in Exhibit 6.8). Let's investigate those charges in greater detail.

The first charge in this category is for the firm's book intangibles. Those are specific purchased intangible assets that are recognized and valued at the time of acquiring other companies, for things like trademarks, patents, franchise rights, copyrights, customer lists, noncompete agreements, and so forth. Think of these as tangible intangibles. These are not hard assets you can touch, but they are identifiable and they are expected to increase the company's profits (unlike goodwill, which is a pure premium paid to buy

23		2011TFQ3	2012TFQ3
91	Intangible Capital Charge	8.5%	9.0%
94	Book Intangibles Charge	1.0%	1.0%
97	R&D Charge	5.0%	5.7%
100	R&D Expense % of Sales	4 0%	6 5%
103	R&D Expense	$ 40.0	$ 81.3
104	Ad & Promotion Charge	2.5%	2.3%
107	Ad & Promo Expense % of Sales	2 2%	1 6%
110	Ad & Promo Expense	$ 22.0	$ 20.0

EXHIBIT 6.8   Intangible Capital Charges (level 5)

profit but not to contribute to it; as such, it is excluded from productive capital and is handled at the very bottom of the EVA Margin schedule).

In fact, accountants value the purchased intangibles at the time of acquisition by discounting the extra profit that they are projected to earn for the firm. Some of the assets, like brand names, are expected to increase profits forever (as compared to the profit that would be earned absent the brand identification). Assets like those are never amortized, so the only charge is the cost of the capital that has been assigned to them. Others, like trademarks or noncompete agreements, are expected to contribute to profits for only a finite period. The charge for those assets therefore covers amortization of the asset over its estimated life as well as the cost of capital on the net unamortized balance—in other words, it includes the period charge to replenish the asset and sustain the profit after the trademark or noncompete agreement has expired.

I concede that the valuations accountants assign to purchased intangibles are not precise, and may even be biased (EPS-manic managers want to put more of the purchase price in goodwill and less in purchased intangibles, since goodwill is not amortized). Even so, the amounts recorded in capital and the amortization of the assets are at least approximately correct and represent a real cost to maintain the current profit stream. Another reason to include the charges in this section is that buying intangible assets and creating them by investing in them inside the firm should be weighed as alternatives, a view that is encouraged by combining these charges and charges for R&D and ad and promotion spending under the same heading.

As for the sample company, the charges for all of its purchased intangibles amounted to 1 percent of sales in both periods. Compared to the charges we've seen for working capital and PPE, it's relatively small potatoes. But it is not negligible—heck, a 1 percent increase in pretax margin doesn't come easily to almost any company—and in any case, it is important. It brings purchased intangibles out of an obscure and neglected corner of the balance sheet right onto the firm's profit margin schedule where it simply cannot be ignored. It is now a visible and totally comparable cost statistic that can be benchmarked against competitor firms and across internal divisions. Moreover, its presence on the profit margin schedule will undoubtedly force managers to justify increasing it, and there are only two ways for them to do that.

One is by proving there will be an offset on the margin schedule, such as from increasing product prices and expanding the firm's gross margin. The other avenue would be off the margin schedule itself; the return from purchasing intangibles could also come from stimulating more abundant growth in sales at positive EVA Margins. It is EVA Momentum that needs to be preserved, not EVA Margin, and the EVA Momentum Pyramid permits those kinds of judgments and comparisons to be made in a common currency, all on a percentage-of-sales scale.

While purchased intangibles were simply maintained at a constant 1 percent of sales, the sample company significantly stepped up its R&D investment program in relation to its sales. R&D spending more than doubled, from $40.0 to $81.3 (line 103), or rose from 4 percent of sales to 6.5 percent (line 100). The charge to EVA, however, is not based on the spending. As has been discussed, it is based on amortizing the spending (over five years is the standard default) and tagging the cost of capital onto the unamortized balance. That charge, as shown on line 97, was 5 percent in the first year, or a full percentage point *higher* than the spending rate that year (because it included interest at the cost of capital on prior spending carried forward). In the most recent year, when management ramped up the spending, it was the opposite—the charge to the EVA Margin was 5.7 percent of sales, or 80 basis points *lower* than the 6.5 percent spending rate (because the spending hike is amortized over time). This is a good example of how EVA smooths out spending shifts, giving managers the time needed to generate a return from investing in innovation while eventually holding them accountable for covering the full cost with interest.

The same observations apply to the sample company's ad and promotion spending, but in reverse. As shown on lines 107 and 110 (and by design of the illustration), management cut the marketing spending by 10 percent in the most recent period, which reduced the ad spending rate from 2.2 percent to 1.6 percent of sales. But the 0.6 percent cutback did not simply fall into the lap of EVA. With ad and promotion spending being amortized over three years with interest, the EVA charge fell by far less, by just 0.2 percent of sales, or by one-third of the spending cut. The managers are still being charged for a portion of the marketing spending that is carried over from prior periods and that is—or should be—contributing to profits and the profit margin in the current period. This illustrates how managers are discouraged from cutting the spending unless it is strategically wise to do so. These are all fabricated numbers, of course, but all this applies to actual companies, as we'll see in a minute.

On net, the charge for intangibles increased by half a percentage point. Again, that is not necessarily a bad thing, but to make the cost increase worthwhile, management would need to be convinced that there was at least a half percent of EVA Momentum coming from compensating sources.

At this point we again arrive at the key pretax EVA Margin statistic (line 112 in Exhibit 6.4), but perhaps now with a far better appreciation for how it consolidates all operating efficiency and balance sheet asset productivity levers into a decisive, fully loaded net margin score, including intangible assets, and how they are acquired, nurtured, and turned into tangible profits. Now it's time to get real.

AMAZON UNDER THE EVA MARGIN MICROSCOPE

Let's repeat the same exercise with Amazon. It will go a lot faster the second time. I have provided a condensed breakout and a deeper dissection of Amazon's EVA Margin elements starting with the table in Exhibit 6.9 and continuing again into greater depth, covering the mid-2007 through mid-2012 interval. I'll start with the summary schedule.

AMZN's EVA Margin, the middle row in the table in Exhibit 6.9, followed a parabolic curve. It started out at 2.7 percent of sales and then climbed to a peak of 3.6 percent for the mid-2009 year before steadily descending to 2.4 percent in the last reported period. It was always positive while not always improving. Sales, though, marked a steady ascent, surging from $12 billion to $54 billion over the span. Sales growth was so phenomenal—35 percent in the last year alone—that EVA increased every year despite the EVA Margin slippage, albeit at a slower EVA Momentum pace more recently.

The pretax EVA Margin is usually a good place to start to get a read on the business fundamentals that tend to fall to the EVA bottom line—abstracting from the corporate charges, that is. As would be expected, it followed a parabolic pattern similar to the one evident for the bottom-line EVA Margin. Now at just 3.8 percent, the lowest point in the six-year span, the pretax margin appears to be caught in a vise, squeezed between a relatively fixed EBITDAR margin running in the 14+ percent range and a soaring charge for productive capital that is now a good 1.5 percent higher than has been typical. More details, you say? Here they come.

The chart in Exhibit 6.10 provides a wealth of performance details at a glance. Learn to read it and you will be a better manager, better investor,

EVA Margin and Momentum

AMAZON.COM INC
Benchmark: Russell3000   Ticker: AMZN

Fiscal Year Ends: DEC
Currency: U.S. Dollar
Scale: Values in Millions

	2007TFQ2	2008TFQ2	2009TFQ2	2010TFQ2	2011TFQ2	2012TFQ2
EBITDAR Margin	15.0%	14.1%	14.9%	14.2%	14.0%	14.4%
Productive Capital Charge	9.4%	8.3%	9.0%	8.3%	8.9%	10.6%
EVA Before Tax Margin	5.6%	5.8%	5.9%	5.9%	5.1%	3.8%
Corporate Charges	2.9%	2.6%	2.3%	2.5%	2.0%	1.4%
EVA Margin	2.7%	3.2%	3.6%	3.4%	3.1%	2.4%
x Sales	$12,194	$17,132	$20,509	$28,665	$40,277	$54,326
EVA	$ 329	$ 544	$ 731	$ 984	$ 1,262	$ 1,305
ΔEVA	$ 50	$ 216	$ 187	$ 253	$ 278	$ 43
EVA Momentum	0.5%	1.8%	1.1%	1.2%	1.0%	0.1%

EXHIBIT 6.9 Amazon's EVA Margin and Momentum

EVA Margin and Momentum

AMAZON.COM INC
Benchmark: Russell 3000   *Ticker: AMZN*

Fiscal Year Ends: DEC
Currency: U.S. Dollar
Values in Millions

	2007TFQ2	2008TFQ2	2009TFQ2	2010TFQ2	2011TFQ2	2012TFQ2
Sales Growth Rate	31.8%	40.5%	19.7%	39.8%	40.5%	34.9%
EBITDA Margin	6.1%	6.1%	6.2%	6.7%	5.4%	4.4%
EBITDAR Add-Backs	8.9%	8.0%	8.7%	7.5%	8.6%	10.1%
COGS (Adjusted)	76.9%	77.5%	77.4%	77.4%	77.6%	76.7%
SG&A (Adjusted)	8.1%	8.4%	7.7%	8.4%	8.5%	8.9%
EBITDAR Margin	15.0%	14.1%	14.9%	14.2%	14.0%	14.4%
Productive Capital Charge	9.4%	8.3%	9.0%	8.3%	8.9%	10.6%
Productive Cap Intensity (Prod Cap/Sales)	0.15	0.13	0.15	0.13	0.15	0.19
× Productive Capital Charge (% of Prod Cap)	64%	63%	61%	65%	59%	56%
Working Capital Charge	−0.5%	−0.3%	−0.2%	−0.4%	−0.2%	−0.1%
Cost of Capital Before Tax	15.4%	15.3%	14.9%	15.0%	14.8%	13.7%
Working Capital DOH	−11	−8	−5	−8	−5	−3
+ Receivables Days	0	6	12	12	15	14
+ Inventory Days	22	22	23	23	25	28
− A/P Days	40	42	47	50	52	52
Funding Ratio (AP/Inv+Rec)	176%	150%	133%	142%	129%	122%
PPE Charge	4.2%	3.0%	3.2%	3.0%	3.6%	4.9%
Gross PPE (Adjusted) per $1 Sales	0.14	0.12	0.12	0.12	0.14	0.15
Depreciation Rate	17.3%	15.8%	15.9%	14.6%	14.5%	20.5%
Remaining Life (Net/Gross PPE)	74%	69%	69%	67%	70%	83%
EVA from Operations Margin	11.3%	11.3%	11.8%	11.6%	10.6%	9.7%
Intangible Capital Charge	5.8%	5.5%	6.0%	5.7%	5.5%	5.9%
Book Intangibles Charge	0.1%	0.2%	0.2%	0.2%	0.3%	0.3%
R&D Charge	4.1%	3.8%	4.1%	3.8%	3.6%	3.7%
Ad & Promo Charge	1.6%	1.5%	1.7%	1.7%	1.7%	1.9%
EVA Before Tax Margin	5.6%	5.8%	5.9%	5.9%	5.1%	3.8%
Corporate Charges	2.9%	2.6%	2.3%	2.5%	2.0%	1.4%
EVA Tax Rate (% EVA Bef Tax)	50.7%	45.1%	41.2%	38.9%	37.2%	37.0%
Other EVA	0.4%	0.3%	0.5%	0.2%	0.3%	0.3%
EVA Bef Goodwill/Unusual Items	3.1%	3.5%	3.9%	3.8%	3.5%	2.8%
Goodwill/Unusual Items Charge	0.4%	0.3%	0.3%	0.4%	0.4%	0.4%
Goodwill (Adjusted)/Sales	0.02	0.02	0.02	0.03	0.04	0.04
Cum Unusual Items After Tax/Sales	0.03	0.02	0.02	0.01	0.01	0.01
EVA Margin	2.7%	3.2%	3.6%	3.4%	3.1%	2.4%
× Sales	$ 12,194	$ 17,132	$ 20,509	$ 28,665	$ 40,277	$ 54,326
EVA	$ 329	$ 544	$ 731	$ 984	$ 1,262	$ 1,305
ΔEVA	$ 50	$ 216	$ 187	$ 253	$ 278	$ 43
EVA Momentum	0.5%	1.8%	1.1%	1.2%	1.0%	0.1%

EXHIBIT 6.10 A Wealth of Performance Details

better consultant, and better board member. You might also need a new prescription for your glasses. This is the new standard of financial excellence at its most granular (not quite; there are even deeper shafts in the EVA Margin schedule to mine, but not at this time).

This schedule is so detailed that it actually backs up one step from the EBITDAR margin. It starts off with the classic EBITDA margin on the second line from the top, and then shows the total sum of the add-backs to get to the EBITDAR margin. The add-backs, recall, are for items like rent expense and R&D and advertising and promotional spending, which are all significant at Amazon and becoming more so. As a result, the conventional EBITDA margin is making the company look less profitable than it really is.

For example, while the conventional EBITDA margin fell precipitously in the past year, from 5.4 percent of sales to 4.4 percent, Amazon's EBITDAR margin actually *increased*, rising from 14.0 percent of sales to 14.4 percent. Why the difference? There are a number of factors, but for one, the EBITDA margin was burdened with a 1.1 percent increase in the R&D spending rate that period, whereas the EBITDAR margin is measured before R&D spending—for just this reason. I could cite other reasons, but the point is that Amazon's EBITDA margin is crying wolf and the EBITDAR margin isn't falling for it. This is an exquisite example of why EBITDAR margin is such an improvement on the EBITDA version. It eliminates sources of noise and better reveals a firm's true cash operating profit margin. It helps management to avoid reaching false conclusions and making bad decisions.

I need to digress and cover a feature of the EVA schedule that hasn't been explained before. It is a quick way to explain the productive capital charges, which is as the multiplicative product of the two lines that are shown just beneath it on the schedule. The first factor is the *productive capital intensity* (the overall ratio of productive capital to sales) and the second one is the average *rental rate* on the productive capital (a composite of the cost of capital rate, the depreciation rate on PPE assets, and the amortization rate on intangibles). The insight is that if capital is used more intensely, or if it becomes more costly to finance and replenish it, the productive capital charges will increase as a charge to the EVA Margin. Let me explain a bit more about the two elements before applying the breakout to Amazon.

Surprisingly, there is no evidence to show that companies with lower productive capital intensity earn more EVA as a general rule. Capital-intense firms like petroleum giant Exxon Mobil, or even Google with its massive investments in systems, servers, and R&D, manage to do very well on EVA because they are able to generate massive EBITDAR margins. Yet it also is true that, everything else held equal, doing more with less and leveraging productive capital assets can be a key differentiating factor.

Apple, for instance, not only manages to have a better brand, higher customer loyalty, stronger pricing power, and greater innovation prowess than other tech companies. It also runs an extremely lean capital ship, as evidenced by a very low ratio of productive capital to sales—its intensity ratio runs at just about 12 cents to the sales dollar as of mid-2012, down from 16 cents six years ago. Apple operates with essentially no working capital, ties up just 10 cents in PPE assets relative to sales, and over the past six years its charge for R&D (as a percentage of sales) has been cut in half and for ad and promotion spending by two-thirds. A strong, exceptionally well-coordinated supply chain, server farms as download factories, and tremendous yields on intangibles (derived from free word-of-mouth and media-generated advertising, and R&D that is heavy on product development excellence) add up to an incredibly capital-light business model, as is summarized in this statistic. Apparently, you *can* have it all. Or at least one company in the whole world can.

The second factor here is the rental rate. It is the weighted average rate at which the productive assets are depreciating and amortizing, bearing interest at the pretax cost of capital, and turning into a charge against EVA. Risky firms must pay a higher rental rate to compensate for the risk, and firms using fast-depreciating assets must, too. Google's capital charge suffers on both counts, with its high business risk and its considerable capital tied up in rapidly obsolescing servers and R&D (whereas regulated utilities that invest in long-lived generation assets pay a far lower rate to rent their assets and recover their capital).

Let's apply the formula to explain why Amazon's overall productive capital charges are the squeezing part of the vice—the charge rose from 8.3 percent of sales in mid-2008 to 10.6 percent in the most recent period. The short answer, as is shown on the breakout schedule in Exhibit 6.10, is that intensity increased 50 percent, from 13 cents of productive capital per dollar of sales at mid-2008 to 19 cents. That was partly but not completely offset by the emergence of a slightly lower rental rate precipitated by an easing of interest rates and an asset mix shifting toward longer-lived PPE assets and away from shorter-lived, more quickly amortizing intangible assets. On net, though, the charge was higher because capital turned more slowly, as a general statement. Armed with that insight, let's dig in to see where and why.

A notable feature of AMZN's business model is operating with *negative* working capital, which is broken out in Exhibit 6.11. AMZN generates more cash from trade suppliers than it ties up in transactional cash balances, receivables, and inventories, and as a result, AMZN is given a cost of capital *rebate* on the schedule that *adds* to its EVA Margin. This is working capital that really works. Sure, negative working capital also helps cash flow, but that is not a separate consideration. The value of running the business with less capital and more cash flow is always fully measured by EVA, and in this category it is fully accounted for by the negative working capital charge.

One worrisome trend is that Amazon's working capital is becoming less negative. The main culprit is relatively less trade funding; the ratio of accounts payable to the money tied up in receivables and inventories has declined from 176 percent to 122 percent, as shown on the last line on the table in Exhibit 6.11. This could be a disguised price hike from suppliers, coming through the back door as more stringent payment terms. It could reflect a shift in product mix and corresponding changes in vendor terms. Whatever

AMAZON.COM INC Benchmark: Russell 3000	Ticker: AMZN				Fiscal Year Ends: DEC Currency: U.S. Dollar Values in Millions		
	2007TFQ2	2008TFQ2	2009TFQ2	2010TFQ2	2011TFQ2	2012TFQ2
Working Capital Charge	−0.5%	0.3%	−0.2%	−0.4%	−0.2%	−0.1%
Cost of Capital Before Tax	15.4%	15.3%	14.9%	15.0%	14.8%	13.7%
Working Capital DOH	−11	−8	−5	−8	−5	−3
+ Receivables Days	0	6	12	12	15	14
+ Inventory Days	22	22	23	23	25	28
− A/P Days	40	42	47	50	52	52
Funding Ratio (AP/Inv+Rec)	176%	150%	133%	142%	129%	122%

EXHIBIT 6.11 Amazon's Working Capital Charge (Level 5)

the reason, it is a stealthy but real facet of the company's performance that is detected by the EVA Margin radar screen. It is one of the reasons why the firm's capital intensity and overall capital charge has crept up.

A far bigger cost increase is coming through the PPE charge that, despite lower interest rates, is recently the highest it has been over the six-year record. It's 4.9 percent in the most recent year versus only a 3.0 percent charge two years before, for example (see Exhibit 6.12). That's almost a full 2 percent *extra* deduction to the pretax EVA Margin. Why has the charge increased so much? There are three reasons: PPE intensity is up from 12 cents to 15 cents on the sales dollar, the PPE assets are being depreciated more rapidly, and the asset base is on average newer than it was.

There is a story behind this. Amazon is investing heavily to increase the number of fulfillment centers and build out infrastructure for Amazon Web Services (i.e., cloud computing). But as with bookselling on the Internet, Amazon wants to be, or perhaps needs to be, the first to scale. To get there, Amazon nearly doubled capital expenditures from $979 million in 2010 to $1.8 billion in 2011. For a number of reasons, AMZN is investing ahead of the expected revenue stream.

If Amazon was computing its own EVA with the benefit of internal facts and figures, this could be a reason to apply the strategic investment treatment— to hold back a portion of the capital spend and meter it back in over time, with

AMAZON.COM INC Benchmark: Russell 3000	Ticker: AMZN				Fiscal Year Ends: DEC Currency: U.S. Dollar Values in Millions		
	2007TFQ2	2008TFQ2	2009TFQ2	2010TFQ2	2011TFQ2	2012TFQ2
PPE Charge	4.2%	3.2%	3.2%	3.0%	3.6%	4.9%
Gross PPE (Adjusted) per $1 Sales	0.14	0.12	0.12	0.12	0.14	0.15
Depreciation Rate	17.3%	15.8%	15.9%	14.6%	14.5%	20.5%
Remaining Life (Net/Gross PPE)	74%	69%	69%	67%	70%	83%
Cost of Capital Before Tax	15.4%	15.3%	14.9%	15.0%	14.8%	13.7%

EXHIBIT 6.12 Amazon's PPE Capital Charges (Level 5)

interest. That would increase the EVA reported at this time, and would smooth out the EVA stream reported over time (assuming the investments pay off). Even without being formally presented with those figures, however, investors seem to be pricing the stock as if they had been. Remember, AMZN's Market-Implied Momentum (MIM) is running at 1.4 percent. The market is projecting a long run of upper-quartile EVA growth for Amazon despite the decline in its EVA Margin and the increase in its capital intensity in recent years.

The third component of capital costs is one on which Amazon relies heavily—to buy technology, to create technology, and to promote its products and services and create brands. The overall cost of its intangible capital runs in the range of about 5.5 percent to 6.0 percent of sales computed the EVA way, as is shown on the first row in the schedule in Exhibit 6.13. The overall charge is now at the high end—despite a lower cost of capital—because AMZN has stepped up spending on intangibles quite considerably. Over the past two years, R&D spending skyrocketed from $1.4 billion to $3.7 billion, from 5 percent to 6 percent of sales, and ad and promotional spending soared from the $0.6 billion to $1.4 billion, or from 2.2 percent to 2.7 percent of sales. The spending hikes turned into a far lower increase in the charge to EVA, though, because the charges are amortized over time but also for another reason—a more subtle but very important reason: Amazon's sales have been growing so rapidly that by the time the spending is amortized, *it is being charged against a much larger sales base.* To put a figure on it, the pretax charges to the EVA Margin for R&D and advertising and promotion sum to 5.6 percent in the most recent period, whereas the company actually spent 9.4 percent. This shows how EVA correctly rewards growth companies that are growing through high-yielding spending on intellectual capital assets. Again, the conventional metrics just don't get this right at all.

Incidentally, AMZN is hardly alone in aggressive R&D spending. Through midyear 2012, for example, Google's fully loaded pretax R&D charge to its EVA Margin is a whopping 13.3 percent of sales. R&D charges are also material for many established industrial companies that are

AMAZON.COM INC
Benchmark: Russell 3000   Ticker: AMZN   Fiscal Year Ends: DEC / Currency: U.S. Dollar / Values in Millions

	2007TFQ2	2008TFQ2	2009TFQ2	2010TFQ2	2011TFQ2	2012TFQ2
Intangible Capital Charge	5.8%	5.5%	6.0%	5.7%	5.5%	5.9%
Book Intangibles Charge	0.1%	0.2%	0.2%	0.2%	0.3%	0.3%
R&D Charge	4.1%	3.8%	4.1%	3.8%	3.6%	3.7%
R&D Expense % of Sales	6.0%	5.4%	5.4%	5.0%	5.6%	6.7%
R&D Expense	$735.3	$923.4	$1,115.7	$1,439.0	$2,239.4	$3,656.1
Ad & Promo Charge	1.6%	1.5%	1.7%	1.7%	1.7%	1.9%
Ad & Promo Expense % of Sales	1.9%	1.9%	2.2%	2.2%	2.5%	2.7%
Ad & Promo Expense	$229.2	$325.5	$449.1	$639.2	$986.8	$1,439.6

EXHIBIT 6.13   Amazon's Intangible Capital Charges (Level 5)

leveraging innovation and product development. The R&D charge is 2.3 percent of sales at Emerson Electric and 4.2 percent at Rockwell Automation, both of which manage to earn double-digit pretax EVA Margins even after the charge. When it is well spent, R&D is not so much a cost of doing business as it is the ticket to value creation. It is the investment that actually creates EVA through price power and gross margin, customer satisfaction, and sales growth. It hits on both EVA Momentum cylinders.

A TALE OF TWO COMPANIES

The EVA Margin schedule is perhaps even more informative when companies and divisions within companies are pitted against each other. As I said, it is a terrific tool to x-ray business models, and to bring their differences and drivers into sharp focus, especially as a backdrop going into the planning process. As an example, let's use the EVA Margin schedule to analyze a David and Goliath battle for EVA Margin supremacy. The contenders are a lightweight upstart rival in jewelry retailing, the online discounter Blue Nile Inc. (NILE), and the carriage-trade heavyweight, Tiffany & Co. (TIF) (see Exhibit 6.14). Over the four-quarter period ending mid-2012, Tiffany earned more than 15 times the EVA of Blue Nile—$173 million versus just $11 million. While affirming that both companies are EVA positive, which is good to know, the comparison is grossly unfair and not very informative because Tiffany has $3.7 billion in sales and Blue Nile just $361 million. Size-adjusted EVA statistics are needed to fairly and insightfully compare the two.

As it so happens, and as is shown on the summary EVA Margin schedule in Exhibit 6.15, Tiffany is also ahead on EVA Margin in this four-quarter period (over the past five years it has been virtually a tie). Tiffany's EVA Margin ratio is 4.7 percent versus 3.1 percent for Blue Nile. TIF's EVA Margin is at the 74th percentile against all Russell 3000 companies in that period, while

	TIFFANY & CO TIF (2012TFQ1)	BLUE NILE INC NILE (2012TFQ2)
Classic EVA	$MM	$MM
NOPAT	$522	$9
Capital	$5,255	($17)
× Cost of Capital	7.1%	8.4%
Capital Charge	$349	($2)
EVA	$173	$11

EXHIBIT 6.14 The Goliath and David Matchup

NILE clocks in at a very respectable 64th percentile. But the interesting part is how they get there, and how the EVA Margin schedule reveals and neutralizes the differences in their business models, which are substantial.

Tiffany starts off with an intimidating lead. Its EBITDAR margin, on line 18, is nearly 40 percent, compared to a really puny EBITDAR margin of just 4.5 percent for Blue Nile. Brand value, premium prices, and scale economies really shine through at this point. But EBITDAR overstates Tiffany's reach, because its business model requires boatloads more capital than Blue Nile's does, which translates into a way higher charge to its EVA Margin. As shown on line 19, TIF would have to set aside a whopping 31.3 percent of its sales, and NILE a minuscule 0.5 percent of its sales, to cover the pretax productive capital charges. Prime real estate assets, a deeply integrated physical supply chain versus a virtual one, and major investments in brand equity make Tiffany far more capital dense. That's fine, but it means that Tiffany *must* earn a much higher EBITDAR margin just to stay even.

Not surprisingly, then, the race tightens considerably at the pretax EVA Margin line. It is 8.4 percent for Tiffany versus 4.0 percent at Blue Nile. This is a good example of how the pretax EVA Margin consolidates the distributed positive and negative attributes of business models into a reliable performance productivity score. It can even fairly grade companies as diverse as these two on one standardized test.

Tiffany must also cover materially higher corporate charges that are characteristic of a more mature company that has accumulated a lot of luggage

Benchmark Report ⊕evaDimensions

Benchmark: Russell 3000 Currency: U.S. Dollar Scale: Values in Millions	FYE: JAN 2012TFQ1 **TIF**	FYE: DEC 2012TFQ2 **NILE**
Key Measures		
Sales	$3,701	$361
EBITDAR	$1,467	$16
EVA Before Tax (EVABT)	$309	$14
EVA	$173	$11
EVA Margins (% of Sales)		
Sales Growth Rate	15.2%	5.4%
EBITDAR Margin	39.7%	4.5%
Productive Capital Rental Charge	31.3%	0.5%
EVA Before Tax Margin	8.4%	4.0%
Corporate Charges	3.7%	0.9%
EVA Margin	4.7%	3.1%

EXHIBIT 6.15 Tiffany and Blue Nile EVA Margin Comparison

over the years. That means that the decisive bottom-line EVA Margins are even closer, with only a 1.6 percent gap between them. With that as a first look, let's descend down the Pyramid path with the schedule shown in Exhibit 6.16.

The reason TIF's EBITDAR margin is so much higher than NILE's is now evident: its cost of goods sold is only about half as large (line 17). For every dollar of sales, Tiffany deigns to put in only about 40 cents of jewelry

	Benchmark Report ⊕evaDimensions		
5			
6	*Benchmark: Russell 3000*	*FYE: JAN*	*FYE: DEC*
7	*Currency: U.S. Dollar*	*2012TFQ1*	*2012TFQ2*
8	*Scale: Values in Millions*	**TIF**	**NILE**
16	**Sales Growth Rate**	**15.2%**	**5.4%**
17	COGS (Adjusted)	41.2%	80.5%
18	SG&A (Adjusted)	19.2%	15.1%
19	**EBITDAR Margin**	**39.7%**	**4.5%**
20	**Productive Capital Rental Charge**	**31.3%**	**0.5%**
21	Productive Capital Intensity (Prod Cap/Sales)	1.40	−0.05
22	x Productive Capital Charge (% of Prod Capital)	22%	−10%
24	Working Capital Charge	6.4%	−1.2%
25	Cost of Capital Before Tax	11.9%	14.0%
26	Working Capital DOH	197	−32
27	+ Receivables Days	18	3
28	+ Inventory Days	196	27
29	= Inventory Days (COGS)	475	33
30	x COGS (Adjusted) /Sales	41.2%	80.5%
31	− A/P Days	23	69
32	= Receivables + Inventory Days DOH	213	30
33	x Funding Ratio (AP/Inv+Rec)	11%	231%
34	PPE Charge	19.3%	1.7%
35	Gross PPE (Adjusted) per $1 Sales	1.08	0.08
36	Rental Rate	17.8%	20.3%
37	Depreciation Rate	8.9%	13.4%
38	PPE Life Remaining (Net PPE/Gross PPE)	75%	49%
39	Cost of Capital Before Tax	11.9%	14.0%
40	**EVA from Operations Margin**	**14.0%**	**4.0%**
41	Intangible Capital Charge	5.6%	0.0%
42	Book Intangibles Charge	0.0%	0.0%
43	R&D Charge	0.0%	0.0%
46	Ad & Promo Charge	5.6%	0.0%
47	Ad & Promo Expense (% of Sales)	6.2%	0.0%
48	Ad & Promo Expense	$229.8	$0.0
49	**EVA Before Tax Margin**	**8.4%**	**4.0%**
50	**Corporate Charges**	**3.7%**	**0.9%**
83	**EVA Margin**	**4.7%**	**3.1%**

EXHIBIT 6.16 Tiffany and Blue Nile EVA Margin Drivers Comparison

content, whereas Nile injects nearly 80 cents' worth. Blue Nile is actually selling jewelry at a slim markup over cost while Tiffany is really selling prestige, location, service, robin's-egg-blue boxes with white ribbons, sparkling display cases, and matrimonial bliss. Knowing this, I buy my wife jewelry at Blue Nile and present it to her in Tiffany boxes.

TIF's pricing power and production scale put its gross margin leagues ahead of NILE's, but that is offset somewhat by a higher SG&A expense. TIF incurs extra costs to administer the empire and manage the stores. Bear in mind, though, that the SG&A costs reported here exclude advertising, depreciation, and rent expense—all those costs are out of EBITDAR and deducted farther down the schedule. The only costs in this section are people costs and purchased costs. This keeps it cleaner and clearer.

PRODUCTIVE CAPITAL

Tiffany employs tons of capital—its capital base is even larger than its sales—whereas Blue Nile runs on empty, actually with *negative* capital overall. Blue Nile has more funding from the trade than it has tied up in *all* of its business assets. Bankers will hate it but shareholders will love it.

Once again, the statistic that sums up the comparison is the productive capital charge that appears on line 20. We've already noted how large it is for Tiffany and how negligible for the Blue Nile, but now let's get into the details. Tiffany must set aside a whopping 6.4 percent of its sales just to cover the cost of financing its working capital, whereas Blue Nile enjoys a pretax cost of capital *rebate* of 1.2 percent of sales (line 24 in Exhibit 6.16). That's a 7.6 percent spread in favor of Blue Nile, and goes some way to making back the 35.2-point EBITDAR margin shortfall with a working capital windfall.

Blue Nile obtains its working capital rebate through generous trade terms from suppliers and quick inventory turns, stocking only what will be sold in a month. Tiffany, on the other hand, ties up jewelry inventories in a leisurely production pipeline and shimmering in display cases for a total of *nearly 500 days* on average (it is only about 200 days' worth of sales, but 475 days' worth of cost of goods sold). And to compound the investment, Tiffany is able to arrange for only about 11 percent of its receivables and inventory investment to be trade financed. One of the things you are paying for at Tiffany is immediate gratification. The jewelry is waiting patiently in the stores for you and your loved one to come in, fall in love with it, and take it home. At Blue Nile, inventory is only pixels on a computer screen and you have to be willing to wait to get your hands on it. Patience is a virtue, as far as saving money and inventory costs is concerned.

Tiffany is a great company with a tremendous business model and storied history. But still, a 6.4 percent charge for working capital? That's incredibly high. Suppose management discovered a heroic way to slash working capital days by a third (I am just speculating here, mind you). It would take out one-third of 6.4 percent, or about 2.1 percent, from its pretax EVA cost structure. Assuming a 40 percent tax rate, that would add 1.3 percent to the bottom line EVA Margin, add a lot to EVA Momentum, and add a lot to MVA and share price (in the planning chapter we'll run through a full example like this). I am not picking on Tiffany. I am simply pointing out that even a simple illustration like this can help CFOs to get the attention of line teams on how important it can be to improve specific elements of balance sheet asset management.

Now we hit the big kahuna. Tiffany must set aside 19.3 percent of sales to cover the full cost of its physical asset base, while Blue Nile needs to reserve only 1.7 percent even after being charged at a materially higher cost of capital rate (line 34). Why the difference? It's the classic trade-off between bricks and clicks. When you make a purchase at Tiffany, every dollar flowing through the cash register is backed by a $1.08 investment in PPE capital, on average (line 35). Look around, linger, admire the sturdy marble columns and gleaming fixtures, rub your toes in the deep pile, enjoy the plush surroundings, even spill a little coffee if you've a mind to, because you've paid for it. Blue Nile, in contrast, runs the business out of a proverbial shoe box and in the digital matrix. The firm needs only 8 cents of PPE capital per dollar of sales, and most of that is the capitalized programming costs related to developing and upgrading the website, which is the only storefront it has. Another portion of the 8 cents is also due to the present value of rented assets, including warehouses and the company headquarters in Seattle. Those assets may be off the books, but they are not out of the EVA mind.

At this juncture we run into another intermediate EVA Margin measure, called the EVA from Operations Margin. It is EBITDAR less the charges for working capital and PPE. It is EVA net of the supply chain costs. It's the EVA equivalent of the cash conversion cycle. It is suitable for evaluating plant managers in an industrial business and store managers in a retail trade. It covers the total pricing, product mix, and supply chain functions, but ignores intangibles as well as corporate charges.

INTANGIBLES

When I open the *Wall Street Journal* I almost always see an ad for Tiffany on page 2 or 3. I am by now more familiar with Paloma than Pablo. And I am on the mailing list for the diminutive robin's-egg-blue catalog that arrives every so often. The constant reminders don't come cheap. In the four-quarter period tracked on the schedule, Tiffany spent a grand sum of $229.8 million on advertising and promotion, or 6.2 percent of sales. That's all been added back to EBITDAR, but now it is time to pay the piper.

But not all at once, of course. With its consistent and well-crafted advertising and promotion campaign building customer loyalty, repeat business, impulse purchases, and a willingness to part with a great portion of the family fortune at premium prices from time to time, Tiffany has built up a brand value the world over. And so, as you know, EVA treats the brand spending as an investment that is expected to make a contribution to profit over time. It is amortized with interest (by default, over a total of 12 quarters). The EVA charge for it was an amount equal to 5.6 percent of sales as compared to nothing (or least nothing reported) for Blue Nile, which relies on word of mouth and Internet searches and essentially costless e-mail blasts to direct traffic to its site, where the main attraction is not prestige, but low prices. Tiffany's charge is sizable, to be sure, but essential to its business model. Ultimately it is what's left over that counts, and what's left over at Tiffany is a hefty 8.4 percent pretax EVA Margin that remains *after* deducting the full intangibles charge. Is it the optimal amount of intangibles spending, and is it spent as well as it could be? The schedule does not give the answers, but it asks those questions. And it provides a format where the answers could be explored and quantified, through to the EVA Margin, to EVA Momentum, and to the discounted EVA value of the shares. I take up the process for doing that in earnest in the upcoming planning chapter.

CORPORATE CHARGES

All that remains to explain are the corporate charges that stand between pretax and bottom-line EVA. The charges sum to 3.7 percent of sales at TIF and just 0.9 percent at NILE, as detailed in Exhibit 6.17.

The first charge is a deduction for corporate income taxes computed the EVA way (and expressed in the table as a tax rate on pretax EVA). TIF pays a higher effective tax rate—it has a large deferred tax asset account that must be financed.

	Benchmark Report evaDimensions		
4			
5	Benchmark: Russell 3000	FYE: JAN	FYE: DEC
6	Currency: U.S. Dollar	2012TFQ1	2012TFQ2
7	Scale: Values in Millions	TIF	NILE
48	EVA Before Tax Margin	8.4%	4.0%
49	Corporate Charges	3.7%	0.9%
50	EVA Effective Tax Rate (% EVA Bef Tax)	41.3%	27.2%
57	Other EVA	0.0%	0.2%
78	Goodwill & Cum Unusual Items Charge	0.2%	0.0%
82	EVA Margin	4.7%	3.1%

EXHIBIT 6.17   Tiffany and Blue Nile Corporate Charges

The second item is an offset category called Other EVA that is added to the EVA Margin. It's a grab bag of miscellaneous, noncore, non-sales-related items, computed after-tax at this stage, and including royalty income, adjustments for underfunded retirement plans, less capital charges on miscellaneous assets, plus capital credits on miscellaneous liabilities, and so forth. All told, Other EVA is net EVA neutral for Tiffany (TIF has a large actuarial loss on its retirement plan to finance) and a modest win for Blue Nile.

The third component is a posttax charge to cover the cost of capital on goodwill and restructuring losses that EVA counts as capital. Tiffany has some, and Blue Nile reports none.

If you are interested in learning more about the details behind the corporate charges, please refer to Appendix C. Ordinary mortals may safely skip it.

PERCENTILE RATINGS

Each statistic and almost every performance indicator on the EVA Margin schedule is assigned a percentile rating, as is illustrated with the highlights shown in Exhibit 6.18. In this example TIF and NILE have been benchmarked against the Russell 3000 universe of public companies (with software from EVA Dimensions, it is possible to benchmark results against other market indexes, including the Russell global 9000 and any of a group of 55 standard industry groups or, even better, against a handpicked custom peer group that is compiled on demand).

TIF's EBITDAR margin, for example, was at the 75th percentile of the market universe whereas NILE's was way down at the 5th percentile (line 19). On the other hand, TIF's working capital days were so high that only 1 in 20 companies had more, and NILE's were so low that only 1 in 20 had less (line 26). (The percentiles are coded in the software so that one tinted green is a better outcome for EVA or just plain better, and one tinted red is worse.)

Converting scores into percentiles is helpful in many ways. For one thing, it simply serves to quantify the status of the corporate performance and to put it in perspective. For example, TIF's EVA Margin is logged in at the 74th percentile of the broad market peer group and NILE's at the 64th percentile slot. It is helpful, to say the least, for the board and management and investors to know, with some precision and relevance, where the company stands on the EVA performance scale. In short, it makes the EVA Margin and its supporting cast of driver metrics into usable statistics.

A second application is to isolate the surfer from the wave and more accurately isolate notable trends that are worthy of a response. One of our CFO clients told us that his firm was a top-quartile performer in its peer group. But when his team crunched their numbers through our software, the EVA report card they received was disturbing. They found that they were really in the

	Benchmark Report	eva Dimensions			
	Benchmark: Russell 3000		FYE: JAN		FYE: DEC	
	Currency: U.S. Dollar	50th	2012TFQ1		2012TFQ2	
	Scale: Values in Millions	%tile	TIF	%tile	NILE	%tile
15	**Sales Growth Rate**	8.3%	15.2%	66	5.4%	40
16	COGS (Adjusted)	60.5%	41.2%	69	80.5%	18
17	SG&A (Adjusted)	12.6%	19.2%	39	15.1%	46
18	**EBITDAR Margin**	25.0%	39.7%	75	4.5%	5
19	**Productive Capital Rental Charge**	22.5%	31.3%	35	0.5%	95
23	Working Capital Charge	1.3%	6.4%	5	−1.2%	95
25	Working Capital DOH	47	197	5	−32	95
33	PPE Charge	8.2%	19.3%	22	1.7%	95
34	Gross PPE (Adjusted) per $1 Sales	0.50	1.08	25	0.08	95
36	Depreciation Rate	8.3%	8.9%	45	13.4%	17
37	PPE Life Remaining (Net/Gross PPE)	67%	75%	36	49%	83
39	**EVA from Operations Margin**	7.5%	14.0%	65	4.0%	37
40	Intangible Capital Charge	2.5%	5.6%	39	0.0%	89
41	Book Intangibles Charge	0.6%	0.0%	75	0.0%	75
45	Ad & Promo Charge	0.0%	5.6%	5	0.0%	50
48	**EVA Before Tax Margin**	3.1%	8.4%	68	4.0%	53
49	**Corporate Charges**	2.4%	3.7%		0.9%	
50	EVA Effective Tax Rate (% EVA Bef Tax)	35.2%	41.3%	28	27.2%	73
57	Other EVA	0.3%	0.0%	43	0.2%	48
78	Goodwill & Cum Unusual Items Charge	1.0%	0.2%	73	0.0%	85
82	**EVA Margin**	0.8%	4.7%	74	3.1%	64
83	*EVA Margin–3-Year Average*	0.1%	4.0%	75	4.3%	76
84	*EVA Margin–5-Year Average*	−0.3%	4.0%	77	4.3%	78

EXHIBIT 6.18   Tiffany and Blue Nile Performance Percentiles

second quartile from the bottom on all the relevant EVA Margin (and EVA Momentum) metrics. Apparently, the firm's performance rebound had been quite strong coming out of the 2008–2009 economic downturn, so they had assumed the firm had maintained its relative standing. But in truth, the firm's competitors had improved a lot more than it had. The company's comparative standing had declined a lot, and it was not operating where it needed to be or expected to be. Shocked by what they saw, the CFO and CEO caucused and called an emergency planning session to raise performance targets and plan goals. Company teams used the EVA Margin schedule to help them pinpoint the specific shortfalls and to target a series of initiatives that would yield the greatest improvement in EVA. Now that's what I call putting EVA into action.

EVA AND MVA AT TIFFANY AND BLUE NILE

As a last look, I've furnished the classic EVA/MVA charts for TIF and NILE (Nile goes back only to when the firm went public), and along with charts showing the two main drivers of EVA—sales and EVA Margin. (See Exhibits 6.19 through 6.22.)

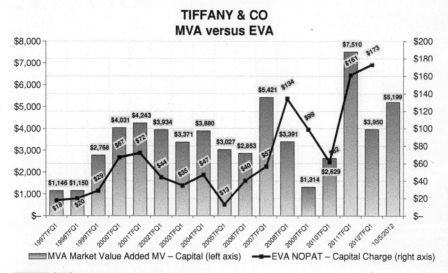

EXHIBIT 6.19 Tiffany's MVA and EVA

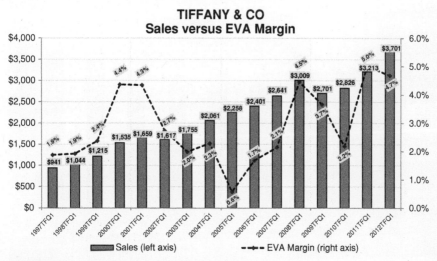

EXHIBIT 6.20 Tiffany's Sales and EVA Margin

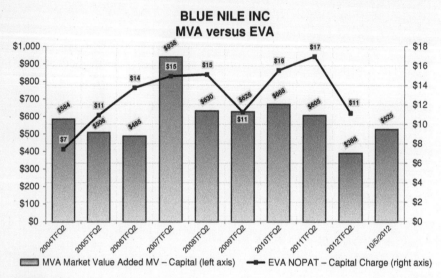

EXHIBIT 6.21   Blue Nile's MVA and EVA

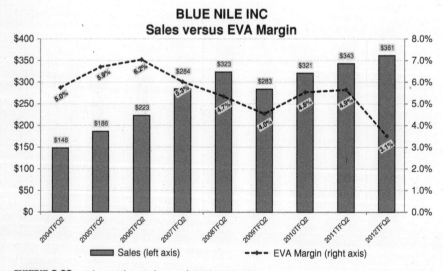

EXHIBIT 6.22   Blue Nile's Sales and EVA Margin

Surprisingly, Tiffany was not doing particularly well on EVA in the early years plotted on the charts. From mid-2000 to mid-2005, its sales and earnings per share (EPS) were growing but its EVA Margin and EVA were shrinking, and its MVA along with it. It is a classic example of where EVA and EPS differ, and EVA wins the argument. Although EVA has improved since then, MVA has shown inconclusive signs of life. The overall impression is that Tiffany has not developed a convincing upward EVA trend, nor has it posted a material long-run advance in owners' wealth. The tale is similar for Blue Nile, or even more so. While its sales and EPS were up, EVA Margin was generally down, and EVA and MVA sideslipped. Again it is clear that an absence of sustained EVA Momentum is a sure formula for wealth stagnation—in principle and in practice.

SUMMING UP THE EVA MARGIN

The EVA-to-sales ratio is the corporate equivalent of a grade point average. It is a summary performance score that neutralizes inherent differences in business models and capital intensity and cuts across all the categories of profitability and productivity that matter, and with each category weighted by how important it is. It elegantly unfolds in stages to reveal the full array of performance levers that managers can use to understand their firm's EVA performance, to spot notable trends, to benchmark with peers, to simulate decisions that involve trade-offs, and in general to gain a detailed understanding of how to tune up their business model and make it capable of generating more EVA profits and putting points on the EVA Momentum scoreboard.

In practice, any one company will personalize the general EVA Margin schedule we've developed. Our clients abbreviate it, reconfigure it, and undergird it with a set of company-specific metrics and milestones. The aim is to end with a comprehensive and multipurpose scorecard that is truly balanced, value aligned, and topped with a single score, and to use it for reviewing actual performance, to help managers to improve the value of plans and projects, and for setting performance targets, which is our next subject.

CHAPTER 7

Setting EVA Targets

One way the EVA ratio metrics pay huge dividends is through their role in setting targets. They are ideally suited for the purpose because, unlike other measures, EVA is value–additive and unaffected by differing business models. The experiences of many companies can legitimately be summed and rank ordered. Historical norms, tendencies, and correlations can be established with statistical significance. The expectations investors have factored into stock prices can be accurately gauged. All of this provides board directors and senior managers a big leg up in setting credible and quite usable performance goals—far more so than with other metrics.

As a practical matter, EVA performance goals need to be specified for a range of applications, and each requires a distinct approach, as outlined in the table in Exhibit 7.1.

One obvious application—which covers the top row in the table—is to set EVA targets as bogeys for determining incentive awards. This is a key

EXHIBIT 7.1 The EVA Target Table

	Strategic (10+ Years)	Medium–Term (3 to 5 Years)	Annual
Incentive plans	NA	Last year's EVA + targeted EVA growth	Last year's EVA (or weighted average EVA)
Business plan outputs	NA	Final plans converted to EVA performance targets	Final budgets converted to EVA performance targets
Business plan inputs	Aspirational EVA growth goal	Minimum expected EVA plan goals	Minimum expected EVA budget goals

to developing true pay–for–performance incentive plans that I'll discuss in a minute.

A second set of applications is developing EVA targets that correspond to the firm's business plans and its budgets, as is depicted on the middle row. Targets for EVA, EVA Margin, and EVA Momentum, and for the present value of the projected EVA, can be derived from the final business plans and used to succinctly express the performance essence of the strategy to the board and investors. This exercise becomes more effective as the process is repeated and management is able to gauge how actual performance and plan revisions compare to the EVA targets established in prior plans.

Management should also compute a set of EVA targets corresponding to its annual budget—broken down by quarter and by line of business—and carry those into the next year to serve as benchmarks for judging actual performance and assessing variances in quarterly performance reviews. The objective is to institute an ongoing management reporting and review process that is inherently EVA–centric and that takes full advantage of the EVA Momentum Pyramid and EVA Margin schedule as tools to help management pinpoint notable trends, shortfalls, and opportunities, and to develop appropriate plan revisions on the fly as a matter of proactive and value–focused corporate control. As these plan and budget targets are really an outgrowth of the planning process, they will be formally covered in the next chapter.

The last set of targets—shown as the bottom row on the table and labeled "Business plan inputs"—are used for planning guidance. Many CFOs find it helps to give line teams and directors a preliminary indication of the EVA performance objectives they expect to emerge from the planning process before the process begins in earnest. In effect, the CFO is making an opening bid on how much EVA the business plans should generate in the upcoming budget year and over a full three– to five–year horizon. Filing a preliminary EVA flight plan like that can help line teams better calibrate their planning efforts and cut down on planning iterations. It also very helpfully reinforces the notion that the ultimate aim of the planning process is to develop the strategies that are best capable of maximizing EVA Momentum, thus implying that everything else—at least in the longer term—is a variable that can be adjusted to achieve the overarching EVA Momentum goal.

Do not confuse what is happening here. Most management teams spend considerable time setting *activity* targets, along the lines of "our markets will expand like this, we will add these products and these facilities, we need to hire these people and take these initiatives," and so forth. This is a vital budgeting, scheduling, and coordinating process, and it must go on. What I am referring to is something different and too often neglected. It is budgeting for value creation, not for activity per se. I am asking managers to ask: "If we do all the activities we've laid out and reach all the mile-stones on our scorecard, what will it add up to in terms of a real economic profit score?" and even before that, to ask at the target setting stage: "What *should* all the activities sum to, and what is the *minimum acceptable* EVA growth trajectory that we need to aim at delivering?" It's a different question than most CFOs ask, but a vitally important one, and answering it requires a different set of inputs than budgeting and goal setting as usual.

There's one more potential EVA goal worth mentioning, which appears in the lower left cell in the table. It is rarely used, because it is so hard to do. The management team climbs to the top of a steep and remote mountain and returns with a strategic vision that is tangibly expressed in terms of a very long–term, even decade–long, aspirational target for growth in economic profit. Although not easy, it is not impossible to do, as I shall prove and illustrate, and the benefits can be truly massive.

Let's begin our discussion, though, in the diagonally opposed cell in the upper right corner of the target table. The question there is how to set appropriate EVA performance targets for annual bonuses. The EVA ratio statistics do not really need to come into play for this application, at least if you take my advice. I argued right from the start that the best way to structure an annual bonus plan is to set it equal to a competitive base bonus award plus a bonus kicker that is some percentage of the spread between this year's EVA and a formula–set target for EVA using lagging EVA results, where the simplest formula is just to set the target to the prior year's EVA. In view of the fact that EVA Momentum runs pretty close to zero for the modal firm in the market—the Russell 3000 median has averaged 0.2 percent a year—setting the EVA target to the prior year's actual EVA is actually sensible for many companies. It is simple, it is effective, and it is economically justified.

Although I covered this in the first chapter, I think it is worth revisiting the two big benefits that a bonus plan like this brings to the table that are above and beyond its simplicity and the incentive it introduces for managers to pay attention to EVA. One is that the EVA performance targets are decoupled from the budget or business plan goals. The idea is to pay for results, not intentions. Managers are no longer motivated to hold back and hedge, but are instead powerfully motivated to think for the long term and stretch for the outstanding performance achievements. Put simply, managers are motivated to think and act like charged–up and engaged owners, because they are paid like owners.

Another advantage to setting performance targets by formula is that it reduces tension and enhances collaboration. The board compensation committee and top management are no longer pitted as adversaries to negotiate annual performance targets, and top managers can count on subordinates to be more open, more strategic, and more capital conscientious in planning, and less engaged in posturing for short–term advantages. Everyone's on the same team when points are scored by increasing EVA and adding value.

EVA is the only measure where an automatically adjusting formula for setting the target can be used. EVA has been defined to eliminate or at least minimize accounting distortions—one–time events and tax gyrations are smoothed, reserve accruals are reversed, discretionary spending on intangibles is written off over time, and allowances are made for the time it takes strategic investments to ramp up. EVA is immune to the jarring distortions that afflict other measures and that require human intervention and judgment to be applied in setting targets for them. As I have said, simple measures make for complex conversations—about how to set targets for them in an ever–changing world. But with EVA, the goal is always very simple—more is better than less—so the target, and the bonus plan, can be very simple and thus very effective.

Another reason performance targets for EVA can be set so simply is that the capital charge in EVA automatically ratchets up or down as more or less capital is invested. It sets aside a priority return for the owners on any new capital that they furnish before management can start to earn any more bonus pay. Directors can relax, knowing that EVA has already done the negotiation for them when it comes to capital expansion. A director might protest by saying, "But we do not want to pay for just earning the cost of capital." EVA agrees. If new investments only just cover the cost of capital, there is no improvement in EVA and no extra bonus is paid. EVA will increase only to the extent that the cost of capital is exceeded. If it is exceeded only slightly, it won't turn into much of an added bonus. The bonus is directly proportional to how much value has been added by adding EVA, and there is nothing wrong with that.

Another safety valve, as it were, for the board is that if the formula–set EVA performance target turns out in hindsight to be too low or too high, and management is unfairly rewarded or penalized, the formula catches up the next year. The performance target going forward automatically incorporates the EVA of the prior year. A little patience is required, but only a little, to let the automatically adjusting formula work its magic. If this remains a significant concern, a feature can be added whereby a large part of any very large bonus is deferred and paid out over the next two to three years while being subject to forfeiture if EVA takes a big turn for the worse. I call it the contingent carryforward and cancellation clause. I wrote about it and recommended it in my 1991 book, *The Quest for Value*, and it remains a very good idea.

Sometimes I am asked how EVA performance goals correlate to earnings per share (EPS). They don't, but that is not a deficiency in EVA. It is a deficiency in EPS. If there was a direct and predictable link between EPS and

EVA, then you might just as well use EPS. But that's the whole point: there isn't. For any given EVA goal, EPS could grow faster or slower, but generally faster to an arbitrary degree that does not matter because the firm's P/E multiple will absorb the difference. For instance, a company's EPS could certainly grow faster than its EVA, almost without limit, by simply taking on more investments that just cover the cost of capital. In that case, EPS inflates where EVA just stands still. EBITDA is of course even worse—far worse, ridiculous in fact—because investments that generate *any* cash flow at all push it up, since there is never any charge for capital.

Management could borrow to buy back stock or to pay out surplus cash and gin up EPS without any effect on EVA. Management could sell assets and generate one–time gains in EPS that EVA considers as an ongoing reduction in capital. Management could temporarily cut back on reserve provisions, including tax reserves or credit reserves, or ease back the throttle on discretionary R&D and marketing, and give EPS a goose that EVA would not find funny. And so on into the night. The point is, EPS is a decidedly different, far more malleable, much less reliable measure than EVA, which is why setting a target for EPS is so difficult and why EPS bonus plans are so inferior.

To elaborate, suppose you prepare a business plan and take care to forecast all the ingredients that go into EPS. Then you can also compute the EVA implied by that same plan. But do not think that the EPS and EVA forecast so derived are somehow linked and equivalent. As I've said, there are any number of alternative EPS paths that will get to the same EVA, and any number of alternative EVA paths that would generate the same EPS. If you modify the forecast in such a way that the EPS projection changes but EVA remains the same, the value of the plan is the same, because value is always based on discounting EVA, as I have shown and will demonstrate more completely in the next chapter. The firm's price–to–earnings (P/E) ratio must therefore change in the opposite direction and in direct proportion as the EPS changes. They must just offset one another. Again, do not make the mistake of assuming the P/E multiples are fixed, and that stock prices move along with EPS. Stock prices follow economic value, EPS follows accounting rules, and the P/E multiple is there to pick up the slack.

As I have said before, simple measures like EPS—or EBITDA, ROI, or operating margin, for that matter—make for complicated conversations about how to set targets. There is actually no simple or sensible way to do it. If you go down that path, you are lost before you start. But with EVA, where more of it really is better than less, a bonus target to earn more EVA this year than last, while it sounds simplistic, is actually the most sophisticated and sensible way to do it. Boards should relax and let the care that goes into the EVA measure, the capital charge protection, and the automatic resetting of the EVA performance targets do the talking for them—at least insofar as annual bonus awards are concerned.

Now let's shift our gaze to the more difficult and interesting question of how to set targets for medium–range incentive plans. These are typically based on cumulative performance against three–year targets. Over longer horizons like that, it is reasonable for boards and top management to build an expectation for growth in EVA into the performance target. Over longer horizons, business cycles smooth out and a business's fundamental trajectory emerges more clearly. It is also the case that some companies are clearly positioned to increase EVA more than others over longer time frames, an expectation that is factored into their stock prices. Apple and Amazon, for example, have such strong franchises that their boards would be justified in incorporating a minimum EVA growth goal into the formulas for setting the EVA performance targets, and then to pay a larger, more motivating share of truly outstanding performance if the actual EVA growth exceeds the minimum growth goal.

Let me expand on that. The EVA performance target I recommend for each year in a three–year bonus plan is still the prior year's EVA, whatever that turns out to be, but now adding in an expected EVA growth increment each year. It is still a formula. It is still set in advance. It still has all the desirable features of the annual plan. The only difference is that the performance target incorporates a preset growth goal for EVA.

To take an example, let's first look at a three–year bonus plan that does not factor an EVA growth goal into the performance target. Suppose the performance target is simply the prior period's EVA, and suppose EVA increases from $100 to $110, $120, and $130 over the next three years. If that happened, the EVA targets would just be the prior year's EVA (i.e., the targets would just lag the actual EVA by one year). The EVA targets would be $100, $110, and $120, and thus the cumulative outperformance would be $30—the $10 excess each year summed over three years. That being the case, if the board wanted to invest $3 in the incentive plan to reward the team, the plan would be structured to pay 10 percent of the cumulative excess.

Suppose, though, that after studying the firm's EVA Momentum track record, its outlook, and the EVA Momentum implied by its stock price, the board mandates that a minimum annual EVA growth goal of $5 be added on top of the prior year's EVA. Assume again that EVA of $110, $120, and $130 materialize. Then the EVA performance targets would equal the lagging EVA plus five bucks—they would be stepped up to $105, $115, and $125 with the $5 growth mandate. The cumulative outperformance this time is just $15—it's half of $30 because $5 was added to the targets each year. The compensation committee can now ratchet up the incentive sharing rate. The bonus plan can now share 20 percent of the cumulative excess EVA above the targets instead of just 10 percent that was appropriate in the absence of the growth goal. It's a better incentive plan because it is a more leveraged plan. In exchange for cutting management out of a portion of the growth in EVA that is expected as a matter of course, the board can afford to motivate management with a larger share of the upside value added.

It's possible to have too much leverage, of course. In fact, I recommend caution here. Do not set the EVA growth goal so high that it is unrealistic and demotivating. Do not even set it so that it matches investor expectations for EVA growth reflected in the current share price. Set the growth mandate lower than that. Set it to less than the Market–Implied Momentum (MIM) rate. Setting the required performance bar higher doesn't actually make the EVA performance go higher. If that were true, set it to infinity. Setting the growth goal at a more conservative target, maybe half of a realistic EVA Momentum expectation or MIM rate, for example, and thus with plenty of legroom to exceed it, is generally the best way to get real buy–in and a real commitment and enthusiasm among the management team to reach and stretch and actually maximize EVA—which is the real goal here. It will certainly be a lot more challenging, and all around more rewarding than a bonus plan based on cumulative EPS or EBITDA or ROI against negotiated targets.

Remember, also, even for rolling three–year incentive plans, I recommend that the performance target for each year be based off the EVA actually achieved in the prior year (plus the growth increment), so that if management for some reason greatly exceeds the target one year (or falls way short), the standard of excellence for the next year is set higher (or lower). This is an important protection built into the plans. When there is an unexpected surge in EVA, the growth is fed back into the performance target, albeit with a lag. The target always catches up with the actual EVA so that the long–term expected bonus is always equal to the target bonus award, yet all the while there is an incentive to increase EVA as much as possible. This self–corrective feature is why Ball Corporation could have essentially the same EVA bonus plan for 20 years and running.

In these examples I have expressed an EVA growth mandate in money terms. As we'll see, EVA growth targets are actually established using the EVA Momentum statistic, a percentage growth goal, but it is always a simple matter to make the conversion (or the bonus plan can be converted to measure and grade performance purely in terms of EVA Momentum rather than going back and forth). For example, say a minimum growth target of 1 percent EVA Momentum is established. That says that the growth mandate is $1 million in added EVA for every $100 million in lagging sales. It's as simple as that.

In sum, the challenge for medium–term incentive plans is to establish the projected EVA Momentum rate that looks reasonable and achievable, that stacks up favorably against peers and the company's market potential, and that is consistent with the stock price and owner expectations. That's a tall order, and it will require judgment. Having reliable facts at hand is certainly a prerequisite. They're coming.

I hesitate to mention it, but it is also possible to set EVA bonus performance targets as a function of the performance of a peer group. In a bonus plan like this, the EVA performance target is set equal to the company's prior EVA plus an adjustment for the EVA movement in the peer group. The adjustment could simply equal the firm's prior sales times the EVA Momentum achieved by the median firm in the peer group in the period. For instance, if the firm's prior EVA was –$100 and its sales were $10,000, and the median peer EVA Momentum turned out to be +2 percent, then the target for judging the firm's EVA in the current year would be –$100 + ($10,000 × 2%) = +$100. In other words, we'd expect to see a big improvement in EVA before paying any upside bonuses because the median peer firm came on so strongly. On the other hand, if the median peer had a bad year—perhaps this is 2009 when EVAs typically tumbled with the market meltdown—management would not be penalized for even a dramatic downturn in EVA given that it was a common industry experience. If the median firm's EVA Momentum was, say, –2 percent, then the EVA target that year would be –$100 + ($10,000 × –2%) = –$300.

One firm that follows an approach like this is Advance Auto Parts. Portions of its proxy describing the plan are reproduced here.

LONG–TERM INCENTIVE COMPENSATION PLAN FOR ADVANCE AUTO PARTS

Our executives receive long–term incentive compensation intended to link their compensation to the Company's long–term financial success.

We introduced performance–based vesting into our long–term incentive program in 2008. EVA was adopted as the performance measure because we believe it is the measure most strongly aligned with the creation of long–term stockholder value. For purposes of this program, EVA is defined as operating profit after taxes ("After–Tax Operating Earnings"), less a charge for cost of capital as calculated on our total debt and equity ("Total Invested Capital") during the three–year performance period.

The Company utilizes an independent consultant to prepare objective EVA performance calculations for the Company and its peer group companies for each performance period. Grants of performance–based SARs [stock appreciation rights] and restricted stock made in 2009 and 2010 will be earned based on our EVA performance as compared to the EVA performance of the companies in our peer group for the 2010–2012 and 2011–2013 performance periods.

AutoZone	LKQ Corp.	Sherwin–Williams
Bed Bath & Beyond	OfficeMax	Tractor Supply
Dollar General	O'Reilly Automotive	Uni–Select
Dollar Tree	Pep Boys Manny Moe & Jack	Wesco Intl.
Family Dollar	PetSmart	Williams–Sonoma
Fastenal	RadioShack	W.W. Grainger
Genuine Parts		

We believe the use of a peer group for these grants increases alignment of long–term incentive compensation earned by executives with stockholder value created relative to that of the peer companies. For the 2008, 2009, and 2010 grants, a minimum absolute level of EVA performance for the respective three–year performance period must be achieved in order for any performance–based award to be earned. The awards granted in December 2011 do not include a minimum absolute level of EVA for the performance period because the Committee believes the EVA performance relative to the defined peer group is an adequate performance requirement and the awards are already aligned with our absolute EVA performance because they are in the form of SARs and restricted stock.

As the Company's EVA performance exceeds the 40th percentile of peer group companies and approaches the 80th percentile of peer group companies, more SARs and shares of restricted stock vest. Executive officers may receive additional SARs and shares of restricted stock up to a maximum of an additional 100 percent of the target level award if the Company's EVA performance meets or exceeds the EVA performance of 80 percent of the peer group companies.

April 16, 2012 Proxy Filing of Advanced Auto Parts, Inc.

The Advance Auto Parts board chose to index the performance targets in order to reward management when it outperforms its peer group and to insulate management from downturns that are out of its control—which are real advantages. The drawback is that the bonuses cannot be computed until the year is up and data on the peer–group performance is available (though projections throughout the year can help fill that gap). A benefit of setting the EVA performance target by a formula using lagging EVA is that the target is totally predictable in advance of the year and even stretching out for multiple years. Managers can compute the bonus they are accumulating each quarter through the year, and they can simulate the bonus they would earn over the full life of a forward plan. That is an important benefit, but it comes with exposing management to industry cycles. As in many things, there is no one right answer, only trade–offs the board will have to weigh.

Before moving on, I am obliged to state, once again, that neither I nor EVA Dimensions is in the business of actually designing incentive plans for our clients. We certainly provide guidance and insights into best practices based on our experiences. Our software tools and databases are also incredibly helpful in setting the targets and gauging performance relative to custom peer groups and simulating the valuation impact. But we do not design bonus plans. That is a business servicing right I left behind at Stern Stewart when I spun out and acquired the EVA Dimensions business in 2006.

The last target I want to discuss is an inspirational stretch target for long–term growth in EVA—a growth goal extending out over a decade. Such long–term targets are seldom used, but can be incredibly powerful. Granted, not all companies will need or want to do this. For some, it is just too early in their life cycles. Others may not have the ability or confidence to tackle such a proposition. But it can be an amazing stimulant and risk–management propellant that really gets the top team—and directors—thinking out of the box and anticipating change before it needs to happen.

One company that has done this, and done it very well, is Coca–Cola. As is depicted in the chart in Exhibit 7.2, taken from a management presentation to investors (page 23), Coke uses EVA Momentum as the means of structuring and stimulating internal conversations about business strategy and, in this case, for communicating the essence of its long–range strategic vision to its board and investors.

Coke's management sat down as a senior leadership team several years ago to chart out a long–term strategic plan that they call the "2020 Vision." The gist of it is expressed in Exhibit 7.2. It conveys the salient fact that management's foremost financial goal—the one at the top of the pyramid—is to achieve long–run growth in economic profit (i.e., in EVA) in excess of 10 percent a year, on average and over a decade ending in 2020. It is not exactly EVA Momentum, but it is the same idea—maximizing sustained

EXHIBIT 7.2 Coca–Cola Depicts Its Vision with EVA Momentum
The information contained on this slide was included as part of a presentation dated August 2012. A copy of the full presentation, including important information about certain forward–looking statements, is available at http://d11wft0f0qzya1.cloudfront .net/2a/e6/ddfba0314dbebe11cc4d8b927556/IR-Overview.pdf.

growth in economic profit is the key strategic planning target and the measure of the overall quality and value of the plan. It is the apex measure, the *Unum*, the one. And it is a fantastic stretch target to announce. But why did management do it?

For one, publicly stating a long–range EVA growth goal credibly conveys top management's commitment to and confidence in actually achieving it. As an investor, you know their hearts are in the right place, and their heads are in the EVA game. Management is clearly focused on delivering measurable value added above other measures. You can have all the investor meetings you like and not get anywhere near the mileage you would from making a public commitment like that.

An inspirational long–range EVA goal also helps energize the company's troops. It counterbalances the tendency to go heads down on the quarter and the year at hand, and promotes proactive engagement in the question of how to engineer a quantum leap forward in economic profit performance over a longer horizon. It opens new vistas in thinking about growth opportunities, in thinking about risk, and in thinking about how to improve EVA, with all the levers it offers.

More concretely, it motivates managers to ask: "How much can we improve our EVA Margin, and can we get it to the point where sales growth is a valuable lever if we are not there yet? How much real profitable growth remains in what we are doing? At what point do we have to branch out, and how would we best do that? What role could or should acquisitions play?"

The long–term goal creates an environment where instead of protecting turf and fighting zero–sum political games, managers realize the real opportunity for personal growth lies in building valuable businesses. And the greater the extent to which the top team can paint an exciting EVA growth story, the more likely it is to attract the talent and the ideas to get there, and the more willing investors will be to pay a premium for the stock—and sooner rather than later. The idea is: let's create a virtuous cycle of value creation.

Coke actually goes a lot further than just communicating the overall Momentum goal—although that alone is very striking. What makes the goal particularly credible is that management proceeds from the *Unum* to the *Pluribus*, from the one mission to the many metrics, telling the world how it plans to do it, at least in broad strokes, at the outset dividing the EVA growth goal into the two main categories I have advocated (on the chart, Coke puts productivity gains on the right and profitable growth on the left, but it is the sum that matters, not the layout). They've laid the EVA Momentum math on the table for everyone to see.

It is arresting, too, that Coke's management is able to assign specific proportions and targets to the Momentum components—30 percent is slated to come from productivity gains and 70 percent from profitable growth. That's sensible, though. Coke's EVA Margin is already so high that further improvements are not going to be easy, although Coke will try—3 percent of the 10 percent growth in EVA is due to come from making the business engine run smoother and cleaner. The bulk of the opportunity—accounting for 7 percent of the 10 percent EVA growth—is due to come from making the engine run faster by scaling and extending the firm's fantastically profitable business model.

Coke's management has also personalized the Momentum schedule—as I always advocate—in this case into five subcategories that tie to the firm's long–range objectives and business model, with Momentum quotas assigned to each, and supplemented with specific underlying winning metrics. It is a fantastic example of what I have in mind. It is a strategic scorecard that consolidates all elements into an overarching financial goal and that

We are On Track and Delivering Results

Measure	2020 Vision	2010 & 2011 Results
Volume Growth	Ahead of Long-Term Target	✓
Revenue Growth	Ahead of Long-Term Target	✓
Economic Profit Growth	Target 10%+ CAGR	✓
Share Gains	Value Share Gains Ahead of Volume Share Gains	✓

EXHIBIT 7.3 EVA Momentum on the Coca–Cola Scorecard
The information contained on this slide was included as part of a presentation dated August 2012. A copy of the full presentation, including important information about certain forward–looking statements, is available at http://d1lwft0f0qzya1.cloudfront .net/2a/e6/ddfba0314dbebe11cc4d8b927556/IR-Overview.pdf.

deconstructs to reveal all the relevant strategic and operational drivers that make up the plan. Please, study it at your leisure. I think it represents an ideal hybrid of the balanced scorecard and EVA.

It is worth noting, although it is little off the subject at hand, that EVA Momentum is not just a financial tool that Coke uses to quantify and communicate the goals of its strategic plan to key constituencies, although it is plainly that. It is also a format Coke's management apparently employs to organize how it thinks about strategy, and how line teams are engaged in a collaborative effort to develop the best possible long–range plans—where *best possible* now has a clear and unambiguous meaning. It is to achieve the greatest sustainable growth in quality EVA profits of which the organization is capable. And when Coke management goes about reviewing the firm's actual performance, EVA Momentum is the key financial metric on the checklist (see Exhibit 7.3). It is a closed–loop system, with value alignment, accountability, and simplicity throughout.

Although Coke's announced target is specifically for a growth rate in EVA, I will argue that in general it is best to set EVA growth targets or performance goals in terms of Momentum. For one thing, a growth rate is meaningless where EVA is negligible or negative, which is true of at least half the companies on the market. Coke can get away with it because it happens to be endowed with a very positive EVA (and Coke adopted the growth goal before EVA Momentum really came on the scene), but for many companies, and certainly many divisions within companies, that is not true. Another reason to prefer EVA Momentum is that it provides all the analytical machinery to manage the growth in EVA—the Momentum Pyramid and the EVA Margin schedule, for example—whereas the growth in EVA does not.

With this backdrop, let's now formally turn to the question of how to set EVA Momentum targets—whether for a long–term aspirational goal as Coke has done or as a preliminary business plan and budget targets or as an expected growth component to bake into medium–range incentive plan targets.

My counsel is to always start with the EVA Momentum math. Run a few simple scenarios to get a feel for the zip code you are in. For instance, suppose your company currently has an EVA Margin of 1 percent. Suppose an analysis of competitor profitability and market position and opportunities for improving the underlying drivers suggests that the EVA Margin could reach as high as 4 percent over five years, and suppose further that 10 percent sales growth is a reasonable stretch expectation. Then the corresponding five–year plan goal is to produce a per annum average EVA Momentum of 1 percent—0.6 percent per year from expanding the EVA Margin by 3 percent over the five years, plus 0.4 percent from the 10 percent sales growth rate at the ending 4 percent EVA Margin. The EVA Momentum math makes it a straightforward exercise to simulate strategic financial goals as an outgrowth of planned productivity improvements and expected sales growth.

Of course, this simple logic should be used only to get a first–pass, ball-park indication. Management will need to vet the goal with a detailed understanding of opportunities to improve the EVA Margin and to exploit the growth potential in its markets. In addition, though, and as a reality check and to gain perspective, management should also place its EVA Momentum goal in the context of the statistical track record for momentum and the expectations for it that can be read from stock prices. Let's now dig into those reference points.

The distribution of EVA Momentum achieved by the Russell 3000 companies for rolling four–quarter intervals is plotted on the upper left chart in Exhibit 7.4 for the decade and a quarter ending in mid–2012. It's the

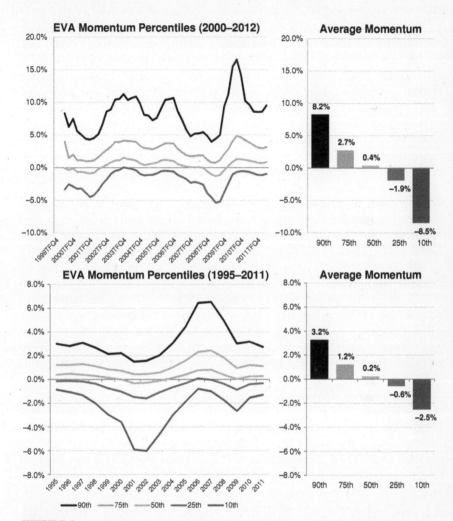

EXHIBIT 7.4 The EVA Momentum Record—One–Year versus Five–Year Intervals

continuous track record of EVA ups and downs by period. The bottom chart, though, is more relevant for setting targets. It presents the average annual EVA Momentum achieved over running five–year intervals from 1995 through 2011 fiscal years. At any point it is computed by taking the five–year trailing change in EVA and dividing by sales six years back, and then dividing by 5 to convert it to an annual average rate. It's equivalent to the annual EVA Momentum that would have been computed from business plans set forth five years before—which makes it a relevant benchmark for setting long–range targets.

The bottom chart also *excludes* certain companies in order to make the results even more relevant for setting plan targets. Biotech companies are left out because as a group they dominate the upper and lower EVA Momentum reaches. They either catch a fever or catch a cold. Thirteen of them averaged momentum over 50 percent per annum and 14 under –100 percent over the five–year span ending mid–2012, for example. All oil and gas wildcatters—simply defined as oil and gas firms with revenues under $1 billion—are excluded from the sample because they explode like supernovas if they strike oil, and turn to white dwarfs if they don't. And in like spirit, all firms with revenues under $100 million are removed because the successful ones that break out of the venture stage skew the EVA Momentum results in the upper reaches. And for this purpose all financial institutions, including real estate firms, have been set aside to focus on just operating companies. What remains are about 1,750 companies that represent the EVA Momentum distribution for reasonably established materials, manufacturing, consumer, services, technology, transportation, distribution, and utilities firms.

Compare the bottom and top charts. EVA Momentum is far more compacted around the median when it is averaged over the five–year spans than when it is measured year to year (note that that the five–year scale is about half that of the annual chart). For example, EVA Momentum for the 90th percentile firm averaged 8.2 percent per year measured year by year, but it was only an average of 3.2 percent per year over running five–year spans. The 10th percentile averaged –8.5 percent by year and it was an average of –2.5 percent over five years. Some of the compression reflects the design of the two sample sets; a number of the more explosive biotech, wildcat, and start–up outliers have been excluded from the five–year record but not the one–year record. Another reason is that business–cycle swings tend to flatten out over longer horizons. Standing here today, the economic downturn of late 2008 and into 2009 has only a slight lingering effect on the five–year EVA Momentum from mid–2007 to mid–2012, for instance. And also, more significantly, hot performers tend to cool as their markets mature and competition becomes more intense, and weakly performing companies are galvanized to improve, restructure, and reverse a bout of unsatisfactory Momentum results.

The tendency for extremes to gravitate toward the middle is called regression to the mean, and it is everywhere in nature, including in the tendency of companies that deviate from the norm to be magnetically attracted to the center. And this is the primary reason why the five–year EVA Momentum provides the most useful reference points for setting planning targets—not just because companies plan out five years, and not just because five–year intervals tend to average out the business cycle. The chief reason is that reversion to the mean is a real force to be reckoned with. The average of the average EVA Momentum over five years is thus the relevant statistical norm, and for convenience it is shown again in Exhibit 7.5.

Median EVA Momentum—the gravitational center of the EVA Momentum universe—has averaged just 0.2 percent per annum over rolling five–year intervals. The firm running in the middle of the pack has delivered only a very slight rise in its EVA over time, as economic theory and mean reversion predict. Accordingly, setting a strategic EVA Momentum goal of zero percent or just slightly positive may sound puny, but is in fact quite reasonable for many companies. It's the management equivalent of the Hippocratic oath—to do no harm. To grow sales while just covering the cost of capital and without decreasing EVA is to meet the market mission at a minimum, and will outperform about 40 percent to 50 percent of the firms on the market at any time.

A more ambitious goal would be the 75th percentile—which calls for a sustained five–year average EVA Momentum of 1.2 percent. The 90th

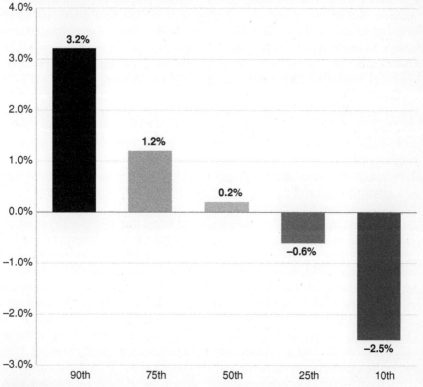

EXHIBIT 7.5 Five–Year Cumulative Average EVA Momentum by Percentiles

percentile runs at a 3.2 percent per year average rate. Memorably, these are 1 percent and 3 percent more than the median rate. An extra 1 percent EVA Momentum may not seem all that consequential, but it really is. Depending on the company, sustaining an extra 1 percent EVA Momentum each year over five years is worth anywhere from a 25 percent to a 100 percent increase in stock price!

Let's run the math. Suppose sales are $100. An extra 1 percent EVA Momentum per year sums to 5 percent more over five years, which leads in steps to an extra $5 in EVA by the fifth projection year. If the cost of capital is 8 percent, the present value of the extra $5 in EVA in perpetuity is $62.50 per every $100 in current sales. That overstates the value a bit, because it takes five years to build up to the full extra EVA, but you get the idea. Even a little extra EVA Momentum goes a long way to adding value if it is sustainable.

The impact of increasing EVA Momentum is not the same for all firms. A bump up in Coca–Cola's momentum adds a lot less to its stock price than for the modal firm on the market. Coke is so profitable, and so valuable, and so conservatively financed, and its equity market capitalization is so massive, that its stock price simply responds far less to a given tick in its momentum than most of the stocks of most other firms. I've estimated that Coke's Momentum Leverage Ratio (MLR), as I call it, is only about 23×. This means that a 1 percent annual increase in momentum sustained over five years is worth a 23 percent higher stock price today.

MLRs for most companies, by contrast, fall in a range of 30× to 80×. The general observation is that generating an extra 1 percent EVA Momentum, moving from the 50th to 75th percentile in EVA growth quality, can be profoundly valuable; going to the 90th percentile, immensely so. I strongly suggest you estimate your company's Momentum Leverage Ratio. It will show you how important it is to get the EVA Momentum target right and how rewarding it can be if you achieve it. You will see how to estimate it in the upcoming planning chapter.

The table in Exhibit 7.6 gives a feel for firms that recently knocked on the threshold of upper–quartile EVA Momentum. It lists all firms falling between the 74th and 76th percentiles for EVA Momentum over the five years ending in fiscal 2011. It is a motley crew. The group includes IT giants like Accenture and IBM, healthcare companies like Becton Dickinson, industrial firms like Timken and Valmont, retailers like AutoZone and Overstock. com, casinos, utilities, transport companies, and many more, with sales from $100 million to over $100 billion and EVA Margins from −5.4 percent to +13.4 percent. And which company, by pure chance, claimed the exact 75th percentile slot? Tiffany & Co., with average annual EVA Momentum of 1.1 percent—very close to (just a little shy of) the typical 1.2 percent EVA Momentum pace of the 75th percentile performer since 1995.

Company	Industry	Percentile	2011 EVA Mo 5-Yr Cum Avg	2011 Sales	2011 EVA Margin	2011 EVA Momentum
HACKETT GROUP	IT Services	75.9%	1.2%	$225	−1.8%	1.5%
WESTERN REFINING	Oil Gas & Consumable Fuels	75.9%	1.2%	$9,071	4.7%	5.2%
ACCENTURE	IT Services	75.8%	1.2%	$27,353	6.7%	1.8%
NEUSTAR	IT Services	75.8%	1.2%	$620	13.0%	−1.4%
DEERE	Conglomerates & Machinery	75.7%	1.1%	$29,466	6.1%	2.5%
ISLE OF CAPRI CASINOS	Hotels Resorts & Cruise lines	75.6%	1.1%	$968	0.2%	1.3%
MULTIMEDIA GAMES	Hotels Resorts & Cruise lines	75.6%	1.1%	$128	−2.4%	11.1%
PRECISION CASTPARTS	Aerospace & Defense	75.5%	1.1%	$7,215	9.6%	1.9%
HELEN OF TROY LTD	Household Durables	75.5%	1.1%	$1,182	2.9%	0.6%
ICU MEDICAL	Health Care Equipment & Supplies	75.4%	1.1%	$302	8.9%	1.8%
OVERSTOCK.COM	Internet & Catalog Retail	75.3%	1.1%	$1,054	−1.9%	−1.7%
EXLSERVICE	IT Services	75.3%	1.1%	$361	3.8%	1.2%
TIMKEN	Conglomerates & Machinery	75.2%	1.1%	$5,170	2.9%	3.5%
BECTON DICKINSON	Health Care Equipment & Supplies	75.2%	1.1%	$7,829	9.9%	0.9%
VALMONT INDUSTRIES	Conglomerates & Machinery	75.1%	1.1%	$2,661	3.6%	1.8%
EL PASO ELECTRIC	Electric Utilities	75.1%	1.1%	$914	4.0%	1.1%
TIFFANY	Specialty Retail	75.0%	1.1%	$3,643	5.8%	1.5%
VIACOM	Media	74.9%	1.1%	$14,914	8.8%	15.7%
PEGASYSTEMS	Software	74.9%	1.1%	$417	0.3%	−1.1%
CHURCH & DWIGHT	Household & Personal Products	74.8%	1.1%	$2,749	6.3%	0.2%
CARMIKE CINEMAS	Media	74.8%	1.1%	$482	−4.3%	2.5%
INNOSPEC	Chemicals	74.7%	1.1%	$774	4.2%	0.9%
AUTOZONE	Specialty Retail	74.7%	1.1%	$8,073	8.7%	1.7%
GRAHAM	Conglomerates & Machinery	74.5%	1.1%	$103	7.2%	5.0%
PORTLAND GENERAL ELECTRIC	Electric Utilities	74.5%	1.1%	$1,813	4.0%	1.6%
CHESAPEAKE UTILITIES	Gas Utilities	74.5%	1.1%	$418	4.0%	0.3%
IRON MOUNTAIN	Commercial Services & Supplies	74.4%	1.1%	$3,015	1.9%	1.4%
PRICESMART	Food & Staples Retailing	74.4%	1.1%	$1,714	1.9%	0.8%
INTL BUSINESS MACHINES	IT Services	74.3%	1.1%	$106,916	7.3%	1.8%
DSW	Specialty Retail	74.2%	1.1%	$2,024	0.7%	2.0%
THERMO FISHER SCIENTIFIC	Life Sciences Tools & Services	74.2%	1.1%	$11,726	−3.2%	0.5%
GENESEE & WYOMING	Freight Transportation	74.1%	1.1%	$829	3.7%	2.4%
BROOKDALE SENIOR LIVING	Health Care Providers & Services	74.1%	1.1%	$2,458	−5.4%	1.6%
WOODWARD	Conglomerates & Machinery	74.0%	1.1%	$1,712	4.0%	2.3%

EXHIBIT 7.6 Companies at the 75th Percentile in Five–Year Momentum

The 90th percentile performers comprise an even more elite group. The average five–year EVA Momentum for the 90th percentile firm was 2.7 percent a year over this five–year interval, which is a little lower than typical (recall that the average over all five–year cycles since 1995 has been 3.2 percent). It is still clearly over the 75th percentile mark, in this case, by an annual average EVA Momentum pace of 1.6 percent per annum. And you know what that means: a lot more EVA and a lot more added value were produced by these firms. The table in Exhibit 7.7 lists firms in the vicinity of the 90th percentile slot, which is occupied by another retailer, Pier 1 Imports. Its EVA Margin ended up nowhere near as high as Tiffany's, but the company came from much further behind. Pier 1, frankly, was resurrected from a near–death experience.

Company	Industry	Percentile	2011 EVA Mo 5-Yr Cum Avg	2011 Sales	2011 EVA Margin	2011 EVA Momentum
AMERICAN WATER WORKS	Utilities-Other	91.0%	3.0%	$2,666	−1.0%	1.1%
COACH	Textiles Apparel & Luxury Goods	90.9%	3.0%	$4,159	17.6%	3.2%
STILLWATER MINING	Metals & Mining	90.9%	3.0%	$906	4.1%	9.9%
INTERDIGITAL	Communications Equipment	90.8%	3.0%	$302	31.9%	−19.2%
SS&C TECHNOLOGIES	Software	90.7%	3.0%	$371	−12.9%	2.2%
STAMPS.COM	Internet Software & Services	90.7%	3.0%	$102	−30.2%	9.0%
AGILENT TECHNOLOGIES	Life Sciences Tools & Services	90.6%	2.9%	$6,626	8.5%	4.3%
CONCEPTUS	Health Care Equipment & Supplies	90.6%	2.9%	$127	−10.4%	−6.8%
ATMEL	Semiconductors & Equipment	90.5%	2.9%	$1,803	0.2%	6.1%
NETAPP	Computers & Peripherals	90.5%	2.9%	$6,233	9.4%	−0.1%
ARUBA NETWORKS	Communications Equipment	90.4%	2.9%	$397	0.3%	4.1%
J2 GLOBAL	Internet Software & Services	90.3%	2.8%	$340	18.5%	6.4%
MAXWELL TECHNOLOGIES	Electronics and Office Equipment	90.3%	2.9%	$157	−7.9%	2.1%
ALLEGIANT TRAVEL	Airlines	90.2%	2.8%	$779	4.8%	−2.1%
FLIR SYSTEMS	Electronics and Office Equipment	90.2%	2.8%	$1,544	7.3%	−2.0%
LORILLARD	Tobacco	90.1%	2.7%	$4,452	26.2%	2.4%
LAS VEGAS SANDS	Hotels Resorts & Cruise lines	90.0%	2.7%	$9,411	4.5%	8.5%
PIER 1 IMPORTS	Specialty Retail	90.0%	2.7%	$1,534	2.5%	2.8%
CRYOLIFE	Health Care Equipment & Supplies	89.9%	2.7%	$120	2.7%	−0.8%
OCLARO	Communications Equipment	89.9%	2.7%	$467	−20.4%	−3.5%
ANSYS	Software	89.8%	2.7%	$691	6.3%	5.6%
PERRIGO	Pharmaceuticals	89.8%	2.7%	$2,755	4.6%	2.4%
SUN HYDRAULICS	Conglomerates & Machinery	89.7%	2.7%	$204	14.6%	9.9%
II–VI	Electrical Equipment	89.6%	2.7%	$503	8.2%	7.5%
LINEAR TECHNOLOGY	Semiconductors & Equipment	89.6%	2.7%	$1,484	34.4%	12.3%
BRUKER	Life Sciences Tools & Services	89.5%	2.7%	$1,652	3.9%	−0.1%
DREAMWORKS ANIMATION	Media	89.5%	2.6%	$706	2.5%	16.8%
EDWARDS LIFESCIENCES	Health Care Equipment & Supplies	89.4%	2.6%	$1,679	8.4%	1.6%
PIONEER NATURAL	Oil Gas & Consumable Fuels	89.4%	2.6%	$2,294	6.3%	0.1%
WATERS	Life Sciences Tools & Services	89.3%	2.6%	$1,851	15.8%	3.6%
MICROCHIP TECHNOLOGY	Semiconductors & Equipment	89.2%	2.5%	$1,383	18.8%	−3.6%
NEOGEN	Health Care Equipment & Supplies	89.2%	2.5%	$184	7.5%	−0.5%
JDA SOFTWARE GROUP	Software	89.1%	2.5%	$691	0.6%	1.5%
WALTER ENERGY	Metals & Mining	89.1%	2.5%	$2,571	5.9%	−8.5%
MICROSOFT	Software	89.0%	2.5%	$69,943	24.8%	3.9%

EXHIBIT 7.7　Companies at the 90th Percentile in Five–Year Momentum

In fiscal 2006 Pier 1 had sales of $1.6 billion, but an EVA Margin of *minus* 11.2 percent, an EVA *loss* of $180 million, and an MVA of just $54 million. Its market value barely exceeded its book capital, and even that was a generous valuation given the circumstances. The company was hurting, badly. And now? For its most recent fiscal year ending February 2012, Pier 1's EVA Margin was *plus* 2.8 percent and EVA was $38 million in the black. MVA hit $1.24 billion as the stock surged to $17.17 at its 2012 fiscal year close from $6.79 at year–end 2006. Now that is wealth creation par excellence.

The firm recruited Alex Smith, a 30–year retail veteran, as president and CEO in February 2007. He ran a basic turnaround playbook: get Pier 1 back to its roots as a great merchant, restructure and rightsize, and execute like crazy. Stores were closed, leases renegotiated, the headquarters building sold for a profit, catalogs and online sales were killed, and marketing was slashed, but great people were hired. The number of buyers, planners, and "allocators"—the specialists responsible for stocking Pier 1 with one–of–a–kind merchandise and keeping the assortment just right—was tripled. It is called resource allocation. Put money where it will produce the most EVA.

Pier 1 has done an outstanding job to get where it is, but here's the rub. The entire EVA Momentum—and then some—over the five years was due to the improvements in the EVA Margin. It has been all productivity gains and no growth. Unsure of the firm's next steps, investors have now pegged the stock at a MIM value that predicts EVA will increase at only a pedestrian 0.2 percent EVA Momentum rate going forward. That would be consistent with generating 5 percent to 7 percent sales growth at the current 2.8 percent EVA Margin. That's not terrible. As I said, aiming for any positive EVA growth isn't fundamentally bad. But it sure is a comedown from the 90th percentile EVA Momentum of the past five years. Pier 1 offers a great example of the regression to the mean phenomenon. A turnaround, once accomplished, can leave an even harder task, and often a question mark, in its wake.

Although tech firms tend to dominate around the 90th percentile, a notable exception is the amazing Sun Hydraulics, at the 89.7th percentile. It is a Sarasota, Florida, manufacturer of valves that generates sales of around $200 million with 700 employees. The success key so far has been a highly informal management style that puts great faith in decentralizing decisions to an empowered and very carefully hired workforce. From 2006 to year–end 2011, its sales were up 40 percent and EVA was up to $30 million from $11 million. The firm's EVA Margin was a truly outstanding 14.6 percent, compared to an already very solid 7.6 percent EVA Margin five years before. MVA tripled, from $150 million to $450 million. Still, the market thinks the time for basking in the sun is over. The forward–looking EVA Momentum implied by the firm's share value is not good. Sun's stock is currently priced for *minus* 0.2 percent EVA Momentum—another example of convergence magnetically pulling incremental EVA growth to the flat–line norm—or worse. It's a firm to watch, if only to see how far its unique management model can go, particularly now that the market is betting against it.

Putting aside Sun and Pier 1 and a very few others, the 90th percentile club is dominated by software, semiconductor, electronics, health care, life sciences, pharmaceutical, communications, and Internet—the intellectual capital concerns. On this scant but suggestive evidence, it seems that to produce a truly outstanding, upper–decile EVA Momentum performance, a firm has got to be either riding (or even better, driving) a real innovation wave, engineering a superb turnaround, hiring really great people and setting them loose, or possessing a truly unique approach to managing and growing a business. Running a business like everyone else, only trying to do it a little better, may get you to the 75th percentile. But the 90th percentile? Forget about it.

Sector clearly matters. The potential for increasing EVA is certainly shaped in some degree by industry characteristics. Witness the table in Exhibit 7.8, which lists the firms with sales over $1 billion that generated the highest five–year Momentum for the period ending mid–2012 in each of 52 industries that EVA Dimensions regularly tracks (I am switching here from looking at Momentum measured over five reporting years to Momentum spanning five trailing four–quarter years ending in mid–2012, which is more up–to–date). Momentum ranges from a 22.8 percent per annum average for Apple to a slightly negative EVA Momentum for Jones Lang LaSalle—the best–performing real estate management firm.

The industries represented at the top of the table are chiefly involved in the newer tech sectors, while the ones at the bottom hail from the long–established, less differentiated, and more intensely competitive end of the spectrum. Even the best paper company, Domtar (#44), put up just a 1.2 percent Momentum average; the best airline, JetBlue (#46), delivered only 1.2 percent, and the best food and staples retailer, Whole Foods Market (#48), rang up but 0.6 percent. Those are not bad results, but they are the very best results in those businesses. The evidence confirms the intuition: some sectors are more amenable, and others more challenging, for generating sustained EVA growth.

Momentum also varies within industry groups in ways that should influence how performance targets are set. As examples, the two charts in Exhibit 7.9 plot the distribution of the five–year EVA Momentum ending mid–2012 for all 74 software and all 95 specialty retail firms in the Russell 3000 with five years of data, regardless of size.

The software group portrait is representative of tech firms in general. One typical trait is an above–average performance profile. The group *median* EVA Momentum is 1 percent, well above the 0.2 percent that is the 50th percentile norm. Momentum also rises steeply from left to right, from lower to upper percentiles, with distant outliers at either end. Plus and minus outcomes are widely dispersed, as competing strategies either win big or lose big. It's do or die in businesses like these. The specialty retail firms exhibit a contrasting pattern that is typical of more established businesses—modest and more normal performance. The median EVA Momentum is 0.3 percent and the slope from left to right is far gentler, with only one outlier on the upside—Winmark, an emerging franchisor of retail store concepts with only $50 million in revenues. Established businesses like retailing provide fewer degrees of freedom to break out one way or another. Put another way, the 10th to the 90th percentile EVA Momentum wingspan is about 2 percent in retail and is much wider, about 6 percent, among the code writers. It takes more Momentum to reach

	Company (as of Mid-Year 2012)	Industry	(A) Cum Avg EVA Mo 5 TFQs (B)+(E)/5	(B) Δ EVA Margin 5 TFQs (C)−(D)	(C) EVA Margin	(D) EVA Margin 5 TFQs Back	(E) Profitable Growth 5 TFQs (C)x(F)	(F) Sales Growth 5 TFQ Cum
1	APPLE	Computers & Peripherals	22.8%	7.5%	19.1%	11.6%	106.2%	558%
2	PRICELINE.COM	Internet & Catalog Retail	18.4%	24.1%	22.9%	−1.3%	67.8%	296%
3	VERISIGN	Internet Software & Services	16.4%	20.5%	−186.2%	−206.6%	61.6%	−33%
4	JDS UNIPHASE	Communications Equipment	14.1%	150.5%	−391.3%	−541.8%	−79.9%	20%
5	CF INDUSTRIES	Chemicals	11.7%	18.0%	22.0%	4.1%	40.6%	184%
6	CELGENE	Biotechnology	11.7%	−3.2%	17.8%	21.1%	61.6%	346%
7	MASTERCARD	IT Services	8.2%	13.7%	28.9%	15.2%	27.4%	95%
8	DISCOVER FINANCIAL	Diversified Financial Services	7.0%	19.9%	26.6%	8.7%	14.9%	52%
9	PUBLIC STORAGE	Real Estate	6.3%	31.0%	2.9%	−28.1%	0.3%	9%
10	HOLLYFRONTIER	Oil Gas & Consumable Fuels	4.5%	−0.9%	6.4%	7.3%	23.5%	367%
11	AMERICAN TOWER	Professional Services	4.5%	27.1%	−5.0%	−32.1%	−4.7%	94%
12	ORACLE	Software	4.4%	2.2%	18.4%	16.2%	19.5%	106%
13	LAS VEGAS SANDS	Hotels Resorts & Cruise lines	4.2%	4.8%	5.0%	0.4%	16.3%	324%
14	HEALTHSOUTH	Health Care Providers/Services	4.2%	19.8%	5.1%	−14.6%	1.1%	22%
15	ALTERA	Semiconductors & Equipment	4.1%	9.0%	27.5%	18.6%	11.7%	43%
16	CNO FINANCIAL	Insurance	3.7%	6.0%	−37.7%	−43.8%	12.4%	−33%
17	PIER 1 IMPORTS	Specialty Retail	3.4%	16.7%	2.8%	−13.9%	0.0%	1%
18	AVIS BUDGET	Freight Transportation	3.3%	16.9%	−1.3%	−18.2%	−0.2%	17%
19	PERRIGO	Pharmaceuticals	3.3%	9.6%	5.9%	−3.8%	7.0%	119%
20	CROWN CASTLE INTL	Wireless Telecommunication Services	3.1%	33.3%	−17.1%	−50.5%	−17.6%	103%
21	TYCO INTERNATIONAL	Conglomerates & Machinery	3.1%	15.3%	−2.6%	−18.0%	0.1%	−2%
22	PPL	Electric Utilities	3.0%	3.3%	9.2%	5.9%	11.4%	125%
23	AMERICAN WATER WORKS	Utilities - Other	2.9%	13.9%	2.0%	−11.9%	0.6%	33%
24	EDWARDS LIFESCIENCES	Health Care Equipment/Supplies	2.8%	7.6%	8.9%	1.3%	6.2%	70%
25	FOSSIL	Textiles Apparel & Luxury Goods	2.7%	4.6%	6.1%	3.4%	8.7%	107%
26	CHARTER COMMUNICATIONS	Media	2.6%	14.4%	−4.8%	−19.3%	−1.4%	28%
27	NU SKIN ENTERPRISES	Household & Personal Products	2.4%	5.9%	8.1%	2.2%	6.1%	76%
28	CLIFFS NATURAL RESOURCES	Metals & Mining	2.3%	−1.4%	5.5%	6.8%	12.7%	232%
29	STANDARD PACIFIC	Homebuilders	2.3%	6.4%	−7.2%	−13.7%	4.9%	−67%
30	MCDONALD'S	Restaurants	2.3%	7.9%	13.8%	5.9%	3.3%	24%
31	ALTRIA	Tobacco	2.1%	19.5%	27.8%	8.3%	−9.0%	−32%
32	POLARIS INDUSTRIES	Leisure Equipment & Products	2.0%	3.4%	8.4%	5.1%	6.7%	80%
33	COCA-COLA	Food & Beverage	2.0%	−0.3%	12.6%	12.9%	10.2%	81%
34	BLACKROCK	Non-Spread Financials	1.9%	7.5%	1.1%	−6.4%	1.7%	159%
35	TEMPUR PEDIC INTL	Household Durables	1.8%	3.3%	12.9%	9.6%	5.6%	43%
36	FASTENAL	Trading Companies/Distributors	1.8%	3.2%	10.1%	6.9%	5.6%	56%
37	DELPHI AUTOMOTIVE	Auto & Suppliers	1.7%	9.7%	3.3%	−6.4%	−1.1%	−34%
38	B/E AEROSPACE	Aerospace & Defense	1.5%	2.1%	5.4%	3.3%	5.5%	101%
39	WEIGHT WATCHERS	Diversified Consumer Services	1.5%	1.8%	16.6%	14.9%	5.6%	34%
40	LEVEL 3 COMMUNICATIONS	Diversified Telecommunication Services	1.5%	12.7%	−10.9%	−23.5%	−5.2%	48%
41	IRON MOUNTAIN	Commercial Services & Supplies	1.5%	6.6%	3.4%	−3.1%	0.7%	20%
42	ROPER INDUSTRIES	Electrical Equipment	1.4%	3.8%	6.3%	2.5%	3.3%	52%
43	SEI INVESTMENTS	Capital Markets	1.4%	11.1%	21.1%	10.0%	−4.2%	−20%
44	DOMTAR	Paper & Packaging	1.3%	5.9%	1.9%	−3.9%	0.6%	29%
45	NATIONAL OILWELL VARCO	Energy Equipment & Services	1.2%	0.2%	5.5%	5.4%	5.7%	103%
46	JETBLUE AIRWAYS	Airlines	1.2%	5.6%	0.2%	−5.4%	0.1%	85%
47	AMPHENOL	Electronics and Office Equipment	0.8%	1.1%	5.5%	4.4%	2.9%	53%
48	WHOLE FOODS MARKET	Food & Staples Retailing	0.6%	1.2%	2.5%	1.2%	2.0%	81%
49	CHICAGO BRIDGE & IRON	Construction	0.6%	1.6%	4.0%	2.5%	1.6%	39%
50	SOUTHWEST GAS	Gas Utilities	0.4%	2.2%	3.5%	1.2%	−0.3%	−9%
51	WELLS FARGO	Commercial Banks	0.3%	−5.3%	5.5%	10.8%	6.6%	120%
52	JONES LANG LASALLE	Real Estate Management	−0.2%	−2.3%	2.1%	4.5%	1.3%	62%

EXHIBIT 7.8 The Leaders in Five–Year Momentum, by Industry

the 75th percentile in the software industry both because the median performance level is higher—it is generally a more profitable business for a variety of reasons—and because the really successful firms are able to stake out more open running ground for increasing EVA. Novelty creates opportunities for both bigger EVA Margins and bigger addressable markets.

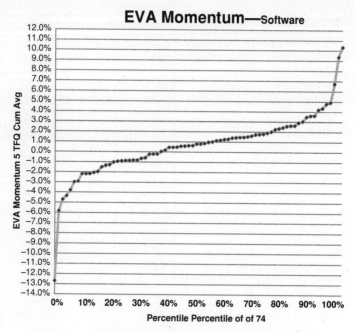

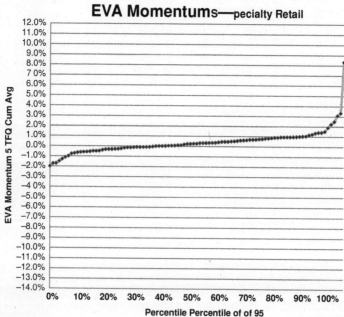

EXHIBIT 7.9   Five–Year EVA Momentum in Software and Specialty Retail

To sum up, an examination of historical performance through an EVA Momentum lens can provide a wealth of interesting insights for corporate strategists to ponder and for CFOs to use in grounding forward–looking plan goals in the statistical reality of what firms have actually accomplished. It is relevant to consider the EVA Momentum for the whole market because, in the end, competition puts all companies in the same business—the business of earning and increasing EVA. The longer–term, lifetime experiences of all companies, including the gravitational pull of convergence, are relevant for every company. In the short term, though, business cycles, sector membership, and sales size do matter. Some business sectors are more amenable to producing economic profits, even if at more risk, and smaller companies, if they are successful, have a natural advantage in generating outsized gains.

To close out this section, the chart in Exhibit 7.10 shows the EVA Momentum distribution for food and beverage companies, which includes

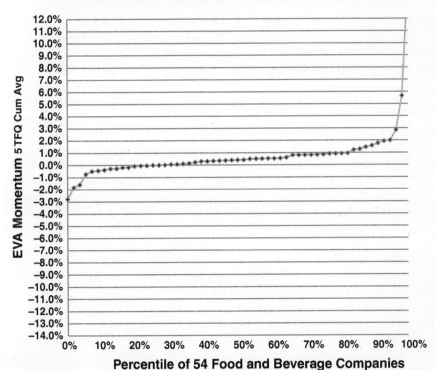

EVA Momentum—Food and Beverage

EXHIBIT 7.10   Five–Year EVA Momentum in Food and Beverage Companies

Coca–Cola (KO ticker). It exhibits the by now familiar pattern and profile expected in a mature business. Median EVA Momentum is modest at about 0.4 percent, and the slope is fairly sedate—by the standards of Momentum—exhibiting a 10th to 90th percentile wingspan of about 2.5 percentage points. In contrast to the retailers, though, two firms stand out as real upside outliers (see Exhibit 7.11). Green Mountain Coffee Roasters (distributor of Keurig) percolated at 15 percent Momentum per annum, and Monster Beverage bubbled away at 5.7 percent Momentum per year—impressive by any standard, and certainly off the charts in this business. Green Mountain's sales, for instance, increased tenfold over the five years, and its EVA Margin expanded to 6.7 percent from 1.8 percent. Unless you expect to catch lightning in a bottle, those accomplishments are not really relevant to setting a long–range plan target, though. The median, and 10th to 90th percentile band, is

Now let's come at momentum from a totally different angle. Investors have formed a judgment about future performance and factored it into stock prices. The judgment is reflected in the Market–Implied Momentum (MIM) rate that discounts back to the prevailing stock price. A public company should certainly consult its own MIM statistic as an input to setting plan and performance goals, and private companies should at least examine the MIM expectations for a set of public peers. It's a way to freely piggyback on the research that market participants have done.

It is, as always, advantageous to examine the full market for perspective before examining specific sectors. The charts in Exhibit 7.12 show the history of MIM for the entire Russell 3000. It is frankly off the charts at the 90th percentile, as there is always some group of turnaround plays and venture start–ups priced to explode from a depressed EVA base. The other percentile break points are relevant as guideposts, though.

MIM tends to be countercyclical. When the economy is in the doldrums and EVA profits are depressed, MIM is often at a peak because a recovery is priced into shares. And when an economic expansion gets long in the tooth, investors pull back on the multiples they will pay for EVA profits that they fear cannot be sustained, and MIM heads into a trough.

As the dot–com bubble burst in 2000 and into 2001 and the economy went into recession, projected EVA Momentum rates stayed high or actually increased because corporate EVA profits fell even faster than the stock market did. Investors were projecting a very strong recovery from the depressed EVA base (which in fact happened—at least through 2007). The 2008 market meltdown was different and somewhat rare in that the stock market fell faster than EVA did—at least at the outset—and MIM fell precipitously. But then in 2009, as the predicted downturn in EVA profits materialized, MIM rates sharply rebounded in anticipation of a rebound in EVA profits, which has happened, albeit slowly.

Company (as of Mid-Year 2012)	Industry	(A) Cum Avg EVA Mo 5 TFQs (B)+(E) /5	(B) Δ EVA Margin 5 TFQs (C)–(D)	(C) EVA Margin	(D) EVA Margin 5 TFQs Back	(E) Profit-able Growth 5 TFQs (C)x(F)	(F) Sales Growth 5 TFQ Cum
1 GREEN MTN COFFEE ROASTERS	Food & Beverage	15.0%	4.9%	6.7%	1.8%	69.9%	1,049%
2 MONSTER BEVERAGE CORP	Food & Beverage	5.7%	0.9%	17.1%	16.2%	27.4%	161%
3 DARLING INTERNATIONAL	Food & Beverage	2.9%	3.2%	5.1%	1.9%	11.1%	216%
4 COCA-COLA	Food & Beverage	2.0%	–0.3%	12.6%	12.9%	10.2%	81%
5 BOSTON BEER	Food & Beverage	1.9%	3.3%	9.0%	5.7%	6.4%	71%

EXHIBIT 7.11   EVA Momentum of Select Food and Beverage Companies

On the other side of the business cycle, MIM rates declined from the end of 2005 onward—right in the midst of the prolonged economic expansion. Investors could sense even then that the good times could not last forever—though they clearly did not forecast a complete meltdown, rather just a slackening in the pace of EVA growth. Nobody's perfect.

Putting the cycles aside, there is a notable long–term trend in MIM evident from the chart, namely a secular decline in confidence across all percentile categories. To get a handle on it, focus for a minute on the median MIM, plotted as the second highest line in the chart in the left in Exhibit

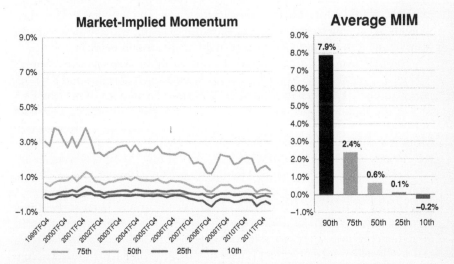

EXHIBIT 7.12   Market–Implied Momentum by Percentile for the Russell 3000

7.12. It was in the vicinity of 0.8 to 1.0 percent up until about the end of 2005 (as I said, that is when MIM began to run out of steam in general). As of mid–2012, however, the market's median MIM stands at the lowest mark on this historical record. Whereas the MIM median has averaged 0.6 percent, it now stands at just 0.2 percent. The dissipation in EVA growth expectations is also evident at the 75th percentile mark. It stood at 1.4 percent as of mid–2012, compared to a long–run average of 2.4 percent. The market is clearly registering a fear that current EVA Margins are not sustainable and that the long–run outlook is not as conducive to sustained EVA profit growth as it has generally been. Any board or management team that is setting a long–range EVA growth target at this time ought to acknowledge the market's concerns and tamp down its growth goals.

What's going on? I will speculate. First, the great wave of digital technology that has propelled profitable growth and permeated the economy for so long is maturing. The business isn't vanishing; the opposite is happening—it is becoming more routine, commoditized, and fungible, with more consumer choices tugging profits out of the system. There's now an iPhone, iPod, iPad, and iPad mini, and more and more capable imitators emerging every day. The old warhorse desktop computers are a dime a dozen. Continued growth in economic profits, at least size adjusted, is looking harder to come by as tech innovations are becoming more commonplace and competitive. Moreover, the expected next wave of innovations—from genetic engineering and nanotechnology and any of a number of ballyhooed ideas—have not yet materialized to fill the void left by the maturing of digital technology. Where's my immortality pill, guys? Large pharmaceutical companies, for example, placed a lot of bets in the wrong places, and now are licking their wounds as patents from their glory days are expiring without new wonder drugs coming to market in sufficient numbers to sustain profits.

Another factor is a greater concentration of the EVA profits. Apple's MIM is 1.7 percent on $148 billion of sales, equating to an expected *$2.5 billion of added EVA per year for at least a decade.* That's a lot of nuclear EVA fuel in the hands of one company. But Apple's gains are taking the wind out of the sales of many other firms. Among the casualties are Research In Motion and Nokia, of course, but also, Dell (MIM is −0.5 percent), Hewlett–Packard (−0.3 percent MIM), and even Best Buy (MIM is zero percent).

Let Best Buy be the lesson. After earning EVA of over $600 million in each rolling four–quarter span of the mid–2005 to the mid–2008 interval, and trading at the time for a MIM of 0.2 percent to 0.4 percent, Best Buy earned a paltry EVA of $2 million on sales of $45 billion for the four–quarter period ending mid–2012. Unable to compete with hugely hip Apple Stores and inexpensive and convenient iTunes downloads, and facing pressure from Wal–Mart in the real world and Amazon in the virtual one, Best Buy's EVA and EVA Margin are, for all practical purposes, zero, and its MVA is priced at essentially zero, too. The discount electronics retailer is trading at just a tad over its book capital. At that price, the market is projecting that Best Buy will simply break even on EVA forever and never generate EVA Momentum or add to its owners' wealth. Let the new management team prove the market wrong, but that is the harsh assessment they are up against.

As the winners in winner–takes–all businesses emerge victorious and claim their crowns, each winner's MIM may rise while precipitating a meltdown for many others. When there are six losers in the tech wars for one winner, the entire MIM distribution collapses. The support struts are kicked out. At one time there were hundreds of auto companies, then a few very profitable ones dominated by one, and now none has a stirring EVA Momentum outlook. Tech is following the same pattern.

But that is not all. The world is flattening. Global competitors are arising on all fronts. Who would have guessed that one of Apple's biggest competitors would turn out to be Samsung, a Korean company? In the future its greatest rival may be some as yet unknown and maybe as yet unhatched Chinese company. The time span in which the market is permitting even the best companies to prosper and spin economic profits is being compressed, and the economic profits (such as they are) are spread the world over. This is not all to be lamented, incidentally. Competition may be forcing EVA profits to evaporate faster and morph into lower prices and higher quality and faster innovations with greater alacrity. The very technology the tech boom is spawning is turning the wheels of competition faster and faster. The consumer wins what the shareholder loses.

There are no doubt many other factors, at least for the United States. A liquefying if not stupefying Federal Reserve policy now in its third round is temporarily depressing interest rates and distorting incentives to save and invest and hire and train. Immigration policies that close doors to highly trained engineers and scientists, looming and as yet unaddressed social liabilities, an increasingly interventionist and activist government, the threat of an explosive Middle East, and an imploding Europe are contours. Add in the prospect of far higher tax rates on capital formation and earned income that will kill supply–side incentives. Make your own list, and it is no wonder that corporate chieftains are holding back on investments, and that the market is expecting EVA Margins to throttle back.

The current depressed MIM rates can also be justified by a strong statistical correlation evident in the EVA data, namely, that higher EVA Margins are generally associated with *lower* EVA Momentum growth expectations. While that is true across the whole market, it is easier to see the connection at first when it is applied to just one sector, as shown on the chart in Exhibit 7.13 for the food and beverage group.

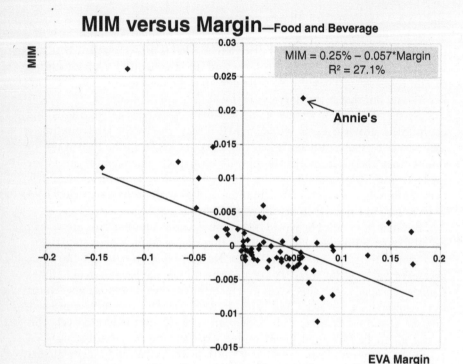

EXHIBIT 7.13   Market–Implied Momentum and EVA Margin in Food and
Beverage Companies

The chart plots the EVA Margin on the *x*–axis versus forward–looking
MIM rates on the *y*–axis for all U.S. food and beverage companies in our database for the most recent four quarters ending in mid–2012. What it shows
is typical. Although there are a few notable outliers—like Annie's, which has
a sizable EVA Margin and very considerable EVA growth expectations priced
into its shares—the bulk of the firms plot along a downward–sloping line. A
bigger EVA Margin is a setup for lower EVA growth expectations, in general.

Why is this so? For one thing, firms with high EVA Margins are vulnerable. The EVA riches they display attract competitors, imitators, and disrup-
tors looking to leapfrog into the next generation. Another reason for the
correlation may be the Innovator's Dilemma. As I've discussed, established
profitable winners tend to fall into the trap of resting on their margin and
return laurels rather than aggressively driving for EVA growth, and the market understands that and fears it. On the other side, firms operating with
weak margins are motivated to restructure, repair, and revive their business
models. The negative slope, in other words, is what you would expect to see

in a world where convergence is the norm—where the strong grow weaker and the lame walk again. The magnetic pull of convergence to the mean is stronger than most people think. It is the market's version of "all glory is fleeting" and "you always get a second chance."

The observation also applies to the economy as a whole. We've already seen how the market tends to price weak EVA Margins to recover and prices in a coming slowdown in EVA Momentum when EVA Margins are peaking, which appears to be happening as I write this book. As of late 2012, the 75th percentile EVA Margin is nearly 5 percent, well above the long-run average of 4.1 percent and near the highest level on record (see Exhibit 7.14). The median EVA Margin tells the same story; it's running at 0.7 percent compared to a long-run average of EVA Margin of 0.4 percent.

In the current climate, business leaders are choosing to hold down discretionary costs and resist hiring, and as a result, the median EBIT-DAR margin is 24.9 percent these days compared to a long-run average of 22.8 percent. Federal Reserve policy is also helping by suppressing interest rates and the cost of capital, which is reducing the capital charge to EVA. For a variety of reasons, the current times are generally very good for EVA Margin, and the market does not expect that to last. The Deloitte CFO Survey in September 2012 summed up the situation very well:

Large companies have looked under every stone for ways to bolster their performance—better focus, scaling back in lower–margin

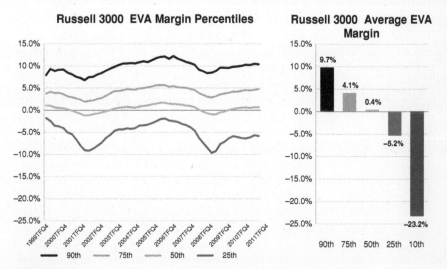

EXHIBIT 7.14 The Course of EVA Margins over Time, and the Averages

*businesses, and getting more efficient in both the front– and back–
office—often with remarkable success. But last quarter's survey
results suggested the returns were beginning to run out. And this
quarter's findings solidified this view, recording the sharpest decline
in expectations we have seen in the two–and–a–half–year history
of the survey.*

MIM is at an all–time low because EVA Margins are about as good as
they can get, growth prospects are feeble, and risk and uncertainty are high.
Whether the cause is impending gloom and doom or just statistical regression to the mean, CFOs and board directors will quite obviously need to
factor the contemporary outlook into the goals they set. The Deloitte CFO
Survey is certainly helpful color commentary. But the most accurate, usable,
and statistically relevant expectations are baked into stock prices—into
MIM, if you know how to read it. And now you do.

In this chapter I've reviewed a variety of data points and techniques that
EVA offers to help directors and top managers set financial performance
goals for a variety of applications. This is an area where EVA really shines.
The care that goes into making EVA a rock–solid measure of corporate
performance gives it a big leg up over all other measures in doing this. It is
the only measure where more is better than less, that irons out accounting
gyrations and distortions, that neutralizes differences in business models
and capital intensity, and that literally discounts to net present value. The
EVA ratio statistics derived from it are thus the only financial performance
measures that can be statistically aggregated, ranked, and correlated with
real meaning and significance.

The payoff is that, for the purpose of setting annual bonus performance
targets, it can be as simple as just rewarding the year–over–year improvement
in EVA. For setting longer–range performance targets, such as incorporating
a growth goal into a midrange bonus plan, on up to an aspirational decade–
long goal like Coca–Cola established, start by running the EVA Momentum
math. Tease out what to expect from a combination of productivity gains
and profitable growth. To do that, you and your team will need to know
your EVA Margins intimately by line of business and the potential for improving them. How do they stack up with peers and with sister divisions?
How far short of best–practice performance standards are they? How can
the "3–P's"—price, product, and process—be leveraged to drive the EVA
Margin higher? Couple all that with an understanding of the growth potential in your markets, and you have the ingredients to cook up a basic EVA
Momentum projection.

Beyond that, cast a wider net. Consult the statistics. Examine the momentum track records and the projected momentum rates baked into the

share prices covering broad market aggregates and your sector peers. Calibrate against companies of your size and business model, taking account of the influence of the current economic climate and general market multiples, and the natural inclination of margins and momentum to converge to the norm. Check your results by evaluating the EVA Momentum and stock price implied by security analyst forecasts and by your own final and approved business plans—which is our next topic. I believe that this framework for setting targets will give you a much richer, more accurate, more relevant, and more actionable set of goals to work toward and pay for than any other.

CHAPTER 8

Put Momentum Into Planning

Where can you expect to derive the greatest benefit from using EVA Momentum? Would it be in reviewing and deconstructing actual performance and comparing it against budget objectives and benchmarking against peers? In setting goals? No, not in either of those, important as they are. The biggest benefit is using EVA Momentum to help line teams to improve the quality and value of their business plans—*during the planning process*.

Yes, the EVA metrics can always be summoned to summarize the financial thrust of the final business plans, as I previously indicated. But here I am advocating something way more important. I am saying there is tremendous value to be gained by bringing the EVA arsenal into the heat of the planning battle as it is being fought and not just as the peace treaty is signed. Give line teams EVA Momentum scorecards as their draft business plans are evolving. Use the scorecards to shape the plan reviews, and to equip the line teams to develop better, more valuable, more EVA-capable business plans.

EVA Momentum is eminently suited to be the financial partner in the planning process. Its function, if nothing else, is to serve as the key financial objective, the measure that everyone works to maximize. Planning reviews are swifter, more incisive, more strategic, and far more shareholder-value aligned when the goal is clear and clearly focused on generating EVA Momentum.

But EVA Momentum is more than just the objective function. It also provides the ideal analytical framework to take preliminary business plans apart and help managers see ways they can improve them to generate even more EVA. The same EVA Momentum Pyramid used to review actual performance does double duty here, this time to isolate the underlying key assumptions and performance factors that are adding to or inhibiting the plan value.

But more than that, the forward plans can be explicitly valued by discounting the EVA profit that they imply. Management can choose the best plans quite directly in terms of their measurable contribution to share value and not just through EVA Momentum as a proxy for the value. Line teams, moreover, are able to interactively simulate how changes in strategies and tactics and priorities ripple through the EVA Momentum Pyramid line items and EVA Margin metrics and flow right into the discounted EVA valuation of their plans. They can see the valuation answer and understand why it is the answer at the same time. It is value-based planning at its clearest and finest.

Valuing the forward plans has ancillary benefits. It enables the CFO to gauge what the firm in total and its common shares are really worth as an input to decisions about issuing or retiring shares at the current price. The valuations also feed right into portfolio reviews, and help to answer such questions as: Which parts of the company are creating the most value or the least? Are we devoting our financial capital and management attention to where it has the greatest impact on our value? What are our divisions worth based on the EVA they can churn out as part of our firm, and how does that internal value compare with what they could fetch on the market?

Sometimes the conclusions are not what the board wants to hear, which is why proving them with EVA can be so critical. It can turn out that the firm's best-performing or most promising business segments present the greatest gaps between exit value and retention value, and are the best candidates for divestiture. That may be a hard pill to swallow, but it is the right answer if the goal is to maximize the value of scarce resources and EVA. Putting the facts objectively on the table helps bring economic reason into what can be emotional questions. EVA facts can counter what Warren Buffett has referred to dismissively as gin-rummy divestitures—just discarding the worst cards at each turn—when the objective always should be to trade up in value, to dispose of businesses that are worth more to others, no matter how far up the food chain their value is to begin with.

Once the planning is concluded, then yes, the final budgets and plans ought to be converted into EVA targets that express the financial essence of the plans to the board and to investors, and management should use them as bogeys for judging performance and adjusting strategies in the next year's quarterly review process. What we are after here is a consistent closed-loop system for planning, target setting, and performance reporting that is completely EVA-based, with accountability, simplicity, and insight hardwired in.

In practice, the bulk of the EVA planning action takes place in the individual lines of business and divisions, and in the iterative review process conducted between corporate and the line teams. For obvious reasons, I am unable to demonstrate that give-and-take with real-world examples. Instead, I'll illustrate it with a couple of hypothetical forecast plans for Tiffany & Co. (TIF) that I prepared with the benefit of a nifty little Excel tool we call Value *Express*. I emphasize that these are not based on an insider view or any conversations with Tiffany management. This is purely an illustration and is just a stand-in for the line-of-business plan analysis that I am advocating.

EVA Summary	2008TFQ2	2009TFQ2	2010TFQ2	2011TFQ2	2012TFQ2	Summary
Sales	$3,075.594	$2,583.853	$2,881.942	$3,416.674	$3,714.946	
EVA	$ 157.168	$ 59.640	$ 85.569	$ 184.734	$ 166.454	
ΔEVA	$ 92.410	$ (97.528)	$ 25.929	$ 99.165	$ (18.280)	
Sales Growth Rate	11.0%	−16.0%	11.5%	18.6%	8.7%	6.9%
Percentile vs Retailing	49	16	59	68	49	44
EVA Margin	5.1%	2.3%	3.0%	5.4%	4.5%	4.1%
Percentile vs Retailing	87	78	75	84	80	82
EVA Momentum	3.4%	−3.2%	1.0%	3.4%	−0.5%	0.8%
Percentile vs Retailing	95	13	50	90	26	70
Cost of Capital	8.3%	7.7%	7.6%	7.4%	6.8%	7.6%

EXHIBIT 8.1 Tiffany's Five-Year EVA Highlights

Let's begin, as you would, by recapitulating recent EVA highlights, as shown in Exhibit 8.1 for Tiffany covering the five-year period ending in mid-2012, where each period is a composite of the trailing four quarters (designated as TFQ).

To refresh your memory, Tiffany is very profitable. Using a weighted average cost of capital of 6.8 percent, which is about 4 percent over the current long government bond rate, TIF earned $166 million in EVA on $3.7 billion in sales over the four quarters ending midyear 2012, for an EVA Margin of 4.5 percent, just a touch above the 4.1 percent average of the past five years. It was higher in 2011, at 5.4 percent, and in 2008, at 5.1 percent, but it is still quite impressive. It is rated at the 80th percentile relative to retailers worldwide.

EVA Momentum averaged 0.8 percent per year over the past five years, or about the 70th percentile among the retailing crowd. Sales growth, though, was relatively slow. At a 6.9 percent average pace, it was only at the 43rd percentile. As you would expect of an aristocrat, TIF's performance is elegant and built for comfort, not speed.

The next step would normally be to get a lot more grounded in the business's performance profile by benchmarking the full array of EVA Momentum drivers against internal and external peers and correlating the financial facts with competitive trends on the premise that you cannot really know where to go unless you first know where you are. Thankfully, I will skip that step in this illustration. A companion exercise at this stage, at least for public companies, is to get a feel for the EVA performance expectations that are baked into the current share price, and to gain an appreciation for the key financial performance variables that are most influential in driving the company's value. Let's do that now for Tiffany.

Exhibit 8.2 presents a summary of a simple get-acquainted, first-pass five-year forecast for Tiffany. As a matter of convenience, it is derived from the median estimates of a pool of 11 equity analysts who actively followed the stock as of October 2012. In practice, you could just as easily use your

TIFFANY & CO	2012TFQ2	Summary	2013TFQ2	2014TFQ2	2015TFQ2	2016TFQ2	2017TFQ2	
Sales Growth Rate	8.7%	6.9%	8.6%	9.4%	9.8%	9.8%	9.8%	
EVA Margin	4.5%	4.1%	4.3%	4.7%	5.1%	5.4%	5.6%	
EVA Summary	2012TFQ2	Summary	2013TFQ2	2014TFQ2	2015TFQ2	2016TFQ2	2017TFQ2	Summary
Sales	$3,714.946		$4,033.261	$4,412.678	$4,846.233	$5,322.385	$5,845.320	
EVA	$ 166.454		$ 173.762	$ 207.184	$ 244.735	$ 285.738	$ 328.003	
ΔEVA	$ (18.280)		$ 7.308	$ 33.422	$ 37.551	$ 41.003	$ 42.265	
Sales Growth Rate	8.7%	6.9%	8.6%	9.4%	9.8%	9.8%	9.8%	9.5%
Percentile vs Retailing	49	44						53
EVA Margin	4.5%	4.1%	4.3%	4.7%	5.1%	5.4%	5.6%	5.0%
Percentile vs Retailing	80	82	83	85	87	88	89	86
EVA Momentum	–0.5%	0.8%	0.2%	0.8%	0.9%	0.8%	0.8%	0.9%
Percentile vs Retailing	28	70						72
Cost of Capital	6.8%	7.6%	6.8%	6.8%	6.8%	6.8%	6.8%	6.8%

EXHIBIT 8.2 The Consensus Forecast of Tiffany's Next Five Years

prior year's business plan or a simple extrapolation of past trends as a starting scenario, but this will serve admirably as a base case.

The consensus projection is that Tiffany will increase sales at a 9 percent to 10 percent clip, above its recent average pace. The forecast EVA Margin is derived from the analyst estimates for operating margin and capital expenditures, and from applying a handful of other assumptions to extrapolate things like working capital and advertising spending. The result is that Tiffany's EVA Margin is projected to steadily increase from 4.5 percent to 5.6 percent—to reach just a little higher than the best EVA Margin attained over the past five years.

The model combines the sales and EVA Margin projections to forecast that Tiffany's EVA will just about double over the five years—from $166 million in the past four quarters to $328 million at the end of the plan. I emphasize once more that sell-side equity analysts are for the most part not forecasting EVA—that is their loss. Our model is simply deriving the EVA metrics from the basic income statement and balance sheet figures that they do forecast and bringing light into their dark world.

Let's now compute the overall average EVA Momentum projected over the life of the plan. Just take the $162 million *increase* in EVA that is projected over the five-year forecast and divide that by the $3.7 billion in sales in the last history period. The ratio is the cumulative EVA Momentum forecast over the five years. It is 4.4 percent. Divide that by 5, and the average projected EVA Momentum pace per year is about 0.9 percent. That is the key metric that summarizes the overall quality and value of the plan in one statistic. The bigger it is, the greater is the projected increase in EVA over the plan and on average per period, and thus the greater will be the discounted present value (PV) and stock price corresponding to the plan. It's the key statistic that the management team should home in on to grade and compare plans. It is the plan performance statistic that all team players should be challenged to maximize as the key financial goal of the planning process. It's the one, the *Unum*, and it is bordered in the table to draw your attention to it.

The 0.9 percent EVA Momentum average implied by the consensus plan is just slightly over the 0.8 percent Momentum average that Tiffany delivered over the prior five years. The projected Momentum, moreover, qualifies for the 72nd percentile against the accomplishments of the specialty retailer crowd, a performance zone that Tiffany has comfortably occupied in the past. Say it either way, and the plan can be judged credible. It is clearly not a hockey stick plan, as many are. It continues on a more or less business-as-usual slope. To play the devil's advocate, it is also clearly a rich plan. EVA is growing at a pace that runs counter to the tendency of outstanding EVA performers to regress to the mean, to revert back to more normal EVA Momentum rates over time. An astute analyst or business manager would want to question the underlying plan assumptions in detail, but that is beyond the scope of our inquiry at this time. We are simply trying to gain a feel for the implications of aiming at various EVA trajectories as a plan goal.

A key implication is the projected market value of the plan. For instance, is the value in the ballpark of the current stock price, or is there a large gap to explain or close? Discounting the EVA implied by the plan says the stock is worth $60.18 a share, compared to an actual share price of $63.01 at the valuation date. It's quite close to the recent price—just 4.5 percent below it—as would be expected if the market is really valuing EVA (even if the market does not know it is valuing EVA *per se*). Let's now look into the details behind the valuation shown in Exhibit 8.3.

The Value *Express* model determines the value of the plan by discounting the projected EVA from the middle of each of the five forecast years back to present value at Tiffany's 6.3 percent cost of capital, and then adding a terminal value for EVA. It's the exact same procedure that was outlined in

Valuation Details	Summary	2013TFQ2	2014TFQ2	2015TFQ2	2016TFQ2	2017TFQ2	Terminal
Projected MVA = Total Present Value of EVA	$ 4,840.799						
Projected EVA and Terminal Value		$ 173.762	$ 207.184	$ 244.735	$ 285.738	$ 328.003	$ 4,802.380
Present Value Factor at the Cost of Capital		$ 0.968	$ 0.906	$ 0.848	$ 0.794	$ 0.743	$ 0.743
Present Value of Projected EVA and Terminal Value		$ 168.116	$ 187.636	$ 207.474	$ 226.747	$ 243.645	$ 3,567.278
Cumulative Present Value of EVA	$ 4,600.897	$ 168.116	$ 355.752	$ 563.226	$ 789.973	$ 1,033.618	$ 4,600.897
Adjustment for Midyear Discounting	$ 181.910						
Adjustment for Average Capital	$ 57.993						
Projected Share Price	$60.18						
= Economic Book Value per Share	$22.56						
+ Common Equity Adjusted	$ 2,856.465						
+ Common Equity	$ 2,396.490						
+ Common Equity Adjustments	$ 459.975						
/ Shares Outstanding	126.64						
+ Projected Price–Book Spread (MVA per Share)	$37.94						
+ Common Equity Revaluation	$ 4,805.112						
+ Projected MVA	$ 4,840.799						
− Option Value After-Tax	$ 35.688						
− Revaluation of Prior Claims & Nonop Capital	$ –						
+ Revaluation of Nonoperating Capital	$ –						
/ Shares Oustanding	126.64						
− Interim Dividends (from valuation to current date)	$ 0.32						

EXHIBIT 8.3 The Details Behind the Valuation of Tiffany's Consensus Plan

Chapter 2, but let's go over it again now that we have our hands on a real company. By default, the model assumes that EVA will no longer grow after the fifth forecast year. It assumes that the corrosive effects of time, risk, and entropy will constrain the company to just maintain EVA as a level perpetuity after being granted five years of EVA growth, which, as I've said, is a fairly typical assumption. Sales may continue to increase thereafter, and operating profit, EBITDA, and EPS may go on expanding, but the supposition is that Tiffany is part of a cohort of firms where EVA can be actuarially expected to go flat line and EVA Momentum to go to zero after half a decade has passed. You are not stuck with that assumption. The Value *Express* model lets users modify the default setting and project extended periods of EVA growth, or decline, beyond the forecast period. For now, though, we'll stick with the default assumption.

To determine the value of extending EVA as a level perpetuity, the EVA forecast in the fifth forecast year is capitalized at the cost of capital (just divided by it). That solves for $4.80 billion. That terminal value is then discounted a full four and a half years back to the present value, using a PV factor of 0.74, as is shown in the table. The EVA valuation is also adjusted to account for midyear discounting and the use of average capital to compute EVA (don't ask). The overall, adjusted, present value sum of the projected EVA for the first five years and the terminal value extension is $4.84 billion. That's the predicted MVA of the plan, the total value added over all resources, and predicted franchise value of the business.

Incidentally, when modeling business unit plans, the analysis would stop right here, at the MVA line. The goal would be to find the plans that produce the most MVA at each business unit level, which would sum to the greatest possible corporate MVA and would thus lead to highest possible share price. But for the consolidated company, we can carry the valuation right through to the stock price.

To do that, a few adjustments need to be made to the corporate consolidated MVA projection. The after-tax cost of exercisable stock options (based on Black-Scholes), $35.7 million in TIF's case, is subtracted. There is also room in the model at this point to fold in the value of off-balance-sheet assets and to deduct an upward revaluation of liabilities (such as from a reduction in interest rates), but I'll ignore those details here for simplicity. The net MVA remainder is then divided by the common shares outstanding—126.64 million shares in Tiffany's case.

The result: EVA predicts that Tiffany should trade for a net franchise value, or market-to-book premium, of $37.94 a share, on top of its common equity book value of $22.56 per share (as adjusted, for instance, to add back unamortized advertising spending to book value), for the total price of $60.18 a share. According to the plan, Tiffany is worth almost three times book value because investors are not buying book value; they are buying the business, and the business includes the present value of EVA per share. As an aside, here is a nice little proof that accountants make the wrong assumption when preparing financial statements. Investors are buying a business and the going-concern value, not a balance sheet set of liquidating assets.

The valuation backs up the EVA Momentum story. The plan does not appear a stretch at all. Given the current stock price, the plan is actually even a little light on the performance that the market is apparently projecting into it, but it is clearly in the neighborhood. This confirms that investors truly hold the company in high regard. On the other side, it tells management that it needs to aim even higher than this plan if it wants to make its stock price sparkle.

So far, we've looked at just one potential plan forecast for Tiffany, derived from consensus estimates, and even that, I submit, provided useful insights that would be of real value to the management team—even if at a fairly high level. But let's not stop here. It is usually a good idea for the CFO to examine a few alternative scenarios to get a feel for the sensitivities of key assumptions and to identify the most important value drivers, and then to share those insights with the management team before everyone dives into the planning process.

An interesting plan variation to start with is the zero Momentum case. What would the company be worth if we take away all growth in EVA? In other words, what would the stock be worth based just on CVA instead of MVA? To simulate that, I held TIF's EVA Margin constant at the 4.5 percent rate it earned in the prior history period and set the projected sales growth rate to zero. That puts EVA at an even $166.454 million a year—in other words, no growth, no EVA Momentum, by design. (See Exhibit 8.4.)

The present value of extending the current EVA profit forever is a CVA of $2.759 billion, quite a comedown from the $4.841 billion MVA projected in the consensus plan. It corresponds to a stock price of only $43.74—a 27 percent tumble from the consensus valuation of $60.18. That should come as no surprise, because we just erased 0.9 percent a year from Momentum. Now it's nada. As we've seen, a Momentum shift of just 1 percent a year sustained over five years has a highly multiplicative effect on the valuation. The lesson is that TIF's management really needs to deliver on a fairly sizable EVA Momentum commitment just to keep its stock price on par with the market.

I don't see the zero Momentum forecast as realistic. Tiffany's sales will grow, of course. If that is so, is it even conceivable that Tiffany might grow its sales and not grow its EVA? Yes, that is possible. All it would take is for Tiffany's EVA Margin to fade away at the same rate that its sales are forecast to grow, so that the two effects would cancel and EVA would go flat line. Something like that is very likely to happen someday, if not starting right now.

TIFFANY & CO	2012TFQ2	Summary	2013TFQ2	2014TFQ2	2015TFQ2	2016TFQ2	2017TFQ2	
Sales Growth Rate	8.7%	6.9%	0.0%	0.0%	0.0%	0.0%	0.0%	
EVA Margin	4.5%	4.1%	4.5%	4.5%	4.5%	4.5%	4.5%	
EVA Summary	2012TFQ2	Summary	2013TFQ2	2014TFQ2	2015TFQ2	2016TFQ2	2017TFQ2	Summary
Sales	$3,714.946		$3,714.946	$3,714.946	$3,714.946	$3,714.946	$3,714.946	
EVA	$ 166.454		$ 166.454	$ 166.454	$ 166.454	$ 166.454	$ 166.454	
ΔEVA	$ (18.280)		$ –	$ –	$ –	$ –	$ –	
Sales Growth Rate	8.7%	6.9%	0.0%	0.0%	0.0%	0.0%	0.0%	0.0%
Percentile vs Retailing	49	44						17
EVA Margin	4.5%	4.1%	4.5%	4.5%	4.5%	4.5%	4.5%	4.5%
Percentile vs Retailing	80	82						84
EVA Momentum	–0.5%	0.8%	0.0%	0.0%	0.0%	0.0%	0.0%	0.0%
Percentile vs Retailing	26	70						39
Cost of Capital	6.8%	7.6%	6.8%	6.8%	6.8%	6.8%	6.8%	6.8%
Valuation Summary		Projected						
Projected Share Price		$43.74						
Current Share Price		$63.01						
Target Shareholder Return		–30.6%						
Projected MVA = PV of EVA		$2,758.8						

> **The Zero Momentum Case:**
> What is Tiffany's value, assuming there is no growth in EVA?
> MVA is $2.8 billion, and share price is $43.74, or 27 percent below the consensus price.

EXHIBIT 8.4   The Zero Momentum Case

Assume for a moment that the Margin deterioration started now. How would we see that play out? If sales grew 10 percent a year, let's say, then Tiffany's EVA would stay the same so long as 10 percent of the prior year's EVA Margin evaporated each year. In this example, the Margin would run down from 4.5 percent where it is now to 4.05 percent ($0.9 \times 4.5\%$) in the first projected year, to 3.645 percent ($0.9 \times 4.05\%$) the next year, and so on, getting ever smaller but never getting to zero, such that the decline in the EVA Margin each year would just offset the incline in sales and EVA would go sideways forever.

There's another way for a zero Momentum scenario to play out. Assume that the EVA Margin earned on the *existing* sales is unchanged, but that the *incremental* EVA Margin is zero on all new sales. Then the sales growth adds nothing to EVA and Momentum is zero. The effect would be the same—EVA runs flat forever, and the Margin deteriorates forever, getting ever closer to zero but never reaching it. Both these zero Momentum tracks, by the way, would produce continuing growth in sales, EPS, EBIT, and EBITDA, but without any increase in shareholder wealth.

Let's move to a second plan variation. Let's find out how much Tiffany's value would increase if, starting with the consensus plan, the forecast EVA Margin is set 1 percent higher in each year. What's the Margin elasticity, to borrow a fancy economics term? The answer, as shown in Exhibit 8.5, is that the share valuation climbs to $67.06, or about 11 percent more than the consensus value. That's elasticity of 11:1. A 1 percent increase in Margin per year over five years increases the current share price by 11 percent.

TIFFANY & CO	2012TFQ2	Summary	2013TFQ2	2014TFQ2	2015TFQ2	2016TFQ2	2017TFQ2	
Sales Growth Rate	8.7%	6.9%	8.6%	8.6%	8.6%	8.6%	8.6%	
EVA Margin	4.5%	4.1%	5.7%	5.9%	6.2%	6.4%	6.6%	
EVA Summary	2012TFQ2	Summary	2013TFQ2	2014TFQ2	2015TFQ2	2016TFQ2	2017TFQ2	Summary
Sales	$ 3,714.940		$ 4,033.261	$ 4,412.678	$ 4,846.233	$ 5,322.385	$ 5,845.320	
EVA	$ 166.454		$ 166.454	$ 166.454	$ 166.454	$ 166.454	$ 166.454	
ΔEVA	$ (18.280)		$ 63.695	$ 31.635	$ 36.687	$ 41.369	$ 46.616	
Sales Growth Rate	8.7%	6.9%	8.6%	9.4%	9.8%	9.8%	9.8%	9.5%
Percentile vs Retailing	49	44						53
EVA Margin	4.5%	4.1%	5.7%	5.9%	6.2%	6.4%	6.6%	4.5%
Percentile vs Retailing	80	82						95
EVA Momentum	–0.5%	0.8%	1.7%	0.8%	0.8%	0.9%	0.9%	1.2%
Percentile vs Retailing	26	70						78
Cost of Capital	6.8%	7.6%	6.8%	6.8%	6.8%	6.8%	6.8%	
Valuation Summary		Projected						
Projected Share Price		$67.06						
Current Share Price		$63.01						
Target Shareholder Return		6.4%						
Projected MVA = PV of EVA		$ 5,712.4						

The +1 percent EVA Margin Case:
What is Tiffany's value, assuming the forecast EVA Margin is 1 percent higher each year? MVA is $5.7 billion, and share price is $67.06, or 11 percent above the consensus price.

EXHIBIT 8.5   The +1% EVA Margin Case

You may be surprised the effect is not larger than that, but remember, Margin is not really what counts in valuation. Momentum is what counts, because Momentum measures the growth in EVA, and it is EVA that discounts to the value. It is, to remind you again, the *Unum*, the one, after all.

In this case, although 1 percent was added to the Margin each year, only 0.3 percent was added to Momentum per year: it increased from 0.9 percent in the consensus plan to 1.2 percent in this plan. Sure, increasing the Margin added a lot to Momentum in the first year, as it came through as a one-time productivity gain. After that, though, there was no *further* increase in the Margin. Beyond the first year, the increase in Margin only continued adding to Momentum after being multiplied by the sales growth rate, which significantly dampened the effect. It only *added* value on the *new* sales added each year. The result was that Momentum increased by an *average* of only 0.3 percent per year, as I said, and that is what determined the increase in Tiffany's market value.

Now we have the ingredients to compute the Momentum elasticity— the Momentum Leverage Ratio (MLR) that I introduced in the preceding chapter. If a 0.3 percent increase in the average Momentum rate translated into an 11 percent increase in Tiffany's share price, then you can figure that a 1 percent increase in the Momentum pace would produce about a 30 percent gain in share price (I get that using more precise figures). Tiffany's MLR is 30×. That's how important Momentum is to the shareholders—1 percent more Momentum equals a 30 percent greater share value. As noted in the preceding chapter, that's at the low end of the 30× to 80× range found for most companies. That's because TIF, like Coca-Cola, is already a high-performing, high-Margin, highly valued company, which dampens the impact of adding more Momentum at the margin.

The next simulation examines the trade-off between profitability and growth. Management teams wrestle with this question all the time. Is it better to drive for more growth or for more profitability? What are the general terms of trade between the two? It's good to know the answer *before* jumping into planning, don't you think?

To get a grip on it, this case asks how much additional sales growth would be required to match the value generated by stepping up the Margin by 1 percent. As shown in Exhibit 8.6, it would take a 4.2 percent increase in Tiffany's sales growth rate *each year* at the original forecast Margin to match the $67 share price from stepping up the EVA Margin 1 percent a year.

The takeaway is that it would take a *lot* more growth for Tiffany to get to the same place. To see why, think in terms of Momentum once again. To reach the same value, EVA has to end up in the same place in five years, which means EVA Momentum has to be the same in both cases. We've already seen that an increase in Margin adds to Momentum twice—as an upfront productivity gain and through increasing the value of the growth over time. It's a double-barreled, large-bore blast. Sales growth, by contrast, is a single-shot, small-caliber gain. It flows into EVA only through one narrow channel—after being multiplied by the Margin.

TIFFANY & CO	2012TFQ2	Summary	2013TFQ2	2014TFQ2	2015TFQ2	2016TFQ2	2017TFQ2	
Sales Growth Rate	8.7%	6.9%	12.8%	13.6%	14.0%	14.0%	14.0%	
EVA Margin	4.5%	4.1%	4.3%	4.7%	5.1%	5.4%	5.6%	
EVA Summary	2012TFQ2	Summary	2013TFQ2	2014TFQ2	2015TFQ2	2016TFQ2	2017TFQ2	Summary
Sales	$ 3,714.946		$ 4,189.289	$ 4,759.334	$ 5,426.840	$ 6,187.965	$ 7,055.839	
EVA	$ 166.454		$ 180.484	$ 223.460	$ 274.056	$ 332.208	$ 395.929	
ΔEVA	$ (18.280)		$ 14.030	$ 42.976	$ 50.596	$ 58.152	$ 63.722	
Sales Growth Rate	8.7%	6.9%	12.8%	13.6%	14.0%	14.0%	14.0%	13.7%
Percentile vs Retailing	49	44						64
EVA Margin	4.5%	4.1%	4.3%	4.7%	5.1%	5.4%	5.6%	5.0%
Percentile vs Retailing	80	82						86
EVA Momentum	−0.5%	0.8%	0.4%	1.0%	1.1%	1.1%	1.0%	1.2%
Percentile vs Retailing	26	70						78
Cost of Capital	6.8%	7.6%	6.8%	6.8%	6.8%	6.8%	6.8%	6.8%
Valuation Summary		Projected						
Projected Share Price		$67.07						
Current Share Price		$63.01						
Target Shareholder Return		6.4%						
Projected MVA = PV of EVA		$ 5,713.0						

The Sales Growth Case:
How much extra sales growth is required to produce the same EVA and value as adding 1 percent to EVA Margin?
It takes an extra 4.2 percent sales growth each year.

EXHIBIT 8.6 The Sales Growth Case

The valuation bias in favor of increasing profitability over increasing growth is real, yet it is something that line teams often misapprehend. They often exhibit a penchant for growth because growth is fun and seems obviously valuable, whereas profitability improvements are hard work and not as visible. But the EVA Momentum math does not lie. It is just a restatement of discounted cash flow (DCF) and net present value (NPV), after all. The truth is, it is almost always more important to increase profitability than to achieve even a lot more growth.

The relative value of growth and Margin does depend quite a bit, though, on the company and its circumstances. At one extreme, suppose a company is operating with a zero or near zero EVA Margin, which is true of many. Then even an infinite amount of extra sales growth could not catch up with a 1 percent improvement in EVA Margin. At the other extreme, suppose a company has a sky-high 20 percent EVA Margin. Then even a light flurry of additional sales growth will generate a veritable blizzard of added Momentum. The Momentum math is such that you really need to run simulations for each line of business to get a feel for it. The underlying truth, though, is that more EVA Momentum, however achieved, produces a greater discounted present value and stock price. It's the perfect proxy for the added value of the plans, and of the value added or lost by plan alternatives, as we will soon see even more clearly a little later on.

The last simulation in this section is one where the model solves for the EVA trajectory, and hence the projected EVA Momentum, that discounts to the company's stock price at the time of the analysis, in this case, to $63.01 for Tiffany. As shown in Exhibit 8.7, a Momentum average of 1.0 percent a year is needed to get to that value. It is just 0.1 percent more per year than the 0.9 percent indicated by the consensus plan. It's only a little more because the consensus price was only a little under the current price.

The 1.0 percent Momentum is Tiffany's MIM—the Momentum rate implied by the company's share valuation. To determine it using Value *Express*, I iterated the model to converge on it, but there are exact formulas to compute it. It is a data point we compute daily for 9,000 global companies.

We don't have to settle just for knowing the market's expectation for EVA Momentum, by the way. If we are able to make a plausible assumption for sales growth, we can solve for the EVA Margin that is consistent with the market's projected Momentum. For instance, if we assume that the consensus sales growth forecast is reasonable, then, as shown in Exhibit 8.7, TIF would need to increase its EVA Margin to 6 percent by the end of the five-year plan to deliver the MIM bacon as compared to the 5.6 percent EVA Margin projected in the consensus plan—again, not a great deal more than the consensus, but it is 1.5 percent higher than the 4.5 percent Margin Tiffany is recording at the present time.

TIFFANY & CO	2012TFQ2	Summary	2013TFQ2	2014TFQ2	2015TFQ2	2016TFQ2	2017TFQ2	
Sales Growth Rate	8.7%	6.9%	8.6%	9.4%	9.8%	9.8%	9.8%	
EVA Margin	4.5%	4.1%	4.8%	5.1%	5.4%	5.7%	6.0%	
EVA Summary	2012TFQ2	Summary	2013TFQ2	2014TFQ2	2015TFQ2	2016TFQ2	2017TFQ2	Summary
Sales	$3,714.946		$4,033.261	$4,412.678	$4,846.233	$5,322.385	$5,845.320	
EVA	$ 166.454		$ 193.290	$ 225.258	$ 262.530	$ 304.951	$ 353.174	
ΔEVA	$ (18.280)		$ 26.836	$ 31.968	$ 37.272	$ 42.421	$ 48.223	
Sales Growth Rate	8.7%	6.9%	8.6%	9.4%	9.8%	9.8%	9.8%	9.5%
Percentile vs Retailing	49	44						53
EVA Margin	4.5%	4.1%	4.8%	5.1%	5.4%	5.7%	6.0%	5.4%
Percentile vs Retailing	80	92						88
EVA Momentum	−0.5%	0.8%	0.7%	0.8%	0.8%	0.9%	0.9%	1.0%
Percentile vs Retailing	26	70						76
Cost of Capital	6.8%	7.6%	6.8%	6.8%	6.8%	6.8%	6.8%	6.8%
Valuation Summary		Projected						
Projected Share Price		$63.04						
Current Share Price		$63.01						
Target Shareholder Return		0.0%						
Projected MVA = PV of EVA		$5,202.8						

> **The Market-Implied Momentum Case:**
> How much EVA growth is required to discount to Tiffany's $63 share price on the valuation date?
> Five-year average EVA Momentum of 1.0 percent is required, which is 76th percentile versus specialty retail peers.

EXHIBIT 8.7   The Market-Implied EVA Momentum Case

At this point in the analysis it would not be a stretch for a CFO to announce plan goals to guide the line teams in their planning exercises. Taking account of the simulations we have run so far, for instance, Tiffany's CFO could quite reasonably tell the line teams that the final plans that emerge from the planning process will need to show consolidated EVA Momentum of at least 1 percent a year on average over the five-year plan, and an EVA Margin of at least 6 percent by plan's end. And in making such an announcement, the CFO would also ideally say that, if push comes to shove, let's be willing to leave some of that Margin goal on the table if that is what it takes to put up more points on the Momentum scorecard, for it is Momentum, not Margin, that drives value, and it is Momentum, not Margin, that will determine our bonus awards.

Private companies and operating divisions obviously cannot look at consensus estimates or solve back to their stock price. But they can still look at their own history, look at their prospects, check out public peers, use the Momentum math, and run the simulations within Value *Express* as I have demonstrated here to get a handle on suitable plan goals.

So far we've used a simple model to simulate plan valuations and sensitivities. We've forecast just two variables—sales growth and the EVA-to-sales Margin—to forecast EVA, and from that, we've derived Momentum and stock price as by-products. How is it possible such a simple model can determine the discounted cash flow net present value of a business without ever actually forecasting the balance sheet or cash flow? It is possible because the cost of all the capital that has been or will be invested is implicitly netted from the EVA Margin and removed from the projected EVA. This is a simple math transformation that makes DCF valuations a lot easier and more obvious.

The model thus enables a CFO or business planner or line manager to focus on the two key questions that determine the value of any business. How big and how profitable will it be? How fast can we grow top-line sales and what bottom-line economic profit margin can we earn? It's a very appealing way to turn discounted cash flow NPV analysis into a familiar and practical sales-based and margin-based planning and valuation framework. Although the model is simple to understand and use, the valuations that come from it are realistic and the insights are quite reliable.

With preliminary simulations like these in hand and a better appreciation for plan performance goals and trade-offs and potential priorities—and not just for the consolidated company, but ideally for each line of business— planning can begin in earnest. Line teams formulate and submit first-pass plans for review. For the EVA-focused firm, the plan submissions are first converted into summary scorecards for a bird's-eye view. The report features the planned EVA and EVA Momentum, plus the main drivers—sales, sales growth, and EVA Margin—and the MVA valuation of the plan from discounting EVA. The business plans are added up, and the consolidated EVA Momentum forecast is gauged against the overall corporate EVA Momentum goal to see how big a gap remains to be bridged. The company's value is also determined from discounting the consolidated plan for EVA and, if public, compared to the firm's actual share price.

The next step is to drill down into the plans in some detail. The underlying assumptions and key drivers for each business plan can be examined and benchmarked, and opportunities to improve the plans can be brought to the surface using the EVA Momentum Pyramid structure. Armed with those insights, divisional line teams go another round on their plans and return with even better ones. It is an iterative give-and-take, but one that is resolutely focused on how to generate the greatest possible EVA growth over a three- to five-year span, with particular detail around the next year ahead.

As I am unable to illustrate the recommended process with actual line-of-business plans, I will again draw on Tiffany's data to create and examine a series of more detailed business plans to give you a feel for what this looks like in practice. The first step, as always, is to review the actual performance track record, but this time digging deeper into underlying financial drivers of the EVA Margin and profitable growth, ideally supplemented with an examination of related nonfinancial metrics that cast light on the financial outcomes—something I will not pursue in this illustration.

The next step is to crack the shell and examine the inner albumen of the forward plan submissions. If I may be forgiven a crass advertisement, Value

Express is capable of converting essentially any forward plan for income statement and balance sheet elements into a raft of underlying financial ratios that capture the essence of the plan and that lead up to EVA Margin, and thereon to EVA, EVA Momentum, and the valuation of the plan. It is then a simple matter to examine the essential drivers of the plan and to vary them—either one at a time to assess the incremental impact of a single plan element or by altering a suite of them to simulate the value of pursuing alternative strategies.

I've done that with the consensus forecast for Tiffany. Exhibit 8.8 is a Value *Express* view of the plan that lays bare the underlying assumptions that determine the EVA Margin, EVA Momentum, and the projected EVA.

The sales growth forecast is the same as before, reflecting the median consensus estimate. As for the productivity drivers, consensus estimates are being used for some variables (which are denoted with a flag in the upper right corner of the cells) and a model buildout is used for others (again, in a real application, the drivers would just be derived from the assumptions contained in the business plans instead of being extrapolated or pulled in from analyst estimates).

The consensus estimate calls for Tiffany's EBITDAR margin to *weaken* about a half percentage point over the five-year plan, from 39.4 percent in

TIFFANY & CO	2012TFQ2	Summary	2013TFQ2	2014TFQ2	2015TFQ2	2016TFQ2	2017TFQ2
Sales	$ 3,714.946		$ 4,033.261	$ 4,391.523	$ 4,795.404	$ 5,251.496	$ 5,767.467
Sales Growth Rate	8.7%	6.9%	8.6%	8.9%	9.2%	9.5%	9.8%
Sales Growth Rate—3-Year Trend	13.3%	6.2%					
Market Share	0.3%	0.2%					
EBITDAR Margin	39.4%	37.0%	38.6%	39.0%	39.0%	38.9%	38.9%
Working Capital Charge	6.5%	6.8%	6.4%	6.3%	6.3%	6.2%	6.2%
Working Capital DOH	206.7	197.7	204.9	203.1	201.3	199.5	197.7
PPE Charge	19.3%	17.3%	18.7%	18.7%	18.3%	18.0%	17.8%
Gross Property, Plant and Equipment							
1. Gross PPE (Adjusted)/Sales	1.09	0.96	1.06	1.06	1.04	1.02	1.01
2. Capital Expenditures	$ 225.379	$ 158.208	$ 267.300	$ 224.600	$ 255.300	$ 277.000	$ 334.000
+ Increase in PV of Rents	$ 118.622	$ 224.626	$ 122.689	$ 296.242	$ 87.744	$ 346.862	$ 170.318
+ Acq-Sales-Impairments-Retirements+/–FX	$ (225.379)	$ (86.434)	$ (82.197)	$ (88.353)	$ (97.003)	$ (101.924)	$ (112.363)
Depreciation Rate	9.0%	9.0%	9.0%	9.0%	9.0%	9.0%	9.0%
Reduction of Accum Depreciation							
1. % of Trailing Gross PPE (Adjusted)	5.0%	3.9%	2.0%	2.0%	2.0%	2.0%	2.0%
2. $ Retired/Reduced	$ 198.207	$ 115.474	$ 82.197	$ 88.353	$ 97.003	$ 101.924	$ 112.363
Gross PPE (Adjusted)	$ 4,109.866	$ 3,242.166	$ 4,417.656	$ 4,850.147	$ 5,096.188	$ 5,618.126	$ 6,010.082
Net PPE (Adjusted)	$ 3,128.942	$ 2,343.509	$ 3,351.798	$ 3,690.998	$ 3,839.102	$ 4,252.972	$ 4,529.386
PV of Rents	$ 2,351.555	$ 1,617.624	$ 2,474.244	$ 2,770.486	$ 2,858.230	$ 3,205.092	$ 3,375.411
PPE Life Remaining %	75%	72%	76%	76%	76%	76%	76%
PV Rents—% of Gross PPE Adjusted	56.6%	47.1%	56.6%	56.6%	56.6%	56.6%	56.6%
Intangible Capital							
Ad & Promo							
1. Ad & Promo Expense % of Sales	6.3%	6.2%	6.3%	6.3%	6.2%	6.2%	6.2%
2. Ad & Promo Expense	$ 234.756	$ 193.912	$ 253.950	$ 275.471	$ 299.674	$ 326.937	$ 357.698
Tax							
Standard-Actual Tax Rate	5.2%	5.2%	5.2%	5.2%	5.2%	5.2%	5.2%
Deferred Tax Liab (Asset)—Net Total Adj							
1. Def Tax Liab(Asset) (% of Productive Cap)	–4.3%	–4.3%	–4.3%	4.3%	–4.3%	–4.3%	–4.3%

EXHIBIT 8.8   The Underlying Assumptions in Tiffany's Consensus Plan

the latest four-quarter period to just under 39 percent, which is somewhat surprising because considerable progress is being projected at the EVA Margin line. A management team that was focused on EBITDAR would miss the real appeal of a plan like this one.

Here is an example of a plan value that falls outside the EBITDAR countinghouse. Working capital is projected to ease back from 206.7 days to 197.7 days, which is the prior five-year average. The effect of excising nine days from cash conversion and turning working capital roughly 5 percent faster is to add 0.3 percent to the pretax EVA Margin. That's a nice gift, kind of like a sterling silver key ring. It still leaves a sizable pretax charge of 6.2 percent emanating from the working capital account, but it's a part of the EVA Margin improvement story that the EBITDAR margin completely overlooks.

The biggest driver of the EVA Margin improvement, according to this consensus view, is greater efficiency in turning the firm's long-term physical assets into customer and shareholder value. The key assumptions in the plan are: (1) capital expenditures follow the consensus estimates, which are running generally in the $250 million to $300 million range; (2) the current mix of leased assets to total assets continues at 56.6 percent (so that as capital expenditures add to property, plant, and equipment [PP&E] each year, a like amount of newly rented assets come on the books to maintain the proportion); (3) assets are depreciated on average over 11 years (i.e., a 9 percent depreciation rate); and (4) 2 percent of gross PP&E assets are retired each year (again, these are just formulaic assumptions created by the model for illustration; in an actual application, the variables would all reflect the specific assumptions contained in management's proposed business plan).

The model simulates the results of these assumptions in terms of the key PP&E metrics we examined for Tiffany's past performance. For instance, PP&E intensity (shown as the first line in the PP&E section of Exhibit 8.8) is forecast to ease back from $1.09 of PP&E per $1 of sales in the latest period to just a $1.01 of PP&E in the last projection. Said another way, and simply inverting those ratios, Tiffany will supposedly progress from generating 91.7 cents of revenue per each $1 invested in gross PP&E assets (including rented ones) to generating 99 cents in revenue per gross PP&E dollar. Either way you say it, the expectation is that there's more bang for the buck, there's more financial throughput through the plant base (or computers are moving to the cloud, or any number of things; a knowledgeable analyst or manager would need to fill in the color commentary here).

Taking all the PP&E assumptions into consideration, the combined PP&E charge for depreciation and the pretax cost of capital on owned and rented assets is projected to recede from 19.3 percent of sales in the preceding history period to 17.8 percent in the fifth forecast year. That's a full

1.5 percent pretax productivity gain, and at an assumed 40 percent standard tax rate, it hands off a huge 0.9 percent after-tax pop to the EVA Margin bottom line. That's not a key ring—that's a diamond ring.

In fact, the bulk of the valuation action in this forward plan is coming right out of the projected reduction in this PP&E line item charge. Now we know. And were we the Tiffany top team, we'd now also know to pepper this business plan with questions like: Is this real? Why is this happening? Are we generating more sales per square foot? How much is from pricing and product mix? Are we better managing store construction and repairs and maintenance? What could prevent us from accomplishing this? Can we do even better than this, or are we pushing too far on this one string? What are the trade-offs? And so forth. Knowing where the added value lies is a key to making sure the value is added.

The Value *Express* model also makes other assumptions to complete the EVA Margin computation. For instance, and again by way of illustration, it assumes that Tiffany maintains an advertising budget of around 6.2 percent of sales (matching its historical average), which the model dutifully amortizes over three years with interest; it assumes that Tiffany's tax provision rate on earnings before interest and taxes (EBIT) continues to be about 5 percent less than the assumed 40 percent standard tax rate assumption; and it assumes the company maintains a net deferred tax asset that reduces its EVA. Although not shown here, the model also charges TIF for the cost of capital on a retirement funding deficit of about $400 million, and assumes that no goodwill is added and no additional unusual losses or gains are recorded.

When all these ingredients are stirred in the pot, the result is exactly what we've already seen for the consensus plan, namely, the EVA Margin increases to 5.6 percent and EVA increases to $328 million. The projected Momentum is, once again, an annual average rate of 0.9 percent. It's the same plan, and it has the same value. The difference is that we are able to see more deeply into the drivers that define the plan so we can pinpoint the key levers, assess its risk, focus on the right questions, and, were we Tiffany's top management team, entertain an internal dialogue about how to make it better. In short, the Value *Express* model has helpfully connected *Pluribus* and *Unum*. It has tied the many business plan assumptions and levers to the EVA measures and valuation insights that matter. Quite helpful, I say.

Exhibit 8.9 recapitulates the consensus plan, but this time lingering to break out the EBITDAR margin (which is falling), the productive capital charge (which is falling even faster with the working capital and PP&E efficiencies), and the key pretax EVA Margin (which is on the rise, and that is what counts). It also shows the projected EVA Margin, EVA Momentum, the present value of EVA, and the stock price, consistent with what we've already seen for the consensus plan. With some modification, this represents

EVA Summary	2012TFQ2	Summary	2013TFQ2	2014TFQ2	2015TFQ2	2016TFQ2	2017TFQ2	Summary
Sales	$3,714.946		$4,033.261	$4,412.678	$4,846.233	$5,322.385	$5,845.320	
EVA	$ 166.454		$ 173.762	$ 207.184	$ 244.735	$ 285.738	$ 328.003	
ΔEVA	$ (18.280)		$ 7.308	$ 33.422	$ 37.551	$ 41.003	$ 42.265	
Sales Growth Rate	8.7%	6.9%	8.6%	9.4%	9.8%	9.8%	9.8%	9.5%
Percentile vs Retailing	49	44						52
EVA Margin	4.5%	4.1%	4.3%	4.7%	5.1%	5.4%	5.6%	5.0%
Percentile vs Retailing	80	82						86
EVA Momentum	−0.5%	0.8%	0.2%	0.8%	0.9%	0.8%	0.8%	0.9%
Percentile vs Retailing	28	70						72
Cost of Capital	6.8%	7.6%	6.8%	6.8%	6.8%	6.8%	6.8%	6.8%

Valuation Summary	Projected
Projected Share Price	$60.18
Current Share Price	$63.01
Target Shareholder Return	−4.5%
Projected MVA = PV of EVA	$4,840.8

The Consensus Forecast Case—In Detail:
Consensus Momentum is 0.9 percent annum, and consensus Margin reaches 5.6 percent.
EBITDAR Margin slips 0.5 percent but the productive capital charge slips 1.4 percent—the value is on the balance sheet.

EXHIBIT 8.9 The Consensus Forecast Case—In Detail

a basic version of the EVA scorecard that management can use to put all its plans on a common summary template.

With more projected drivers at its disposal, Value *Express* is able to compute more output variables, including the net operating profit after taxes (NOPAT), capital, capital investment, and free cash flow implied by the plan. It also happily discounts the projected free cash flow to a present value using the same midyear discounting factors as were applied to value EVA, and uses the same assumptions to determine the value of cash flows extending out beyond the forecast horizon—namely, that since EVA is not expected to grow after the fifth year, any investment after the fifth year is a zero NPV proposition that can be safely ignored. The terminal value of free cash flow is thus simply the NOPAT forecast in the fifth year capitalized in perpetuity. The results are shown in Exhibit 8.10.

Following this procedure, the discounted free cash flow value of the company as a business enterprise is a total of $10.257 billion. When the existing $5.416 billion capital base is removed, the remainder is $4.841 billion. That is the projected market value of the cash flows less the already invested capital. In other words, that is another way to measure the MVA of the plan. And although it is measured by discounting the cash flow this time, it is once again *identical* to the present value of the forecasted EVA, to the penny, as the schedule in Exhibit 8.10 shows.

I've already explained why this is and must be, but it is also hard coded into the DNA of the Value *Express* model so you can never get it wrong. It is also a critical check that the model has got the debits and credits right, for the only time this does work is if any adjustments made to capital or NOPAT are strictly balanced, as any good accountant would insist they be.

Free Cash Flow	Summary	2013TFQ2	2014TFQ2	2015TFQ2	2016TFQ2	2017TFQ2	Summary
NOPAT	$ 411.681	$ 543.150	$ 608.313	$ 676.914	$ 751.814	$ 832.503	$ 682.539
– Incr in Capital	$ 380.647	$ (15.857)	$ 945.305	$ (36.075)	$ 1,028.657	$ 96.523	$ 403.710
+ FCF due to NOPAT, Capital Adjustments	$ 0.825	$ –	$ –	$ –	$ –		$ –
Free Cash Flow FCF NOPAT –In	$ 31.860	$ 559.008	$ (336.992)	$ 712.989	$ (276.843)	$ 735.980	$ 278.828
Valuation Details	**Summary**	**2013TFQ2**	**2014TFQ2**	**2015TFQ2**	**2016TFQ2**	**2017TFQ2**	**Terminal**
Projected MVA = Total Present Value of FCF	$ 4,840.799						
Projected FCF and Terminal Value		$ 559.008	$ (336.992)	$ 712.989	$ (276.843)	$ 735.980	$ 12,237.179
Present Value Factor at the Cost of Capital		0.97	0.91	0.85	0.79	0.74	0.74
Present Value of Projected FCF and Terminal Value		$ 540.843	$ (305.197)	$ 604.435	$ (219.689)	$ 546.697	$ 9,089.956
Cumulative Present Value of FCF	$ 10,257.046	$ 540.843	$ 235.646	$ 840.081	$ 620.393	$ 1,167.090	$ 10,257.046
Less:Capital Most Recent Actual	$ 5,416.246						
Projected MVA = Total Present Value of EVA	$ 4,840.799						
Projected EVA and Terminal Value		$ 173.762	$ 207.184	$ 244.735	$ 285.738	$ 328.003	$ 4,802.380
Present Value Factor at the Cost of Capital		0.97	0.91	0.85	0.79	0.74	0.74
Present Value of Projected EVA and Terminal Value		$ 168.116	$ 187.636	$ 207.474	$ 226.747	$ 243.645	$ 3,567.278
Cumulative Present Value of EVA	$ 4,600.897	$ 168.116	$ 355.752	$ 563.226	$ 789.973	$ 1,033.618	$ 4,600.897
Adjustment for Mid year Discounting	$ 181.910						
Adjustment for Average Capital	$ 57.993						
Projected Share Price	**$60.18**						
= Economic Book Value per Share	**$22.56**						
+ Common Equity Adjusted	$ 2,856.465						
+ Common Equity	$ 2,396.490						
+ Common Equity Adjustments	$ 459.975						
/ Shares Outstanding	126.64						
+ Projected Price –Book Spread (MVA Per Share)	**$37.94**						
+ Common Equity Revaluation	$ 4,805.112						
+ Projected MVA	$ 4,840.799						
– Option Value After–Tax	$ 35.688						
/ Shares Oustanding	126.64						
– Interim Dividends (from valuation to current date)	$ 0.32						

EXHIBIT 8.10 The Valuation Details of Tiffany's Consensus Plan

Any way you look at it, the value of the consensus forecast is $60.18 a share. Either of the two EVA methods—the simple Margin-times-sales method we first used, or the ground-up forecast method we've just reviewed—are far more intuitive and informative than the relic DCF method, don't you agree? Again, DCF gives the same valuation answer as EVA, but without the insight, accountability, consistency, or simplicity.

Now that we've concluded a detailed analysis of the base-case plan (in this illustration, the consensus forecast is meant to function as a stand-in for a first-pass plan submitted by a line team), it's time to develop and examine alternatives, with the goal of raising the projected EVA performance bar and deriving more EVA Momentum from the plan. The alternative scenarios could represent competing views of a risky world to stress-test the valuation and help management develop contingency plans, on up to a Monte Carlo type of simulation. Or they could involve tweaking the plan with a few select initiatives and refinements. Or they could incorporate bold new strategies that entail a range of trade-offs, where some performance metrics improve and others deteriorate, and the question is: is this a better strategy, all things considered? That is precisely where the EVA metrics can be so incredibly helpful, because they consolidate the individual and often countervailing pluses and minuses into a set of reliable scores.

This is the time for the hard, thoughtful, creative analytical work, involving a detailed investigation of markets, technology, competition, emerging consumer trends, and so on. The idea, though, is that after the brainstorming and strategic analysis are concluded and a financial forecast representing a revised plan has been developed, it can be uploaded into Value *Express* and converted into the Best-Practice EVA model for the purpose of measuring its value and diagnosing its financial drivers. It is necessarily an iterative and interactive process. Left brain talking to right brain, back to left, and so on.

I will now walk through two hypothetical alternatives for Tiffany that I dreamed up for the sake of illustration. The first revision focuses quite simply on slashing Tiffany's incredibly high working capital with a weed whacker and accelerating turns and cash conversion by about 40 percent, dropping days on hand from 197.7 days to just 120 days. It is an extreme and unrealistic proposition, I am fairly certain, but it is an interesting lesson in how a single performance dimension can be isolated and valued and its importance highlighted to the management team.

There are dual Momentum Pyramids shown in Exhibit 8.11, with the one on the left characterizing the consensus plan and the one on the right the revised working capital productivity plan. Note that the cutback drops the pretax working capital charge in proportion, by about 40 percent, from 6.2 percent to 3.7 percent. That adds 2.5 percent to the pretax EVA Margin and 1.5 percent to the EVA Margin bottom line. EVA Margin is forecast to reach 7.1 percent by the fifth forecast year, compared to 5.6 percent in the base-case consensus forecast. Those are all huge improvements, and they all stem from reducing working capital.

How does the working capital move play through EVA? EVA steps up to $417 million in the fifth forecast year compared to $328 million in the original consensus case. Momentum ramps up from 4.3 percent to 6.7 percent over the five years, an overall increase of 2.4 percent. Of that, 1.5 percent is due to expansion in the EVA Margin, as would be expected from cutting the working capital charge, but there's another 0.9 percent in added Momentum coming through the profitable growth channel, from making the projected sales growth all the more profitable. Although it emanates solely from a supposed improvement in balance sheet efficiency, the positive impact is felt across both dimensions of the Momentum formula.

The revised plan's MVA is $5.953 billion, compared to about $4.841 billion in the base case. The working capital initiative increases owner wealth by about $1.1 *billion*. From a cash flow point of view, that comes from the present value of the cash freed up by the reduction in working capital. But in the EVA world, the added value is, as always, due to the present value of the extra economic profit and EVA Momentum that the revised plan generates.

The $1.1 billion bump up in MVA is worth $8.78 per share. Put that on top of the consensus value of $60.18 a share, and the revised plan is worth $68.96 a share, an increase of 14.6 percent. But then you already knew it was in that ballpark. As noted, EVA Momentum increased by 2.4 percent

Consensus Base Case

Projected Share Price $60.18
Target Return -4%
MVA $4,841

5 Yr EVA Momentum	4.3%
EVA Momentum	
ΔEVA/Trailing Sales	
$328 — $166 / $3,715	

Productivity Gains	1.1%
Δ(EVA/Sales)	
5.6% - 4.5%	

Profitable Growth	3.2%
(EVA/Sales) x Sales Growth	
5.6% x 57.3%	

	2012TFQ2	2017TFQ2
Sales	$ 3,715	$ 5,845
COGS (Adjusted)	41.8%	NA
SG&A (Adjusted)	18.8%	NA
EBITDAR Margin	39.4%	38.9%
Productive Capital Charges	31.5%	30.1%
Working Capital Charge	6.5%	6.2%
Working Capital Days	206.7	197.7
PP&E Rent Charge	19.3%	17.6%
= Gross PP&E per $1 Sales	1.09	1.01
x Rental Rate	17.6%	17.7%
= Depreciation Rate	9.0%	9.0%
+ PP&E Life Remaining	75%	76%
x COC Bef Tax	11.4%	11.4%
Intangible Capital Rent Charge	5.7%	6.2%
Book Intangibles Charge	0.0%	0.0%
Ad & Promo Charge	5.7%	6.2%
EVA Before Tax	8.0%	8.7%
Corporate Charges	3.5%	3.1%
Tax Rate	40.9%	38.5%
Other EVA	0.0%	0.4%
Goodwill and Unusual Charge	0.2%	0.1%
Goodwill (Adjusted)/Sales	0.00	0.00
Cum Unus Items/Sales	0.03	0.02
EVA Margin	4.5%	5.6%

WC Productivity Case 2

Projected Share Price $68.96
Target Return 9%
MVA $5,953

5 Yr EVA Momentum	6.7%
EVA Momentum	
ΔEVA/Trailing Sales	
$417 — $166 / $3,715	

Productivity Gains	2.6%
Δ(EVA/Sales)	
7.1% - 4.5%	

Profitable Growth	4.1%
(EVA/Sales) x Sales Growth	
7.1% x 57.3%	

	2012FQ2	2017TFQ2
Sales	$ 3,715	$ 5,845
COGS (Adjusted)	41.8%	NA
SG&A (Adjusted)	18.8%	NA
EBITDAR Margin	39.4%	38.9%
Productive Capital Charges	31.5%	27.7%
Working Capital Charge	6.5%	3.7%
Working Capital Days	206.7	120.0
PP&E Rent Charge	19.3%	17.8%
= Gross PP&E per $1 Sales	1.09	1.01
x Rental Rate	17.6%	17.7%
= Depreciation Rate	9.0%	9.0%
+ PP&E Life Remaining	75%	76%
x COC Bef Tax	11.4%	11.4%
Intangible Capital Rent Charge	5.7%	6.2%
Book Intangibles Charge	0.0%	0.0%
Ad & Promo Charge	5.7%	6.2%
EVA Before Tax	8.0%	11.1%
Corporate Charges	3.5%	4.0%
Tax Rate	40.9%	38.2%
Other EVA	0.0%	0.4%
Goodwill and Unusual Charge	0.2%	0.1%
Goodwill (Adjusted)/Sales	0.00	0.00
Cum Unus Items/Sales	0.03	0.02
EVA Margin	4.5%	7.1%

EXHIBIT 8.11 Tiffany's Consensus Plan versus the Working Capital Productivity Plan

over the five years, which is an average increase of just about 0.5 percent per year. Multiply that 0.5 percent annual increase by Tiffany's 30× Momentum Leverage Ratio, and the predicted stock price lift is 15 percent versus the 14.6 percent computed earlier. The difference is just rounding. Again, every change in performance or strategy predictably impacts value via its impact on EVA Momentum.

Incidentally, this case poses a real problem for the EBITDA crowd. TIF's share price is projected to increase by almost 15 percent with the revised plan, yet EBITDA and EBITDAR haven't changed at all. It's a pure balance sheet initiative. But if the valuation is higher—and it is, because the EVA (and cash flow) is higher—then TIF's enterprise multiples must increase as a result. That is perfectly understandable as a function of the improvement in EVA. But what can the EBITDA crowd say? They are just left to mumble voodoo incantations about an inexplicable expansion in the enterprise multiple.

Let's take one final stab at improving the business plan before putting the pencil down. Suppose that management builds on its working capital initiative and hatches a new bold strategy, with results portrayed in the right-side chart in Exhibit 8.12. The new plan calls for significantly ratcheting up spending on advertising and marketing over the five-year plan (upping the fifth-year spend rate from 6.2 percent of sales to 7.2 percent of sales) in order, let's say, to become the preeminent source of prestige jewelry in the Asian market and other key developing markets (I am just making this up). EVA accommodates the strategic shift by amortizing the product launch and brand spending over three years, with interest, spreading out the cost to better match the proposed benefit.

The payoff comes in from more sales, a larger margin, and faster turns (as are evident on the right-hand Momentum Pyramid), as follows:

- The expansion plan tags 3 percent onto sales growth per year, or about 23 percent more over five years.
- Exerting pricing power in impressionable developing markets boosts the gross margin and thus the EBITDAR margin by 1 percent (which is just exactly offset by the assumed 1 percent increase in advertising and marketing spend).
- The revised plan is also expected to generate more sales per square foot of retail space (they're breaking down the doors to buy), which speeds the overall fixed asset turns by 5 percent (gross PP&E drops from a buck and a penny in the prior plan to 96 cents per sales dollar in the new plan). Although the new strategy calls for more capital expenditure spending and additions to leased assets, which reduces the average age of the PP&E base somewhat, the overall yield on the PP&E assets is higher.

WC Productivity — Case 2

Projected Share Price **$68.96**
Target Return **9%**
MVA **$5,953**

5 Yr EVA Momentum 6.7%

EVA Momentum		
ΔEVA/Trailing Sales		
$417	— $166	/ $3,715

Profitable Growth 4.1%

(EVA/Sales) x Sales Growth	
7.1% x	57.3%

Productivity Gains 2.6%

Δ(EVA/Sales)	
7.1% —	4.5%

		2012TFQ2	2017TFQ2
	Sales	$ 3,715	$ 5,845
	COGS (Adjusted)	41.8%	NA
	SG&A (Adjusted)	18.8%	NA
	EBITDAR Margin	39.4%	38.9%
	Productive Capital Charges	31.5%	27.7%
	Working Capital Charge	6.5%	3.7%
	Working Capital Days	206.7	120.0
	PP&E Rent Charge	19.3%	17.8%
	= Gross PP&E per $1 Sales	1.09	1.01
	x Rental Rate	17.6%	17.7%
	= Depreciation Rate	9.0%	9.0%
	+ PP&E Life Remaining	75%	76%
	x COC Bef Tax	11.4%	11.4%
	Intangible Capital Rent Charge	5.7%	6.2%
	Book Intangibles Charge	0.0%	0.0%
	Ad & Promo Charge	5.7%	6.2%
	EVA Before Tax	8.0%	11.1%
	Corporate Charges	3.5%	4.0%
x (1−)	Tax Rate	40.9%	38.2%
+	Other EVA	0.0%	0.4%
	Goodwill and Unusual Charge	0.2%	0.1%
	Goodwill (Adjusted) /Sales	0.00	0.00
	Cum Unus Items/Sales	0.03	0.02
=	EVA Margin	4.5%	7.1%

Profitable Growth — Case 3

Projected Share Price **$75.72**
Target Return **20%**
MVA **$6,808**

5 Yr EVA Momentum 8.3%

EVA Momentum		
ΔEVA/Trailing Sales		
$473	— $166	/ $3,715

Profitable Growth 5.7%

(EVA/Sales) x Sales Growth	
7.1% x	80.1%

Productivity Gains 2.6%

Δ(EVA/Sales)	
7.1% —	4.5%

		2012TFQ2	2017TFQ2
	Sales	$ 3,715	$ 6,691
	COGS (Adjusted)	41.8%	NA
	SG&A (Adjusted)	18.8%	NA
	EBITDAR Margin	39.4%	39.9%
	Productive Capital Charges	31.5%	28.8%
	Working Capital Charge	6.5%	4.8%
	Working Capital Days	206.7	155.0
	PP&E Rent Charge	19.3%	17.2%
	= Gross PP&E per $1 Sales	1.09	0.96
	x Rental Rate	17.6%	17.9%
	= Depreciation Rate	9.0%	9.0%
	+ PP&E Life Remaining	75%	77%
	x COC Bef Tax	11.4%	11.4%
	Intangible Capital Rent Charge	5.7%	6.8%
	Book Intangibles Charge	0.0%	0.0%
	Ad & Promo Charge	5.7%	6.8%
	EVA Before Tax	8.0%	11.0%
	Corporate Charges	3.5%	3.9%
x (1−)	Tax Rate	40.9%	38.8%
+	Other EVA	0.0%	0.4%
	Goodwill and Unusual Charge	0.2%	0.1%
	Goodwill (Adjusted) /Sales	0.00	0.00
	Cum Unus Items/Sales	0.03	0.01
	EVA Margin	4.5%	7.1%

EXHIBIT 8.12 Tiffany's Working Capital Plan versus the Profitable Growth Plan

What shows that? The pretax PP&E charge to the EVA Margin is scaled back by 0.6 percent. Under the prior plan it was 17.8 percent and with the new one it is 17.2 percent—still very high, but just not quite so high.

So far, so good. But as is typical of many strategies, it is not better in every dimension. The entry into more remote foreign markets complicates logistics, and a plan goal to reach less well-heeled consumers requires Tiffany to extend more credit and increase receivables. The result is that working capital is put partway back up. It will end the five-year plan at 155 days on hand versus 120 days when management was focused solely on the working capital initiative. The additional working capital puts a 1.1 percent pretax charge back on the EVA Margin books.

The net effect of the crosscurrents is that the projected EVA Margin stands perfectly still (I designed it that way to make a point). It reaches 7.1 percent in the last forecast period, the exact same as was projected in the working capital productivity case. There is no progress there. EVA, though, is projected to go $56 million higher compared to the prior plan, and EVA Momentum is up another 1.6 percent over five years, or another 0.3 percent or so per year. What's that worth? $30\times \times 0.3$ percent, right. The stock price from discounting EVA is up another 10 percent, from $68.96 to $75.72, as predicted. It is a better plan. It generates even more EVA and more owner wealth.

And yet none of the payoff comes from improving the EVA Margin, nor does it come from any improvement in return on capital. It does not come from increasing the conventionally reported operating margin. As was mentioned, the increase in advertising and marketing spending just offsets the projected increase in the gross margin. And the added value is certainly not revealed by the increase in working capital days on hand (compared to the prior plan). Companies preoccupied with maintaining pristine working capital metrics would find this a very hard move to swallow, and those focused on operating margins would find it inconsequential.

But it is a great move nonetheless. Compared to the value of pursuing the working capital initiative alone, the Asian expansion strategy adds another $855 million to the firm's MVA and owner wealth. It carries the stock price to a full 25 percent premium over the original consensus valuation. And it all comes—as the Momentum Pyramid makes crystal clear—from generating more sales growth at a handsomely positive EVA Margin. Although there is no net increase in the quality of earnings, there is an impressive increase in the quantity of quality earnings. It's a contrived example, sure, but it is realistic in the sense that trade-offs are a constant in business decisions, and it does illustrate how ill-advised it is to judge performance, set targets, and meter bonus pay according to the individual micro-metric metrics and in the absence of the definitive EVA score of the business game.

Although this illustration did not show it, there are many conceivable strategies for a firm like Tiffany, which is already quite EVA positive, to step on the accelerator and grow EVA even faster and produce even more franchise value while *diluting* its EVA Margin and reducing its return on capital somewhat. Can that really be advisable? Yes. Any change in strategy that generates more EVA and more Momentum is more valuable no matter what the other metrics may say. And that is not a question of believing in EVA. As long as you subscribe to the view that discounted cash flow is an accurate way to measure the value that the market truly values, then you can always trust the insights from EVA, for the two always discount to the same answer.

Let's bring together the various scenarios we've examined onto the summary chart that follows. It plots the projected average EVA Momentum for the simulations we've considered going left to right, undergirded with salient explanatory statistics, and the corresponding MVA and share price from discounting the EVA projections plotted north to south.

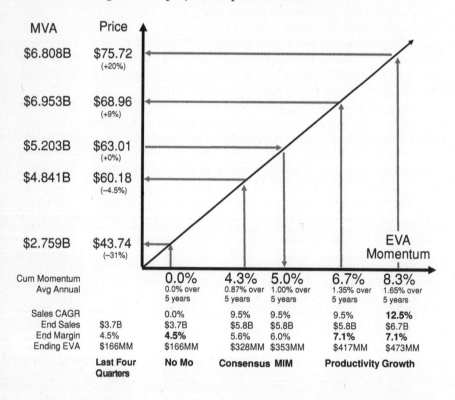

MVA	Price					
$6.808B	$75.72 (+20%)					
$6.953B	$68.96 (+9%)					
$5.203B	$63.01 (+0%)					
$4.841B	$60.18 (−4.5%)					
$2.759B	$43.74 (−31%)					EVA Momentum

Cum Momentum		0.0%	4.3%	5.0%	6.7%	8.3%
Avg Annual		0.0% over 5 years	0.87% over 5 years	1.00% over 5 years	1.35% over 5 years	1.65% over 5 years
Sales CAGR		0.0%	9.5%	9.5%	9.5%	12.5%
End Sales	$3.7B	$3.7B	$5.8B	$5.8B	$5.8B	$6.7B
End Margin	4.5%	4.5%	5.6%	6.0%	7.1%	7.1%
Ending EVA	$166MM	$166MM	$328MM	$353MM	$417MM	$473MM
	Last Four Quarters	**No Mo**	**Consensus**	**MIM**	**Productivity**	**Growth**

The lowest valuation—only about $44 a share—is for the no EVA Momentum case ("No Mo") where we assumed EVA would remain forever stuck at about $166 million. This valuation is about 31 percent under the market price. It gives a feel for a floor on valuation, and an indication of how much value is at risk on actually generating positive EVA Momentum over time.

EVA MOMENTUM IS A PERFECT PROXY FOR THE QUALITY AND VALUE OF FORWARD PLANS

The next rightward step is the consensus forecast, which equated to a $60.18 stock price on an average Momentum pace of a little less than 0.9 percent per annum. If possible, it is nearly always helpful to price out the expectations of analysts who follow the stock and for insights into improving stock price by improving communication—particularly where the company's own plan value well exceeds the consensus valuation.

The arrows are reversed for the middle case on the chart, pointing from price to performance, because that was the case where we worked backward and solved for the EVA Momentum that would equate to the company's actual $63.01 stock price on the October 8, 2012, valuation date. The math showed Tiffany's MIM was an even 5.0 percent over the five years, or an average of 1.0 percent per year. This is an even more relevant bogey for the CFO to use in setting minimum plan performance goals.

The last two are for the simulations we just covered—the one for the working capital productivity initiative and the other for the revised growth strategy. These are obviously just two alternatives among many. The planning goal is to find the best one with the most Momentum.

A diagonal line connects the dots. That's no accident. For all practical purposes, it is always very nearly a straight line. This is key. More Momentum is more EVA, and more EVA is more value added and a higher share price premium on top of the firm's underlying book value. As advertised, *EVA Momentum is indeed the perfect proxy for the quality and value of business plans*. In other words, EVA Momentum reduces the net present value of discounted cash flow and the share price contribution of business plans to a single summary statistic that works in any business (and without actually using cash flow). That is a big deal, don't you think?

By now the implications should be clear as a bell. CFOs should use EVA Momentum and the underlying vital statistics to summarize, rank, and review proposed business plans in terms of their potential for adding value, and, as I have illustrated, they should challenge their line teams to use the available Momentum and Margin tools to deconstruct their proposed plans and to return with better, more EVA-capable, and fundamentally more valuable plans. And on a more elevated plane they should follow the Coca-Cola lead and use Momentum as a general-purpose framework for thinking about strategy, and in support of a truly balanced and value-anchored scorecard, one where company-specific strategic themes and milestones and related winning metrics literally tuck in under the EVA Momentum Pyramid.

When the planning process is concluded, EVA Momentum and its ratio entourage should be used to express the essence of the plan to the board and investors. The final plans, moreover, should be turned into a set of key EVA budget targets, by quarter, by line of business, over the next year. Other metrics can be added as circumstances dictate, and intelligent trade-offs can be made. But the commitment and the incentive should be to deliver the EVA Momentum target, and quarterly performance reviews should be organized to help management to meet and exceed that commitment.

This, to me, is the culmination of value-based corporate management. It is the best practice as far as the financial analysis of the plans is concerned.

CHAPTER 9

Dividing Multiples into Good and Bad

It is one thing to develop a plan and forecast a value. It is another to ascertain how reasonable it is, and how it fits into the valuations of other companies on the market. When we developed the plans for Tiffany, we examined their reasonableness in light of the EVA performance metrics and the underlying drivers and assumptions, and the impact on the discounted valuation, which was all well and good. In fact, I think it is essential. But valuation multiples, properly understood, can also be used as reality checks on the reasonableness of corporate plans and forecasts. Valuation multiples also are a key element in the EVA stock-rating model covered in the upcoming chapter on EVA and the buy side. If nothing else, management should be prepared to respond to its board or to investors when asked to account for the firm's valuation multiples compared to those of peers.

The most popular of the valuation ratios is, of course, the price-to-earnings (P/E) multiple. It also is the worst. P/E has a long legacy, back to a predigital age when computations of any kind were so hard to perform that simple metrics were preferred. That is not an excuse to keep using it now. I have already explained a number of times and in a number of ways that P/E multiples are horribly flawed and should be ignored. You will see further evidence of this in the next chapter when we look at acquisition valuations. I never look at P/E, and don't see why you should. Let's move on. There are better alternatives.

The sensible EVA-based valuation multiples are illustrated for Tiffany in Exhibit 9.1. The right-hand "Projected" column displays the multiples associated with the consensus forecast which, recall, discounted to a $60.01 share price, or just 4.5 percent off the actual price on the valuation date.

The first of these is MVA Spread, the ratio of MVA to capital. We've seen this before, but now let's consider it more fully. It can be computed using the firm's actual MVA, given its share price, and that is shown in the table for Tiffany as of midyear for each of the past three years. It can also

Valuation Summary	2010TFQ2	2011TFQ2	2012TFQ2	Projected
Projected Share Price				$60.01
Current Share Price	$42.07	$79.59	$54.93	$64.01
Target Shareholder Return				−6.2%
Projected MVA = PV of EVA				$ 4,820.50
Capital (Most Recent Actual)				$ 5,416.20
Projected Market Value				$10,236.80
Valuation Multiples	**2010TFQ2**	**2011TFQ2**	**2012TFQ2**	**Projected**
MVA Spread MVA/Capital	88%	159%	76%	89%
Percentile vs Retailing	65	78	64	64
MVA Margin MVA/Sales	107%	221%	111%	130%
Percentile vs Retailing	79	90	79	80
EBITDAR Multiple EV/EBITDAR	6.5	9.3	6.5	7.0
Percentile vs Retailing	40	62	39	42
NOPAT Multiple MV/NOPAT	19.6	25.9	18.5	19.9
Percentile vs Retailing	45	64	40	45
Future Growth Reliance FVA/MV	27%	39%	13%	19%
Percentile vs Retailing	49	50	38	40

EXHIBIT 9.1   Tiffany's EVA-Based Valuation Multiples

be computed using the predicted MVA derived from discounting the forward-plan EVA as a way to judge the reasonableness of the plan. Tiffany's predicted MVA under the consensus forecast was $4.82 billion, and its last reported capital was $5.42 billion. The MVA/capital ratio comes to 89 percent. This means that every $1 in capital in the business would translate into 89 cents of added owner wealth, according to the forecast. How high is that? It is hard to judge as an isolated statistic, but it is at the 64th percentile among the retailing crowd, as reported in the table. On that score, the multiple is on the high side, but not egregiously high. It is what would be expected for a company of Tiffany's quality, and it is also in line with the percentile rank for the multiple in prior years.

A sister ratio—the MVA Margin, or the ratio of MVA to sales—is 130 percent under the consensus plan. Each $1 of current sales translates into $1.30 in franchise value. Tiffany's MVA Margin ratio is pegged at the 80th percentile among retailing peers compared to the 64th percentile for the MVA Spread. Why the difference?

Tiffany, as we have seen, operates a business model that is far more capital intense than most retailers, which deflates the ratio of wealth creation per dollar of invested capital. Remember, though, that in the EVA model, capital is a cost, not a divisor. That's why we tend to deemphasize the MVA/capital ratio in favor the MVA/sales ratio as a valuation metric, for that is the valuation multiple that ties directly to the sales-based EVA performance ratios. Without going into the gory details, a company's MVA/sales ratio is always equal to its current EVA Margin and the present value of its projected EVA Momentum, divided by the cost of capital. It is the capitalized value of profitability and profitable growth. In this case, TIF's 80th percentile MVA Margin ratio quite understandably corresponds with its 80th percentile EVA Margin and the 72nd percentile EVA Momentum projected in the consensus plan. If the EVA Margin and Momentum metrics are sensible and achievable, then the MVA Margin, and actually all other valuation multiples, must be as well. I will have more to say on this theme.

Another valuation ratio of note is an adjusted (read *improved*) enterprise valuation multiple. Traditional enterprise multiples are computed as enterprise value divided by EBITDA. This one is computed as the firm's enterprise value, *including* the present value of rented assets, divided by the EBITDAR metric, which is measured prerent expense, as opposed to the conventional EBITDA figure, which is measured postrent expense. This is an even more totally unlevered valuation multiple than the EBITDA version. The classic enterprise multiple is distorted when the mix of leasing and owning assets varies, but this one sees through it (and thus it is the one used in the EVA stock-rating model, as will be discussed). TIF's valuation according to the consensus plan is 7.0× trailing-four-quarter EBITDAR, which places this multiple at the 42nd percentile among the retail crowd. That's a far lower rating than the MVA multiples, which clocked in at the 64nd to 80th percentiles. Why the discrepancy?

Here's the answer. TIF's EBITDAR is inflated—*relative to those of other retailers*—because TIF has relatively more of the expenses that are not deducted from EBITDAR but that the market truly considers to be important. Hence, its multiple of EBITDAR is lower. Like EBITDA, EBITDAR is measured before deducting depreciation, and TIF has gobs of depreciation of its asset base as compared to other retailers. EBITDAR is also before amortization of intangibles, and TIF has substantial amortization of advertising spending. Most significant, EBITDAR is before interest, including especially the full cost of capital charge that EVA takes into account and that applies to its considerable base of owned and rented assets and also to its immense investment in working capital and in brand equity. And TIF has a particularly high EVA tax rate from its hefty deferred tax asset account. In all those ways, EBITDAR substantially overstates the EVA profit the market is really valuing to a more extreme extent than it does for other retailers, so that the valuation multiple of EBITDAR is understandably lower than its MVA ratios relative to its peers. EBITDAR or its bastard cousin EBITDA are both truly earnings before many things that count, and that the market obviously factors into valuations. Again, if, the EVA performance metrics are reasonable, then the valuation is reasonable. Do not start to doubt the valuation because the multiple seems out of line. Figure it out. There is almost always a sensible way to explain why the multiple diverges.

The next multiple down the list is a step in the right direction. It is the ratio of market value to net operating profit after taxes (NOPAT). It is 19.9× for TIF's consensus plan, or 45th percentile. Besides cleaning up sundry accounting distortions, NOPAT differs from EBITDAR in that it is measured after taxes (at the smoothed tax rate and considering the benefit of deferring tax payments), and it is measured after setting aside the depreciation and amortization of wasting assets that must be replenished or replaced to keep the profits flowing.

As a result, NOPAT comes a lot closer to the distributable cash flow that the market really values. This is because NOPAT measures the *net* cash flow the firm generates after setting aside a necessary allowance to recover and maintain the capital, as opposed to EBITDA or EBITDAR, which are *gross* cash flows, and thus inherently unsustainable. Granted, the reported depreciation and amortization costs are not perfect measures of the true replenishment costs. But the reported charges are almost always a more accurate indication of the real cost than to assume the charges are null, which is what EBITDA and EBITDAR do. Our research shows conclusively that NOPAT multiples better explain and predict stock prices than the cash flow multiples do.

To be specific, recall that NOPAT is in principle the free cash flow that would be available as an annual liquidating distribution assuming there is only investment to maintain the status quo and no investment for growth. Under those assumptions, a firm's intrinsic market value would be just its normalized NOPAT profit divided by the cost of capital. It is its NOPAT capitalized as a level perpetuity. For Tiffany, given its 6.3 percent cost of capital, the basic NOPAT enterprise multiple should thus be 15.9× (1/6.3 percent), just the inversion of the cost of capital.

Tiffany's actual NOPAT multiple is 19.6×, or 4× NOPAT higher, because the firm's market value goes further than just capitalizing NOPAT and also includes the present value of the forecasted growth in EVA. Put another way, 4× of the 19.6× multiple, or about 20 percent of it, is implicitly due to the value of the projected growth in EVA. All this helps us to understand the NOPAT multiple better, and why it is better than any of the cash flow multiples. And yet, for all that, the NOPAT multiple is not an especially efficient way to home in on the key valuation question, which is: how much of the company's market value depends on, and is at the risk of, EVA growth? Granted, the answer to the question is contained in the NOPAT multiple, but it is hard to isolate it, which brings us to the next and final multiple of interest.

The culminating EVA ratio shown in Exhibit 9.1 is Future Growth Reliance (FGR)—the percentage of the market value attributable to the growth in EVA, and a sister to the Market-Implied Momentum statistic. In this case, it is the percentage of the forecast market value that is attributable to the consensus forecast for growth in EVA. Tiffany's projected EVA growth reliance is 19 percent, which is only the 40th percentile among peers. It is another indication that the plan is not exceptionally aggressive, at least as far as the proportion of the value that is contained in the projected EVA Momentum. That's nice to know, but then, how does that conclusion square against the much higher MVA multiples we've seen? And how does it square against the 0.9 percent EVA Momentum that was forecast in the consensus plan, which was rated at the 72nd percentile compared to the Momentum accomplishments of its peer group? It seems too low, perhaps?

It is not. Remember, the value used to compute all the multiples is the same—it is derived from discounting the consensus EVA plan. So if any one multiple appears out of line, then you just need to figure the reason for the discrepancy rather than questioning the valuation.

Here's the explanation. Recall that MVA comes from the present value of current EVA plus the present value of projected growth in EVA. The preponderance of Tiffany's MVA is in the first bucket. It is so profitable right out of the starting gate, with an 80th percentile EVA Margin, that the lion's share of its MVA is derived from its embedded EVA and not as much, *relatively speaking*, comes from the EVA growth component. TIF illustrates the rule that where MVA is high and FGR is relatively low, you have a company that is already quite profitable and whose projected EVA growth is simply less important by comparison, no matter how good it may be on its own terms. It is the perfect portrait of an established aristocrat—an apt description of Tiffany, eh?

This illustrates an important rule. You can read the MVA/sales and FGR ratios in tandem to get a full stereoscopic view of a company's valuation, and dispense with all the others. Suppose you performed a valuation of a forward plan and found it translated into a relatively low MVA/sales ratio but a relatively high FGR ratio. What would that indicate? That the company's EVA is currently underwater; it is expected to improve significantly, but will nevertheless stop short of ever reaching high ground. It is a firm deep in the valley that is expected to climb to a base station and no higher.

What if both ratios are high? That's really terrific. The valuation multiples are telling us the company is currently an EVA Margin star and is a prospective big-time EVA Momentum winner. It is a great company that is forecast to become greater still. It's like a phenomenally talented midcareer athlete with years of outstanding performances still to come. It's Roger Federer after winning the 2006 U.S Open, his ninth of 17 slams, and counting. Again, the two ratios taken together give you an efficient and reliable way to understand and benchmark the valuation story. There really is no need for P/E or an enterprise multiple in any form. They are at best redundant, and almost always inferior.

So concludes our short detour into the world of valuation multiples. A personal goal for this conversation was to demonstrate just how slippery and opaque multiples can be. There's a lot going on inside the ratios, and if you look closely at the conventional ones, they are so flawed that it is really hard to gain any reliable insights from them. I fear that CFOs and CEOs and investor relations (IR) directors spend a lot of time going in circles on those, and it is largely fruitless. If you are to look at any, I urge you to consult the EVA valuation multiples I have explained. They are more efficient, and they are more dependable.

I will go further, though. I am suggesting that less reliance be placed on valuation multiples in general. Up to now, valuation multiples have been the best available means to judge the overall quality of a plan or the degree of stretch in it. *But now it is possible to judge the forecasts directly.* The projected EVA Momentum and EVA Margin statistics that characterize the plans can be benchmarked against the profiles of actual corporate ac-complishments, against market-implied rates, and in the context of the EVA Momentum math. Do not abandon multiples. MVA/sales and FGR have a role to play. But you are now able to shift the emphasis toward a quantifi-cation of the EVA performance metrics that so succinctly, completely, and accurately characterize the financial and valuation essence of the plans.

CHAPTER 10

Put EVA into Capital Decisions and Acquisitions

I encounter CFOs who ask me to show them how EVA gives them better insights into business decisions or investment projects. These are often the same CFOs who like to employ an intensely rigorous capital review process. They intentionally throw up a lot of hurdles that make it hard for their line teams to access capital until they can prove that the projected returns are there. I think they are going about it all wrong, asking the wrong questions and getting the wrong answers.

Years ago, while consulting with a Brazilian company that operated a diamond mine as a sideline business, I asked the CEO, "How's the diamond extraction business these days?" "Not as good as it was," was the answer. As the CEO told it, the Brazilian government had put on capital controls that made it difficult to take money out of the country. The result: even more people wanted to take their money out, and one of the best ways was to purchase diamonds at inflated prices and carry them overseas (don't ask how). The demand created by capital flight caused the diamond boom. Then the government wised up and relaxed the controls. Capital could freely flow in or out—at least at that time. Then everyone wanted to bring their money back to invest in Brazil, and the price of diamonds collapsed.

What's the lesson? The harder it is for line teams to get their hands on capital, the more they want it, and the more they will bend the rules to get it, such as by inflating projections or proliferating capital requests or by turning into strong project proponents. Frustrated by what they see as an out-of-control process, CFOs will sometimes impose an overall capital spending limit—they follow Brazil's example and put on capital controls—which only makes matters worse. There's nothing anyone wants more than what they can't have. Every line team feels it has to really puff up the potential payoffs for its projects for fear the other teams are doing it even more. It's mutually assured escalation. It's like putting a pot on the stove, locking a lid tight on top, and turning up the heat. It's an explosive combination. And it's guaranteed to reduce trust, candor, and the quality of the information flow. It leads to a less efficient allocation of capital, not a better one.

The solution is not in introducing more analytical rigor into the capital budgeting process (although there certainly are companies where more is needed). It is not to find a superior analysis tool that will somehow magically reveal the true returns on proposed projects. The answer that really works is to change the attitudes of the managers who propose the projects and the atmosphere within which capital is allocated. And the best way I've found to do that is to use EVA to frame and value the decisions and investments, to measure and evaluate performance, and to meter bonus pay, as I have already described. This holistic approach makes everyone truly accountable for capital and goes much further to improve capital budgeting and decision making than any technical refinements to a discounted cash flow (DCF) analysis.

When I hear a CFO say, "We can't use EVA because we already have so much contention over the cost of capital, and EVA will only make that worse," I know exactly what the problem is. They are in old-school finance. They are jacking up hurdle rates in another feeble attempt to rein in capital spending. But that doesn't work well, either. It just leads to a lot of animosity and pointless arguments over the ninth decimal point of inaccuracy in the cost of capital. Again, the solution is to charge for capital and establish clear rewards for improving EVA. Then, as I have said, you can simplify the cost of capital. Expose managers to the risk in the bonus plan, and there is no need to make the cost of capital the risk management tool.

In an ideal EVA world, the CEO and CFO stand up in front of their entire management team and say, in effect, "Ladies and gentlemen, in the past capital was hard to come by because capital was essentially free. The measures we used did not really make earning the cost of capital a visible and critical responsibility. That put a lot of pressure on us at the head office to function as the capital gatekeepers. The only time there was any real accountability for investing capital was when the decision to invest it was being made, but not after, and because that did not work well, we sweated the decisions, as you are painfully aware. But now we've adopted EVA. Now we are going to charge you for the capital you request, just as if you had rented the assets you say you need to run and grow your business. Now capital is available, as much as you want; please come and get it; we want to generate more profitable growth. Just remember this: The capital you invest comes back to you as a fixed charge cost you must cover. You will be rewarded for exceeding it and penalized for falling short."

Believe it or not, that statement, that process, is the chief way that any company can improve its capital allocation to where the maximization of net present value is naturally wired in.

Having said all this, I do not diminish the importance of corporate over-sight. The corporate office is typically staffed with seasoned executives who are more intimate with the company's overall strategic direction and focus, are compensated more with long-term stock incentives, are less biased to any one division, and also are apt to have more business experience and financial acumen. Bringing that to bear is important. But with EVA the field teams have the incentive to respect that rather than ignore it or try to get around it.

I also want to emphasize that EVA is able to *provide superior analytical insights* into capital budgeting decisions, which I will now review. I don't mean to dodge that point. But as considerable as the advantages are that I will demonstrate, the case for using EVA in capital budgeting chiefly rests on how a holistic application of EVA to all aspects of management can change everyone's attitude toward using capital. That is the real key.

From a technical perspective, let's first acknowledge that the discount-ed present value of EVA is equal to the discounted cash flow NPV of an individual capital project or business decision. That not only works for valuing whole companies or lines of business. It works just as well for evaluating individual projects. Any decision you can model out in terms of a skeletal income statement, balance sheet, and cash flow forecast is a candidate for present value EVA analysis. Doing it that way lets managers get to the NPV answer by modeling out the very same incremental EVA projection that they know will be overlaid on top of their base business's EVA if it is accepted.

And remember, unlike any other measure, EVA is additive. Add a project to any business, and regardless of the business's embedded EVA, it will end up with more or less EVA depending on the EVA of the project. The clear line of sight that sees the EVA of individual projects directly adding into the EVA and the Momentum of the sponsoring divisions and the corporate parent is an enormous advantage compared to other measures.

Not to belabor a point I've covered, but all the other measures, and I do mean all of them—measures like operating margins, growth rates, re-turns, even cash flow—are simply not value additive. Margins and returns can decrease even with positive NPV projects. Growth rates, earnings, and EBITDA can increase even with negative NPV ones. And free cash flow al-ways goes down, at least in the short term, with any new investment. It slays the innocent with the guilty. The disassociation between economic value added and conventional metrics is simply a fatal flaw that dooms them to the dustbin of history. The disconnection creates a tremendous opportunity for ambiguity and misalignment of incentives, and is one of the big buga-boos of modern corporate life. Let's fix that.

As for the analytical bit, there are real advantages to using a souped-up version of EVA Margin to analyze the value of a capital project and the value drivers within it. Instead of just measuring and analyzing EVA Margin by period, or comparing it point to point over a plan horizon as we have done so far, for capital budgeting applications an overall summary EVA Margin is computed based on the projected present value (PV) of EVA and the present value of projected sales. This PV EVA Margin, as I call it, provides a single statistic that is characteristic of the overall profitability and net present value of the project, like an internal rate of return (IRR), only better. It also facilitates understanding the drivers and assumptions with a special present value version of the EVA Margin schedule.

Let's walk through the derivation of the PV EVA Margin, starting with the obvious—the net present value of a project or decision is the present value of the EVA it will generate, by definition:

NPV = Present Value of EVA

Now, divide and multiply by the present value of the forecast sales:

$$NPV = \frac{\text{Present Value of EVA}}{\text{Present Value of Sales}} \times \text{Present Value of Sales}$$

Abbreviate "present value of" to "PV" for simplicity:

$$NPV = \frac{\text{PV EVA}}{\text{PV Sales}} \times \text{PV Sales}$$

Give the present value version of the EVA Margin a name:

NPV = PV EVA Margin × PV Sales

Take a simple example. Suppose that the discounted present value of the EVA projected over the life of an investment project, which is the same thing as its NPV, is $100. That's good because any positive NPV is a good thing. But how good? It's hard to tell with just NPV as an isolated data point. But suppose the discounted present value of the projected sales over the project life is $2,000. Then the PV EVA Margin is 5 percent:

NPV = PV EVA Margin × PV Sales
$100 = 5%   × $2,000

The PV EVA Margin gives us a statistic that is directly comparable to EVA Margin statistics in general. *This is huge.* We now have a means to judge how attractive the project is, or maybe how unrealistic the assumptions are, using a productivity and profitability statistic that is just a variation on the classic EVA Margin metric that is used to judge and diagnose business performance period by period. All of the reference points that apply to EVA Margin from public company data, and that become familiar to line teams as they get to know the EVA Margins of the businesses they manage, are valid and applicable benchmarks for judging the PV EVA Margin projected for an investment project.

For example, we've seen how the 75th percentile EVA Margin for the Russell 3000 universe runs at 4.2 percent over the long term. The PV EVA Margin of this project is even better than that. It is either a great project or the assumptions are overly optimistic. Another perhaps more relevant reference point would be to compare the PV EVA Margin of the project against the EVA Margin of the company itself or of the division sponsor, or against the PV EVA Margins that have been forecast and realized by comparable projects the company has reviewed in the past. For example, if the division sponsoring the project is earning only a 2 percent EVA Margin on a similar cost allocation footing, or if similar investments have generated a –1 percent PV Margin in recent years, why should top management (or the sponsor) believe this project will do better? The case needs to be challenged. The statistic gives context, and context is an aid to judgment. That's an advantage to using EVA that you don't get from cash flow.

The power of the PV Margin, then, is its ability to consolidate the economic essence of a project into a single summary statistic that can be rated and scored, using the familiar EVA Margin construct. And in the same vein, the PV EVA Margin can be also traced to all the underlying component drivers of the NPV, again on a common percentage-of-sales scale, but this time in net present value terms. It is *E Pluribus Unum* and *E Unum Pluribus*, once again.

Let's have a little fun now looking at a strictly hypothetical capital project decision that will illustrate this new methodology. The question to be investigated is a critical one for Claudine's Salt Water Taffy Company, one of the divisions of the Boardwalk Empire, a conglomerate headquartered in Atlantic City, New Jersey.

It seems there are two ways to operate the machines that stretch the saltwater taffy that the company sells. They are fast speed or slow speed, designated as 4× or 3× pull rates. Claudine's brother, Frank, who runs production, argues in favor of 3×, of running the machines on the slow setting. His argument is that 4× wears out the machines too quickly. They depreciate more rapidly and have to be replaced more often, which leads to more downtime costs while the replacements are brought on line. Machines capable of operation in the faster mode are also more costly to purchase up

eva **D**imensions

Claudine's Salt Water Taffy Company
Taffy Pulling Rate Time Line:
Fast Speed (4×) vs. Slow (3×)

Fast Speed: 4x Taffy Pull Rate

Year	0	1	2	3	4	5	6	7	8	9	10	11	12	13	14	15	16	17	18	19	20	21	22	23
Investment ex Up-Front Extra ($USA 000's)	10																							
Extra Up-Front Investment	25								10								10							
Maintenance Downtime (Days)									60								60							
Loss of Sales ($US 000's)									12								12							

Fast Speed: 3x Taffy Pull Rate

Year	0	1	2	3	4	5	6	7	8	9	10	11	12	13	14	15	16	17	18	19	20	21	22	23
Investment ex Up-Front Extra ($USA 000's)	9																							
Extra Up-Front Investment	21												9											
Maintenance Downtime (Days)													60											
Loss of Sales ($US 000's)													9											

- **Faster (4×) Pull Rate requires:**
  - a larger up-front investment
  - more frequent sustaining investments
  - larger sustaining investments
  - 1.5× as many days of downtime
  - $15K more sales lost during down time

- Why would you ever want to run the machines faster and burn up more capital?

EXHIBIT 10.1

front. There is a greater initial capital investment that digs more deeply into cash flow, and raises the temperature of Frank's Scottish blood.

Frank prepares a report to analyze the decision. Since the fast machines need to be replaced every eight years, and the slow ones he favors need to be replaced only once every 12 years, he figures he needs to look at the total cost-benefit equation over 24 years to align three fast-machine cycles and two slow ones. He lays out the assumptions very neatly in the table in Exhibit 10.1, along with his acerbic conclusion cleverly framed as a question: "Why would you ever want to run the machines faster and burn up more capital?" And he might have added, "and hurt our cash flow, increase downtime, incur more lost sales, and burn up our precious capital equipment 1.5× as fast?"

Fortunately, Claudine is no slouch in the finance department. In fact, she has recently been thoroughly schooled in the Best-Practice EVA management system. "Frank, you may be right," she says. "Your arguments sound convincing. But let's run the numbers and see which strategy will increase our family fortune the most."

Her first stab at this is to compute NPV. She dutifully discounts the year-by-year EVA profit forecasts for the two strategies to a present value. Her conclusion is shown in Exhibit 10.2. The left bar each year plots EVA for the fast-running machine and the right bars the slowly turning ones:

"Frank," Claudine cries out, "look at this. There are only two years when the EVA profit of running the machines fast is less than the EVA of running them slow. Those are the two years—8 and 16—when the speedy taffy pullers have to be replaced and the downtime kicks in big time. But even in the first year, when we lay out a lot more money to buy them, the faster machines pull so much more taffy volume that we're way ahead. I've discounted the projections, and the NPV is $4,938 under the slow-speed strategy, and the net present value is $16,356 under run 'em and gun 'em. This just shows all those things you are worried about are way more than offset by the benefits. Your concerns are real, but the payoff is there, on net."

Frank is on the verge of conceding when suddenly, triumphantly, his face lights up. "Aha!" he exclaims. "You've made a big mistake in your analysis, Claudie. You cannot just compare the EVA and NPV straight up. The slower machines generate less output, so we need more of them to meet the projected demand. You'd have to multiply out the NPV of the slow machines to hold sales the same."

He adds, piling on, "Also, come to think of it, I see your EVA answer, I trust you did the math right, and I see the left bar is taller than the right bar, but I really don't see why that is so, which is another reason I'm not really buying in."

eva **D**imensions

Because, Running Fast Generates a Lot More EVA and NPV

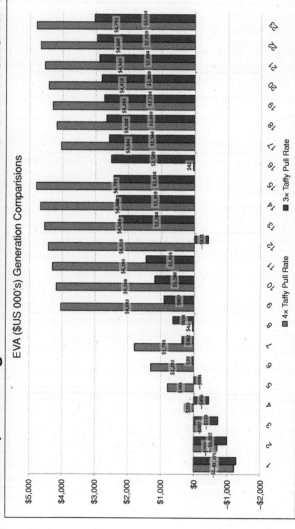

EVA ($US 000's) Generation Comparisions

■ 4x Taffy Pull Rate   ■ 3x Taffy Pull Rate

Just looking at NPV is not right, either, since the 4x run speed covers more sales than 3x—we need to size-adjust the comparison!

EXHIBIT 10.2

"Okay, Frank those are very good points," Claudine says. "So I have an idea that may kill the two birds with one stone. I will compute and analyze the NPV as a percentage of the present value of the sales, so whatever the sales are, the NPV is going to be greater whichever production plan gives us the greater NPV ratio on the sales." A few minutes later, Claudine's desktop computer prints out the PV EVA Margin schedule shown in Exhibit 10.3.

"Franklin, here's the deal. I computed the present value of the sales that are supported by the two production plans assuming no downtime, and expressed all costs as a percentage of that, including the lost sales as a charge so it's not just buried in the present value of the sales. Just look at the top line. The 4× plan supports a discounted sales stream of $187,000 over the 24 years assuming the machines ran all the time, whereas the PV of flat-out sales is only $140,000 for the 3× machines. On that score, you are right. The 4× machines produce one-third more sales than the 3× ones, so we really did need to look at this, size-adjusted. We could not just compare the NPVs straight up. But the answer is right there, on the bottom line. That shows that the present value of the projected EVA, in other words, the NPV relative to the present value of the sales, is a PV EVA Margin of 9.2 percent for the fast machines and 5.6 percent for the slower ones. So Frank, for any given production plan, for any given sales demand, we'd earn a lot more EVA by operating the faster machines. It's very conclusive, Frank."

"Claudine, you're right," Frank concedes. "That proves it. I guess in this case it does make sense to burn through the capital faster, because the return is higher, somehow. But that's what I still want to know: *why* that is the answer. It would actually convince me even a little more, and I might learn something about how to run the business even better, if you could show me what's really driving that conclusion. You know me—I don't just want the machine to work; I want to know *how* it works and how to make it run, er, faster, I guess, or, well, certainly better in any event."

The answers to Frank's questions are on the PV EVA Margin schedule, as you can see in Exhibit 10.3. The lost sales from downtime, for instance, are broken out separately on the second row from the top. Because there are two machine replacements for the run 'em and gun 'em plan, instead of just one for the go-slow plan, it is hit with more lost sales. The downtime takes 1.3 percent out of the present value of the sales that would be produced with flat-out production versus a downtime loss of just 0.6 percent of sales in 3× mode. That is a real cost to run fast, and it's in there, as a charge to the PV EVA Margin. It's the one thing that really goes against the conclusion. But on every other count, the speedy machines win.

eva**D**imensions

Use the PV of EVA Margin Schedule to Size Adjust

	4x Taffy Pull Rate		3x Taffy Pull Rate		
	$US 000's	% of PV Sales	$US 000's	% of PV Sales	Difference
PV of Normal Sales	$187,201	100.0%	$140,400	100.0%	--
− PV Downtime (Lost Sales)	$8,650	1.3%	$3,022	0.6%	-0.7%
= PV Actual Sales	$178,550	98.7%	$137,379	99.4%	-0.7%
PV Normal EBITDAR	$71,963	40.3%	$45,148	32.9%	7.4%
− PV Downtime (Lost EBITDAR)	$4,186	2.3%	$1,373	1.0%	-1.3%
= PV Actual EBITDAR	$67,777	38.0%	$43,776	31.9%	6.1%
− PV of SG&A	$10,713	6.0%	$8,243	6.0%	--
− PV of COGS	$100,060	56.0%	$85,360	62.1%	6.1%
= PV of Manufacturing Overhead	$18,634	10.4%	$18,634	13.6%	3.1%
+ PV of Variable Costs	$81,427	45.6%	$66,727	48.6%	3.0%
Pretax PV of Productive Capital Charges	$56,234	31.5%	$44,010	32.0%	0.5%
= Pretax PV Investment ex Upfront Extra	$22,900	12.8%	$16,010	11.7%	-1.2%
+ Pretax PV Up-Front Extra Investment	$33,333	18.7%	$28,000	20.4%	1.7%
= PV of EVA Before Tax	$11,543	6.5%	($235)	-0.2%	6.6%
− PV of Tax	$2,886	1.6%	($59)	0.0%	-1.7%
+ PV of Tax Shield of Depreciation	$7,698	4.3%	$5,114	3.7%	0.6%
PV of EVA	$16,356	9.2%	$4,938	3.6%	5.6%

- This is a PV EVA Margin schedule. All line items are the present value over the forecast, and expressed as a percentage of sales.
- Running fast machines (4x) does incur extra downtime costs 0.7 percent of sales and 1.3 percent of EBITDAR, but ….
- Manufacturing overhead, and energy, labor variable costs are 6.1 percent lower.
- Although the 4x machines are more expensive, the capital charge is 0.5 percent of sales lower → the capital burns faster but more efficiently.
- The extra investment also produces higher tax shields.
- The 4x fast machines are *far* more EVA productive—5.6 percentage more EVA per every $1 of sales.

EXHIBIT 10.3

Specifically, run fast is better than go slow for three main reasons: (1) it saves on supervisory costs and operator costs (which vary by machine, not output); (2) it generates a slightly greater volume of sales output per dollar of capital tied up in the machines (i.e., the PP&E intensity is lower); and (3) the government subsidizes the extra investment in the faster machines with depreciation tax shields. In other words, if you burn the capital faster, you burn the people slower, and you do not burn it faster compared to the sales volume it produces—if anything, a little less.

Incidentally, the PV EVA schedule shows not just the individual driver elements but also the present value versions of the EBITDAR Margin and the pretax charge for the productive capital (the only capital here is the machines, because Claudine is paid at point of production, and there is no working capital investment in this case, because the local bosses insist on cash on the barrelhead). As I said, it's the same very familiar EVA Margin schedule, but now applied to summarize and analyze the drivers in net present value terms.

In this example, the amount of sales was not a variable. In many decisions and investment projects, sales would be a variable. This is why, in general, the PV EVA Margin is merely a profitability indicator characteristic of the overall project economics, akin to an internal rate or return (IRR), but like IRR it is not the measure that management should aim to maximize (it was in the example because sales were fixed, and the question was how to minimize the production cost, but that is a special case). The goal is always to maximize NPV by maximizing the present value of the EVA. So if one investment program was forecast to generate a PV EVA Margin of 5 percent on $2,000 in PV sales, for an NPV of $100, and an alternative, more aggressive investment plan was projected to earn a PV EVA Margin of 3.75 percent on twice the sales, for an NPV of $150, it's the latter plan that is preferable. It generates a 50 percent greater NPV, it contributes more to owner wealth, and it would add more to the EVA Momentum of the sponsoring division.

Choosing the larger-scale investment project does assume two things, however. It first assumes that additional capital can be obtained at the cost of capital rate. For publicly traded companies with access to debt and equity markets, that is a valid assumption, but for a private company with no wish to go public, it might not be. Capital might be limited to internally generated cash. In that case, everything I've said so far about EVA applies except for one thing. The cost of capital used to measure performance and measure value needs to be hiked up a couple of percentage points above what a market-based cost of capital would be. That will motivate line managers to sweat more capital out of existing operations and to reject investments at the margin they would otherwise accept. That puts the correct opportunity cost on the capital, given its relatively greater scarcity in the private firm. The alternative—measuring and rewarding free cash generation—is not a good solution because it slays the innocent with the guilty, it stops all projects in their tracks regardless of how high the returns may be, and it puts a premium on projects that get cash back fast rather than those that generate the greatest NPV relative to the true incremental internal opportunity cost of the capital.

A second assumption in choosing the more aggressive (faster-production) plan is that the risk is the same as the less ambitious strategy—that there is the same certainty of actually generating the projected sales and NPV return on sales as in the more conservative plan. That may not be the case; it may be less certain of success (of course, it is also possible that the more aggressive investment plan is *more* certain; it may increase the probability of being first to reach critical scale, may offer customers a lower markup over costs in exchange for attracting more volume, and may involve other investments in quality, convenience, features, innovation or brand that make it more likely to succeed at that scale, for example). Many CFOs try to account for perceived uncertainty by hiking up the cost of capital, but that is simply reducing all the richness of the risk analysis to a very slender reed. Hike up the cost of capital by how much, and why? It is generally better to answer those questions head-on by creating a set of alternative forecast scenarios for EVA and the present value of EVA and PV EVA Margin that reflect the downside of what could happen, and then to apply judgment. This is particularly useful when the investments are staged and have options that need to be explored and priced in.

We've also developed an EVA-based capital-at-risk ratio that can be helpful in quantifying the degree to which assumptions can shrink while still preserving value. I call it the NPV Spread. It is the PV of EVA (i.e., NPV, once again) divided by the present value of the investment spending projected to occur over the life of the project and discounted at the cost of capital. It is like the PV EVA Margin except that instead of using the present value of sales as the divisor, the divisor is the present value of the capital investments as and when they are forecast to be made. For example, if the PV of EVA was forecast to be a $100 NPV, and the present value of the forecasted capital investments by year, discounted at the cost of capital rate, was $800, then the NPV Spread ratio is 12.5 percent. That says that every dollar of invested capital translates into 12.5 cents of added owner wealth if the plan is met, or, put another way, it says there is a 12.5 percent cushion on top of the capital investment by which assumptions can shrink while preserving the investors' capital.

Preserving capital, as defined in this ratio, is a tougher test than you may think. It requires the project to recover the investor's principal—the money it has committed to the project—and also to provide the cost of capital return on the investment. If I just gave you your money back 10 years from now with no return, you would not consider that to be preservation. You'd consider that an erosion of your wealth. In like spirit, the NPV Spread ratio does not turn positive until NPV turns positive, and NPV is not positive until the principal invested in a project is recovered *and* the return on the investment at least matches the cost of capital. The ratio is not positive until investors get their money back with interest, which is the obligation that must be met as far as the market is concerned. To worry about just getting back the principal and not earning interest on it is an arbitrarily less ambitious goal, with no economic substance and not worth measuring.

I contend that the NPV Spread is actually better than internal rate of return (IRR) for helping management to assess how much of a risk cushion is built into the forecast assumptions, and should be used in place of it. IRR, as you may recall from your finance text, is the interest rate that discounts all of the forecast cash flows to a zero net present value. Here's the hitch: the IRR calculation always assumes that all intermediate cash flows thrown off by the project can be reinvested at the computed IRR rate, which is not at all the correct assumption to make. IRR is simply a terribly flawed statistic at root. The correct assumption, of course, is that intermediate cash flows can be reinvested at the cost of capital, if only by retiring the firm's debt and equity. The NPV Spread ratio makes that assumption. It is based on the PV of EVA/PV of the investments, discounting each at the cost of capital. It assumes that the time value of money is the cost of capital all the way through, which makes it an inherently superior risk metric.

Another advantage to using the NPV Spread to represent the risk cushion is that it preserves the consistency that I argue is so critical for simplicity. It ties right back to EVA and to the present value of the EVA, and should be explained in that way. I have said we want to get rid of the return on investment (ROI) metric. Likewise, please delete IRR from your vocabulary. If you want something equivalent, but better, in the EVA world, look at the NPV Spread, please. And remember, if the NPV Spread is zero, that is not the same as IRR being zero. It is better than that. If the NPV Spread is zero, that is the same as the IRR equaling the cost of capital. The NPV Spread is more akin to IRR less cost of capital (COC), or the IRR net of the cost of capital, if you will. It is the excess return over the required return. Actually, to be perfectly specific, it is the dollar excess return on the capital, discounted to a present value. It is the total present value risk cushion expressed as a percentage of the investment at risk. Think of it in that light.

Be aware that the NPV Spread, like any return measure, is not a measure to maximize. The goal is not to maximize safety. It is to maximize wealth creation, NPV, and the present value of EVA, as always. NPV Spread is a measure that should be used to quantify the risk posture of the investment and fit it into a risk budget. For instance, some firms establish minimum NPV Spreads for projects in various risk classes as a risk control mechanism, which I think is more sensible than fiddling with the hurdle rates.

PRICING ACQUISITIONS

From an EVA point of view, acquisitions are no different than any other investment decision. It is a question of adding value to the capital, where the capital invested in an acquisition is the purchase price. But unfortunately, when investment bankers are brought into the room, common sense goes out the window and voodoo valuations hold sway. The language of the bankers and their sell-side analyst accomplices is so often couched in terms of earnings per share (EPS) dilution and accretion and multiple expansion and contraction (bring your Slinky), it is worth a moment to ponder, again, why this is just so silly.

EPS doesn't count because, again, the buyer's P/E multiple typically changes in the wake of acquisition transactions and *generally to counter the change in EPS*. If EPS goes up, it is simply more likely that the P/E ratio goes down, and vice versa. This is not a ramrod rule, but it is a very strong tendency, for reasons I will explain in a moment. This fact of life makes EPS a wholly unreliable measure of the merits of a transaction. Please, boards, stop looking at it, and demand better, more thoughtful, more sensible analysis from your advisers. The stakes are too high to base major decisions on a highly flawed accounting metric.

One reason P/E drops is that many acquisition buys are debt financed. We've already covered the distortions that arise when operating decisions—like buying a business—and financing decisions are commingled. In this case, adding leverage adds risk to the shareholders, and they will be compensated by pricing the stock postdeal at a lower multiple of the pro forma riskier earnings. That alone renders the EPS impact of a transaction a misleading measure of its merits.

It's worse than just that, though. It's not just mixing up the leverage that distorts EPS. It's mixing up the business multiples that really confounds EPS (and its sister, the enterprise multiple). As the buyer's and seller's businesses and business prospects are fused, their multiples are just as certainly commingled. The buyer's P/E multiple is either advanced or suppressed by the multiple the seller brings to the table. And this is the major reason EPS is just so utterly distorted as an indicator of the economics of a proposed transaction.

Consider this. If a company with a high multiple buys one with lower P/E in a stock exchange, its EPS is almost guaranteed to go up. That's because the seller's shares convert into a lesser number of the higher-multiple buyer shares, while the earnings of the two companies combine. The consolidated earnings are spread out over fewer shares, and presto, the buyer's EPS goes up. It is important to understand that the buyer's EPS increases regardless of the identity of the high-P/E and low-P/E firms in the example. Apple could buy Exxon with stock and Apple's EPS would go up. It is purely an arithmetic consequence, and it has no economic merit or substance.

To see how really absurd and inept EPS is as a measure of value, turn the deal around and have the lower-P/E shares retire the higher-multiple ones. This time, have Exxon issue stock to buy Apple. The math reverses, and the buyer's EPS goes down. It looks like a bad deal when Exxon bites Apple, but good if Apple gobbles up Exxon, but it is the same deal (if we assume that regardless of which firm buys or which sells, the same management team runs the combined company with the same strategies). It cannot be good one way and bad the other. What resolves the paradox? No matter which firm issues the paper, the consolidated firm is the same (or, it is assumed to be the same to make the point), and it has the same consolidated value, the same consolidated earnings, and thus the consolidated P/E multiple *must be the same* regardless of which way the deal goes, because it ends up being exactly the same company.

That being the case, a high-P/E buyer must *always* suffer a reduction in its multiple as it blends down toward the average of the two multiples, and the low one must ascend up to it. EPS doesn't count, because the P/E ratio is *mathematically* bound to offset it. Think of it this way. When you buy a company, you buy not only its earnings, but also the *quality* of its earnings. You acquire its risk, its return, its EVA, its growth prospects, and so on. In a nutshell you are buying its P/E multiple. Inevitably, the buyer's P/E naturally shifts toward the seller's, and that tends to offset the EPS dilution or accretion the merger creates. If you dilute high-octane gasoline with low-octane fuel, the octane rating—in this case, the earnings power rating, the P/E multiple—is diluted. It is just in the nature of the chemistry of how business multiples combine.

Still not convinced? Check out the graph in Exhibit 10.4. It plots the percentage accretion or dilution in EPS going left to right and the percentage change in P/E multiple going north to south from the 66 largest stock-for-stock deals over the period from 1993 to 2003. Yes, it is a bit dated, but I have no reason to believe the market has become less sophisticated since then. What it shows is stunning. It shows a downward slope, meaning that the more a buyer's EPS went up, the more its P/E came down, and the more its EPS was diluted in the wake of a deal, the more its P/E climbed, just as the math says it must, but there is the data.

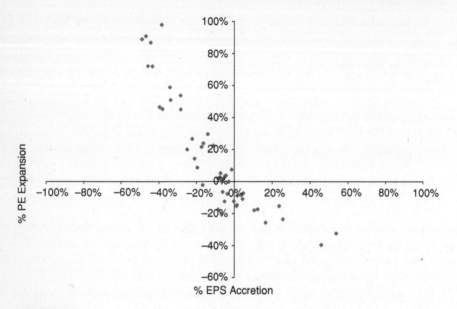

EXHIBIT 10.4

EPS DOESN'T COUNT; IT IS OFFSET BY P/E

Here are a couple of examples drawn from the study. When Halliburton acquired Dresser Industries for $8.1 billion in stock, Halliburton's EPS fell 11 percent, but its stock price increased 9 percent as its P/E expanded by 22 percent. And when Bank One acquired First Chicago, Bank One's EPS increased 12 percent, but its stock price fell 7 percent as its P/E multiple fell 17 percent. In both cases, the P/E ratio moved to more than counter the EPS move, and turned the deals around.

The most generous interpretation of the data would be that EPS was a completely misleading and random indicator of the value of the transaction—but in fact, it is worse than that. As the examples I cited suggest, the slope of the line is so negative that EPS movements were generally *more than offset* by changes in the P/E multiple. If EPS increased 10 percent, the P/E multiple tended to decrease 10.5 percent, for example, and vice versa. The stunning conclusion is that, at least in those deals, and that was all of the major ones over a long period of time, the more EPS increased, the more the buyer's share price decreased. If EPS was an indicator at all, it was in the opposite direction than what most boards assume it to be. One implication is clear: boards should stop paying top management bonuses on EPS.

Another is that boards, and management teams, really need a more reliable way to assess the true merits of proposed transactions, for it is clear that earnings per share just don't come close to the mark.

On that score, let me first explain how I define a successful transaction. It is one in which on the date of the announcement, the buyer's as well as the seller's stock prices both go up. This is not how investment bankers define successful transactions. For them, it is all those that happen, because, like a Las Vegas minister, their fee is based on matrimony. Of course, we will only really find out if a merger is successful many years later. But the initial stock price reaction is important for two reasons.

First, it's like the newspaper you read in the morning. It's the first draft of history. It's what you have as a judgment on the decision as it is made and the facts are released to the market. It is like a report card for the senior year in high school. A low grade point average at that time doesn't necessarily consign the student to a miserable life, but hey, it's not a good sign.

Another reason the initial stock price reaction matters is that it is the best objective judgment of investors who follow the stock about how the deal will *eventually* work out. Studies have shown the initial reaction is not biased; you cannot make money shorting all the acquirer stocks that go up in price and buying those that fall as major merger deals are announced. The market doesn't get it wrong, on average. But more than that, other studies have shown that the more the buyer's stock price falls in the wake of a trans-action, the greater the likelihood the bought company will subsequently be spun back out and the responsible CEO lose his or her job. Just think about America Online/Time Warner. Stock price way down, and now AOL is out and both of the presiding CEOs are out.

The easiest and most accurate way to value an acquisition is to recognize that it involves an exchange of value, not an exchange of earnings. You want to get more value than you give up. You want to measure the total value that the seller brings to the buyer, and deduct the total value that the buyer pays to the seller. The difference is the value added to the buyer. It is the MVA or NPV of the transaction, if you will. And the best prediction of the buyer's share price is that it will rise or fall by the MVA per postdeal share outstanding. The chart in Exhibit 10.5 depicts this.

In this example, the target company is public and trades for a market value of $1 billion. It is assumed that the company is fairly valued in the sense that the current market value is an unbiased and reasonably accurate view of the present value of the EVA profit that the target is capable of earning on its own. If the target was intrinsically undervalued in the market—if the EVA it would earn all by itself was worth more than $1 billion—then that would also be a potential source of value to a buyer.

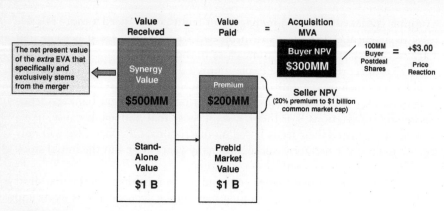

EXHIBIT 10.5 The Exchange of Value in an Acquisition

However, can a sometime corporate buyer better detect the real value of a target company than the professional investment community that is paid to find undervalued stocks? Can a hedgehog who plays the valuation game occasionally outfox all the foxes on Wall Street who are professionally compensated to find undervalued shares? Maybe, if you are Warren Buffett or John Malone. But for mere mortals, probably not. Besides, if the justification for the deal is that the target is undervalued, then don't pay a takeover premium to buy the company; just buy the stock and wait for your insight to be realized in the market, or better, just buy options on the stock.

Of course, if you are acquiring a private company, you have to form an understanding of what the target business is fundamentally worth before the acquisition pixie dust is sprinkled onto the business plan. And of course, a projection of EVA should be used to measure that stand-alone value. But for the acquisition of a public company (and absent any leaked word of the seller's intention to sell or a buyer to buy), it seems best to assume the seller's intrinsic value is reflected in its share price.

The exchange of value formulation thus boils down to this. The only way that a buyer can sensibly pay the premium over market value that is required to induce a transaction is to create a synergistic value above the target's stand-alone value that can be split with the selling shareholders. And what precisely is synergy value? Simple. It is the present value of the *extra* EVA that specifically and exclusively stems from the merger and that the two companies could not produce by contracting with each other, or on their own, or that the shareholders could not produce on their own.

For instance, it is *not* a synergy to reduce risk by combining off-cycle businesses, because shareholders can diversify the risk for free simply by holding both stocks in their portfolios. It is *not* a synergy to increase leverage and retire equity, even if it is the buyer raising the debt to retire the seller's equity, since the seller and buyer could borrow and buy back shares on their own. It is also *not* a synergy to simply participate in the growth that a promising target company brings to the table. The value of that growth is already reflected in the target's stand-alone value and is not a reason to pay a premium of any kind. It takes something extra and special to qualify as a synergy.

Let's not make this a mystery. EVA itself points the way. A synergy is something that predictably increases the consolidated EVA in one or more of the many ways that EVA could increase in any business, which are: (1) to cut operating costs intelligently (for instance, overhead costs, distribution costs, even taxes, by stepping up deductions or more fully utilizing carryforward losses or foreign tax credits); (2) to accelerate profitable growth above what the seller and buyer could accomplish independently or by contracting with each other (such as by raising prices with greater market power, accelerating product development by collaboration, scaling growth through a shared platform, etc.); and (3) to purge assets and activities that don't earn the cost of capital (such as by consolidation of redundant assets, product lines, etc.). To the greatest extent possible, the synergies have to go beyond flowery aspirational potentialities. The synergies should be backed by hard facts and expectations that will quite clearly flow through the income statement and balance sheet into EVA. The synergies should also be substantiated by a detailed plan that outlines the steps the buyer will take to integrate the seller over the first one to three years. It's the standard operating procedure, but now under the hard glare of the EVA klieg light.

Synergies can also be managerial and organizational in nature, letting great managers and superior management processes roam over a greater territory of opportunity and assets to manage. In this sense, EVA is a synergy, too. If your firm is an accomplished practitioner of Best-Practice EVA and the seller hasn't a clue, you can create value by making the seller swallow the EVA medicine after being brought into the fold.

Some synergies are hard to lay out with precision. They may be in the vein of expanding options for growth or gaining a stepping-stone into a broader capability set. Fine, write those out, put those in a little blue box with a white question-mark ribbon, and return to it once you've got the hard facts of the valuation analysis nailed down to see if you need to open it.

I hate to be a party pooper, but there are negative synergies, too, that must factor in as a deduction, such as when the two cultures cannot coexist and key people or key accounts defect.

By now you've seen what projecting and discounting EVA look like for a business plan or for a capital project. It's the same exercise here, and not worth repeating in an example. Suffice it to say, you need to bring all your EVA acumen to bear. You need to develop a base-case plan for the seller that is realistic and that realistically reconciles to its existing market value if it is public (and no word of intentions to sell have leaked), taking account of security analyst expectations, its EVA Margin and Momentum trend, competitive position, and the likely convergence of Momentum to the mean—don't forget that. In the example in Exhibit 10.5, this analysis leads to the conclusion that the stand-alone market value of the target is $1 billion, as it stands on the chart.

Next you need to overlay all the measureable synergies on top of the base case. You can measure the present value of the extra EVA directly and incrementally, or you can fold the synergies right into the base-case plan and use the combined EVA forecast to value the target company with synergies. In the example, the present value of the synergistic EVA is $500 million, which means that the value of the seller to the buyer is a total of $1.5 billion. Just as EVA is additive, the present value of EVA is additive. Synergy value adds right on top of the base-case value.

Suppose the buyer in this example pays a total of $1.2 billion to consummate the deal. That puts the selling shareholders ahead by $200 million, or by a 20 percent premium compared to the $1 billion stand-alone value they had before, and the buyer is ahead by the $300 million balance. If there are 100 million buyer shares outstanding postdeal, the prediction is the buyer's share price will increase by $3 a share. If the buyer's accountants inform us that the deal will dilute EPS, then we simply conclude the buyer will sell for an even higher P/E multiple. Again, in the economic model, it is EVA that determines the value, it is accounting that determines EPS, and the P/E multiple is there to pick up the slack. It is just a plug.

An insight that this way of thinking brings is that, for an acquisition to be successful in terms of boosting the buyer's as well as the seller's share price—a so-called win-win transaction—there must be real and realizable synergies, and the buyer must show price restraint and not pay more than all of the synergistic value to the seller, which is always a great temptation in the heat of battle. Again, EVA facts can help to check emotions and enthrone reason in decisions. And it is the EVA facts, not the EPS fantasy, that can best guide managers and boards to what they can truly afford to pay without overpaying.

Let's assume for a moment that the world is perfectly rational and that all potential buyers go through a similar economic logic. Then any one buyer should be willing to bid up the total value to just match what the purchaser thinks the seller is worth to it, including the value of the synergies it foresees realizing, but no more. A higher price would only end up harming its shareholders, and would represent an unconscionable wealth transfer from the buyer to the seller shareholders, in this ideal world.

If all buyers behaved like that, and dropped out at the bid that left them just breaking even on MVA, the market-clearing premium offered to the seller would equal the value of the synergies that could be developed by the *second most* value-adding merger partner, leaving only the most value-adding merger partner as able to pay the auction premium and emerge with a gain. The market is not that perfect, but at some level a system of checks and balances exists that encourages businesses that are for sale, like any other scarce resource, to flow to their highest valued use. This being so, it is helpful to look at the value through the eyes of other potential bidders and ask: are we the best merger partner? Are we able to create the most value through the combination, and do we have a good plan for achieving that? If the answer is no, save the time and move on.

In the example, I said that the total value paid was $1.2 billion, and we saw how the deal value, the MVA, could be judged just knowing that—just knowing the total value of the financing package and not the specific financing elements. To be specific, though, the total value paid consists not only of all the debt and equity the buyer issues in the deal, but also all liabilities it assumes and cash it uses, whether on its books or on the seller's books, and all reckoned at postdeal market value. The point is, a buyer needs to total up all the value that is being paid to get its hands on the total value acquired, and it is the difference that will accrue to the buyer's shareholders as the residual claimants.

An advantage of this approach is that you are forced to focus on the total value paid and not the form of the payment. You are not tempted to mix operating and financing decisions. For example, it makes no difference to the deal economics if the total value paid is in the form of all equity at a $1.2 billion postdeal value, or all debt at a $1.2 billion postdeal value, or anything in between. The MVA to the buyer is the same, either way. The buyer's EPS will of course be profoundly different depending on the financing mix that is employed. The difference does not matter, though, because, again, the P/E multiple will plug the difference and bridge the gap.

The next time you are scrutinizing an acquisition and the impact on EPS comes up in the boardroom discussion with investment bankers, don't forget to ask the embarrassing question: "I see that you have prepared a rather precise calculation of the pro forma EPS, but what will happen to our P/E multiple?" That's when the voodoo comes out. That's when the bankers start shaking their rattles and rolling the dice and alluding to their trading desks and how "the market" will react, as if they know "the market" personally. It is certainly entertaining, even if it is not a very productive use of the board's time.

CHAPTER 11

EVA and the Buy Side

Shortly before America Online (AOL) acquired Time Warner in 2000, Geoff Colvin, then an executive editor of *Fortune*, called me with a request. He wanted to know how EVA valued AOL. This was long before the advent of EVA Margin and Momentum and our software tools, so I spent a few hours (now I could do it in seconds) pulling out the facts, which frankly stunned me.

At the time AOL had a market value of around $180 billion, as I recall, and only about $10 billion in capital measured the EVA way. AOL traded for an MVA premium of about $170 billion, which as you now know should equal the present value of the EVA profit the firm is capable of earning, or else the stock is mispriced. AOL by my reckoning was earning an annual EVA at the time of $300 million, and with a 10 percent cost of capital, the present value of its embedded EVA was about $3 billion. That left only another $167 billion of MVA to be accounted for by the present value of the growth in EVA that was to come. I breathlessly solved for how fast EVA would have to grow to discount to the valuation. It was (are you ready for this?) an increase of $1.6 billion a year, every year, *forever*. Completely impossible, of course.

I said to Geoff, "There may be a new economy, but there's not a new economics. Two and two still must equal four. EVA growth of that magnitude is simply inconceivable. AOL looks just ridiculously overpriced, according to EVA." And Geoff wrote this up in a column in *Fortune* magazine, pointing out how absurd the valuation was.

It so happened that the article hit the newsstands on the very day it was announced that Time Warner, the parent of *Fortune*, would be acquired for AOL stock (it was incidentally a deal where AOL's EPS increased 131 percent, because its multiple was so much greater than Time Warner's, but AOL's P/E plunged so far, by 67 percent, that shareholders were left 24 percent worse off. It was one of those rare deals where the market priced in *negative* synergies, one plus one equaling less than two, and was right about that). Several years later, after the dot-com bubble had burst and Time Warner shareholders were left holding highly watered-down paper, Colvin penned another *Fortune* column titled, "Don't Blame Steve Case." Case was the AOL CEO who engineered the deal, and Colvin's point was that he had actually gotten a good deal for *his* owners in comparison to what happened to other Internet stocks in the crash, and that the guilty party was really his ultimate boss, Time Warner chief executive Gerald Levin, who had been so foolish as to take AOL stock in payment.

I tell this story because it planted a seed in me. Although I had been occupied over the years chiefly with how to use EVA to improve corporate performance and governance, I became intrigued by the idea that EVA could be used to pick stocks systematically. It took a lot of work over many years, developing the database, testing and developing the model, and the like. But roll the camera forward and we've succeeded well beyond my expectations. And that is principally due to the incredible job my professional colleague (and now my spouse) Ling Yang did in turning the concept into a workable product that we call PRVit (pronounced "prove it," and standing for performance-risk-valuation investment technology). PRVit rates 9,000 global stocks each day on a 0- to 100-point buy-sell scale based on each firm's ability to earn and increase EVA compared to its current market value and after adjusting for risk.

PRVit has been officially rating stocks on Bloomberg since 2006, and since late 2009 it has been featured on Fidelity.com in an abbreviated retail version. But more importantly, PRVit is now the foundation for a separate equity research wing of EVA Dimensions that is staffed with a crack team of experienced Wall Street analysts under the leadership of Craig Sterling, whom we hired from Credit Suisse. Our team assists institutional investor clients in making better buy-sell decisions with the power of EVA by bringing all of the analytical tools and databases in our arsenal to bear. They are already having a big impact since the service was launched in January 2012. One indication is that the team is already in the "broker vote"—which is the preferred means by which fund managers compensate research providers through an allocated share of their trading commissions—at a substantial majority of the largest active U.S. equity managers. The interest is global, and we'll locate offices around the world over the next several years.

I believe this represents an extremely important development. The entire premise of PRVit is that stock prices are magnetically drawn to their fundamental EVA values, and that money can be made as they move closer to it. While I've shown through the course of this book that the market really marches to an EVA drum, the statistical evidence showing PRVit works is yet another indication that MVA really does follow EVA, and that increasing EVA is really the right goal for corporate managers to pursue.

A second reason the development of PRVit is important is that there has always been a concern among CFOs and CEOs that if they talk the EVA language they won't really be understood on Wall Street. Our team is helping to close that communication gap. They are educating fund managers about the advantages of viewing stocks and corporate performance through an EVA lens as they walk them through our analysis of their portfolios or delve into stocks or themes they care about. A frequent reaction once fund managers understand EVA is: "Please bring us EVA-emergent companies." Translation: many of the buy-side managers we advise are eager to meet new corporate adopters of EVA because they realize it can help management increase the firm's stock price through performance improvements.

In the past it was impractical for investors to use EVA, no matter how much they might have wanted to. There were no databases or analytical tools or a professional research team to support it. But that has all changed. And if the early returns are any indication, in two to three years EVA will be viewed as one of the dominant models of investing analysis. The same attributes that make EVA and the EVA ratio metrics and the analytical tools we've developed so appealing for corporate teams apply equally well to researching stocks. The clarity, the consistency, and the insight of EVA can be a huge advantage to investors who have limited time to research stocks and find the right ones to buy or sell. That being the case, CFOs who want to be ahead of the curve will also want to learn to converse in terms of EVA and evaluate the buy-sell pressure on their stock through the PRVit model before they find that investors are asking them about it.

Let's take a closer look at the PRVit model itself. As I said, it is based on the idea that stocks are gravitationally pulled to their intrinsic EVA value, and if they are off the fundamental value line, there is money to be made predicting they will return to it. Another way to say it is that the PRVit model is premised on what I like to call value at a reasonable price (VARP), as in: can a stock be bought at a discount to its real value, or is it trading for unwarranted premium to it? You have no doubt heard of growth at a reasonable price (GARP). Why limit the application? Whatever the stock, be it growth or value, small capitalization or large, the investing question is always really the same: Is a stock trading for more or less than it is really worth? If less, buy it; if more, sell it or sell it short; and do both with more conviction the farther a stock deviates from the fair-value line. The grid in Exhibit 11.1 visually portrays the answer to the VARP question.

On the vertical axis we plot an index of what a stock is really worth (i.e., its true intrinsic value) based on EVA, on a percentile scale *versus all other companies*. Since we are unable to project and discount EVA for every stock to measure its intrinsic EVA value (at least at this time), we've developed a way to proxy for true worth by using a battery of metrics to size up

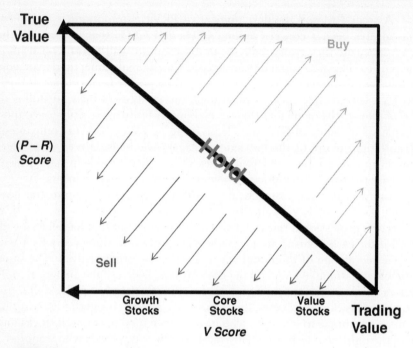

EXHIBIT 11.1   The VARP Grid

a company's ability to earn and increase EVA and adjust it for risk. On the horizontal scale we plot a composite index of the firm's valuation multiples, again on a percentile scale and as compared to the multiples for all other companies, but in reverse order—highly valued stocks plot more leftward. That way, all the stocks that plot along the diagonal stretching from the upper left to the lower right are essentially fairly valued—they are trading for a set of valuation multiples that statistically correspond to their intrinsic value as judged by their risk-adjusted EVA performance score. And if you plot the data for the entire market on this grid, you will see that there is a strong tendency for stocks to cluster around that diagonal line. In general, the more risk-adjusted EVA performance there is, the higher the market valuation is. That is expected, of course, and confirms that the market is really attempting to value EVA, even if imperfectly so.

It is the "imperfectly" part that PRVit attempts to exploit as a stock-rating model. Companies that plot off the fair-value line are the ones that PRVit says are over- or undervalued. The best bargains plot in the upper right zone—where stocks can be bought for less than their true value—and the ones to sell or sell short appear in the lower left zone—where stocks are trading for more than their true value. The PRVit score quantifies how far above or below the fair-value line a stock lies. If a stock trades right on the line, its PRVit score is 50 out of 100. It's a hold. The farther the stock plots into the upper right zone, the more its PRVit score approaches 100; and the farther into the lower left zone, the more it approaches a zero PRVit score.

I hasten to add that PRVit is not perfect, and it is not personal. We are only using a proxy for fair value that is based on assuming that past EVA trends and risk signals accurately predict future performance. That is largely true but not perfectly true, for many reasons. A second point is that PRVit is based purely on a statistical numerical analysis. There is no human judgment involved, so if you don't like your rating, please, don't blame me. I cannot do a thing about it, except by helping you to improve your EVA by using EVA.

Quantifying the PRVit score involves a couple of steps. The first is measuring a company's performance strength by its "P score," its riskiness with an "R score," and its valuation multiples in a composite "V score," where each score is expressed on a percentile scale versus all other companies in the public stock universe we track (we'll see the ingredients of those scores in a minute). The PRVit score is then computed by measuring a ratio of true value to trading value for each company (where true value is represented by the firm's (P − R) score, its risk-discounted EVA performance score, and trading value by its V score), and then expressing the ratio on a percentile scale, as follows:

$$\text{PRVit score} = \frac{\text{True value}}{\text{Trading value}} = \frac{(P - R)}{V} = \frac{0 - 100}{100}$$

Raw PRVit scores are measured against a full market universe of stocks for the broadest statistical relevance. A complication, though, is that at any time, the PRVit ratings for the set of stocks making up an entire industry group can be biased high or low. As of October 2012, for instance, specialty retail stocks were generally assigned lower PRVit scores than average. The industry's median PRVit score was only 39 on the 100-point scale. This can be seen in the left-hand chart in Exhibit 11.2, which plots the PRVit matrix, or VARP grid if you will, for the 109 specialty retail stocks in the Russell 3000 at that time.

Note that the stocks tend to plot along the diagonal, as would be expected in a market that is generally valuing risk-adjusted EVA performance. However, the retail stocks as a group sag into the lower left zone. A preponderance of the stocks plot below the fair-value line. As I said, the median rating is 39 and the average rating is 43, as shown in the table below the grid. What explains why that is happening?

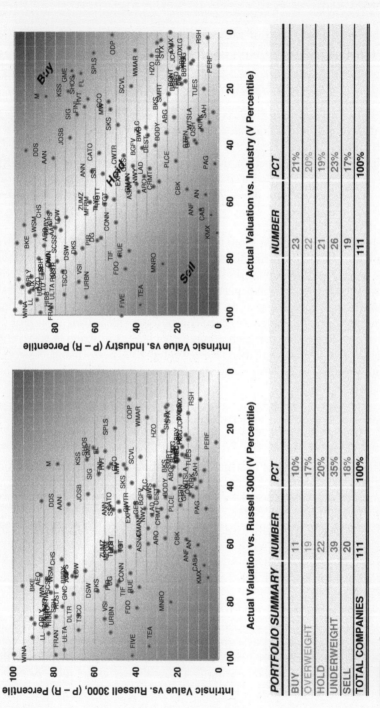

EXHIBIT 11.2 The PRVit Matrix for Specialty Retailers

PORTFOLIO SUMMARY	NUMBER	PCT
BUY	11	10%
OVERWEIGHT	19	17%
HOLD	22	20%
UNDERWEIGHT	39	35%
SELL	20	18%
TOTAL COMPANIES	111	100%

	NUMBER	PCT
	23	21%
	22	20%
	21	19%
	26	23%
	19	17%
	111	100%

The answer is that investors at this time are generally forecasting a brighter outlook for specialty retailers than for most industry groups, which means that the retailers' valuation multiples based on trailing earnings are higher than most. When the forward-looking V score is relatively high based on brightening prospects and the (P – R) score is comparatively low looking at the trailing EVA results, the entire industry group slides into the lower left zone and is weighted toward lower PRVit scores than is typical across the entire market. Industry *median* PRVit scores are thus more a question of the industry outlook and profit cycle than they are an indication of a fundamental misvaluation. In fact, our research shows you cannot make money trading on it. Highly rated sectors do not outperform lower-rated ones, as a general rule.

PRVit shines, though, in predicting the winners and losers for stocks *within* industry groups. It can tell you which retailer is a better buy than another, but not that it is time to switch into retailers and out of oil and gas stocks, for example. To isolate the insight and remove the noise, a second PRVit score is computed that removes the industry bias and exposes the intrinsic mispricing of stocks as against their relevant peer set. Quite simply, the raw PRVit scores (and the component P, R, and V scores that go into them) that are initially measured against the full market universe are reranked solely against industry peers. Those adjusted scores are displayed on the right-side chart for the specialty retailers in Exhibit 11.2.

As advertised, the reranking process shifts the scores up and to the right so that they are evenly distributed on both sides of the fair-value divide by design. There are now essentially the same numbers of buys as sells across the industry, and the average (and median) PRVit score within the industry has been reset to 50 (which means the median PRVit score for all stocks is also centered on 50 and there is no built-in bias to buy or sell stocks in general). The industry-adjusted PRVit score is a pure measure of a stock's investing merits compared to others in the same industry facing the same or similar cycles and outlook. These are the official PRVit scores, and the buy-sell ratings that EVA Dimensions issues are based on them. For instance, companies posting industry-neutral PRVit scores between 80 and 100 are rated as buys and those scoring between 0 and 20 as sells.

With this as a background, let's take an example and look at how PRVit scores AutoZone (AZO), an auto aftermarket retailer that uses EVA as a key performance and compensation metric. I hasten to add that the PRVit score has nothing to do with AutoZone's use of EVA per se. There is no extra quality rating or any other rating associated with that (except that, if using EVA helps a company to earn more EVA, then it would increase the PRVit performance score, but only in that way).

To cut to the chase, PRVit rates the stock quite highly, and has for some time, and over that time, AZO's stock has performed very well, as PRVit predicted it should (you did not think I would show you one where it did not work, at least not at the outset, right?). PRVit rates AZO a 70 against the whole market and 82 when judged in industry. It's the industry score that matters, and that qualifies AZO as one of 21 stocks rated as buys among specialty retailers.

But first, let's see how PRVit rates AZO against the entire Russell 3000 universe. We're by now somewhat familiar with the Russell 3000 metrics, and this makes for a more general discussion as opposed to a retail-centric discussion. It will then be a relatively simple matter to convert that raw market score into an industry-neutral PRVit score.

For its fiscal year ending August 2012, AZO generated an EVA of $1.0 billion on $8.6 billion in sales, which is obviously very good. PRVit quantifies just how good that is in context of all other Russell stocks, as shown in Exhibit 11.3. AZO's results appear in the first column, its percentile rating versus the Russell universe is in the right column, and the 25th, 50th and 75th percentile break points for each metric are displayed between them as reference points.

AZO's overall **Performance Score** is pegged at the 93rd percentile of all Russell 3000 companies as of the report date (October 19, 2012). That's an outstanding, A+ performance rating. It is a function of statistically combining two subscores: a profitability score running at the 93rd percentile, and an EVA Momentum trend score that qualifies for the 79th percentile. The performance score is thus a composite indicator of how successful a company has been at earning and increasing EVA, which are—or should be—the main drivers of its MVA. Let's look at the two subcomponents and the foundational metrics that are used.

The **Profitability Score (P1)** gauges EVA as a return on sales and return on capital. AZO earned a 9.4 percent EVA Margin over the most recent four

93	Performance Score (P)				Higher is better
93	**P1 Profitability**	Financial strength in generating a return on capital over the full cost			
		AZO	**25th**	**50th**	**75th**	**% Russell**
	EVA Margin (EVA/Sales)	9.4%	−4.4%	1.0%	5.1%	87
	EVA Spread (EVA/Capital)	20.4%	−2.7%	1.1%	5.0%	95
79	**P2 Trend**	The growth rate in the firm's economic profit (its EVA)			
		AZO	**25th**	**50th**	**75th**	**% Russell**
	EVA Momentum (vs Cap)	2.7%	−0.8%	0.8%	2.7%	75
	3-Year Trend (ΔEVA/Cap)	3.1%	0.0%	0.9%	2.5%	79
	Last Quarter (ΔEVA/Cap)	2.9%	−0.9%	1.0%	3.2%	72

EXHIBIT 11.3   AutoZone's Performance Score

quarters, which we know is really upper-crust. As is reported in the table, AZO's EVA Margin is at the 87th percentile versus the Margins reported by all Russell stocks—really impressive when you consider that AZO has nothing like the legacy or brand or prestige of Tiffany, for instance. It comes down to pure operational excellence. AZO's EVA as a yield on its capital is rated at an even higher percentile versus the Russell universe because as a retailer it has comparatively less capital in relation to sales than most other companies. By using both ratios as indicators, PRVit is better able to compare companies and sectors that vary in capital intensity and to come up with a more accurate reading on profitability per se.

The **Trend Score (P2)** is a composite rating of the firm's EVA Momentum measured over three time intervals—over the past year, as a three-year trend (computed by running a regression line through the EVA earned over the past four years), and for the most recent reported quarter compared to the same quarter the year before. Each of the three contains information about the company's direction. In combination they trace out the full arc of the EVA curve and give a rounded view of the EVA Momentum trajectory from a strategic to a tactical view. AZO passes all three litmus tests. Its Momentum has been quite consistently near the 75th percentile over all three time spans. The statistical average of the three readings comes together in a 79th percentile trend score.

To pile on the riches, AZO is assigned a very low **Risk Score**; as shown in Exhibit 11.4, its risk profile is judged to be only at the 17th percentile, which adds confidence that its performance is real and sustainable and not just a fluke or highly conditional. As opposed to the performance scores, *lower* risk scores increase the PRVit score. Less risk is more reliability.

Risk is a function of two subscores—a volatility score that for AZO is running at the "it does not exist" 0th percentile, and a vulnerability score coming in at the 54th percentile, higher but still midrange versus the typical firm.

17	Risk Score (R)					Lower is better	
	0	R1 Volatility				Variability in stock price and the EVA profit margin	
			AZO	25th	50th	75th	% Russell
		Stock Price Volatility	19%	29%	37%	48%	5
		EVA Margin Variability	0.3%	1.9%	4.0%	10.6%	1
	54	R2 Vulnerability				Leveraged, negative cash flow firms are suspect	
			AZO	25th	50th	75th	% Russell
		Free Cash Flow Rate	21%	7%	1%	−9%	6
		Op Cash Gen Return	25%	54%	25%	12%	49
		Total Debt/Total Capital	100%	8%	26%	44%	99
		Total Debt/EBITDAR	2.5	0.8	1.9	3.5	61

EXHIBIT 11.4 AutoZone's Risk Score

The **Volatility Score (R1)** gauges the degree of unpredictability inherent in the firm's business as reflected in the standard deviation of its stock price and in the quarterly variations in its EVA Margin over the past three years. The greater the fluctuations, the less predictable the firm is deemed to be and the less confidence is attached to any observations of its EVA performance. On both counts, though, AZO comes through as rock solid. I like to call it a wysiwyg stock—what you see is what you get. It is a transparently reliable EVA performer.

The **Vulnerability Score (R2)** considers how able a firm is to finance growth and withstand economic turbulence. Firms with stronger cash flow and less leverage have more financial strength and staying power, and are assigned a *lower* R2 score. Cash flow is assessed two ways. The first is in terms of free cash flow after all investment spending, as a percentage of capital. The more positive it is, the less dependent a firm is on external markets to finance growth, the briefer is the duration of its cash flows, and the better positioned it is to buy back stock. Investors get their money back sooner, which reduces risk.

The second cash flow measure is one we call the operating cash flow yield. Operating cash flow is free cash flow measured *before* deducting capital expenditures, lease additions, and acquisition spending. It is an indication of the underlying strength of operations that is not penalized for rapid plant expansion or acquisition investments. It is reduced, however, by an uptick in working capital. It knocks out accounting accruals that can gin up near-term earnings. It does not count sales that are not collected and inventories that are not sold. It excludes accrued costs building up into working capital accounts that will turn into earnings charges down the road. Weak operating cash generation can thus be an early warning indicator for profit challenges down the road.

The two cash flow metrics combine to give a more rounded view of cash flow strength than either alone gives. AZO is a good example of that. It is particularly strong on its free cash flow generation compared to other companies, but is not as strong on its operating cash return. Both ratios are needed to tell the cash flow story. Note, though, that the cash flow measures are risk measures in the PRVit model—they are *not* performance measures. As I have stressed, performance is always a question of earning and increasing EVA. Cash flow counts only as something that needs to be financed, that reflects the duration of the bet, or that betrays a reliance on balance sheet accruals to puff up reported earnings. It is a risk measure only.

Besides cash flow, the other factor considered in determining the vulnerability score is leverage, which is reported at 100 percent for AZO. To minimize its cost of capital and maximize its EVA, AZO's management sensibly maintains a fairly leveraged balance sheet that requires management to borrow cash it does not need against the expansion of its balance sheet in order to buy back even more stock than its free cash flow suggests would be possible. AZO has bought so much of its stock at prices way above book value that it runs with negative book equity, and its debt-to-capital ratio is over 100 percent (we limit it to 100 percent for reporting it). Using leverage (judiciously) to reduce the cost of capital is good for EVA and it is good for the P score, but it does introduce a financial risk that is accounted for here.

The risk, though, is not actually measured by the capital structure leverage ratio; that is displayed on the report for information only. The leverage ratio that enters the model is the debt repayment horizon. It is based on how long it would take to repay the debt and the present value of the rents out of EBITDAR—out of pretax, predepreciation, preinterest, and prerent cash flow. As is displayed in the PRVit report, it would take AZO 2.5 years to pay back its obligations assuming the EBITDAR earned over the trailing four quarters persisted. That's a relatively long time by market standards. It's a 60th percentile risk factor versus the Russell 3000. It is a pain point in the risk score and a blemish in an otherwise pristine risk profile. In the end, though, it is overwhelmed by the rock-solid stability in the firm's EVA Margin and its stock price, and even more in the P score, which is where the benefit of the leverage translates into a lower cost of capital and more EVA.

At this point the model pauses to compute a percentile proxy for intrinsic value by combining (P – R) into one score for all Russell companies, and then calculating the percentile for each firm. AZO's 93rd percentile performance score, less its 17th percentile risk score, puts its (P – R) score at the 87th percentile relative to the Russell 3000. That's its **Intrinsic Value Score**. It says that AZO should be more valuable than 87 out of 100 firms on the market. That is the score that is plotted on the vertical axis of the PRVit grid.

The last ingredient needed to complete the VARP recipe is V. Where does the stock trade? How highly valued is it? What valuation multiples are being placed on the firm, and then, last, how do those compare to the firm's intrinsic value score on a percentile scale? Not surprisingly, the market holds AZO in very high regard. As shown in Exhibit 11.5, AZO qualifies for an

89	Valuation Score (V)					Lower is better	
	90	V1 Wealth Ratios				Valuation multiples to book capital (as adjusted)	
			AZO	25th	50th	75th	% Russell
		MVA Margin	173%	–5%	39%	127%	81
		MVA Spread	356%	–5%	31%	115%	92
	72	V2 Wealth Multiples				Valuation multiples to cash flow, earnings, EVA	
			AZO	25th	50th	75th	% Russell
		EBITDAR Multiple	8.8	5.5	7.4	10.2	63
		NOPAT Multiple	18.0	14.6	19.3	26.4	43
		Future Growth Reliance	3%	–24%	12%	54%	43

EXHIBIT 11.5 AutoZone's Valuation Score

89th percentile **Valuation Score**. That, too, is the result of two subscores: a wealth ratios score, which rates price-to-book multiples and positions AZO at the 90th percentile, and the wealth multiples score, which gauges price-to-flow ratios—valuation multiples of earnings, cash flow, and EVA—that slots in at the 72nd percentile. As I've said, the V score is a composite index of valuation multiples, and in that diversity, there is strength to discern how high is up.

The **Wealth Ratios Score (V1)** gauges MVA as a percentage of sales and capital. Those are, as expected, very high for AZO. MVA is 173 percent of sales and over 3.5 times capital. The company has been quite successful at creating wealth because it has been quite successful at creating and growing EVA. While that is terrific for the shareholders who held the stock over the years, it does nothing for any investors who are thinking about coming into the stock now. For them, it is a price to be paid, not a reward, which is why the higher the V score, the lower the PRVit score.

Note that the V1 score, which gauges MVA to sales and capital, is analogous to the P1 score, which gauges EVA as a percentage of sales and capital. Basically PRVit is asking whether the firm's EVA is being correctly reflected in its MVA, with dangling modifiers. And if we just put the EVA and MVA scores on the scales in a straight-up comparison, we see that AZO's MVA is being priced at the 81st and 92nd percentiles of sales and capital whereas its EVA scores higher, at the 87th and 95th percentiles of sales and capital. That face-to-face comparison shows that MVA is lower than the firm's EVA suggests it should be, an impression that is amplified when the firm's positive EVA Momentum score and low risk score are also taken into account.

The **Wealth Multiples Score (V2)** takes another tack on considering where the stock is priced, and considers three valuation multiples in the process. Of the three, the enterprise multiple, in this case, the so-called EBITDAR multiple, while it is statistically relevant, is actually the least effective of the trio at predicting or explaining stock prices. You can see why here.

AZO's EBITDAR multiple is assigned a higher percentile rating than its NOPAT multiple and its Future Growth Reliance (FGR, remember, is the percentage of market value over and above the value of embedded EVA, so it is akin to a multiple of EVA). Why is that? Because a lot of AZO's value comes through in the rapid turns of its inventory and store capital—just the opposite of Tiffany. Its capital-lean business model means that its NOPAT and its EVA are higher than its EBITDAR is—because the capital costs deducted from them are lighter—which means that the valuation multiples based on NOPAT and EVA are somewhat dampened by comparison. As I have stressed before, valuation multiples are always rather slippery and in any event are more reliably assessed in profit measures that reflect the total costs and benefits of the business model that investors take into account in pricing the stock. That is why valuation is always better assessed as a multiple of NOPAT, which is measured net of the depreciation and amortization of capital that EBITDAR ignores, and even more, of EVA, which also brings the cost of capital into the valuation multiple picture.

And it is this last metric, the Future Growth Reliance ratio, that is so stunningly out of line for AZO. Only 3 percent of the company's aggregate market value is counting on and is at risk of growth in EVA. That is less reliance on EVA growth than is true for the median firm on the market. In fact, it is only at the 43th percentile. And yet over the past quarter, year, and three years running, AZO consistently racked up EVA Momentum results near the 75th percentile break line.

All the scores that enter the PRVit model have now been discussed and are awaiting final assembly. The last step is to compute and rank the ratio of intrinsic value to trading value, specifically, the $(P - R)/V$ ratio. As mentioned before, the PRVit ratio for AutoZone corresponds to a 70th percentile score against the entire Russell market, and when that is reranked exclusively against the raw PRVit market scores for other specialty retailers, it improves—it is shifted to an industry-neutral score of the 82nd percentile, which corresponds to a buy rating. The scores are all depicted on the PRVit grid so that without getting lost in the details—in fact, at a glance—you can appreciate the judgments and insights that PRVit renders. The grids are shown in Exhibit 11.6.

The intersection of the intrinsic value score on the vertical axis and valuation score running right to left on the horizontal axis is the PRVit score positioning on the grid. When viewed against the full market, on the upper chart, AZO's PRVit score intersects in the upper right zone (I concede it looks like it plots on the line or a little in the lower left zone, but the actual score, 70, is in the upper right zone; the plot is just an approximate representation of the score, and the program that generates it doesn't always put the dot precisely where it should be, frankly).

The lower grid plots the PRVit scores after reranking them against the specialty retailer peer group. When you rank AZO's PRVit score just against its grade and not the whole school, its intrinsic value score rises 7 percentile points and its actual valuation score rises only three points, which puts its PRVit score 12 points deeper into the upper right zone. Again, AZO looks to be an even better buy when you narrow the investment options to the group of specialty retailers. That is the firm's formal PRVit score, and the buy-sell signal we bank on.

Now that the mechanics have been covered, you can appreciate the PRVit score in another light—namely that it is, in effect, a turbocharged earnings yield ratio. It pushes investors into stocks that look capable of generating high returns on the value paid. But there are very significant differences between the PRVit yield and traditional earnings yield (which is just the inversion of the P/E ratio). First, the earnings that count in the PRVit

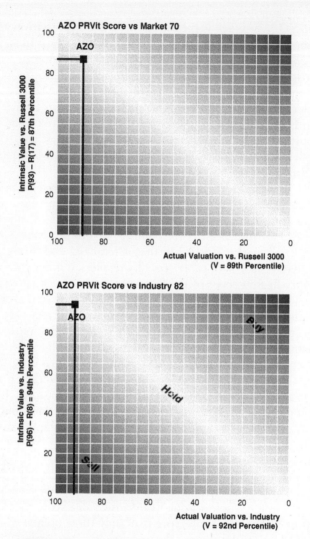

EXHIBIT 11.6   The PRVit Matrix for AutoZone

yield are EVA earnings, not EPS or EBITDA earnings. Only high-quality
earnings enter the PRVit rating. Accounting-inflated earnings or investment-
generated earnings don't count at all. Another distinction is that the yield
is derived not just from the firm's current profitability. It also includes a
sophisticated assessment of the growth trend in EVA. The full arc of the
EVA Momentum curve is a factor in the P score, as has been shown. And
as a result of this, it is not just a static measure of yield, but a dynamic

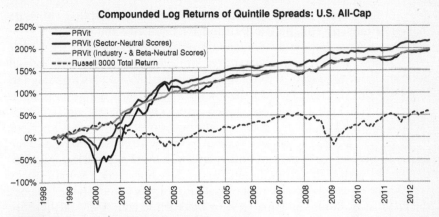

Compounded Log Returns of Quintile Spreads: U.S. All-Cap

— PRVit
— PRVit (Sector-Neutral Scores)
— PRVit (Industry - & Beta-Neutral Scores)
---- Russell 3000 Total Return

EXHIBIT 11.7   How PRVit Performed Since 1998

indicator of the overall return that puts growth stocks and value stocks on a fair footing. Third, the earnings yield is risk-adjusted. PRVit asks whether the yield is likely to be sustainable, and judges that with the temperature settings for a variety of measurable risk factors. A final point of distinction is that the yield measured in the PRVit score is not technically a return on value, but a return on a composite index of valuation multiples. All told, it is a diversified mix of measures rolled into one indicative buy-sell score. By gosh, it is *E Pluribus Unum*, once again.

The PRVit model digs far more deeply, consistently, correctly, and statistically into the real fundamentals of business performance and valuation multiples than the run-of-the-mill stock screener, which is a good reason to believe that, while stocks are generally aligned with their risk-adjusted EVA earnings potential, PRVit can ferret out opportunities to make the market an even more perfect EVA valuation engine. That is what the evidence seems to suggest.

As I have said, PRVit has a published track record on Bloomberg dating back half a decade. We are also able to simulate how PRVit would have rated stocks going back further to span more market cycles. As shown in Exhibit 11.7, if you had bought the top 20 percent of PRVit-rated stocks, shorted the lowest 20 percent, and rebalanced monthly, you would have substantially outperformed just passively investing in the Russell 3000 universe[1] (there

---

[1] This is not really the correct comparison, frankly, as the long/short PRVit strategy is market neutral—it should be compared with an uncorrelated cash return. But that is quibbling. The valuation insights are so good that PRVit can apparently win a handicapped race.

are various flavors of PRVit tracked that vary by how much they eliminate market or industry risk, but all of them have predictive ability).

The chart in Exhibit 11.8 zooms in on the year ending in September 2012. It shows the returns generated from portfolios formed with Russell 3000 stocks divided into 20 bins rank ordered by PRVit scores from high to low. Over this short time period, the top three bins clearly did better than all others, and the lowest three fared much worse. Over longer periods, as predictions accumulate, the top four to eight bins, covering the top 20 percent to 40 percent of PRVit-rated stocks, tend to outperform the market, and the lower 20 percent to 40 percent underperform. There's pretty clear evidence that stocks with high ratings do tend to produce higher returns than stocks with lower ratings. It's not perfect of course. Not every stock in the bin goes the PRVit way. But if you are a CFO or IR director, your firm's PRVit score is not a ruling you should dismiss out of hand.

Incidentally, PRVit also works globally. Exhibit 11.9 is the same chart, but now plotting the returns from the 20 portfolios formed by ranking all 9,000 stocks we cover in our global database each month according to their global PRVit Prime scores (PRVit Prime scores are determined by measuring the raw PRVit scores against the entire 9,000-company universe, then using regression to eliminate the common effect of country and sector on

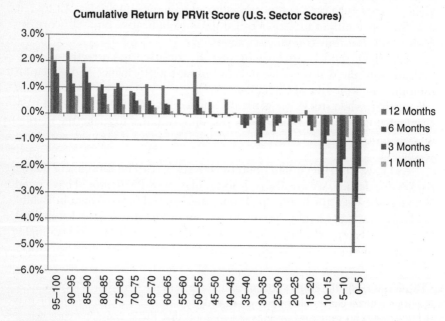

EXHIBIT 11.8   PRVit's Performance for the Year Ending in September 2012

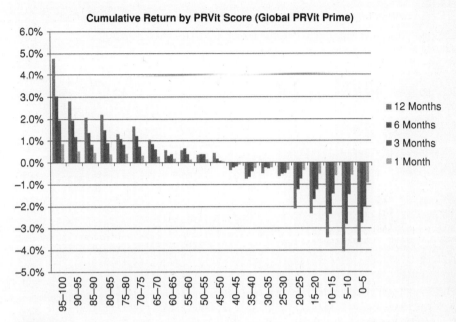

Cumulative Return by PRVit Score (Global PRVit Prime)

- ■ 12 Months
- ■ 6 Months
- ■ 3 Months
- ■ 1 Month

EXHIBIT 11.9   PRVit's Global Performance for the Year Ending in September 2012

the scores; it is a pure measure of the mispricing of a stock after abstracting from the country and industry it is in). Once again, the returns line up with the PRVit scores.

How did PRVit fare with AutoZone? Pretty well, as it turns out. The plot in Exhibit 11.10 shows that AutoZone was able to maintain a PRVit score generally in or very near the buy zone all the way from 2007 to October 2012, a time when AZO proved to be a very good investment indeed.

This raises an interesting question: How did AutoZone manage to retain such a high PRVit rating over the years as its stock price and its V score climbed higher and higher? The short answer is an ever-ascending performance pattern in terms of expanding the EVA Margin and generating EVA Momentum. Exhibit 11.11 has the key results, as are reported on page 3 of the PRVit report.

AutoZone managed to more than double its EVA over the past five years (line 7) as the firm's EVA Margin steadily increased from 6.4 percent to 9.4 percent (line 10). EVA Momentum was consistently positive and over 1 percent in each of the past three years (line 13). The performance improvements lifted the P score to the 93rd percentile from only the 75th percentile five years back and were the reason AZO was able to hold on to its high PRVit rating even as its stock price climbed from $121 to $369.

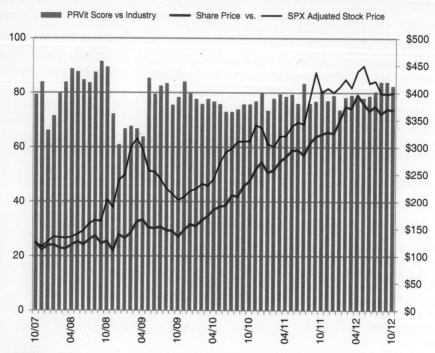

EXHIBIT 11.10   PRVit's AutoZone Ranking and the Stock's Performance

Incidentally, when the question of valuation is on the table, all the EVA tools are fair game, and our investor team brings them all into play. For instance, beyond the PRVit score, what does the EVA Momentum math say, and how does that compare to the Market-Implied Momentum (MIM) rate that is baked into the firm's stock price?

Consistent with the almost nonexistent Future Growth Reliance we observed, AutoZone's MIM was just 0.1 percent as of the report date, meaning that the stock is priced for almost no growth in EVA. And yet that certainly has not been the historical record. If management can keep up anything like its past EVA Momentum trend, the stock will turn out to be a great bargain. A skeptical investor, though, could ask: But how much higher could the EVA Margin go, given it is so high already, and won't that limit the potential for future growth in EVA if productivity gains are taken off the table? That's a good question.

Suppose AZO's EVA Margin has peaked. Then we can ask how fast AutoZone's sales would have to grow at the current 9.4 percent EVA Margin rate to match the 0.1 percent Momentum rate in the stock. Run the math. It would take sales growth of only a little more than 1 percent per annum

Performance

AZO's exceptionally strong return on capital and its impressive EVA profit trend combine for a first-rate, 93rd percentile P score.

	2007TFQ4	2008TFQ4	2009TFQ4	2010TFQ4	2011TFQ4	2012TFQ4	19-Oct-12	Average
1 Sales	$6,170	$6,523	$6,817	$7,363	$8,073	$8,604	$8,604	$7,258
2 EBITDAR (EBITDA+Rent+R&D+Ad+Etc.)	$1,452	$1,537	$1,598	$1,791	$2,002	$2,168	$2,168	$1,758
3 NOPAT (Net Operating Profit After Tax)	$687	$731	$754	$861	$981	$1,064	$1,064	$846
4 Capital (Net Operating Assets)	$3,631	$3,720	$3,828	$3,873	$3,984	$4,194	$4,194	$3,872
5 Return on Capital (ROC) (NOPAT/Capital)	19.1%	20.0%	18.7%	22.3%	25.3%	26.8%	26.8%	22.0%
6 Cost of Capital (COC)	8.2%	8.0%	7.5%	7.3%	7.1%	6.4%	6.4%	7.4%
7 EVA (ROC − COC) × Capital	$392	$440	$453	$577	$707	$811	$811	$563
8 Company Type	Star	Star	Star	Star	Star	Star	Star	
9 EVA Spread (EVA/Capital = ROC − COC)	10.9%	12.1%	11.3%	15.0%	18.3%	20.4%	20.4%	14.6%
10 EVA Margin (EVA/Sales)	6.4%	6.7%	6.7%	7.8%	8.8%	9.4%	9.4%	7.6%
11 EBITDAR Margin (EBITDAR/Sales)	23.5%	23.6%	23.4%	24.3%	24.8%	25.2%	25.2%	24.1%
12 Sales Growth	3.7%	5.7%	4.5%	8.0%	9.7%	6.6%	6.6%	6.4%
13 EVA Momentum (ΔEVA/Sales)	0.3%	0.8%	0.2%	1.8%	1.8%	1.3%	1.3%	1.0%
14 EVA Momentum (ΔEVA/Capital)	0.6%	1.3%	0.4%	3.1%	3.4%	2.7%	2.7%	1.9%
15 3-Year Trend (ΔEVA/Capital)	-0.1%	0.8%	0.8%	1.5%	2.4%	3.1%	3.1%	1.4%
16 Last Quarter (ΔEVA/Capital)	1.3%	2.7%	-0.6%	3.8%	3.7%	2.9%	2.9%	2.3%
P Performance Score	75	86	91	94	93	93	93	89
P1 Profitability Score	87	89	91	92	93	93	93	91
P2 Trend Score	45	69	74	86	84	79	79	73

EXHIBIT 11.11 AutoZone's Key Performance Figures

to do it, which seems inconceivably slow. Surely AZO will expand faster than that. If so, the inescapable conclusion is that AZO is being priced for a fairly significant deterioration in its EVA Margin. So let's look at this the other way around.

Suppose sales are forecast to grow at, say, 7 percent, in line with the historical trend (see line 12 in Exhibit 11.11). How much would the EVA Margin have to drop to match the Market-Implied Momentum rate of 0.1 percent? It would have to decay a little less rapidly than the sales are forecast to grow, to leave a slight 0.1 percent Momentum in the balance. If you run the math exactly, the Margin would have to ease back about 30 percent over five years, or from 9.2 percent to 6.4 percent. That's about 3 percent after tax, or 5 percent pretax assuming a 40 percent standard tax rate. The simple simulation indicates that investors would have to be fairly severe pessimists about the business model to dislike the stock at the current price. They would have to be assuming that the EVA Margin is vulnerable and likely to retreat substantially after years of advancing, and that competitive pressure and Margin convergence are right on the horizon. Time will tell if that is so, but PRVit and the Momentum math clearly and quickly put the key facts on the table that the analyst, and management, should ponder.

Before discussing the corporate applications, and to reinforce our knowledge, let's see how well PRVit rates Tiffany, shown in Exhibit 11.12. Not well at all, as it happens. TIF's PRVit score is just 16 against the market and 11 against the specialty retailer peer group (yes, it's in the same group as AZO). While reranking against the industry generally lifts PRVit scores of specialty retailers, it decreased the score for Tiffany. It all depends on where the company's statistics fall against the full industry distribution. Any way you look at it, though, PRVit rates Tiffany a sell. Tiffany plots deep in the lower left zone on the PRVit grid. This time the grid accurately reflects the PRVit id. The plot is spot on.

After all the work we performed in the planning chapter modeling a bright future for Tiffany, what is the PRVit model telling us in dissent? First, PRVit is based on judging actual results, and plans are just projections. Caveat emptor. Management must be optimistic, whereas the market must be skeptical. Also, look at the PRVit acid test, as I call it, for a shortcut insight. Pit Tiffany's P1 score against its V1 score for a straight-up EVA-to-MVA comparison. Tiffany's EVA performance ratios are running at the 74th percentile, but its MVA wealth ratios run a tad higher, at the 77th percentile. That's the opposite of the relationship we saw at AutoZone. In Tiffany's case, MVA is running somewhat ahead of EVA, not behind it.

Another concern that PRVit calls out in the P2 trend score is that Tiffany's EVA weakened over the past year and also, critically, in the last quarterly sounding. For the second quarter of 2012 compared to the second

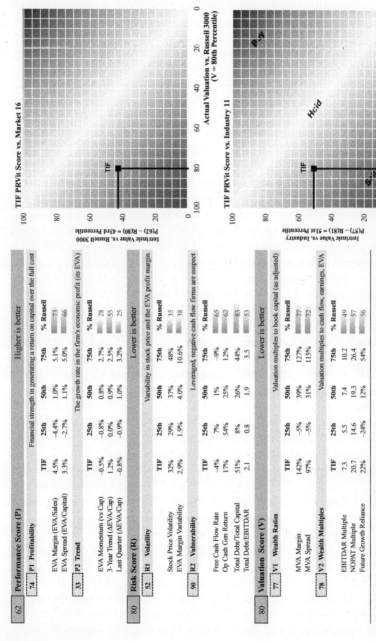

Performance Score (P) 62					
P1 Profitability 74				Higher is better	
Financial strength in generating a return on capital over the full cost					
	TIF	25th	50th	75th	% Russell
EVA Margin (EVA/Sales)	4.5%	-4.4%	1.0%	5.1%	73
EVA Spread (EVA/Capital)	3.3%	-2.7%	1.1%	5.0%	66
P2 Trend 33					
The growth rate in the firm's economic profit (its EVA)					
	TIF	25th	50th	75th	% Russell
EVA Momentum (vs Cap)	-0.5%	-0.8%	0.8%	2.7%	28
3-Year Trend (ΔEVA/Cap)	1.2%	0.0%	0.9%	2.5%	55
Last Quarter (ΔEVA/Cap)	-0.8%	-0.9%	1.0%	3.2%	25

Risk Score (R) 80					
R1 Volatility 52				Lower is better	
Variability in stock price and the EVA profit margin					
	TIF	25th	50th	75th	% Russell
Stock Price Volatility	32%	29%	37%	48%	35
EVA Margin Variability	2.9%	1.9%	4.0%	10.6%	38
R2 Vulnerability 90					
Leveraged, negative cash flow firms are suspect					
	TIF	25th	50th	75th	% Russell
Free Cash Flow Rate	-4%	7%	1%	-9%	65
Op Cash Gen Return	17%	54%	25%	12%	62
Total Debt/Total Capital	51%	8%	26%	44%	83
Total Debt/EBITDAR	2.1	0.8	1.9	3.5	53

Valuation Score (V) 80					
V1 Wealth Ratios 77				Lower is better	
Valuation multiples to book capital (as adjusted)					
	TIF	25th	50th	75th	% Russell
MVA Margin	142%	-5%	39%	127%	77
MVA Spread	97%	-5%	31%	115%	72
V2 Wealth Multiples 78					
Valuation multiples to cash flow, earnings, EVA					
	TIF	25th	50th	75th	% Russell
EBITDAR Multiple	7.3	5.5	7.4	10.2	49
NOPAT Multiple	20.7	14.6	19.3	26.4	57
Future Growth Reliance	22%	-24%	12%	54%	56

The PRVit Matrix: depicts a company's PRVit score by plotting its intrinsic value score—what PRVit rates the firm is truly worth based on its risk-adjusted performance (i.e., its comparative P − R score) against its actual valuation score, which reflects the company's current trading multiples. Companies rated "Hold" plot along the diagonal, which is where the firms' actual valuation multiples align with their intrinsic values. "Buys" plot in the upper right zone, which is where PRVit rates the firms as worth more than their current share values, and "Sells" appear in the lower left zone, where the firms' (P − R) scores fall short of their V scores. The top grid rates the firms against the entire market, and the lower one ranks them against industry peers (which is the basis for the official PRVit score).

EXHIBIT 11.12 Why PRVit Is Down on Tiffany

quarter of 2011, Tiffany's EVA Momentum was negative, and only at the 25th percentile of all Russell 3000 firms. The most recent news in Tiffany's EVA data is that EVA is heading south, something that escaped our attention in the strategic planning chapter because we were focused only on performance data over a full year or four quarters. Now PRVit is appropriately waving a bright red flag on that deteriorating score.

Another flag is being raised, perhaps surprisingly, on the risk score. Compared to AZO, TIF is more volatile, both in stock price and in fluctuations in its EVA Margin—it is a retailer of luxury goods, after all, not steady auto aftermarket supplies. It may not have registered before, but Tiffany's EVA Margin got walloped in the mid-2008 to 2010 market meltdown while AZO skated right through. Tiffany's cash flow metrics are also weaker. Being more capital intense, TIF has to invest more capital as it grows. That is a burden that every capital-intense business model will have to carry. All things considered, TIF is assigned an 80th percentile risk score versus all Russell 3000 companies. That may seem an overly harsh judgment. After all, none of the individual risk metrics reached so damning an indictment. Why then is the overall risk score so severe?

This is probably a good time to mention a wrinkle in the PRVit model. Our research uncovered a subtle correlation that needs to be taken into account. As it turns out, the more profitable a company is, the lower its risk metrics tend to be. Profitable companies often have established franchises that enable them to earn profits more consistently and with less volatility than firms that are locked in highly competitive, fragmented, and less profitable businesses. Profitable companies also tend to have stronger cash flow metrics because they generate more cash internally, and that also enables them to pay off their debt faster and often to use less of it. If you plot out raw R scores against P1 scores for the whole market, you'd see R trending down as P1 goes up—which means we'd essentially be counting profitability twice if we did not make an adjustment.

We use a regression model to adjust the risk score upward for profitable companies. And because TIF is so profitable—its P1 is at the 74th percentile—it gets tagged with a sizable upward revision (the same upward revision applied to AZO, even more so since it is more profitable, but it was not as noticeable because its underlying risk metrics were so low to begin with). Put another way, Tiffany exhibits a far higher risk profile for a company of its profitability class than you'd expect. It is not as risky in an absolute sense, but it is riskier than expected after accounting for how profitable it is. That is an attribute of Tiffany's business model that escaped our attention before, and that management might want to address as a planning opportunity. The question would be: "How can we reduce our business risk profile as an avenue to becoming a more attractive investment?"

A final few points of note concern Tiffany's V2 score—its cash flow and profit multiples—which are judged to be rather high, at the 78th percentile against the market. First, TIF's EBITDAR multiple is *lower* percentile rated than its NOPAT and EVA multiples, whereas for AZO it is the opposite. To repeat, TIF's EBITDAR multiple is low because its EBITDAR so overstates the profit that the market is really valuing by entirely leaving out the cost of the capital that TIF uses so much of. It is another example of why the enterprise multiple is the least important and most undependable valuation multiple in the model. As for TIF's Future Growth Reliance, it is well over the market median. TIF is priced as an EVA growth stock, and 22 percent of Tiffany's market value is at risk of EVA growth, compared to only 3 percent for AZO. Yet AZO has the far better EVA Momentum track record.

Statistical cross talk between P1 and V2 is another complicating factor that we've been forced to deal with in the model. As we saw in the target setting chapter, the market tends to project that companies already earning high EVA Margins are less likely to continue growing EVA than ones with lower EVA Margins. Whether it is due to competitive convergence or cyclical reversals, the link is statistically significant and must be eliminated in order to avoid double counting (or at this point it would be triple counting) a firm's profitability in its PRVit score in another unintended way. A regression model is used to adjust the V2 valuation multiples score upward for profitable companies. Although Tiffany's multiples are quite pedestrian by the standards of the whole market, they are judged to be upper-quartile when benchmarked against companies of its profitability class. Put another way, the market is pricing the stock for way more sustained growth in EVA than is typical of a firm that is earning a 4.5 percent EVA Margin. The same upward adjustment was made to AZO's V2 score, but again, it was not as noticeable since its multiples were so low to begin with.

All things considered, PRVit is raising a set of legitimate concerns about Tiffany's value as an investment. If Tiffany's stock price was lower, and therefore its V score was lower, then of course, at a price, it would be viewed as attractive to own. If Tiffany's EVA hadn't tripped up recently and its EVA Margin was higher and its EVA Momentum was more consistently impressive, then Tiffany's P score would be higher, and it could be attractive to own at the current price. Earning and increasing EVA are always a key to increasing share price. And the buy-sell decision is always a question of whether one can buy value at a reasonable price. Is the PRVit judgment an absolute indictment of Tiffany as an investment? No; no model is perfect. But PRVit does assemble of wealth of insights into a set of statistical scores that are helping investors and an increasing number of CFOs to home in on the key performance-risk-valuation insights and reach more incisive conclusions about true worth and the key questions that need to be answered.

Incidentally, EVA and PRVit are useful not only to zero in on one stock at a time. Our equity research team is firing the EVA arsenal at a broad range of topics that fund managers care about, from investigating whole sectors at a time and x-raying and comparing the business models of peer firms, to researching investing themes such as which stocks will fare best and worst when interest rates rise again, to which firms are best positioned and best priced to emerge from a cyclical downturn, and so on. It certainly is not all based on PRVit or even mainly based on PRVit. But it is always based on EVA, and it is always providing ready and reliable insights not easily obtainable elsewhere.

One example of the custom research our team is performing is shown in Exhibit 11.13. It's an analysis of early-stage biotechnology stocks, which are notoriously hard to value. The approach the team took was to look at the EVA Margin time line for a sample of 15 early-stage biotech companies that had successfully brought products to market. As the chart shows, the median firm ended up earning a 20 percent EVA Margin once up and running.

The team then looked at another set of unproven emerging biotechnology firms and computed the revenue that each would need to generate five years down the pike at the assumed 20 percent EVA Margin in order to discount to their current share prices. The interesting finding was that the consensus revenue forecast was above the EVA-derived revenue requirement for 15 emerging biotech companies, the upper block of companies in Exhibit 11.14, and was under it for the 10 in the lower block. It's an important confirmation that the market apparently had gotten the valuations right on average, and that the 20 percent EVA Margin assumption was reasonable. For the investors, though, it was also extremely helpful that EVA could show them where the value looked like a stretch and where it appeared more assured.

Although PRVit was developed to help investors make better decisions, it is also finding a home with CFOs and IR directors. Many of them are interested, to say the least, in seeing the same EVA information and rating scores as are being furnished to institutional investors by the EVA Dimensions research team. They want to be on the same page. Beyond that, they tap into PRVit for an objective reading on how EVA is scoring their company's performance, risk, and valuation against peers and the market as a whole. They are using it as part of the information packet they furnish to their board each quarter. It's a format they find convenient to keep directors abreast of how the firm is performing and being valued relative to peers, and the outlook for the stock.

One CFO I know looks at it another way. He believes that as more pure quant funds are getting into his stock, and as even fundamental investment firms are increasingly turning to front-end quantitative screens to help them

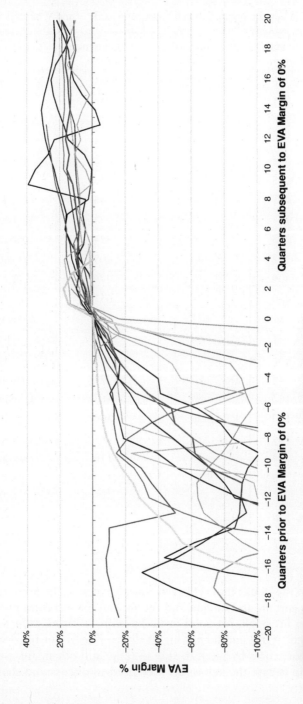

EXHIBIT 11.13 EVA Margin Pattern for Successful Biotech Companies

EXHIBIT 11.14 Where Emerging Biotech Value Seems Likely and Where It's a Stretch

Ticker	TFQ Revenue	2017 Implied Revenue	2017 Consensus Estimate	2020 Consensus Estimates
MSB AU	38	991	1,971	2,966
PCYC	81	2,234	913	3,230
INCY	168	841	1,418	1,433
IDIX	39	252	191	742
DNDN	303	149	633	637
ALNY	83	331	216	757
ONXX	457	1,766	1,786	2,176
NPSP	127	201	533	Unavailable
EXEL	248	35	324	Unavailable
GHDX	222	346	409	606
CPHD	309	1,018	776	1,223
ALKS	480	594	657	797
ARNA	30	437	638	Unavailable
IRWD	71	650	494	692
ITMN	23	795	460	834
CRIS	29	42	41	Unavailable
BMRN	162	1,385	1,363	Unavailable
THRX	140	790	566	706
ISIS	124	528	284	Unavailable
SVNT	14	502	116	Unavailable
IMGN	16	827	167	372
ARIA	26	2,595	827	1,980
MDVN	110	1,546	634	847
SGEN	167	1,776	576	866
REGN	762	5,705	2,902	2,751

winnow down the stocks they will even consider owning, he needs a way to pull back the curtain and understand the measurable pressure points that are bearing on his stock, for good or ill. He calls PRVit his "Quantitative-Pressure Gauge" (QPI) and he has his IR director chart out the evolving P, R, V, and PRVit scores by week to stay in tune. Still others are using it to help them help isolate the key issues they need to discuss and shape their investor relations messaging, and as a way to prep for meetings with the growing group of investors who are looking at investing decisions through an EVA lens.

Speaking of which, investors are increasingly asking us, "What are the hallmarks of a real EVA company?" They realize that many firms compute EVA or something similar, but they also know that to really benefit, a company must do more than just measure it. In case you are interested, here's the short five-point checklist that I submit:

1. EVA is the management's overarching financial mission—it is not just one measure among many, but the one that really counts.
2. EVA is defined to remedy material accounting distortions and more accurately measure real economic substance and to surface better decisions.
3. All decision making is EVA-based—projecting, analyzing, and discounting EVA is the key.
4. EVA is accountable and motivating—it is the central measure in management reporting and analysis, and the key measure if not the sole measure in a formula-based bonus plan.
5. EVA is well understood and well used throughout the company, from the boardroom to the shop floor.

In the next chapter I cover success factors and implementation steps in far greater detail. But for investors, that short checklist gives them a quick way to separate the Best-Practice EVA firms from the pretenders.

CHAPTER 12

Become a Best-Practice EVA Company

My objective in writing this book was, first, to persuade you that the greatly enhanced EVA ratio framework is superior to all conventional metrics for measuring, understanding, and improving the financial performance of an enterprise. EVA, EVA Momentum, and EVA Margin always give the right answer because, by definition, they always are the same as the net present value of cash flows that is the true determinant of value. All the other measures and ratios that business has relied on for decades are incomplete, often inconsistent with one another, and hopelessly flawed because they routinely provide incorrect answers that lead to poor decisions. The EVA framework, in contrast, is internally consistent and always leads to the right answers because EVA is the one and only measure for which more always is better than less.

My ultimate goal, however, is to persuade you to *use* EVA to the fullest and to rewire how your company thinks, plans, decides, and communicates, and even pays its managers and workers. I sincerely believe that adopting Best-Practice EVA is the surest way for every company to achieve the greatest success in its chosen markets and produce the greatest wealth, not just for shareholders but for customers, employees, and all its other constituencies. The way to do that most effectively is not adding the bits and pieces you find appealing. To be most effective, Best-Practice EVA implies a commitment to go all the way with EVA.

That does not mean, however, that you have to throw out everything else right away and plunge into EVA on the strength of my arguments alone. The process I am about to describe for adopting Best-Practice EVA is just that, a process. I am confident that as you and your team go through it, the process itself will dispel any doubts about the superiority of the EVA framework long before you have taken any irreversible steps. The doubts will fall away as soon as you see a few examples within your own company where

EVA and your current financial procedures arrive at different conclusions. I *know* that the EVA conclusion will be the superior one, and I know that will be clear to you as well, because the transparency of EVA will show exactly why its answer is the economically superior one. Even so, some may decide to simply put EVA in place alongside their conventional planning and analysis activities—at least for a while. That's okay, because it will just be a matter of time until the superiority of the EVA information becomes obvious, and in the meantime, EVA will furnish valuable intelligence and a fresh perspective and guard management against blind spots.

The Best-Practice system I advocate calls for three great substitutions. The first is to elevate EVA to the status of being the profit performance measure that really counts in your company and is the final arbiter of how you make decisions and tell your story. There should be no ambiguity here. The goal is not to maximize EVA subject to maintaining tolerable book income or cash flow. It is to maximize EVA, period.

Committing to an EVA focus is not the radical move it appears. I am not trying to be provocative here, just ruthlessly practical. Most people think focusing on EVA is a radical move because they misconstrue the divergence between EVA and earnings per share (EPS). Most CFOs, for example, assume that by focusing on EVA they may leave their EPS in the dust. But what really should concern them is the exact opposite. By focusing on EPS (or operating profit or EBITDA), they may well leave their EVA in the dust. Remember, EVA deducts the full cost of capital, where EPS doesn't. There's no charge in EPS for the most expensive capital of all, the return expectations of shareholders. Charging for all capital makes EVA the most demanding profit performance measure, not the least. It is quality earnings, not commodity earnings. Therefore, when a company increases its EVA profit, it almost always increases its EPS (I say almost always because there are other accounting adjustments to EVA that could intervene, but each has been discussed in turn, and each was shown to favor EVA, like writing R&D off over time instead of expensing it).

So it's not that EVA fails EPS, but that EPS fails EVA. It is incredibly easy to inflate and manipulate EPS while decreasing EVA and reducing shareholder wealth. That's why you really should focus on increasing EVA, and let EPS just take care of itself. The same goes for operating profit and EBITDA, only a lot more so. They are both measuring earnings before many things that count. What is the point of even considering them except as stepping-stones to EVA?

The second great substitution I advocate is to stop using discounted cash flow analysis, and use EVA instead. I've hit this pretty hard throughout the book, but let me state the case again briefly. When you literally stop discounting cash flow and start using EVA as the main valuation and decision engine, supplemented by the full EVA tool kit of measures and ratios, decisions are clearer, more informed, more accountable, and more cohesive because the decisions link right back to how performance is measured. EVA gives you everything that cash flow does, but so much more. So why use cash flow?

The third great substitution is to toss out or at the least subordinate all the conventional financial ratio metrics in favor of the new trio of EVA ratio metrics we've developed at EVA Dimensions. I've shown how classic operating margins or EBITDA margins are just cogs in the EVA wheel and line items in the EVA Margin schedule. I've gone a lot further and blasted ROI, ROC, and RONA to smithereens. I implore you to retire return on capital and the DuPont ROI formula—with honor and full pensions. They have helped over the years. But it is time for the centenarians to retire in favor of the new EVA ratios.

Let me make the case for the EVA focus I am advocating with an analogy. What is the appeal of the Apple iPhone or Apple products in general? Most agree that simplicity is a huge part. For Steve Jobs and his chief designer, Jonathan Ive, simplicity is lack of clutter, intuitively obvious functionality, with a modicum of sophistication and attention to detail tossed in for good measure. It is perhaps best exemplified with the single button, just one, on the front of the iPhone. It's the same with Best-Practice EVA. *One* measure is used pervasively, consistently, and passionately to express the corporate financial mission, review performance, guide decisions, allocate capital, price acquisitions, set goals, and meter bonus pay, and for communication with the market. The consistent and comprehensive use of EVA for all those corporate applications is what makes EVA simple, effective, and powerful.

The iPhone's simplicity is more than just the one button, though. It is also how that one button accesses all the applications. It's a pristine window into the digital world. It is the same with EVA. It is one measure that opens into the many. It elegantly unfolds in steps to reveal all the elemental measures and performance factors and strategic milestones that contribute to value. I have called it *E Pluribus Unum* and *E Unum Pluribus*—from the many to the one, and from the one to the many. That's the mantra I have recited and that is successfully exploited with the EVA ratio metric set.

In brief, I am calling for CFOs to start fresh and end simple, with EVA at the core. What does it take, then, to be really successful with Best-Practice EVA? I can reduce it to three things.

The **first** is fairly obvious, and would be true of any major initiative. It's willpower. It is about gaining a real commitment to EVA, where commitment flows from knowledge about it and from comfort and experience in using it, and from seeing others using it too, frankly. The commitment has to emanate from the top down. The board must be on board with EVA. The CEO's commitment to it is critical, of course. And the CFO must be willing to be the real keeper of the EVA flame.

If the commitment to EVA really is there, go public with it if your company is public. Tell investors that you are a bona fide Best-Practice EVA outfit, and prove it. Show them you've checked all the boxes. It's not one measure among many. It is the measure that counts, for example. It's the process of how you use EVA and your degree of commitment to it that investors need and want to hear. They do not need you to disclose your EVA figures. EVA Dimensions does that already. They want to know your heart beats to the EVA drum and that your head is in the right place.

The **second** critical success factor is to actually purge and purify, to use EVA widely and deeply, wiring it into and throughout all aspects of management. *Deeply* means that EVA is the riveting focus of attention, and that all other measures and methods have been retired from service or subsumed under the EVA banner. Put an EVA stake deep into the ground. *Widely* means EVA is used pervasively. On the crossbar, it threads through, unites, speeds, and simplifies all aspects of the management process, making it simpler, more accountable, more cohesive, and more capital conscientious. Performance reporting is EVA based, planning is EVA based, capital budgeting and acquisition analysis are EVA based, and setting targets is EVA based. It's all based on EVA.

For EVA to fill all those roles, it needs to be a versatile but dependable player. It must truly be a continuous improvement performance metric. It must be defined so that good decisions add to it and bad ones subtract from it. It should resist gaming and reflect strategic value and not tactical opportunism. The same measure should work looking forward for making net present value (NPV) decisions and for looking backward to measure, analyze, and reward performance. All those features are inherent to the EVA framework. But in applying the framework to your specific company, it is crucial to spend some time up front to get the EVA measure right. The formulas for measuring and revising the cost of capital and the adjustments that will be made to repair reported accounting distortions need to be thought through and tested. The measure should be so airtight that it is capable of simplifying conversations about setting targets and quelling arguments about the decision goals. You want to reduce all of the ongoing disputes into a one-time up-front pow-wow to define EVA, and then to live with the definition you've selected for at least a three-year period.

The **third** success factor is also obvious. Pay for it. Make bonuses and advancement up the corporate ladder a function of earning and increasing EVA. This does not have to be done right away, but as soon as possible. And ideally, decouple the EVA incentive pay from budget targets. Put the incentive plan on autopilot and liberate your team to stretch and dream and achieve and to think and to act like owners because they are really paid like owners—by giving them a share of the value they add instead of paying them for beating negotiated intentions.

How do you get there? In five steps that I call the "5-Ps"—**Pilot, Prepare, Prototype, Practice, Perform.**

Pilot: The best way to get started is to take Best-Practice EVA for a test drive—which is my cue for a modest advertisement. Simply furnish EVA Dimensions with basic financial data in an Excel spreadsheet for your company and its lines of business, covering past and planned performance, and a list of public peers, and our team will run it through our software tool kit for you. We'll derive the EVA, EVA Margin, and EVA Momentum ratio statics and build out the Momentum Pyramid for your company and your public peer set. We'll analyze and value the existing forward plans, and possibly a major investment or acquisition decision. We'll upload security analyst and consensus forecast models for your company (if public) and public peers to give a reading on the market's expectations for EVA. In short, we will show you how it works and illustrate the insights it offers, and give you a thorough, well-documented and generally quite informative presentation covering all aspects of Best-Practice EVA. Your team does not have to be tied down running the software at this stage. You concentrate on absorbing the insights and pondering the value of moving ahead with the Best-Practice EVA program.

Prepare: Assuming you want to keep going, this step maps out the proposed adoption process in some detail and breaks it into appropriate modules with milestones. This is also an occasion to install the EVA software on your computers and get your team trained to use it. It is also a good time to dig into the cost of capital, and figure out how to define EVA your way by testing the corrective accounting adjustments. Choose a definition for EVA that strikes an optimal balance. Keep it as simple and close to reported accounting as you can, but also make it function as a legitimate continuous improvement metric that bridges decision-making and reporting applications. Review the recommendations with the leadership team, and then lock and load the chosen definition into the EVA software system to ensure company-wide conformity.

Prototype: The EVA Dimensions software tools provide a complete set of Best-Practice EVA reports, templates, and decision modules that have been refined over many years of client applications. They provide any new adopter with an enormous head start. But that is not to say there is no work to be done. Almost every company modifies them in three ways.

The first is by *personalizing* the reports to address the needs of various constituencies. The board of directors will need only a summary view of the company's MVA and market expectations and updates on corporate and line-of-business performance through an EVA lens. The management committee will require access to another layer of detail, and the individual line teams will need the ability to drill down deeply. The planning or IR departments may want to see yet another take on the EVA data points. The question is: how can the salient EVA insights best be harvested, organized, and communicated to the various user groups through a set of customized reporting templates?

A second task is *integrating* company-specific metrics and milestones into the EVA Margin and EVA Pyramid schedules. As I've said, the objective is to end with a truly balanced and value-anchored scorecard with the EVA metrics perched at the top. It takes a little creative work to figure out the best way to insert company-specific financial and nonfinancial metrics into the EVA templates. Mocking up proposed solutions is a helpful step at this stage.

The last step is *automation*—making it as easy as possible to generate the EVA reports in a timely manner. Though it is discussed at this stage, automation is typically postponed until the reports have been vetted through one full management cycle. In fact, some companies find the software so capable and the semimanual process of using the EVA software so painless that they continue to use it as the main EVA analysis engine and forgo any intense information technology (IT) integration effort.

Practice: Some companies want to move onto the Best-Practice EVA program as soon as they can—and for that, there is no better way than the software solution we've crafted to get it up and running. Most CFOs, however, decide to take a full year to shadow it before formally switching over to it, and I think that is generally a good strategy. It provides more soak time on the concepts and more time to spread knowledge about the EVA ratio model, and it lets the finance and planning teams get comfortable administering the program with hands-on opportunities to learn by doing. It also creates more opportunities to build the consensus for EVA at the top of the house before going live.

The practice program tends to run down two tracks. The first one is what we call the Rhythm of Financial Excellence and is depicted in Exhibit 12.1.

The cycle can start anytime, but let's assume it commences with development of a financial intelligence information packet as background for the strategic planning process. The objective is to provide the senior leadership team with a robust and penetrating EVA ratio analysis of the company and its lines of business relative to public peers, and an understanding of performance expectations, arming them with essential financial facts that can help inform their thinking about strengths, weaknesses, and opportunities, and the overall plan performance goals and priorities that they will want to

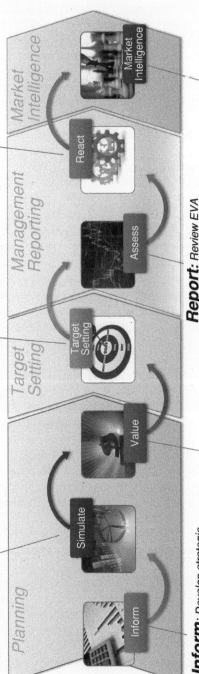

Stimulate: Analyze and value draft business plans, prepare summary scorecards, to stimulate better plans during plan review process.

Target: Convert plans and budgets into quarterly and long-range targets for EVA, EVA Margin, EVA Momentum by line of business.

React: Refine plans, refocus resources, recalibrate targets.

Market Intelligence: Quarterly update of public peer benchmarking, security analyst forecast models, PRVit rating.

Inform: Develop strategic insights into performance trends, value drivers, best practices, gaps and opportunities, and market expectations through an EVA lens as a backdrop to initial strategy discussions.

Value: Summarize the value and EVA Momentum implied by the final plans for review with the board, leadership team, and investors.

Report: Review EVA Momentum and drivers versus budget targets and prior year, by line of business, by quarter.

Planning | Target Setting | Management Reporting | Market Intelligence

Inform · Simulate · Value · Target Setting · Assess · React · Market Intelligence

EXHIBIT 12.1 The Rhythm of Best-Practice EVA Financial Excellence

establish. Usually this is a midyear exercise. It is a semiannual refreshing of the comprehensive analysis that normally concludes a year, and it immediately precedes commencement of the formal planning exercise.

Once planning begins in earnest, the next step is to upload and analyze the draft business plans and process them into EVA report cards that enable the line teams to generate more EVA-capable plans and initiatives. This is typically an iterative process, and in the practice year it is also a terrific opportunity to educate the line teams about the EVA metrics and how to use them to increase the value of their plans. Once concluded, the EVA essence of the final plans is summarized and reviewed with directors, and the budgets are converted into EVA targets by line of business and by quarter for the next year.

That sets that stage for the next important practice round. It is to upload and review actual results against the EVA budget targets at the end of each quarter and for the trailing year, using a fully fleshed-out EVA Momentum Pyramid adorned with company-specific metrics and milestones to structure the variance analysis. As I have suggested, a cascading set of ever more detailed reports is prepared for review with directors, the management committee, and the line teams. The review process is a natural segue into rethinking the plans, reprioritizing the agenda, and rerunning the EVA tool kit to refresh the cycle, particularly in firms that use rolling budgets and forecasts.

The final regular rhythm is to look outward and gather market and competitive intelligence. It is to take stock of the firm's evolving MVA and Market-Implied Momentum (MIM) as part of the quarterly reporting package, and, once public peers have reported their quarterly financials, it is also to gauge performance, value, and expectations relative to the competition and by extracting insights from the PRVit reporting package.

At every step along the way, the templates used to communicate the EVA insights are refined based on feedback. The objective is to end the year with a set of scorecards and analysis formats that are well understood and well integrated into the ongoing management calendar, and ready to go live in the next year.

Many firms add one more element to the practice round. It is to develop and track a shadow EVA bonus multiplier as the year unfolds. That is typically based on grading the firm's actual EVA as the year goes on against budget or against the prior year or a peer set. Another part of the simulation is to see how the actual EVA performance results would hypothetically feed into resetting the EVA performance goals that would be used in the next year's bonus plan—assuming it is all based on an automatic adjusting formula. Management teams that go this route also typically perform a back-test analysis of the EVA bonus multiplier that would have applied to the company and for its compensation peer group over the past five or 10 years. The look back helps to provide a feel for how the program would have operated, and it also tends to establish, by plotting out the data points, that there would have been a strong link between the EVA-based incentive rewards and the stock price results. Again, EVA Dimensions does not design the plans, but our clients get a lot of mileage from using the EVA software tool kit to simulate how performance would translate into pay as a backdrop to rolling out formal EVA bonus plans.

The second main track in the practice round is to use EVA to address a range of ad hoc decision questions as they arise through the year, as illustrated in Exhibit 12.2.

Acquisitive companies, for example, want to see how EVA applies to the valuation of acquisition candidates. The objective is to thoroughly understand the "exchange of value" pricing model built into our software and how that compares to the conventional but flawed "exchange of earnings" approach. Another objective is to understand how the strategic investment treatment applies to acquisitions—in other words, to a determination of how much of the purchase price should be held back and over what time frame it should be metered back into capital in order to smooth out the impact on EVA while maintaining accountability.

Once a few practice rounds have been fired at acquisitions, many companies also formally link their acquisition tools to the EVA software systems we've developed. It is a fairly simple matter to port the output from an acquisition-forecasting engine into the EVA engine, and then to fashion the EVA output into an acquisition scorecard format that the CFO and leadership team will find most appealing. This is one of the steps to making sure EVA threads through and unites all aspects of decision making and management reporting. The consistent use of EVA is a key to making it simple, powerful, and accountable.

A similar procedure applies to the evaluation of capital projects and business decisions. Run a few of them through the EVA software model, and review the insights in the present value (PV) EVA Margin schedules. Start measuring and using the NPV Spread as the indicator of the risk cushion, and set minimum targets for it by risk class of the investments. Port existing capital budgeting tools into the EVA software tools. Customize the EVA output to fit your preferences. Get so comfortable with the EVA analysis and insights that you are willing to stop discounting cash flow and to put all your efforts into analyzing and valuing EVA instead. Rewrite and reformat your capital budgeting manuals and decision-valuation tools so they, too, are EVA focused. That is another step to making EVA successful by making it so central.

M&A Valuation

- *Acquisitions viewed as an exchange of value—total value received less total value paid.*
- *Synergies are valued as the PV of extra EVA arising from combination.*
- *EVA valuation multiples reconciled with flawed accounting indicators.*
- *Postdeal EVA is accountability is created.*

Portfolio Review

- *Reliably assess value sources and drains across major business lines.*
- *Measure, benchmark, analyze EVA and determine intrinsic value.*
- *Correlate to public market valuations.*
- *Assess implications for resource allocation, portfolio rebalancing.*

EVA Visibility

- *Measure EVA at deeper divisions—cutting across product lines, customer segments, departments, functions, regions.*
- *Reveal angels and demons customers and lines of business, and simulate remediation strategies—price, purge, policy, process, position, etc.*

NPV

- *DCF and IRR are replaced with projecting, discounting, and improving EVA.*
- *The PV EVA Margin schedule is used as principal analytical tool and statistically compared to actual EVA Margins.*
- *The PV EVA Spread (PV EVA/PV Capital Investment) is principal risk cushion index.*

Investor Relations

- *Upload and analyze implications of security analyst and consensus forecasts.*
- *Use market-implied momentum to asses expectations built into share price.*
- *Use PRVit for insights into intrinsic value of company, peers, sector.*
- *Run EVA dashboard for peer comparisons.*

Treasury

- *Project capital requirements and determine impact on key financial ratios.*
- *Use FRS valuations as input to decisions to raise/retire equity.*
- *Optimal capital structure reduces the cost of capital and increases EVA Momentum.*

EXHIBIT 12.2 Best-Practice EVA Executive Decision Support Applications

This step also presents a terrific opportunity to develop EVA Nuggets and use them for team training. EVA Nuggets are mini case studies that illustrate how to think about decisions in the new EVA light and how to formally use projections of EVA to reach better outcomes by considering all the trade-offs that exist in the decisions that the company's managers typically face. The Claudine's Salt Water Taffy Company production decision case we reviewed is an example. We have seen our clients creating Nuggets for decisions about working capital and supply chain issues; for questions about investing in brands and innovation; for addressing pricing, product, and customer profitability opportunities; and on up to really strategic choices and transformations. The best Nuggets dovetail with the success keys that top management has identified for the company's strategy, so that both initiatives—EVA and the business strategy—reinforce each other and improve the chances for success on both counts.

Another typical application, especially for diversified firms, is to conduct portfolio reviews by combining the EVA analysis with strategy analysis to determine the best candidates for growth, or for restructuring, new management, consolidation, or divestiture. A divestiture, incidentally, is also viewed as an exchange of value, but with the roles reversed. It is a question of asking whether the net after-tax sale proceeds exceed the internal value of the business unit based on the EVA it can be expected to earn in the incumbent's hands—and ignoring any bookkeeping gain or loss recognized in the process.

An initiative that is typically postponed into year 2 is to drill EVA analytics down even deeper into the business performance well, to ask: what EVA are we earning or losing as we slice a business into distinct markets, customers or customer types, products or product lines? The idea is to create more visibility into the EVA profitability drivers and, so armed, to be able to revise prices, change features, fire customers, reallocate resources, and redesign products and services in order to expand the EVA Margin and generate more EVA Momentum from the business.

Treasurers and investor relations directors also use the practice year to get comfortable with EVA and incorporate it into applications that matter to them. Treasurers typically find a value in consulting the EVA analysis of the company's forward plan and the PRVit analysis of the stock as an input into timing share buybacks or their willingness to issue shares. IR directors, too, use the EVA and PRVit analysis of the company and its peers to gain a better understanding of the firm's intrinsic value.

Perform: What's next? Execute. Repeat the process but for real. Continue to enhance the applications and reports and make them more concise and personal. Drill deeper with EVA analytics to unearth even more granular insights into how to improve EVA and create EVA Momentum. Continue to surface and celebrate EVA Nuggets, bringing the best examples into company newsletters and the like to share EVA success stories and keep the EVA flame burning brightly.

If you haven't done it, tell the world you are a Best-Practice EVA company. Meet with a targeted set of buy-side investors who are favorably inclined toward EVA-emergent firms. Prove to them you are a genuine EVA firm. Here's the five-point checklist, one more time, in brief essence:

1. EVA is your overarching financial mission.
2. EVA is a legitimate continuous improvement metric and reliable decision guide.
3. All decisions are EVA-based.
4. EVA is accountable and tied to incentives.
5. EVA is well understood—it is ingrained in the culture, from the boardroom to the shop floor.

As for initiating an EVA profit sharing bonus plan, do that, of course. My recommendation: in the first year, set the EVA performance targets to the agreed budget targets for EVA. Have one final round of budget negotiations as a way to fairly transition onto the plan. But let everyone know that thereafter, the EVA performance targets will be reset by formula so that, from day one, everyone is motivated to maximize the EVA Momentum they deliver and the wealth that they create.

That is the name of the business game, after all, and EVA Momentum is the right way to keep the score.

THE DECISION AND STRATEGY TO ADOPT BEST-PRACTICE EVA

An Interview with Hugh Johnston, Chief Financial Officer, Pepsico, Inc.

a. Please give a little background on why Pepsi has decided to adopt EVA.

PepsiCo has always focused on driving shareholder value through growth, efficient deployment of capital, and effective portfolio management. What I like about EVA is the simple way it integrates these concepts, both for performance reporting and decision support.

b. What are the main benefits you are looking to achieve?

We're using it to achieve a few things. First, we're using it to support our decision making: where we should invest, how much we should invest, and what changes we should make to our portfolio of businesses. Second, we're using it as a performance management tool.

What I've observed is, by driving EVA into the organization, the trade-off discussions I have with our business units are very balanced. EVA gives us a comprehensive common language and set of measures to arrive at the optimal shareholder-value based outcome.

c. What are the main steps you are taking to do it?

We're working with EVA Dimensions and are currently using their EVA software to break apart PepsiCo's historical and projected EVA growth by business to better understand the relative source of value creation across our portfolio and to identify areas of opportunity to drive additional value. We anticipate this analysis to influence our portfolio investment decisions going forward.

d. Do you see using the new EVA ratio metrics, the EVA profit margin and EVA Momentum, as part of the solution?

Absolutely. These ratios are a helpful way to dissect EVA across our businesses and across our competitive set. They provide insights into the drivers of a given business' EVA creation relative to others and as such, help the organization focus on where the opportunities are.

We're in the process of implementing EVA with EVA Dimensions; over time, I expect that the tools and metrics will become quite common in our vernacular at PepsiCo.

e. You've already publicly announced the decision—how has that been received by investors?

Investors appreciate management teams that balance growth, efficiency and returns. Investors may have different models and their own shorthand in how they think about these topics, but I'm finding that the EVA framework is a very effective way to discuss these topics in a comprehensive, integrated way that has a clear link to shareholder value creation.

The Best-Practice
EVA Software Toolkit

Software tools developed by EVA Dimensions make it easy and affordable to bring Best-Practice EVA in-house for a test drive or to put it into place. The chart in Exhibit A.1 presents the product architecture.

At the foundation is a comprehensive database of EVA metrics computed in accordance with our Best-Practice EVA standards and covering 9,000 global companies that is updated daily by EVA Dimensions. Users can access the metric insights for any of those firms through a set of three desktop Excel tools we call *Express*. **PRVit** *Express* is for calling up PRVit scores, reports, and value at a reasonable price (VARP) grids for one company at a time or for an entire industry group. **EVA** *Express* enables a user to download up to 20 tickers at a time and examine and compare their actual performance over the past decade, and close up by quarter, for the whole gamut of key EVA performance statistics and the underlying drivers, along with wealth creation and expectations statistics, such as we reviewed for Tiffany, Blue Nile, Amazon, and the like. We think it is the finest financial analysis engine on the market. The third one, **Value** *Express*, is for forecasting and improving the net present value and EVA Momentum of forward plans and acquisitions, as we saw illustrated in the planning chapter.

Above the line is a supplemental software system called **FRS**, standing for the Financial Radar Screen. It's the software engine that automatically converts custom company data into Best-Practice EVA. Simply deposit actual or forward-plan forecast income and balance sheet financial data for a company, its internal business units, acquisition candidates, and capital projects onto the preformatted Excel spreadsheet, push a few buttons, and presto, the EVA cake is baked. The raw financial data is automatically transformed into real economic insights with the power of EVA.

A single screen exists in FRS that enables users to customize how they want the software to calculate the results. Users control the tax rates and cost of capital, select and set the precise accounting adjustments they prefer, and store them in the model. For example, users indicate whether they want rents to be capitalized or expensed, and whether they want R&D to

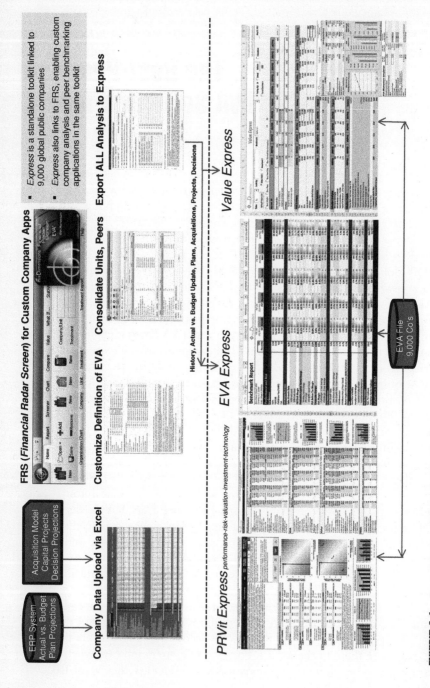

EXHIBIT A.1 Best-Practice EVA Software Tools

be expensed or amortized, and over what time frame. This is where you ensure that EVA strikes the optimal balance between simplicity and relevance, and becomes the continuous improvement metric that works best for your company.

FRS also consolidates public peers and internal business units into custom benchmarks. As it does that, FRS computes the 10th, 25th, 50th, 75th, and 90th percentile break points for all the key EVA metrics and the related financial drivers. That enables users to see the real statistical significance and trends in their data and not to be misled by viewing the results out of context.

Last, and this is a major feature, FRS and *Express* interconnect. All of the company-custom analysis that you can examine on-screen in FRS can also be automatically exported into the familiar and flexible Excel *Express* tools. There they can also be combined with company metrics and milestones, or fed into company reporting tools, and the goal of achieving truly balanced scorecards can be realized.

The software tool kit is the simplest, most productive, and least expensive way to bring Best-Practice EVA in-house. We designed it for that purpose.

Corrective
Accounting Adjustments

EVA PENETRATES ACCOUNTING DISTORTIONS
TO REVEAL ECONOMIC TRUTH

Accounting rules frequently misrepresent economic reality and distort performance comparisons over time and across companies. A fundamental reason is that accounting statements are biased to the perspective of lenders, and not to owners or business managers. The very word *assets* betrays a creditor's concern for securing debt repayment under the worst of circumstances, and after share owners have essentially lost everything. In a going concern, by contrast, any so-called assets are actually liabilities. Assets tie up capital that must be financed at the cost of capital, thus reducing EVA and diminishing franchise value. A firm that ties up more assets on its balance sheet is perhaps more bankable, but it is less valuable as a business enterprise than another that earns more profit with fewer assets. Another source of distortion is that accounting statements incorrectly mix operating performance and financing decisions, when they should be kept apart. Or take the practice of expensing R&D outlays, justified under the principle of conservatism. In truth, R&D spending is the font of economic growth, customer satisfaction, and productivity gains. Without it, we'd stand still. R&D is patently a form of capital investment, and should be recognized and managed as such, not written off as a period loss. The following table presents the full range of adjustments that EVA Dimensions applies to reported financials in order to arrive at a more consistent, comparable, complete, and correct measure of real economic profit. The adjustments are applied to the entire 20-year reported financial records of 9,000 public companies around the world, and updated daily.

Refinement	Rationale/Benefit
Capital is the total sum of debt and equity funds raised from investors or retained from earnings and invested in net business assets.	Managers manage capital, not equity. EVA is based on an entity, not equity, view. It is unaffected by the debt/equity mix but depends solely on the quality of capital management. It values shares by valuing the business's enterprise and franchise value, and measuring share price as the residual claim on that value.
Noncontrolling interests are excluded from capital and from earnings.	Noncontrolling interests are viewed as suppliers or trade creditors, not owners. EVA measures the economic profit attributable to the parent company shareholders, and the present value of EVA is the value added to their investment in the business.
Surplus cash is discharged from capital, and the associated investment is excluded from earnings.	Marketable securities invested at market prices are assumed to be EVA neutral, by definition. EVA is unaffected by cash hoarding or distributions; it accurately measures the underlying business performance.
Leased assets are treated like owned; the present value (PV) of rents is added to capital; the interest component of rent expense is added back to earnings and the weighted average cost of capital on the PV of rents is deducted in its place.	The lease/buy mix is neutralized so that the management of the assets matters and not how the assets are financed. Also, this treatment gives a more accurate reading of leverage.
R&D and ad spend are added to capital and amortized over time (default for R&D is over five years, except 10 years for pharma and biotech; default for ad spend is over three years, except over five years for pharma and biotech); interest at the cost of capital on the unamortized balance is included in the capital charge.	EVA does not rise when managers cut the spending to make a short-term budget goal, nor does it plunge when managers invest more funds to create intangible assets; it neutralizes buy or build decisions for technology and brands; EVA is value neutral—same present value by writing off over time with interest as expensing.

Refinement	Rationale/Benefit
Impairment charges are reversed, added back to earnings and to capital, as if the charges never occurred.	EVA is impaired, not the balance sheet, by investments that cannot cover the cost of capital.
Restructuring costs are considered to be investments that add to balance sheet capital.	Nonrecurring charges do not obscure underlying business performance. A restructuring is EVA positive if benefits outweigh the incremental costs. Losses (or gains) on asset sales are irrelevant—what matters is whether the after-tax proceeds, invested at the cost of capital, generate a greater profit than would retention of the asset—which is the question EVA answers.
Tax provision is smoothed by applying a standard normal corporate tax rate.	One-time tax rate fluctuations (from refunds, penalties, judgmental changes in deferred tax asset valuation reserves, and the like) are smoothed and booked into a created deferred-tax account.
Interest saved by the net balance sheet deferral of tax, including created deferred taxes from above, reduces the tax on EVA.	Net business assets exclude deferred tax assets, making things simpler. All tax issues are consolidated into one truly effective, time-value-adjusted tax rate.
Operating reserves and deferrals (bad debt reserve, LIFO reserve, warranty reserve, deferred income) are included in capital, and the period changes are booked into NOPAT and EVA.	Penetrates earnings management and reveals timing of recurring cash flows from operations.
Accumulated other comprehensive income (AOCI) hedge gains or losses are excluded from capital.	There is no gain or loss in a true hedge and no impact on EVA.
Retirement cost/liability distortions are purged.	Service cost replaces the reported retirement cost; the net funding deficit times the cost of capital reduces EVA, so that the present value of EVA fully deducts the funding gap to the firm's value (and vice versa for a funding surplus).

Refinement	Rationale/Benefit
The weighted average cost of capital to measure EVA is based on a three-year average D/E blend, not the proportions recently employed.	Unlike EPS and ROE, EVA does not mix operating and financing decisions, and it is impervious to transitory changes in capital structure, such as when a firm borrows to finance a major acquisition.
The weighted average cost of capital to measure EVA is based on the average unleveraged beta for the company's principal line of business (industry).	Betas for individual companies are measured with error. The industry average unleveraged beta is generally a more accurate estimate of the underlying business risk that enters into the cost of capital.
The weighted average cost of capital to measure EVA is based on an expected 4 percent market risk premium (MRP) over the rate prevailing on 10-year government bonds as a relatively risk-free reference point.	Studies for U.S. market show a 4 to 6 percent MRP, but past averages likely overstate the future. Over the past 85 years, the United States has been a survivor, outlier market; liquidity, information flow, and wealth increased, which likely *reduced* the actual demanded risk premium but misleadingly *increased* the *measured* premium; the United States is coming to the end of its demographic baby boom times.

Accounting for Corporate Charges in Detail

The report in Exhibit C.1 breaks out the detailed line items behind the corporate charges for Tiffany (TIF) and Blue Nile (NILE). It is not exhaustive of the items in this section, but it is usefully illustrative. Let's walk through the corporate charges line by line.

The biggest difference in the corporate charges between TIF and NILE is taxes, but it is not as straightforward as it appears. Not only does TIF have a higher tax rate, but the rate applies to a larger pretax EVA Margin. TIF's 41.3 percent tax rate on its 8.4 percent pretax EVA Margin is equivalent to a charge of 3.5 percent of sales, whereas NILE's 27.2 percent tax rate on its 4.0 percent pretax EVA Margin is a charge of just 1.1 percent of its sales. As this illustrates, companies cannot really be judged according to the size of their corporate charges because the charges might be bigger only because the pretax EVA profit margin is bigger. It's the tax rate that reveals if the tax strategy has added value.

Why is TIF's effective tax rate above the assumed standard tax rate of 40 percent? After all, TIF's tax provision over the years has been consistently less than the assumed 40 percent rate, principally because of foreign source income. Remarkably, the normally hyperconservative accounting community is quite liberal in permitting companies to just ignore the extra U.S. tax that would be owed on repatriation of foreign income if management claims that the earnings will be permanently reinvested overseas. Under EVA, by contrast, the tax provision is computed as if all operating income, including foreign source income, was taxed at a standard U.S. tax rate of 40 percent, but since that tax was not actually paid, the accumulated deferred portion is credited with the cost of capital and applied as a reduction in the effective EVA tax rate. For Tiffany, the time value of postponing tax on foreign source income was 4.9 percent of pretax EVA in that year, as is reported on line 54.

More than offsetting that benefit, however, TIF carried a sizable deferred tax asset on its balance sheet. As is typical, payroll and other compensation have been accrued as an expense for book purposes but have not yet

	Benchmark: Russell 3000 Currency: U.S. Dollar Scale: Values in Millions	50th %tile	FYE: JAN 2012TFQ1 TIF	%tile	FYE: DEC 2012TFQ2 NILE	%tile
5	Benchmark: Russell 3000					
6	Currency: U.S. Dollar	50th	2012TFQ1		2012TFQ2	
7	Scale: Values in Millions	%tile	TIF	%tile	NILE	%tile
8	**EVA Before Tax Margin**	3.1%	8.4%	68	4.0%	53
9	**Corporate Charges**	2.4%	3.7%		0.9%	
10	EVA Effective Tax Rate (% EVA Before Tax)	35.2%	41.3%	28	27.2%	73
11	= Standard Tax Rate (STR)	40.0%	40.0%		40.0%	
13	– Cap Chrg: Cum Std - Actual EBIT Tax (% of EVABT)	2.6%	4.6%	56	16.6%	80
14	– Cap Chrg: Def Tax Liab (Asset) (% of EVABT)	0.0%	–5.9%	17	–3.8%	20
16	Def Tax Liab(Asset) per $1 of Prod Cap	1.6%	–4.5%	5		NA
17	Other EVA	0.3%	0.0%	43	0.2%	48
18	= Miscellaneous Op Income After Tax	0.0%	0.1%	62	0.0%	57
24	+ EVA From Investments—Equity	0.0%	0.0%	0.0%	0.0%	0.0%
27	– Cap Chrg: Investments—Other	0.0%	0.0%	0.0%	0.0%	0.1%
29	– Cap Chrg: Other Operating Assets	0.2%	0.5%	25	0.0%	76
31	+ Cap Chrg Saved: Funding (Misc Liabs)	0.7%	1.3%	67	0.2%	21
33	– EVA Due Noncontrolling Interests	0.0%	0.0%	NA	0.0%	NA
35	– Cap Chrg: PEB Funding Losses (Gains)	0.0%	0.8%	5	0.0%	50
36	Cum PEB Funding Losses (Gains) AT		$429.72		$0.00	
37	**EVA Before Goodwill and Unusual Items**	2.3%	4.9%	65	3.1%	55
38	Goodwill & Cum Unusual Items Charge	1.0%	0.2%	73	0.0%	85
39	Goodwill (Adjusted)/Sales	0.12	0.00	83	—	90
40	Cumulative Unusual Items After Tax/Sales	0.01	0.03	44	—	70
41	Strategic Add Back	0.0%	0.0%		0.0%	
42	**EVA Margin**	0.8%	4.7%	74	3.1%	64
43	EVA Margin—3-Year Average	0.1%	4.0%	75	4.3%	76
44	EVA Margin—5-Year Average	–0.3%	4.0%	77	4.3%	78

EXHIBIT C.1 Tiffany's and Blue Nile's Corporate Charges in Detail

been paid or deducted on the tax books. A more significant reason is that TIF realized a $120 million gain on an asset sale/leaseback transaction. The gain was taxed up front but is being deferred for financial reporting. On net, TIF has already paid several hundred million dollars more in tax than its tax provisions have shown, and the cost of capital to finance that increased the company's effective rate by 5.9 percent (line 55), bringing the overall effective tax rate to over 40 percent.

The second category, labeled "Other EVA," is not a corporate charge but an offset to it. It is a net add-back to EVA coming from a sundry pool of items. The income and expense items are reported after tax. Moreover, if the items stem from capital charges or credits, they are computed using an after-tax cost of capital because at this stage the EVA elements are being measured after tax.

For Tiffany, the Other EVA grab bag is almost exactly zero, but only because of a coincidental confluence of debits and credits. It consists of the following:

1. Net nonoperating income amounting to 0.1 percent of sales (line 59).
2. Less a capital charge on sundry non-revenue-producing assets, 0.5 percent of sales (line 70).

3. Less a 0.8 percent after-tax cost of capital charge to close a sizable retirement funding gap (line 76). Management reports a net actuarial loss of nearly $200 million at the close of this period, but compared to the on-balance-sheet liability, the total funding gap is $430 million (line 77). Funding that at the cost of capital creates the charge.
4. Plus a 1.3 percent EVA Margin benefit stemming from the cost of capital saved by using sundry accrued liabilities to fund the business and defray capital (line 72). Those include the accrued liabilities for payroll and other operating expenses, and also the sizable deferred gain on sale.

Think this last one through. As noted, Tiffany has previously undertaken a sizable sale and leaseback transaction. Under EVA, the leased-back assets are treated as if they were owned and put back on the balance sheet. The estimated present value of the lease payments has been added to capital and included in PP&E in an amount that would presumably closely approximate the value of the asset at the time of the sale. Ironically, this means that the capital charge credit for the deferred gain coming through on the Other EVA line above is simply offsetting the added capital charge from including the stepped-up leased asset in PP&E capital. To a first approximation, the two cancel, and there is no net effect to EVA from swapping an owned asset into a leased asset. In reasonably efficient and competitive markets, owning and leasing are financing substitutes, *except for taxes*. And in this case, because the gain on the sale was taxed up front, the net effect of the transaction was to prepay taxes that would otherwise have been paid over the life of the asset. Bottom line: the cost of capital charge on the advanced tax payment makes Tiffany's EVA *lower* than it otherwise would be as a result of the transaction. Ah, a thing of beauty—that EVA should penetrate the fiction and reveal the reality of even so gossamer a thread as that.

EVA BEFORE GOODWILL AND UNUSUAL ITEMS

A third corporate charge is still to come, but at this point we draw a line and record another intermediate EVA Margin. It is called EVA Before Goodwill and Unusual Items (line 78). It is what EVA would be if all acquisitions had been consummated without paying goodwill premiums and if there had been no one-time restructuring costs. It is a measure of what the go-forward EVA Margin might be on incremental business assuming those sunk costs are truly irrelevant and unlikely to recur. That is one possibility. You can be the judge. But the EVA Margin schedule says to have it both ways. Measure EVA both before and after the most abstract forms of capital, and derive whatever meaning you attach to each.

GOODWILL AND UNUSUAL ITEMS CHARGES

EVA is measured after all capital costs, including the after-tax capital charge on unimpaired goodwill and on the cumulative nonrecurring losses and charges, net of gains and credits, after tax. Those two charges come to naught for Blue Nile, and are 0.2 percent of sales for Tiffany,[1] which is minuscule for a large company. Visa, BlackRock, Boston Scientific, Time Warner, and Symantec are among the firms that have accumulated so much goodwill and in some cases one-time restructuring investments that the charges in this category alone are over 10 percent of sales. Some of those firms have been very successful despite having such a large charge. BlackRock, for instance, has been able to successfully integrate and enhance the money management firms it has acquired where virtually all the purchase prices have been recorded as goodwill. Others, like Time Warner, were not so lucky. The merger with AOL turned out to be ill-timed, extremely pricey, and ill-conceived. The CEOs responsible did not last long.

The last line on the schedule prior to the EVA Margin is the so-called strategic investment add-back (line 82). That is where the cost of capital saved by holding out a portion of acquisition premiums or investment ramp-ups would appear. It is not automatically populated for public company data because we have not yet figured a sensible way to estimate it. But our individual clients use this account to accommodate major investments with delayed returns (as was described in Chapter 3, Accounting for Value).

---

[1] Tiffany actually reports about $14 million of goodwill in its annual balance sheet, but the amount is so immaterial it is not broken out on the quarterly filings we are using; the goodwill is therefore included in the capital charge for other assets included in Other EVA.

Glossary

NOPAT is **net operating profit after taxes**. It is *operating profit* before any interest or financing charges are deducted, measured *net* of period charges for depreciation and amortization, and *after taxes* computed using a smoothed normal tax provision, net of the cost of capital saved from deferring taxes, and *after corrective adjustments* to remedy accounting distortions. As such, it estimates the free cash flow from operations that is distributable after ensuring that tangible and intangible assets needed to sustain the profit can be replenished.

Capital is **net business assets**. It is all assets used in business operations, net of trade funding from accounts payable and accrued expenses. It is also equal to the total amount of debt and equity raised from investors or retained from earnings. Capital is measured after making adjustments to remedy accounting distortions. For instance, it is measured net of excess cash, net of deferred-tax assets, and net of pension and retirement assets, but including leased assets, and after capitalizing and amortizing research and development (R&D) and advertising spending over time. EVA Dimensions' reports display the amount of capital in place as of the end of each period, but the amounts used in the computation of EVA and return on capital are averages of capital.

Cost of capital (COC) is the **minimum rate of return required to compensate lenders and shareholders for risk**. It is not an actual cash cost that a company must pay or that accountants record. It is an invisible but nevertheless very real opportunity cost—the cost to investors of giving up the opportunity to invest their capital elsewhere. It is thus equal to the rate of return that the firm's lenders and shareholders could *expect* to earn from buying a portfolio of stocks and bonds that matches the blended risk profile of the firm's debt and equity. It is estimated in three steps, starting with the relatively risk-free yield prevailing on 10-year government bonds that sets a minimum return requirement for all companies, then adding a premium to compensate investors for bearing the firm's business risk (i.e., for the inherent variability in NOPAT profit over a business cycle), and third, subtracting a discount to reflect the benefit of using tax-deductible debt as a capital structure component in place of pure equity.

Capital charge is **NOPAT needed to earn the cost of capital return on the firm's capital**. It is determined by multiplying the cost of capital times the average amount of capital in the business over the period. It is how large NOPAT would need to be to enable the firm to pay interest on its debts, after tax, and leave a profit remainder that would give its shareholders a minimum acceptable return on the equity they've put in the firm. Only when NOPAT is above that threshold has management truly added value to the resources placed at its disposal, compared to alternative market uses for the capital.

The capital charge can thus be thought of as an objective profit performance target for NOPAT that is set in the market by benchmarking the firm against its capital market competitors, as opposed to being set internally by the board or budget. As management adds more capital, the capital charge profit standard is automatically raised, and as management decides to or is able to withdraw capital from its business, the market-demanded NOPAT profit bar is automatically lowered. The capital charge is thus an empowering mechanism that enables all employees to tell a good decision from a bad one without having to ask headquarters for guidance.

(As a technical matter, the capital charge computed for a four-quarter period is the sum of the capital charges for the four quarters, where each is based on the average capital outstanding over each quarter times the quarterly cost of capital rate prevailing over the quarter; this procedure provides an accurate continuous reading of the hurdle charge, even when capital spending is lumpy over a year; yet it cannot be precisely derived by the data furnished in the EVA Dimensions tables.)

EVA (economic value added) is **NOPAT minus capital charge**. It measures the firm's *economic profit*—the profit remaining after deducting all costs, including the cost of giving the firm's investors a full, fair, and competitive return on their investment in the business. EVA consolidates income efficiency, asset management, profitable growth, and strategic retrenchment into a single, comprehensive net profit score. It is the only profit measure that fully and correctly increases when balance sheet assets decrease. And unlike EBIT, EBITDA, or EPS, EVA does not increase unless growth covers the full cost of incremental capital. It recognizes only quality growth, and ruthlessly reveals the profit shortfalls incurred by firms that purchase growth at the expense of earning a decent return on their investments.

EVA also counters the tendency of companies (or business divisions) that are already earning high margins and returns to milk them—to slow growth in order to maintain high performance ratios. All growth that produces returns higher than the cost of capital will cause EVA to increase, even if existing margins or rates of return are diluted. A goal to increase EVA therefore puts a Bunsen burner under the best businesses to keep scaling, growing, innovating, and investing rather than to rest on their laurels, and, it offers business teams that are navigating tough turnaround lines the opportunity to shine and compete for resources by making the negative EVA less negative.

In short, a focus on growing EVA is the simplest, surest, and most direct way to align management with the mission to maximize the firm's net present value and its stock price, and to provide line teams with all the right incentives and insights into decision trade-offs.

Return on capital (ROC) is **NOPAT/average capital**; it is the **after-tax rate of return on net business assets**. Unlike return on equity (ROE), ROC is unaffected by changes in interest rates or the firm's debt/equity mix. It measures business productivity performance sans financial distortion. ROC is directly comparable to the firm's COC as a benchmark, and as such, it offers an insight into value creation and destruction. When ROC is greater than COC, EVA is positive and value is added to the investors' capital, and when ROC is less than COC, EVA is negative and value is eroded.

One way to think about increasing EVA is thus to strive to earn a higher return on existing capital, to invest capital to support growth over the full cost of the capital, and to release capital from assets and activities that cannot cover the cost of capital. While that's true and helpful, it couches the EVA drivers in terms of managing and investing capital and earning returns on capital. That appeals to the finance crowd, but it is a lot less intuitive to line teams than is a sales-based approach to measuring, analyzing, and improving EVA. It is time to bury return on net assets (RONA) and the DuPont ROI formula, and replace them with the EVA return on sales method (see EVA Margin and EVA Momentum for further details).

EVA Spread is the **ratio of EVA to capital**; it is the EVA yield on capital, and mathematically the same as ROC minus COC (i.e., it is the percentage spread between the return on capital and the cost of capital). Putting it in terms of portfolio management, EVA Spread is the firm's *alpha*—the excess return above a risk-relevant benchmark return. If the spread is zero, the firm is just covering its overall costs and is breaking even on EVA.

EVA Margin is the **ratio of EVA to sales**; it is the firm's true economic profit margin covering income efficiency and asset management. Unlike EBIT and EBITDA margins, which are inflated by the margin requirements of capital-intensive businesses, EVA Margins are not biased in favor of capital-intensive business models, because any added capital is a cost to the EVA Margin. As a result, even firms that differ as much as the capital-mongering chip maker Intel and the incredibly capital-lean consumer staples retailer Wal-Mart can be meaningfully compared in terms of their EVA Margins, whereas they are totally incomparable on other barometers.

EVA Margins also neutralize sourcing decisions. By outsourcing, firms shift the capital costs they would bear on their own balance sheets into the prices they pay to outside vendors. As a result, operating margins decline—a misleading signal—but capital turns speed up, leaving EVA Margin as the reliable arbiter of the relative merits of alternate sourcing strategies.

EVA Margins reveal, as no other margin measure can, the true effective business model productivity that survives at the bottom line, once all costs are netted out, no matter whether the costs are operating costs that enter on the income statement or capital costs that flow from the balance sheet. Broad-based results for the market universe are therefore relevant benchmarks for any firm.

For reference, over the past 20 years, the median Russell 3000 EVA Margin was just 0.5 percent (a sensible economic outcome that indicates business markets are as a rule quite frustratingly EVA competitive, as expected); the 75th percentile firm earned an EVA Margin of 4 percent to 5 percent, on average, and the 90th percentile firm earned 9 percent to 10 percent, on average. It is only the rare firm that earns over a 10 percent EVA Margin (whereas EBITDA margins over 10 percent are commonplace). EVA Margins are also frequently close to zero, or even negative, which is why so many firms that grow sales and book earnings are not really in the business of growing value, an insight they would more readily appreciate if they paid more attention to their EVA Margin metrics.

Besides benchmarking and grading performance, and serving as a guide to business model profitability, EVA Margin can be used as a practical tool to help managers improve performance productivity. Dissecting the Margin and tracing it to the underlying drivers (as is shown on the EVA Margin schedule) can reveal opportunities to construct a higher-performing business model, for example.

The larger point in all this is that with EVA, capital is a cost, an understandable charge to earnings like any other, and not a divisor as it is with an ROI or RONA calculation. Capital is simply a charge to EVA and to the EVA profit margin, conceptually no different than a charge in cost of goods sold. And once the cost of capital has been deducted from profit, management is then free to divide the resulting EVA profit by whatever indicator is most useful and intuitively appealing to help line teams better manage it. A growing number of CFOs are coming to the realization that instead of thinking in terms of RONA and net assets and the DuPont ROI formula, it is easier and more effective to think of EVA as sales times the EVA Margin (EVA/sales), and to think about increasing EVA by looking for ways to increase the EVA Margin and to drive profitable sales growth at a positive EVA Margin—a goal that ultimately leads to EVA Momentum, which supersedes even the EVA Margin as a ratio measure of total performance progress from all sources.

ΔEVA is the **change in EVA, and the best money measure of performance progress over a period.** EVA increases when costs are intelligently cut, with all growth over the cost of capital, and when nonproductive capital is purged and assets turn faster (and also when management adopts a lower-cost capital structure). It decreases when non-value-adding costs are incurred, when capital is frittered away on nonproductive uses, and when management pursues growth that fails to generate an adequate return on the invested capital.

The change in EVA ignores history and registers all value-adding activity at the margin. It is independent of how much capital a company has invested in its past, and independent of legacy assets or liabilities it has inherited. It measures performance progress, whether for a firm that is turning around and making a negative EVA less negative, or for a profitable firm that is scaling, innovating, investing, growing, and adding to its economic profit.

EVA Momentum is the **change in EVA divided by prior-period revenues.** It is the size-adjusted growth rate in economic profit. It is the ideal overall summary measure of performance *progress*. It is the only business performance ratio indicator where bigger is always better, because it gets bigger when EVA does, and thus it can serve as every company's most important financial goal. It is a statistic that can be used to grade overall performance, benchmark with peers, and set targets.

For reference, the median EVA Momentum generated among the Russell 3000 companies has averaged just 0.2 percent (at the margin, EVA growth is hard to come by); the 75th percentile firm generated a sustained average momentum (over five years) of 1 to 1.5 percent, and the 90th percentile firm generated 3 to 4 percent.

It is an applicable measure regardless of inherited assets or legacy liabilities, which also makes it an early indicator of turning points—of performance turnarounds in the making or of fatiguing business models. It is thus an ideal performance measure to span individual divisions in a company and put them on a common scorecard.

It is the only performance ratio with a clear dividing line between good and bad performance. That line is zero EVA Momentum. If EVA Momentum is positive, EVA has increased; if it is negative, EVA has declined.

EVA Momentum is also the single best statistic to quantify the quality and value of a forward plan. Briefly, the bigger the EVA Momentum over the plan, the greater is the NPV, MVA, and share price implied by the plan. More EVA Momentum is more EVA and is a greater discounted net present value, by definition. It's the perfect proxy for CFOs to summarize and grade planned performance across even very disparate lines of business.

EVA Momentum can also help management improve performance and maximize forward-plan value, because it can be taken apart and eventually traced to *all* underlying performance and value drivers, but initially starting with these two: (1) productivity gains, as measured by expansion in the EVA Margin, and (2) profitable growth, as indicated by the product of sales growth and the EVA Margin.

EVA Momentum, in short, provides both a reliable and an encompassing single statistic to quantify performance progress in all relevant, value-adding dimensions, and it provides a window into all the moving parts that move EVA and drive shareholder value. It is the bird's-eye view and boots-on-the-ground view at one fell swoop. It is the best of both worlds.

Productivity gains are measured by the **change in EVA Margin.** Even a firm that does not increase sales can increase EVA and generate EVA Momentum with an *increase* in its EVA/sales margin—from leveraging the *3-P's*, as we call it—*price*, *product*, and *process*—from earning and exerting price power; from fielding an outstanding, EVA-oriented product portfolio; and from enhancing process excellence spanning income efficiency and asset management—all of which are measured right through the EVA Margin schedule.

The overall change in the EVA Margin over a period thus succinctly and accurately summarizes the total net benefit of achievements in all the individual performance elements that appear on the EVA Margin schedule (which besides the EBITDAR and productive capital elements also include the benefit of managing and deferring taxes, restructuring the business, exhibiting acquisition discipline, and integration prowess, to name a few).

Profitable growth is the **product of sales growth and the EVA Margin.** It is the second fundamental way to increase EVA and drive EVA Momentum, by growing sales at positive EVA Margins, or by reducing sales where the EVA Margin is negative—it works both ways because this factor is the multiplicative product of sales growth and EVA Margin. For example, 10 percent sales growth at a 2 percent after-tax EVA Margin contributes 0.2 percent to EVA Momentum.

The implication is that abundant sales growth at a low EVA Margin is inconsequential, but that even modest sales growth at a large EVA Margin can make a sizable contribution to EVA and to added market value. While ultimately it is the overall growth rate in EVA—the EVA Momentum—that determines MVA and franchise value, EVA Margin is a key lever on both sides of the EVA Momentum story (in productivity gains and in profitable growth).

The main insight here is that EVA Momentum explicitly includes the value added from achieving profitable growth, which of course is a critical performance dimension, and it conveniently expresses that value add on the exact same scale as the business model productivity gains. Momentum uniquely enables businesses to directly compare the two and make sensible trade-offs as required—such as possibly to forfeit a portion of the EVA Margin in exchange for even more profitable growth. And yet, and in contrast, measures like RONA and operating margin totally ignore the value of growth. They fight the business battle with one eye closed.

It is quite possible therefore that even experienced business managers do not fully appreciate how much value their profitable business lines are adding, because profitable divisions that achieve even modest sales growth can be the key drivers of the corporate EVA Momentum, even if they are not increasing their returns or their margins. In fact, the profitable divisions could well be adding significant EVA and creating material value even as their margins and returns diminish somewhat, due to the added value of incremental growth over the cost of capital. EVA Momentum and its component drivers can thus make for better insights into total value-adding performance, and thereby lead managers to make better planning and resource allocation decisions than they would by looking at other less effective, less complete, less correct indicators.

Market value is the **value of the firm's debt and equity capital**, given its share price, net of excess cash, and assuming that the book value of liabilities approximates their market value. The debt capital consists of all interest-bearing short- and long-term debt and capital leases, the estimated present value of rents (from capitalizing operating rents at a multiple), and the postretirement net balance sheet funding liability (net of prepaid postretirement assets and accumulated other comprehensive income [AOCI], and net of tax).

Capital is the **sum of all debt and equity capital, net of excess cash and after corrective accounting adjustments.** Because balance sheets balance, it is also equal to the firm's net business assets—the sum of its working capital (leaving out excess cash); net property, plant, and equipment (PP&E); investments; intangibles; goodwill; and other operating assets, again as adjusted for removal of accounting distortions.

MVA (market value added) is the **firm's market value less its capital.** MVA is triply significant.

First, it measures the firm's *franchise value*—its market value as a going concern above putting its assets in a pile, and which is due to all of its distinctive and proprietary assets and capabilities.

MVA also measures the owners' aggregate *wealth* as of a point in time; it compares the present value of the cash that the owners can expect to take out of the business—if only by selling the shares and cashing out the loans—with the total cash they have invested in the business.

Last, MVA is the market's implied estimate of the aggregate *net present value* of all of the firm's capital investment projects—those in place plus those expected to materialize down the road.

MVA, in sum, shows, as no other measure can show, how successful management has been at allocating, managing, and redeploying scarce resources in order to maximize the net present value of the enterprise and thus maximize the wealth of the owners. Increasing MVA, even if only to make a negative MVA less negative, is the real test of corporate success over an interval of time.

Here's the key insight: In principle, a firm's MVA at a point in time is equal to the present value of all the EVA profit it can be expected to earn over its entire future life. Firms that just cover the cost of capital and break even on EVA tend to sell close to book value and to trade for no MVA premium. Only firms that can earn and sustain EVA profit will create a distinct franchise value and reward their owners with added wealth. And thus increasing EVA is the key to creating wealth, to adding more to a firm's market value than the firm invests in its capital till.

An implication is perhaps startling: Corporate managers should dispense with discounted cash flow analysis, and should instead project, analyze, and discount EVA to measure and improve the net present value of plans, projects, and acquisitions. The NPV value is the same for a given forecast, whether from discounted cash flow or from discounting EVA, but the EVA method provides more ready insights into the full range of value drivers and key assumptions, and, unlike cash flow, it can be used to measure actual performance and strengthen accountability for generating results that add to shareholder value.

CVA (current value added) is the **value from capitalizing the firm's current EVA in perpetuity.** It is the MVA, or franchise value, that the company would have if the firm was simply able to sustain its most recent EVA forever and was incapable of growing it any further. It is measured by taking the trailing EVA and dividing it by the cost of capital, which is the formula to determine the present value of a level payment that recurs year after year, ad infinitum (adjustments are also made for midyear discounting and using average capital in the computation of the capital charge).

FVA (future value added) is the **present value of the projected *growth* in EVA over the prevailing level.** The market's estimate for FVA is derived simply by subtracting CVA from MVA—from removing the portion of MVA that is due to capitalizing the current EVA in perpetuity. The larger the FVA remainder, the more the market is registering confidence that management has positioned the company for sustained growth in EVA (and vice versa). The relative degree of confidence is expressed in the Future Growth Reliance (FGR) ratio, which is the percentage of the firm's aggregate market value that is in the hands of FVA—of expectations for future growth in EVA—and also, indirectly, in the Market-Implied Momentum (MIM)—the EVA growth rate that is implicitly baked into the share price.

MVA Spread is the **ratio of MVA to capital**. It measures the efficiency with which investors' capital investment has translated into a franchise value and into an aggregate net present value premium. An MVA Spread of 50 percent indicates that every $1.00 of invested capital has turned into $0.50 in added wealth. Looked at another way, the ratio quantifies a risk cushion, the market value premium percentage to invested capital that will fend off an erosion in the investor's principal investment due to an unforeseen drop in the firm's EVA earning power.

NPV Spread is the **ratio of NPV to PV of projected capital investment**. It is computed by measuring the present value (PV) of the EVA profit that is forecast for a decision or investment, which measures its NPV, and dividing that by the present value of the capital invested in the decision or project year by year. The larger it is, the more risk cushion there is. It is the recommended alternative to internal rate of return (IRR), which erroneously assumes all intermediate cash flows can be invested at the IRR, which is incorrect. Beware, though, it is not the measure to maximize—EVA and NPV are. It is a measure to consider the risk and fit the project into a risk budget. For instance, some firms establish minimum NPV spreads for projects in various risk classes as a risk control mechanism.

MVA Margin is the **ratio of MVA to sales**. It measures how efficiently and prodigiously sales translate into franchise value. As a mathematical insight, just as MVA is in principle the present value of projected EVA, which divides into CVA and FVA, a firm's MVA/sales ratio should equal its current EVA Margin plus the present value of its projected EVA Momentum, divided by the cost of capital. It is the capitalized value of profitability and profitable growth.

Future Growth Reliance (FGR) is the **ratio of FVA to market value**. It is the percent proportion of the firm's market value that is derived from, and depends on, growth in EVA. The greater the reliance, the more confidence the market is placing on the company's ability to rebound from a cyclical downturn or strategically drive EVA expansion.

Market-Implied Momentum (MIM) is **EVA profit growth rate that is impounded into the company's stock price** or, more specifically, that is reflected in its FVA, the portion of overall market value that is attributable to the present value of expected EVA growth.

MIM is a more reliable indicator of consensus market expectations than the so-called consensus earnings per share (EPS), which is, after all, not a true consensus, but is an opinion survey of sell-side analysts, ignoring the buy side, for EPS, a measure that hardly tells the whole value story. MIM, by contrast, literally discounts to the share price, and as such, it represents the market's true outlook for the firm given the information that investors have collectively factored into its share value.

CFOs use their MIMs to understand and monitor market expectations, to set a bogey for judging the company's actual EVA Momentum, and to help them set minimum plan and compensation performance targets in terms of EVA growth goals.

Market-implied EVA improvement is the annual EVA buildup that cumulates over 10 years and discounts back to the current share price—technically, to FVA (the portion of the firm's value that implicitly derives from expected growth in EVA). To determine it, the indicated MIM rate is multiplied times current period sales, which converts the expected growth rate into a money measure of expected EVA improvement. Multiply that by 5 to estimate the five-year forward-plan EVA improvement goal the company must achieve to be on track with market performance expectations.

Free cash flow (FCF) is **NOPAT less the period change in capital**—it is the cash generated by the business that is free of, or net of, all the capital invested in net business assets. It is total cash operating receipts minus total cash operating disbursements, no matter whether the disbursements were recorded as expenses that reduced NOPAT or as expenditures that added to balance sheet capital. It is the net distributable cash flow generated by, or required by, the business, and as such, it is by definition also equal to all cash transactions with all providers of capital to the company.

A company that generates more NOPAT than it reinvests in capital expansion generates positive FCF to pay interest on its debts, to retire debt, pay dividends, buy back stock, or accumulate a war chest of cash that permits more of the same down the road. A company that invests more in growth capital than it earns through its NOPAT winds up with a negative FCF that must be financed by raising new debt or equity or by drawing down surplus cash. Moreover, any cash it pays out in interest or dividends or share buybacks cannot really be paid; those outlays only add to the cash deficit that must be financed.

As a consequence, and by definition, discounting a projection for FCF to a present value determines the aggregate market value of the firm's outstanding debt and equity securities, for it discounts the anticipated cash transactions to and from the investors over the life of the business at the appropriate blended cost of capital rate.

Yet ironically, FCF in any one year, or even over longer intervals, is not a reliable of measure of performance. That's because, as long as a company is investing in positive NPV projects and strategies with attractive returns above the cost of capital, the more investments it makes, and the lower or more negative its free cash flow goes, the greater its NPV, MVA, and stock price will be. It is simply not possible to tell whether a firm is more or less valuable by generating more or less free cash over a period of time.

That's not just a theory. It is a stock market fact. The evidence proves it (furnished upon request). Bottom line: FCF measures the magnitude of cash liquidity or funding deficit over a period—it is a treasury measure—but it is most decidedly *not* a performance measure. And this applies to all cash flow measures, however defined.

The conclusion: Cash is not king. EVA is king. Management should always aim to maximize the present value of EVA and the firm's franchise value and owner's wealth, and just let the cash flow chips fall where they may. At least that is the ideal.

Companies that are genuinely cash constrained, like private companies, should still use EVA, but just measure it using a higher cost of capital than for a pubic, liquid firm. That will sweat more cash out of the balance sheet, and cut off projects that would otherwise get done, in order to force a balance between available cash and cash investment opportunities.

FCF generation is the **ratio of FCF to capital.** It is the rate at which the firm generates or consumes cash in its business activities, net of all investment spending, expressed as a yield on (average) capital. It is mathematically equivalent to the return on capital (NOPAT/average capital) less the growth rate in capital (call that GCap, and it equals ΔCapital/average capital); that is, FCF generation by definition equals ROC – GCap.

For example, a firm that earned an ROC of 15 percent and invested in capital at a GCap growth rate of 10 percent has an FCF generation rate of +5 percent. It is generating a positive net distributable cash yield on its capital. In sum, where ROC > Gcap, FCF generation is positive, and the company is internally cash sufficient and generates more than enough profit to fund growth. And if ROC < GCap, FCF is negative and external funding must be sought (or cash reserves taken down).

FCF generation is a measure of net cash liquidity and funding need, but like FCF, it is *not* a measure of performance. It is a measure of liquidity generation or net funding need only.

EVA Margin schedule is a **special format to compute the EVA Margin and connect it to all the underlying productivity indicators** that are familiar to managers and that they can manage. It puts all pluses and minuses of business productivity performance on a common margin scale, which is a tremendous simplification that enables line teams to more easily spot trends, make decisions involving trade-offs, and prioritize initiatives in terms of added value.

EBITDA Margin is the **ratio of EBITDA to sales.** It is the classic earnings before interest, taxes, depreciation, and amortization cash profit measure, as a percentage of sales.

To be clear, though, as reported by EVA Dimensions, it is measured net of stock-based compensation, for two reasons. One, stock-based compensation is a necessary and unavoidable cost of keeping key people motivated and aligned with creating value. Second, the stock-based compensation charge recognized on financial statements is a legitimate estimate of the expected ongoing cost to the shareholders of diverting a portion of corporate value creation to employees. Though not cash, stock-based compensation is an unavoidable cost of doing business. It is as if the employees were paid in cash, and they returned the cash to buy options in the firm. It is a self-financing expense, but an expense nevertheless that reduces the present value of the company.

EBITDAR add-backs are **all the adjustments to convert EBITDA to EBITDAR—** which is an even cleaner, purer, more comparable measure of cash operating profit.

One add-back is for rent expense, because rent expense is effectively just depreciation and interest paid via a third party. Adding back rent expense makes EBITDAR the same whether an asset is leased or it is owned, whereas EBITDA is always greater if an asset is owned rather than leased. EBITDAR is thus impervious to shifts in the mix of owning or leasing assets.

The other add-backs are for: (1) R&D and advertising spending, which are added back in order to isolate the underlying operating profit before discretionary investments in intangible assets (which under EVA are capitalized and amortized as part of the intangible capital charges farther down the EVA Margin schedule); (2) reported retirement expense less the service cost (service cost is the actuarial increase in the present value of future retirement payments that the firm owes its employees due to service in the period, which better approximates the ongoing expected cost than the reported cost, which is based on numerous questionable assumptions and mixes in irrelevant sunk costs from prior periods); and (3) the changes in bookkeeping reserves for bad debts, LIFO, warranty expense, and so forth (to bring recurring cash flows from operations into the EBITDAR picture instead of stuffing them into balance sheet accounts that can be manipulated).

EBITDAR is **EBITDA plus EBITDAR add-backs**—it is an improved version of EBITDA that is a better, purer, more comparable measure of true cash operating profit. EBITDAR is more reliable than EBITDA for judging a business's pricing power and operating efficiency.

Productive capital charges is the **sum of all depreciation, amortization, and pretax cost of capital charges on the firm's productive capital**—its working capital, PP&E, and intangible capital, both bought and built (R&D and ad spend are capitalized under EVA), but excluding goodwill (which is handled down the schedule as a corporate charge).

The pretax cost of capital—which is a grossed-up version of the familiar after-tax cost of capital—is used to measure it so that the charge is directly comparable with any other operating cost, like cost of goods sold, that is also pretax (a firm that has a weighted average cost of capital of 6 percent after tax and a 40 percent tax rate, for example, is charged at a 10 percent pretax cost of capital rate). An improvement in asset management thus appears quite simply as a reduction in the rental charge and an improvement in the margin, just as if prices had increased or operating costs had been lowered.

The more productive capital a company employs in relation to its sales, and the greater the capital charge rate, the larger its EBITDAR margin must be before economic profit can be created. The productive capital rental charge thus serves as the equivalent of a threshold EBITDAR margin—it is the cash operating profit margin minimum required to earn the cost of capital and generate EVA.

The productive capital charge can be depicted in two ways. First, it is the sum of three component charges—a percent margin charge for working capital; for the PP&E assets owned and rented; and for the intangibles, bought and built, excepting goodwill (the goodwill charge is shown even farther down the EVA Margin schedule, in a separate section). Second, it can also be computed by multiplying productive capital intensity—how much productive capital is being employed per dollar of sales—times the productive capital rental rate—the weighted average rate at which the productive capital is depreciating or amortizing and is incurring cost of capital charges. The two views of the productive capital rental charge enable management to follow trends, benchmark with peers, and isolate underlying competencies and gaps that may need attention.

Productive capital intensity is the **ratio of productive capital to sales**. A higher ratio indicates the firm is tying up more capital in revenue-generating assets to produce each sales dollar it generates—that the business is more capital intensive. There is no evidence to show that companies with lower capital intensity as a general rule earn more EVA, however. Capital-intensive firms like petroleum giant Exxon Mobil, or even Google with its massive investments in systems, servers, and R&D, manage to do very well on EVA because they are able to generate massive EBITDAR margins. Yet it also is true that, everything else held equal, doing more with less and leveraging investments in productive capital assets into even more sales, customer satisfaction, and EBITDAR Margin can be key differentiating factors. Apple, for instance, manages to have a better brand, higher customer affinity, price power, and innovation prowess than other tech companies while still running an extremely lean capital ship, as evidenced by its productive capital-to-sales ratio. A stronger supply chain, better product mix, and higher yields on intangibles do matter, of course, at least relative to peers and in light of the company's business model, and are summarized in this statistic.

Productive capital rental charge is the **ratio of the productive capital charges to productive capital**—it is the consolidated average rental rate applied to the firm's productive capital. It is the weighted average rate at which the productive assets are depreciating and amortizing, bearing interest at the pretax cost of capital, and turning into a charge against EVA. Risky firms must pay a higher rental rate to compensate for the risk. Firms using fast-depreciating assets—for instance, a firm like Google that has considerable capital tied up in rapidly obsolescing servers—must pay a higher rate (whereas regulated utilities that invest in long-lived generation assets pay a lower rate to rent their assets and recover their capital). And firms that invest a large proportion of their capital in intangibles, like for R&D and ad spend that tend to obsolesce rapidly and are swiftly amortized, will generally pay a higher average rental rate for their mix of productive capital assets.

EVA Margin Before Tax is the **EBITDAR margin less the productive capital charges**, as a percentage of sales. It is a key productivity measure that combines income efficiency and asset management, and that neutralizes business model differences. It is suitable for measuring line teams and division heads, as it comes before corporate charges are deducted.

Corporate charges are the sum of taxes computed the EVA way, less Other EVA, plus the cost of capital on unimpaired goodwill and on accumulated restructuring charges. It is the net frictional drag that separates bottom-line EVA from pretax EVA.

EVA tax is computed at an assumed smoothed, standard tax rate, less the cost of capital saved by the net deferral of tax, including taxes deferred compared to the assumed smoothed rate.

Other EVA is a grab bag of sundry income and expense, credit and charge items that are unrelated to sales and direct business operations. It consists of non-sales-related operating income, after tax, plus the EVA from investments carried at cost and at equity, less the EVA attributable to noncontrolling interests, less the cost of capital on miscellaneous noncore assets, plus the cost of capital saved by using noncapital, non-interest-bearing liabilities as funding sources, less the cost of the capital required to close a net unfunded retirement funding loss or gap.

Capital charge on cumulative special items after tax is the cost of capital associated with the accumulated balance of unusual and nonrecurring charges. EVA isolates ongoing operating performance by removing unusual and nonrecurring charges from the firm's NOPAT earnings, but to preserve the integrity of double-entry bookkeeping, the charges are also added back to balance sheet capital, which turns into a capital charge to EVA as a percentage of sales.

In this way a restructuring does not lead to a jarring period expense, but is rather viewed as an investment that can (and should) increase EVA by increasing the firm's NOPAT profit by more that the cost of the capital invested in the restructuring.

Asset impairments (other than goodwill, which are added back to goodwill directly) are also added back to capital and included in the capital charge to the EVA Margin. Under EVA, an impaired asset just stays on the books. It continues to impair EVA with a capital charge in future just as it has in the past, and to serve as a constant reminder that capital has been misallocated. An impairment, as a pure bookkeeping write-down of no economic substance, thus has no net bottom-line impact on EVA as a pure accounting matter.

Losses on asset sales are also added back to earnings, and added back to this capital account. In other words, under EVA, capital is reduced by after-tax sale proceeds, by the net after-tax cash amount recovered in a sale or in liquidation, and not by the meaningless book value of the disposed assets. Consequently, if management sells assets for more than the EVA they are contributing to the firm, then the firm's EVA will increase with this accounting treatment, even as a bookkeeping loss is registered.

Gains are treated symmetrically, and are applied to reduce capital, after tax. Rather than showing a one-time unsustainable earnings hike, a gain on sale is thus converted into an ongoing reduction in capital and in capital charge, thus effectively replacing the earnings lost from the sale of the asset.

The costs of contingencies, legal settlements, and acquisition integration are also removed from earnings and added into this capital account as permanent investments in the organization to maintain its existence and organizational vitality.

All of these adjustments smooth EVA in the period in which they occur and thus enable management to demonstrate the real merits of the decisions, but in subsequent periods they have no effect on the firm's ability to increase its EVA and hence to generate EVA Momentum.

About the Author

Bennett Stewart is chairman and chief executive of EVA Dimensions LLC, a financial technology firm that provides software, data, and training and support programs to enable its corporate clients to test and implement Best-Practice EVA, and that offers EVA-based equity research services to help institutional fund managers make better-informed buy/sell decisions and generate excess returns.

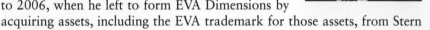

Mr. Stewart was a founding partner of Stern Stewart & Co., the EVA consulting firm, from 1982 to 2006, when he left to form EVA Dimensions by acquiring assets, including the EVA trademark for those assets, from Stern Stewart.

He is the author of *The Quest for Value* (HarperBusiness, 1991), which is described as "the definitive management guide to EVA." He is a recognized expert in the field of value-based performance management, incentive compensation, and accounting for value, and is a frequent speaker and author of articles on topics in those fields.

Along with his colleague and spouse, Ling Yang Stewart, he developed an EVA-based buy-sell rating, screening, and reporting system known as PRVit, standing for the performance-risk-valuation investment technology.

Mr. Stewart serves as chairman of the audit and finance committee of ITC Holdings, Inc., a New York Stock Exchange–listed firm that is the nation's largest independent electric transmission company. He is a member of the board of advisers to the *Morgan Stanley Journal of Applied Corporate Finance*, and is a past chairman of the alumni advisory council for the Operations Research and Financial Engineering Department of Princeton University.

He holds an MBA degree from the University of Chicago Booth School of Business and a BSE degree in electrical engineering from Princeton University.

Index

"AAMCO adjustment," 80
Accountability, 32
Accounting model of value, 65–66
Accounting rules, mandated, 47
Accumulated service cost liability, 77
Acquisitions:
  EPS and P/E, 238–243
  exchange of value in, 239–240
  MVA and, 243
  pricing of, 236–238
  public vs. private company, 240
  synergy value, 240–242
Acquisitive companies, 281
Advance Auto Parts, 164–166
Allen, Franklin, 93
Amazon (AMZN):
  business model and, 15
  cash flow and, 26
  EVA and MVA, 27
  EVA Margin and, 139–146, 147
  EVA ratio metrics, 119–122
  performance targets and, 162
America Online (AOL), 245–246
Amortization costs, 220
Anheuser-Busch, 87, 88
AOL. See America Online (AOL)
Apple Inc.:
  business models and, 15, 107
  cash reserves and, 51
  desktop computers and, 89
  EPS, P/E and, 237
  EVA and MVA, 36, 37
  EVA Momentum and, 178
  global competition for, 185
  iPhone, 275
  iTunes, 184
  market value and, 38
  performance targets and, 162
  ROC and EVA/sales profit margin, 95
Assets:
  book value of, 52

tying up capital, 48
Asset turnover ratio, 126
AutoZone:
  EVA Margin for, 262, 264
  EVA Momentum and, 272
  Future Growth Reliance for, 256–257, 262
  MIM and, 262, 264
  'S' curve and, 93–94
AutoZone PRVit score:
  EVA and, 251
  Intrinsic Value Score, 255
  performance figures and, 263
  Performance Score, 252
  Profitability Score (P1), 252–253
  PRVit ratio/PRVit matrix, 257, 258
  ranking/stock performance, 261, 262
  Risk Score, 253
  Trend Score (P2), 253
  Valuation score, 255–256
  Volatility Score (R1), 254
  Vulnerability Score (R2), 254
  Wealth Multiples Score (V2), 256
  Wealth Ratios Score (V1), 256

Bad debt reserves, 68–69
Ball Corporation:
  EVA bonus plan, 11–14, 163
  EVA/MVA connection for, 20–22
  strategic investments, 80, 81
  TSR and TIR for, 45–46
  value improvement and, 27
Best Buy, 15–16, 34, 184
Best-Practice EVA. See also "5-Ps"
  bonuses/advancement, 276–277
  commitment to, 273, 275–276
  decision/strategy to adopt, 284–285
  executive decision support applications,
    282
  financial drivers and, 209
  five-point checklist, 271, 284
  rhythm of, 279

Best-Practice EVA (*Continued*)
  Rhythm of Financial Excellence, 278–279
  substitution, first, 274
  substitution, second, 274–275
  substitution, third, 275
  synergies and, 241
  using EVA deeply/widely, 278
Beta risk, 74
Biotech companies, 172, 268–270
Bloomberg, 248, 259
Blue Nile Inc. (NILE), 95. *See also* TIF/NILE
  companies
Bonus plans. *See also* Incentive plans
  annual performance targets, 159
  at Ball Corporation, 11–14, 81
  Best-Practice EVA and, 276–277
  EVA performance targets and, 10–11
  shadow EVA bonus multiplier, 280–281
  three-year, 162–163
Book value, 39, 193, 215
Brahma Beer, 87–88
Brand spend, R&D and, 62–68
Brand value, 39
Brealey, Richard A., 93
Briggs & Stratton, 16
"Broker vote," 246
Business cycles:
  Market-Implied Momentum (MIM) and,
    182
  risk premiums and, 3
  swings/long horizons, 172–173
Business model productivity, 123
Business models, 107
Business plans:
  assumptions and drivers for, 201–205
  EVA metrics and, 185
  EVA Momentum and, 215
  forward plans, 185–186, 202, 204,
    215–216
  improving, 211–212
  past trends and, 188
Business sectors. *See* Sectors
Business unit plans, 192
Business valuation methods, 33
BusinessWeek, 89

CAGR. *See* Compound annual growth rate
    (CAGR)
Capital. *See also* Cost of capital (COC)
  allocation of, 224
  charge for using, 42

defined, 2
intangible, 136–139
internally generated cash, 233
negative, 95
one-time gain on sale and, 59
productive, 131–132, 151–152
RONA and, 94
working (*see* Working capital)
Capital account, capital gains/losses, 54–59
Capital charge:
  accountability and, 32
  in EVA calculation, 3–4
  working capital and, 5
Capital decisions:
  Claudine's Salt Water Taffy Company,
    227–233
  NPV Spread and, 234–236
Capital preservation, 234–235
Capital spending limit, 223
Cash, discharging surplus, 51
Cash flow, 25–27. *See also* Discounted cash
    flow (DCF); Free cash flow (FCF)
Cash operating profit, 130–131
Cash operating profit margin, 127
Chase Manhattan Bank, 83
Checklist, five-point, 271, 284
Christensen, Clayton, 88
Claudine's Salt Water Taffy Company,
    227–233, 283
COC. *See* Cost of capital (COC)
Coca-Cola Company:
  business models and, 107
  EVA and, 14–15, 33
  EVA Momentum and, 166–170, 173–174,
    182, 187–188, 215–216
  RONA and, 86–87, 88
COGS. *See* Cost of goods sold (COGS)
Colvin, Geoff, 245–246
Common equity book value, 193
Companies. *See* Firms
Company-specific metrics, 135
Compound annual growth rate (CAGR), 122
Consensus EPS, 105
Consensus EVA plan, 221
Contingency plans, 207
Continuous improvement performance
    metric, 276
"Cookie jar" reserve, 68
Corporate bonds, 74
Corporate charges, TIF/NILE companies,
    153–154

Corporate market value, 39
Corporate oversight, 225
Cost(s):
  amortization, 220
  restructuring, 59–61
  sunk, 102
Cost of capital (COC):
  capital allocation and, 224
  debt leverage and, 45–46
  deducting, 47
  described, 2–3
  EVA setting aside, 25
Cost of goods sold (COGS), 131
Credit Suisse, 246
Credit Suisse First Boston (CSFB), 88
Crown Holdings, 22, 23
CSFB. *See* Credit Suisse First Boston (CSFB)
CSX Corporation, 16
Current value added (CVA), 30, 195
CVA. *See* Current value added (CVA)

DCF. *See* Discounted cash flow (DCF)
Deadbeat loans, 68
Debt leverage, 45–46
Deferred tax liability, 69–71
Dell, 34
Deloite CFO Survey, 187
Depreciation:
  cash flow and, 25
  PPE assets and, 140
  reported, 238
Digital technology, 185–186
Discounted cash flow (DCF). *See also* Cash flow
  EVA Momentum and, 200
  holistic approach and, 224
  market value and, 214
  NPV analysis, 202
  stopping use of, 26, 274–275
Discount Internet retailer, 95
Domtar Corp., 178–179
Dot-com bubble, 12
Downturns, 3
Dresser Industries, 238
DuPont ROI formula/model, 85, 122, 124–125, 275

Earnings before interest, taxes, depreciation, and amortization (EBITDA), 3
Earnings before interest and taxes (EBIT), 3, 205

Earnings per share (EPS):
  accounting model of value and, 65–66
  acquisitions and, 236, 238
  EVA and, 34, 274
  OCI and, 75
  offset by P/E, 238–243
EBITDA, 219–220, 274
EBITDAR:
  cash operating profit, 130–131
  computation of, 134
  EBITDA and, 127
  median margin, 187
  NOPAT and, 219–220
  for Tiffany's (TIF), 148–151, 202, 204, 219
EBITDAR Margin, 127, 128–129
EBITDAR multiple, 256, 267
Ecolab, 44–45
Economic value added. *See* EVA
Enron, 69
Enterprise valuation multiple, 219
E Pluribus Unum and *E Unum Pluribus*, 99–100, 197, 201, 205, 227, 259, 275
EPS. *See* Earnings per share (EPS)
Equifax, 97
Equity analysts, 195
ERISA, 77
EVA (economic value added):
  as additive, 91, 225
  basic calculation, 3, 82
  charge for using capital and, 42
  computation of profit, 1
  discounted present value of, 225
  discounting to NPV, 20
  Momentum and, 205
  monitoring at margin, 33
  target of, 81
  targets, setting (*see* EVA targets)
  timing value in, 70–71
EVA Dimensions, 38, 68, 71, 98, 166, 180, 246, 275, 285. *See also* Software tool
EVA Margin. *See also* PV EVA Margin
  advantages to, 126
  Amazon and, 139–146, 147
  for AutoZone, 272, 274
  biotech companies and, 268–269
  at Coca-Cola Company, 168
  company-specific metrics and, 135
  EBITDAR, 130–131
  EBITDAR/EBITDAR Margin, 127
  EVA Momentum and, 127

EVA Margin (*Continued*)
  EVA Pyramid level 2, 127–129
  EVA Pyramid level 3, 129
  franchise value and, 214
  Innovator's Dilemma and, 186–187
  intangible capital, 136–139
  knowing your, 190
  over time, averages, 187–188
  PPE and, 134–136
  pretax, 129
  principal applications, 126–127
  productive capital, 131–132
  PV EVA Margin and, 227
  summary view of, 123–124, 158–159
  tale of two companies, 146
  TIF/NILE companies (*see* TIF/NILE
    companies)
  working capital and, 133–134
EVA Margin Before Tax, 124
EVA Momentum:
  75th percentile/five-year, 175–177
  90th percentile/five-year, 175, 178–179
  for Amazon, 121, 122
  for AutoZone, 262
  biotech companies and, 172
  at Coca-Cola Company, 166–170,
    174–175, 180, 186–187
  DCF, NPV and, 202
  described, 101–104
  first look at, 109–114
  five-year leaders, 174–182
  food/beverage companies, 182–184
  forward pass and, 215–216
  goal setting and, 173–174
  growth targets and, 167
  maximization of, 123, 127
  median, 173
  no ("No Mo"), 214
  for Pier I, 175, 178–181
  in planning (*see* Planning process)
  projection of, 190
  P score/PRVit score and, 258
  Russell 3000 companies, 171–174
  sector/industry group and, 180–186
  in software/specialty retail, 184
  stock price and, 166
  for Sun Hydraulics, 178–181
  for Tiffany's, 197, 205, 266
  for whole market, 186
EVA Momentum Pyramid. *See* EVA Pyramid

EVA Momentum scorecards, 191, 205, 207,
    209, 216
EVA Nuggets, 283–284
EVA performance expectations, 193
EVA Pyramid:
  business plans and, 207, 216
  level 2, 127–129
  level 3, 129
EVA ratio metrics:
  for Amazon, 119–122
  E Pluribus Unum and *E Unum Pluribus*,
    99–100
  EVA Margin, 105–109
  EVA Momentum, 101–104, 109–114
  Market-Implied Momentum (MIM),
    104–105
  market metrics, 114–119
  overview, 100–101
EVA stock rating model, 83
EVA targets:
  business plan outputs, 161, 170
  EVA Margin and, 170–171, 186–187
  EVA Momentum/Russell 3000, 171–174
    (*see also* EVA Momentum)
  incentive plans (*see* Incentive plans)
  Market-Implied Momentum (MIM) and,
    181, 183, 185, 188
  Momentum Leverage Ratio (MLR), 175
  table of, 161, 170
EVA training, 4
Excel tool, 192
Exxon, 237

Fair-value line, 247–249
FCF. *See* Free cash flow (FCF)
Federal Reserve policy, 186, 188
Fidelity.com, 246
FIFO value, 131, 133
Finance ratios. *See* EVA ratio metrics
Financial excellence, 278 279
Financial objective. *See* EVA Momentum
Financial performance variables, 194
Financing decisions, 48–51
Firms. *See also specific company*
  new economy, 95
  types of, 34–35
"5-Ps:"
  Perform, 283–284
  Pilot, 277
  Practice, 278, 280–283

Prepare, 277
Prototype, 277–278
Five-point checklist, 284
Fixed charge costs, 228
Food/beverage companies, 180–181, 186,
    198. *See also specific company*
Foreign exchange (FX) transactions, 125
Formula-based bonus plan, 11
Fortune, 16, 20, 87, 246–246
Forward pass, 215–216
Forward plans:
    discounting EVA profit, 191
    EVA Momentum and, 215–216
    PPE and, 206
    Value *Express* and, 204
    valuing of, 193
Franchises, 166
Franchise value, 39, 214. *See also* MVA
    (market value added)
Free cash flow (FCF):
    for Amazon, 121
    new investments and, 225
    NOPAT and, 28–29, 30–31, 42
    for Tiffany's, 207, 209
Funding deficit, 75
Future Growth Reliance (FGR):
    for Apple Inc., 36, 37, 38
    for AutoZone, 256–257, 262
    for Tiffany's, 220, 267
Future value added. *See* FVA (future value
    added)
FVA (future value added):
    growth horizons and, 35–36
    growth in EVA and, 32
    to market value (FGR), 36, 38
FX. *See* Foreign exchange (FX) transactions

GAAP. *See* Generally accepted accounting
    principles (GAAP)
Gabelli, Mario, 89, 90
GARP. *See* Growth at a reasonable price
    (GARP)
Generally accepted accounting principles
    (GAAP), 58
Georgia-Pacific, 80
Global competition, 185
Global PRVit Prime scores, 260
Going-concern business enterprise, 39, 48,
    68, 83, 197
Google, 107

Government bonds, 3, 74–75
Green Mountain Coffee Roasters, 35, 180,
    182
Grove, Andrew, 88
Growth at a reasonable price (GARP), 247
Growth horizon, 34–35

Halliburton, 238
Hallmarks of EVA company, 271
Housing bubble, 12
Hurdle rate, 24

IBM:
    Equifax and, 97
    Innovator's Dilemma and, 88–89
IFRS. *See* International Financial Reporting
    Standards (IFRS)
Impairment charge, 52
Incentive plans. *See also* Bonus plans
    EVA target table, 161, 170
    long-term (*see* Long-term incentive plans)
    medium-range, 166–168
    pay-for-performance, 162
Industry groups, 181–187
Information technology (IT), 135, 276. *See
    also* Technology
Innovator's Dilemma:
    EVA Margins and, 193–195
    IBM and, 88–89
    RONA and, 88
The Innovator's Dilemma (Christensen), 88
In-store stocking rate, 94
Intangible capital, 136–139
Intangibles:
    EVA Margin schedule and, 132
    TIF/NILE companies, 152–153
Intel, 88
Internal rate of return (IRR):
    EVA Margin and, 126–127
    NPV Spread and, 235
    pitfalls of RONA and, 93
Internal Revenue Service (IRS), 72
International Accounting Standard No. 36
    (IAS 36), 53
International Financial Reporting Standards
    (IFRS), 52
Internet retailer, 95
Investments, strategic, 79–81
Investor relations (IR), 240, 271
IR. *See* Investor relations (IR)

IRR. *See* Internal rate of return (IRR)
IRS. *See* Internal Revenue Service (IRS)
IT. *See* Information technology (IT)
Ive, Jonathan, 275

Jergens Inc., 66–67, 68
JetBlue Airways Corp., 178–179
Jobs, Steve, 36, 38, 88, 275
Jollibee Foods, 79
Jose Reyes syndrome, 89

Kao USA, 66–67

Leases:
    capitalized or expensed, 94
    treating as if owned, 52
Liabilities, assets as, 48
Line-of-business plans, 198, 206
Loan loss reserve, 68–69
Long-term incentive plans:
    at Advance Auto Parts, 164–166
    at Coca-Cola Company, 166–170

Manitowoc Company, 89–90
Manufacturers, 135
Margin. *See* EVA Margin
Margin elasticity, 199
Market-Implied Momentum (MIM):
    for Amazon, 121
    for AutoZone, 262
    described, 104–105
    EVA growth goal and, 163
    for Tiffany's, 202
Market-Implied Momentum (MIM) and,
        184, 186, 188, 190, 192
Market saturation, 33
Market-to-book premium, 200
Market-to-book spread, 31
Market value:
    MVA and, 29
    of plan, 198
Market value added. *See* MVA (market value
        added)
Massey Ferguson, 61
Measured postrent expense, 219
Measured prerent expense, 219
Metrics, 135. *See also specific metric*
Microsoft, 39, 51, 89
MIM. *See* Market-Implied Momentum
        (MIM)

MLR. *See* Momentum Leverage Ratio
        (MLR)
Momentum. *See* EVA Momentum
Momentum Leverage Ratio (MLR), 175,
        202
Momentum Pyramid, 122
Monsanto, 64–65, 68
Monster Beverage, 183–185
Multiples. *See also* Price-to-earnings (P/E)
        multiple
    dividing good into bad, 217–222
    enterprise valuation, 219
    NOPAT, 220
    stocks and, 40
MVA (market value added):
    acquisitions and, 243
    for Amazon, 121
    for Ball Corporation, 20–22
    cash flow and, 26
    CVA and, 199
    described, 19
    formula, 38
    market value and, 29
    return from increasing, 42
    for Tiffany's, 239
MVA Margin ratio, 218–219
MVA Spread, 217–218
Myers, Stewart C., 93

Negative capital, 95
Net depreciated asset base, 136
Net franchise value, 199
Net present value (NPV):
    EVA and, 20, 25
    EVA Margin and, 126
    EVA Momentum and, 202
    looking forward/backward, 276
    MVA and, 19
    NOPAT and, 31
    profitable growth and, 7
New economy companies, 95
NOPAT (net operating profit after taxes):
    capital charge and, 5
    EBITDAR and, 219–220
    in EVA calculation, 3–4
    excess cash and, 51
    FCF and, 28–29, 30–31, 42
    leases and, 52
    multiples, 220, 256
    profit target, 6

significance of, 29
for Volkswagen, 24
NPV. *See* Net present value (NPV)
NPV Spread, 234–236

OCI. *See* Other comprehensive income (OCI)
Off-balance-sheet liability, 77
On-balance-sheet liability, 77
One-time gain on sale, 59
Operating decisions, 48–51
Operating profit, 130–131
Operating profit margin, 127
Other comprehensive income (OCI), 75, 76
Outsourcing, 96–97, 106

P/E. *See* Price-to-earnings (P/E) multiple
Pension plans, 75, 82. *See also* Retirement cost distortions
PepsiCo, Inc.:
adoption of EVA, 284–285
business models and, 107
taxes and, 71–72
Percentile ratings, TIF/NILE companies, 154–158
Performance improvement categories, 7
Performance metrics, 17, 28, 276. *See also specific metric*
Performance profile, 193
Performance reviews, 216
Pfeifer, Dean, 89
Pier I, 175–177
Planning process:
business plans (*see* Business plans)
Excel tool (*see* Value *Express*)
forward plans (*see* Forward plans)
planning reviews, 190–191
portfolio reviews, 191
for Tiffany's (*see* Tiffany's planning process)
Portfolio reviews, 191
Post-employment-benefit (PRB), 77
Postrent expense, 219
PPE. *See* Property, plant, and equipment (PPE)
PRB. *See* Post-employment-benefit (PRB)
Prerent expense, 219
Present value, 25, 32. *See also* PV EVA Margin
Pretax cost of capital rate, 131–132
Pretax margin, 129

Price-to-earnings (P/E):
acquisitions and, 236–237
EPS and, 238–243
Price-to-earnings (P/E) multiple, 65–66, 76, 217
Principles of Corporate Finance (Myers, Brealey, and Allen), 93
Productive capital, TIF/NILE companies, 151–152
Productive capital charges, 129
Productive capital intensity, 140
Profit:
computation of, 1
performance metrics (*see* Performance metrics)
Profitable companies, 266
Property, plant, and equipment (PPE), 126, 134–136, 204
Proprietary franchise value, 39
PRVit (performance-risk-valuation investment technology):
analysis, 280, 283
custom research and, 268
described, 246
fair-value line and, 247–249
global performance, 260–261
performance since 1998, 259
PRVit matrix/VARP grid, 249
Score (*see* PRVit score)
specialty retail stocks, 249–251
valuation multiples and, 248
VARP and GARP, 247
for year ending Sept 2012, 260
PRVit Prime scores, 260
PRVit score. *See also* AutoZone PRVit score
formula, 249
industry-adjusted, 251
(P – R) score, 249, 251, 255, 258
PRVit yield and, 257–259
(P-R)/V ratio, 257
Tiffany's and, 264–267
V score, 249, 251, 255–256
Public companies, 80, 193
PV EVA Margin. *See also* EVA Margin
advantages to using, 235
derivation of, 226
described, 234
EVA Margin metric and, 227
risk and, 236

QPI. *See* "Quantitative-Pressure Gauge" (QPI)
"Quantitative-Pressure Gauge" (QPI), 270
Quarterly performance reviews, 216
Quarterly reporting, 280

R&D. *See* Research and development (R&D)
Rate-of-return metrics, 97
Ratio metrics, 98. *See also* EVA ratio metrics
Regression model, 266
Regression to the mean, 173
Rental rate, 140
Rent expense, 130
Reported charges, 220
Reported earnings, 75
Reporting, quarterly, 280
Research and development (R&D), 11, 62–68
Research In Motion (BlackBerry), 35, 184
Restructuring costs, 59–61
Retailers, 135
Retirement cost distortions, 73–79. *See also* Pension plans
Return on capital (ROC):
Return on equity (ROE), 78
Return on investment (ROI), 11, 126, 235
Return on net assets. *See* RONA (return on net assets)
Reverse impairment charges, 52–54
Rhythm of Financial Excellence, 276, 277
Risk-adjusted EVA performance, 248–249
Risk metrics, 266
ROC. *See* Return on capital (ROC)
ROE. *See* Return on equity (ROE)
ROI. *See* Return on investment (ROI)
RONA (return on net assets):
Amazon and, 119, 122
Anheuser-Busch and, 87, 88
Christensen on, 88
Coca-Cola and, 86–87, 88
EVA compared to, 86
height of building and, 91–93
internal divisions/asset assignment, 95–96
Manitowoc Company and, 89–90
maximization of, 86
as misleading indicator, 85, 91
new economy companies and, 95
outsourcing and, 96–97, 106

pitfalls of IRR and, 93
ratio metrics and, 97–98
returns from all projects, 102
shortcomings of, 94–95, 125
Russell 3000 companies. *See also* AutoZone PRVit score; TIF/NILE companies
EVA Margin and, 245
EVA Momentum and, 171–174
long-run norms and, 33
Market-Implied Momentum (MIM) percentiles, 183
PRVit scores and, 260
specialty retail stocks, 249–251

Sectors, 178, 181
Selling, general, and administrative (SG&A), 131, 148
Sell-side equity analysts, 196
SG&A. *See* Selling, general, and administrative (SG&A)
Shareholder returns:
EVA and, 41–46
sources of, 36
Share price, from EVA to, 38–41
Smith, Adam, 41
Smith, Alex, 176–177
Software companies, EVA Momentum and, 178, 180
Software tool, 20, 164, 277, 281
Specialty retail:
EVA Momentum and, 174, 178
PRVit ratings and, 249–251
SSCo (simple sample company):
EVA calculation for, 3–4
MVA of, 29
NOPAT and, 4, 28
Sterling, Craig, 246
Stern Stewart & Company, 16
Stock(s):
intrinsic value of, 247–248
multiple and, 40
pricing of, 34
valuations, 210
Stock appreciation rights (SARs), 165
Stock-outs, 94
Stock-rating model, 83. *See also* PRVit (performance-risk-valuation investment technology)
Strategic investments, 79–81
Strategic vision, 166–167

Sun Hydraulics, 176–177
Sunk costs, 102
Synergy value, 240–242

Tax deferral, 69–71
Tax prepayments, 69
Technology, 184–185. *See also* Information
    technology (IT)
10-Q filings, 119
Terminal value, 33
"3-P's" (pricing power, product mix, process
    excellence efficiency), 112, 129, 188
Tiffany & Co. (TIF):
    EBITDAR and, 219, 267
    EVA-based valuation multiples,
        217–218
    EVA Momentum, 172, 174, 266–267
    FGR of, 220
    Future Growth Reliance, 220, 267
    hypothetical forecast plans, 193
    legacy/brand/prestige of, 253
    MVA Margin ratio, 219–219
    MVA of, 221
    MVA Spread for, 217–218
    NOPAT multiples, 220
    Planning (*see* Tiffany's planning process)
    profitability of, 195
    projected EVA growth, 220–221
    PRVit score and, 264–267
    risk profile for, 266
    V2 score, 267
Tiffany's planning process:
    alternative scenarios, 210, 212
    consensus plan/Value *Express*, 195, 298,
        205, 208, 211, 213
    EBIT and, 208
    EBITDAR margin and, 205, 207
    EVA Margin and, 195, 202, 203, 208
    EVA Momentum and, 197, 202,
        208, 214
    five-year EVA highlights, 193–195
    forecast and, 195–196
    free cash flow and, 208, 210
    MIM and, 203–204
    Momentum Leverage Ratio, 200
    MVA projections, 199
    NOPAT and, 208, 210
    PPE metrics, 207
    sales growth case, 202
    valuations and, 214–215

    working capital productivity plan,
        211–213, 215
    zero Momentum case, 200, 202
TIF/NILE companies:
    corporate charges and, 153–154
    EVA Margin comparison, 148
    EVA Margin drivers comparison, 150
    EVA/MVA charts, 156–158
    intangibles and, 152–153
    overview, 146, 148
    percentile ratings and, 154–158
    productive capital and, 151–152
    TIF's EBITDAR margin, 149, 151
Time Warner, 245–246
TIR. *See* Total investor return (TIR)
Total investor return (TIR):
    defined, 41–42
    for Ecolab, 44–45
    formula, 43
    TSR and, 44
Total Quality Management (TQM), 6
Total shareholder return (TSR):
    described, 41
    for Ecolab, 44–45
    formula, 44
TQM. *See* Total Quality Management
    (TQM)
Trade credit, 4
Transportation companies, 135
Trends, 127
TSR. *See* Total shareholder return (TSR)

Valuation(s):
    accounting model of, 66
    of acquisition candidates, 281
    details, 28–38
    framework for, 207
    growth horizon and, 34
    Momentum and, 202
    multiples (*see* Multiples)
Valuation bias, 204
Valuation multiples:
    NOPAT and, 256–257
    PRVit model and, 248
Value:
    accounting model of, 65–66
    creation of, 20, 158, 285
    terminal, 33
Value at a reasonable price (VARP):
    fair-value line and, 247

Value at a reasonable price (*Continued*)
  grid, 249
  Valuation score (V), 255–256
Value-based planning, 20, 216
Value *Express*, 192, 195–196, 201–202, 204, 206–207, 209
Value neutral corrective adjustments, 82
Varity Corporation, 61–62
VARP. *See* Value at a reasonable price (VARP)
Vision. *See* Strategic vision
Vitamin Shoppe, 93, 94
Volkswagen, 23, 24, 27

Wall Street Journal, 16
Wal-Mart, 15, 34, 59, 184

Wealth creation:
  as corporate mission, 41
  EVA as measure of, 22
  fundamental principal of, 20
  RONA and, 86
  sources of, 36
The Wealth of Nations (Smith), 41
Working capital:
  capital charge and, 5
  charge, levels 4 & 5, 133–134
  interest-free credit and, 4
  productivity plan, 209–213

Zero Momentum case, 196–197

Special Bonus – EVA Company Report

Congratulations! As a Best-Practice EVA book buyer, you are entitled to a complimentary download of a special 6-panel report for a public company you select from EVA Dimensions' 9,000 company global database.

To access your free report, first, visit this web address:
http://www.evadimensions.com/learnEVA/BestPracticeEVA/Book/BonusReport

Then, enter this unique number [**BPEVA20130110**] in the entitlement window, select the company you want to view, and after registering as a **Best-Practice EVA** reader, you will be able to view the report on screen, save it, print it, and share it. It's yours to keep.

Learn More
about using Best-Practice EVA at your organization:

Corporate Finance
Software, training and hands-on support that enable corporate CFO teams to take BP-EVA for a test drive or to put it into action right across business units, business plans, and business decisions.

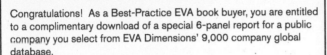

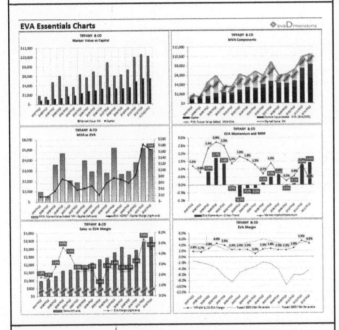

Consultants
*Tap into **Express**, EVA Dimension's acclaimed on-demand toolkit to analyze, project, value and benchmark any of the 9,000 public companies in our global file.*

Investors
EVA Dimensions provides EVA data, quantitative analysis, screens, portfolio reviews, sector analysis, PRVit ratings and custom insights on themes and names that our insitutional investor clients care about.

The special 6-panel report you receive will open a window on the essential EVA insights for the company you choose, covering a 15-year history of:

- The EVA measure of economic profit compared to the MVA measure of owner wealth
- The firm's EVA Margin – it's key measure of business model productivity – benchmarked against market norms
- The track record for EVA Momentum – the measure of the growth pace in economic profit – as compared to the "market-implied" Momentum growth rate that investors implicitly baked into the firm's share price.

All in all, it's a well-documented two-page report that tells the basic EVA story in pictures. You can also visit http://www.evadimensions.com/EVAvsMVA to download the EVA vs. MVA chart for as many companies as you want any time your want – it's an open-access portal to EVA!

Bankers/Buyers
Software and training to put BP-EVA to work to anaylze and value buy-sell transactions

For more information visit
http://www. evadimensions. com/learnEVA/ BestPracticeEVA